One Man in His Time

Serge Obolensky

Copyright ©
All rights reserved.
ISBN: 9798595231565

v. 1

First paperback edition by Mystery Grove Publishing Co. LLC
Reprint of public domain text from McDowell, Obolensky, New York, 1958

NOTE FROM THE PUBLISHER

Serge Obolensky was born in 1890. In his nearly nine decades of life, he would witness and take part in some of the largest events in human history. The death of the Old World, the beginning of the Modern era, two World Wars, the fall of the Russian Empire, and the ascent of the United States into its status a the global superpower. He was a giant figure, who acted with distinction during the titanic power shifts that swallowed so many millions.

The word "elite" is often discussed today, usually with sinister connotations. Serge Obolensky was elite in every sense of the word: part of the titled aristocracy, wealthy, enormous physical courage, savvy in high culture and finance. However, readers will undoubtedly notice the differences between him and the elites they see in the media every day.

It is these differences that have motivated us to republish his work in a more accessible manner. Obolensky first released this book in 1958 under the humble title *One Man in His Time*. In it, he tracks the entirety of his life. Certainly his accounts of time spent as a cavalryman, guerilla or paratrooper are thrilling, but readers have perhaps more to gain from the stories of his childhood, his education as a young man, and his time spent determining how he was going to live his life in exile. As young people today look to see how they will live their lives in a time of great uncertainty, Serge is a candid and reliable guide to the challenges tied with entering adulthood.

Although we strived to recreate the work in its original form with this paperback rerelease, there were many photographs included in the original hardback that we would have been unable to reprint in acceptable quality while keeping prices low. High-quality scans of these photographs have been posted for free on our Twitter page ((@MysteryGrove).

I gratefully dedicate this book to Hellen Hull,
a true friend throughout the years,
and to whom I owe so much

*All the world's a stage,
And all the men and women merely players.
They have their exits and their entrances;
And one man in his time plays many parts*
                                           -As You Like It

ACKNOWLEDGMENTS

The author thanks Robert Cantwell for his editorial assistance and excellent research, and expresses his appreciation to the staff of McDowell, Obolensky, without whose efforts this volume would not have been possible.

The author also commends Rosine Raoul and Charles Criswell, the copy editors; Sidney Feinberg, the designer of the book; Jerome Mulcahy and Al Manso, who aided in design problems and organized the photographic material and art work; and Peter Markovitch, who provided the photographic engravings.

TABLE OF CONTENTS

Chapter 1	Pg. 1
Chapter 2	Pg. 15
Chapter 3	Pg. 27
Chapter 4	Pg. 32
Chapter 5	Pg. 38
Chapter 6	Pg. 45
Chapter 7	Pg. 52
Chapter 8	Pg. 54
Chapter 9	Pg. 61
Chapter 10	Pg. 69
Chapter 11	Pg. 81
Chapter 12	Pg. 89
Chapter 13	Pg. 105
Chapter 14	Pg. 115
Chapter 15	Pg. 122
Chapter 16	Pg. 134
Chapter 17	Pg. 157
Chapter 18	Pg. 181
Chapter 19	Pg. 188

Chapter 20	Pg. 195
Chapter 21	Pg. 212
Chapter 22	Pg. 224
Chapter 23	Pg. 246
Chapter 24	Pg. 258
Chapter 25	Pg. 275
Chapter 26	Pg. 280
Chapter 27	Pg. 302
Chapter 28	Pg. 313
Chapter 29	Pg. 320
Chapter 30	Pg. 326
Chapter 31	Pg. 337
Chapter 32	Pg. 344

Genealogy of Direct Male Descent of the Princes Obolensky

I. Rurik—Grand Duke of Novgorod and Kiev 862. A.D.

II.	Igor—Grand Duke of Kiev	912 A.D.
III.	Svyatoslav—Grand Duke of Kiev	945 A.D.
IV.	Vladimir—Grand Duke of Kiev	980 A.D.
V.	Yaroslav—Grand Duke of Kiev	1054 A.D.
VI.	Svyatoslav—Prince of Chernigov	1076 A.D.
VII.	Oleg—Prince of Chernigov	1115 A.D.
VIII.	Vsevolod—Prince of Chernigov	1146 A.D.
IX.	Svyatoslav—Prince of Chernigov	1194 A.D.
X.	Vsevolod—Prince of Chernigov	1215 A.D.

XI.	Saint Mikhail Chernigovsky	1246 A.D.
XII.	Yurii—Prince Tarussky and Obolensky	
XIII.	Constantin—Prince Obolensky	
XIV.	Ivan—Prince Obolensky	
XV.	Constantin—Prince Obolensky	
XVI.	Ivan—Prince Obolensky	
XVII.	Semen—Prince Obolensky	
XVIII.	Constantin—Prince Obolensky	
XIX.	Mikhail—Prince Obolensky	
XX.	Vassily—Prince Obolensky	
XXI.	Boris—Prince Obolensky	
XXII.	Audrey—Prince Obolensky	
XXIII.	Benedict—Prince Obolensky	
XXIV.	Matvey—Prince Obolensky	1688 A.D.
XXV.	Mikhail—Prince Obolensky	1739 A.D.
XXVI.	Alexander—Prince Obolensky	1712 A.D.
XXVII.	Peter—Prince Obolensky	1742 A.D.
XXVIII.	Alexander—Prince Obolensky	1780 A.D.
XXIX.	Serge—Prince Obolensky-Neledinsky-Meletzky	1819 A.D.
XXX.	Platon—Prince Obolensky-Neledinsky-Meletzky	1850 A.D.
XXXI.	Serge—Né Prince Obolensky-Neledinsky-Meletzky	1890 A.D.
XXXII.	Ivan—Né Prince Obolensky-Neledinsky-Meletzky	1925 A.D.
XXXIII.	Ivan Serge—Obolensky-Neledinsky-Meletzky	1952 A.D.

PART I

Horse Blanket

CHAPTER I

A wide boulevard, with four rows of shade trees on both sides of it, ran from the railroad station at Czarskoe Selo to the park around the Summer Palace of the Emperor of Russia, and the houses of the nobility stood in their own grounds on both sides of the boulevard. My father's house in Czarskoe Selo was the first in the row after leaving the station, and there I was born on October 3, 1890. I was my father's first child; we were in the direct male line of the Obolensky family.

Each summer the Emperor and the Empress left the Winter Palace in St. Petersburg, twenty miles away, for Czarskoe Selo; and the villas filled up with people whose position in Russian life was about like our own. By that I mean they belonged to one of the two hundred princely families of Russia, their wealth was generally in landed estates, their social life revolved around court functions, and their sons went into the army.

Under ordinary circumstances I might have been expected to do the same. My father was Colonel Platon Obolensky, then forty years old, a heavy-set, kindly man who had a military record of considerable distinction and was aide-de-camp to Grand Duke Vladimir. You see, in Russia in those days a boy with a background like mine would almost automatically be trained to become an officer, and if his father was aide-de-camp to a Grand Duke, it meant that he would probably be brought up close to court circles. But I was too young to have had a real life in the Russian court before the war and the Revolution came. Curiously enough, I had no military training whatever until 1914, when I entered the Russian cavalry as a private and was trained in actual combat.

Up to the time I was five or six years old, my mother had complete charge of me and brought me up the way she thought I should be brought up, regardless of tradition or anything else. She was strong-willed, and she had her own ideas.

Mother was born Marie Narishkin. She was a slight, rather frail-looking woman, with thin features and dark hair, much younger than my father. She loved horses, raised thoroughbred trotters on her estate in the district of Tambov and raced them. The Narishkins were a family of courtiers. They had been in evidence at the Russian court from the time of Peter the Great, whose mother was a Narishkin. But the Narishkins never accepted a title. They considered it beneath them. They were brilliant, gay, reckless, good-looking people, art collectors, patrons of artists, gamblers, and they lived abroad much of the time.

Pushkin's famous gambling story, *The Queen of Spades*, was inspired by the life of my great-great-great-grandmother Anna Narishkin. It is a sinister tale about a great lady who never loses when playing cards and who is murdered by an impecunious young officer for her secret. And about the time I was born, Tschaikovsky based one of his last operas, *Pique Dame*, on the same Narishkin family legend.

Mother's father, my grandfather Narishkin, was typical of the family. He lived a very gay life, spending most of his time in Paris, was mixed up with a lot of women, and ran through a couple of fortunes. But he was exceedingly lucky—or maybe he gauged things right, for he came into a new inheritance every time his money ran out. When he died, at a considerable age, he was once again possessed of tremendous wealth. His wife, my grandmother Narishkin, was a tall, imperious woman and one of the most famous beauties of her time.

Mother was not very strong, and I eventually learned that she had lost a child shortly before I was conceived. She had been disappointed by so many miscarriages that when I appeared I was babied, petted, worried about, and spoilt. The worst thing, though, was that Mother had wanted a daughter. She had no intention of changing her feelings just because I turned out to be a son. For the first five years of my life my hair was kept long, and I was dressed in skirts. This was humiliating to me. I even had curls, like Little Lord Fauntleroy. My male cousins pulled my hair and made my life miserable, whilst my girl cousins liked to curl my ringlets, which was just as bad.

But I had a guardian angel in the person of my nurse, Miss Lizzie Arthur, a stout little Scottish woman born in Glasgow. She came to us because her aunt, Mimi Brown, had been the nurse of the Narishkin family, my mother's own nurse. Miss Lizzie lavished her kindness on us all her life, for she remained with us as housekeeper when we no longer needed a nurse. Firm, independent, just, and loving, she saved our young souls from cynicism after our mother left. I barely managed to get her out of Russia at the beginning of the Bolshevik Revolution.

Miss Lizzie was extremely outspoken, but she pronounced Russian words with a rolling Scottish burr, so it was almost impossible to understand her. She spoke English also with an accent that could hardly have been surpassed by Robert Burns himself. The result was that I learned to speak English like some Russian branch of a Highland clan, which highly amused my English friends later on at Oxford.

I had an old donkey, an animal so portly that his neck had a roll of fat on it. His tummy bulged so much that I actually fancied him to be a python who had swallowed something in two parts. They used to place a basket saddle on his back and strap me into the basket; then we waddled through the lanes in the park. Czarskoe Selo was surrounded by a dense belt of fir trees. Inside this perimeter the park was magnificently landscaped. It was heavily wooded in places, and successive empresses had planted shrubs that by my day had turned into small forests of lilac. It was in one of these that the old donkey took it into his head to run away with me.

Miss Lizzie rushed home and alerted the police. The servants were called out to search the woods, and I understand that a whole cortege streamed from the house in their varied costumes and went plunging through the lilac bushes. They found me in a gentle little glade, fast asleep in the basket saddle, while the donkey contentedly nibbled the lilacs.

During the winter we lived in our house on the Mohovaya in St. Petersburg. We occupied the top two floors. The nursery was the next room but one from the end of the long corridor, with Father's dressing room on one side. Opposite this was a big bathroom with two bathtubs in it and two small wood-burning stoves—chip heaters. Beyond Father's dressing room, the corridor led to the Green Room, a big sitting room which opened onto our landing—Miss Lizzie's and mine. Across the landing was the Red Room, another big sitting room. Beyond the Red Room was Mother's bedroom. It was an enormous room, and she always kept it dark and shadowy. It was also the haunt of her poodle, Turk, who always growled at me and bullied my poodle, Filka. Turk didn't bite, but Filka and I never liked that side of the house. Mother's dark room was a creepy place.

From the landing a wide stairway covered with a cerise rug swept down to the first floor. Another aide-de-camp to Grand Duke Vladimir, Prince Chahovskoy, lived there with his two children, who were about my age. On the first landing, there stood an enormous stuffed bear that my father had killed. In his paws the bear held a silver tray on which callers deposited their cards. Beside him stood an old-fashioned Victorian chair with a canopy over it. Down another few steps was the entrance. Our doorman was an enormous man with a very long black beard. His uniform was blue, and he wore a kind of bandoleer, blue, with red and gold ornaments on it. On great occasions he substituted a large red bandoleer for his everyday blue one. I could never find out what it was for. Father was of the opinion that in earlier days it was a sort of scabbard and that it had probably been much smaller then. As he said, there was always meaning to such things. In any event, all the doormen of the big houses wore them, and all had great beards and smart blue uniforms.

At intervals a significant pair of gray trotters and a sleigh appeared before our door. You could tell those were fast horses just by looking at them. The coachman looked enormous in his padded livery. A coach-man like that was what I wanted to be. And in the back of the sleigh, on a carpeted platform, stood a footman wearing a long coat with an immense fur collar. Whenever that sleigh appeared, my curls were put in order, a fur coat was pulled over my skirted clothes, and Miss Lizzie hustled me off to visit my Grandmother Obolensky. Those were her fast trotters, and when they arrived at our doorstep it generally meant that she wanted to see me.

Nothing ever delighted me more. Grandmother's sleigh was very grand, and Father always had slow horses, so those gray trotters with the blue net over them, the fat coachman, the motionless footman and the two-horse sleigh gave me a thrill every time I saw them. I really loved horses, good ones. We sailed out over the snow. The Mohovaya ran perpendicular to the Neva River, which was only a few blocks from our house, and opened into the Sergievskaya, the street on which my grandmother lived. The Sergievskaya ran parallel to the Neva. So it wasn't a very long journey to my grandmother's, really just around the corner. But thanks to Grandmother, who I think had heard how much I enjoyed these rides, we took longer than necessary. Then we turned and approached her house with considerable ceremony. Across the frozen Neva was the outer ring of Peter and Paul Fortress. A short distance upstream, on our side of the river, stood the Winter Palace.

The sleigh stopped before the house. Grandmother had an apartment. We got out and went upstairs. As soon as I came in, some elderly ladies gave me candy and all sorts of things, and they fussed and clucked over me. They were callers—aunts and great-aunts of the family, which was large. I suppose they had heard I was coming. To elderly ladies of Russia, children were always an occasion.

Grandmother herself lived alone except for a lady companion. She was very old, and she was an invalid. A hint of peppermint always pervaded her dim bedroom. There were a great many icons over in one corner, and before them a vigil light that was always burning gave a fading reddish luster to the heavy furniture and the drawn curtains.

I suppose the lack of other Obolensky grandchildren gave me a special importance in Grandmother's eyes. At each visit, her features glowing, she handed me a little present. I'm afraid I was always disappointed. What I really wanted was those trotters. But I adored her, and I think the feeling was mutual.

I know now that I grew up in a world where the relics of different social periods were all around me. Grandmother represented something fundamentally Russian, timeless and changeless, that underlay them all. She was a survivor of a bygone era even then. Her native Russian quality was neither tempestuous nor emotional, which is what Europeans have erroneously come to think of as the Russian temperament—the extreme, in other words. On the contrary, Russia's strength of that epoch, Grandmother's strength, was abiding simplicity, a radiant hospitality, an almost frugal way of life that linked the richest people to the general norm of Russian existence. Wealth was not at all a matter for display. It was used to maintain the outward forms of responsibility and position, the way my grandmother kept those wonderful horses that she never used. Or maybe she kept them up for me.

In Russia you were called by your first name and your father's name. In some circles it was actually a social error to forget the patronym. So I was Serge

Platonovitch—Serge for my own name, and Platonovitch meaning "son of Platon." However, I couldn't pronounce Platonovitch. I said "Paponch," so they called me Paponch or Paponka, the diminutive. Paponka means "horse blanket." Once when a party was setting out from the house at Czarskoe a general whose name I can't remember, but who was commander of the Emperor's Cossack bodyguard, said to Mother, "I'm going to teach Paponka something." He got a tea tray and said "Horse Blanket, you come along with me." He took me up the front stairs, put me on the tray, and let me loose. I came swinging down the stairs, around the curve, with a terrific clatter, to the absolute horror of poor Mother. From then on I found tea-traying down the stairs a superlative pastime. It may have been good training for tobogganing at St. Moritz later on.

Horses made up the abiding interest of my childhood. Father drove what were called English harness horses. And when I say drove, I mean that he drove himself. As an old cavalryman he often dispensed with the services of the coachman and handled his own team. I often think his coaching knowledge may have served him in good stead—nobody knew where he went. But, as I said, he had slower, heavier horses than my grandmother.

Mother, like Grandmother, preferred fast horses. She had a pair of blacks, Atlasnie and Skvoretz—Satin and Blackbird. Satin was a cross between an Arab and a race horse. Mother also had a pair of bays, but she preferred the blacks. They were usually driven as a team, but some-times singly. Sometimes Satin was placed in the shafts and Blackbird was harnessed as a wheel horse or trace horse, a *pristiashka*, harnessed outside the shafts and guided by an outside rein. Blackbird galloped while Satin trotted, and the art of the coachman was to keep the two gaits equal but dissimilar. Blackbird looked as if he were just running alongside to keep tin company.

I liked to dress up as a coachman, so Mother had a blue coachman's coat made for me. What with my hair and skirts, she really went to an enormous amount of trouble. The coat was lined with white rabbit fur. I wore it practically all the time. As a result, the fur molted and soon my clothing was covered with rabbit hairs. Then Mother gave me a little red two-wheeled governess cart for Czarskoe, and the aged donkey, more obedient than before, pulled it around. Our house at Czarskoe Selo was well heated, and we were able to stay there in the autumn until after the snow fell. Mother also gave me a little Finnish sleigh, called a *veica* sleigh, lighter than the Russian sleighs. The donkey was harnessed to it and I drove around the grounds in my molting coachman's coat.

Besides living in St. Petersburg in the winter and at Czarskoe in the summer, we sometimes visited Mother's estate, called Ira, in the district of Tambov, about three hundred miles southwest of Moscow. These trips awed me. The train that carried us south lived in my memory. The engine was supposedly dangerous, and at stations we all stood well back for fear it might explode. Inside the carriage, though, we seemed to be speeding like the wind. I retained an image of the little city of Tambov as colorful and glamorous, and of the trip overland to Ira, a long way to the east, as a prolonged adventure.

Most of the land was flat, with hilly country around the Vorona River, near which the estate lay. Mother had sheep, primarily, and cattle, and she kept about a hundred brood mares.

The house itself was fantastic. It was built in the gayest tradition of Russian rococo architecture, which is saying a good deal. Panels of different colors covered the long front of the house and gave it an al-most medieval checkerboard effect. An ell on one end repeated the pattern, and a dome rose mysteriously beyond the ell, glowing hotly in the southern sunshine. Inside it was all great shaded rooms and long polished halls.

The Narishkins always had a lot of guests. Sometimes Mother, Miss Lizzie and I visited Aunt Lila Narishkin at Hamalise, their summer house near Viborg in Finland. Many of the Narishkin villas were really palaces, but the house in Finland was a big rambling frame structure, about like an Adirondack Mountain lodge. Madame Narishkin—she was rarely referred to as Aunt Lila—was the granddaughter of Barclay de Tolly, the general who with Koutouzoff turned back Napoleon's invasion of Russia.

When her grown children were around her, the effect was unreal, like a theatrical setting in which a number of superlatively handsome people have been gathered—young men, debonair and elegant and faintly cynical, and her daughters, Ella, Marie, and Nathalie, ethereally beautiful, with Madame Narishkin even at her age more beautiful than any of them. Mother was an attractive woman in most company, slight and graceful, but she had a long and inquisitive Grecian nose, a slightly prim appearance, and among those beauties she was an ugly duckling. She was, I must say, totally overshadowed by her ravishing sister-in-law Aunt Lila.

Because Father was aide-de-camp to Grand Duke Vladimir (the brother of the late Alexander III) the children of the Grand Duke were often around our house in St. Petersburg. There were Grand Duke Cyril, Grand Duke Boris, Grand Duke Andre, and Grand Duchess Helen, who became the wife of Prince Nicholas of Greece and the mother of Marina, the Duchess of Kent. They were all older than I.

During the summer all the children of the court were at Czarskoe, and we all played together. Besides the royal family and the children of Grand Duke Vladimir there were the children of the other Grand Dukes, like Grand Duke Dimitri and Grand Duchess Marie, always called The Younger, to distinguish her from the other Grand Duchess Marie; these two were the children of Grand Duke Paul, and about my age.

When there was a court function at the Summer Palace, friends came from St. Petersburg and stayed with us and then the whole party went to court. A slide was put up in an unused ballroom, and while our parents went to the court ball, or whatever it was, we slid down the slide. I recollect that Prince Belosselsky, whose son escaped from the Bolsheviks and came to America, used to come to these court functions and stay at our house, because I remember his valet. The man was a Hungarian named Crouch, who wore enormous handlebar mustaches which he kept waxed and pointed. After the grownups left Crouch used to scare me stiff because he'd glower and turn the points of his long mustache straight ahead and charge right at me.

These important occasions, with Father in his uniform, and Mother wearing a tiara, were interesting to us children—people coming and going, brilliant uniforms, much jewelry, and fine horses and carriages. Mother was a vivid, ardent, sociable woman—really a young girl—and she loved people, crowds and parties, balls, music and dancing, and grew radiant and animated: I liked to watch her dress.

She had whole sets of jewelry, from tiara and earrings down to brooches, necklaces and stomachers. It was fascinating for me to watch her prepare for her state occasions. There was a concealed safe in her dressing room that was far taller than I was. Whenever it was open and its trays upon trays of chamois leather were exposed, I used to pull up a chair and stand upon it. I loved to look at the jewels. I was particularly fascinated by the deep, glowing blue of the sapphires. But I also loved the rubies and emeralds. I was less interested in the diamonds and the pearls.

My parents' bathrooms were at opposite ends of a corridor in the house on the Mohovaya in St. Petersburg, and when they were getting ready to go to a court function I was kept busy running from one end of the corridor to the other to see how their preparations were coming along. Father shaved himself. He had seven razors, each razor with the name of a day of the week on the handle. I liked to watch him lather his face and shave neatly around his large mustache and nose. A small chip fire was always kept burning in Mother's bathroom. I had a small tub in a corner, because the big bathtub was too large for me to bathe in, and I was indignant whenever she locked me out of our bathroom while she bathed.

In those days my parents were always together. Father and Mother were quite social. But Father was basically the more serious of the two, although he possessed a great hidden twinkle that often seemed about to burst out. There was a deep difference between them. Father had a good business head, and for all his liberal ways was highly practical. Mother was hopeless at finance, and extravagant. When she had to leave Russia many years later, she left not with one but with all her jewels. For a start, she had seven tear-drop emeralds, in fact, a whole emerald parure. With this she bought herself *one* Rolls-Royce, which even in those days was a bad rate of exchange, particularly when the emerald set was my inheritance. Nevertheless, she lived well for the rest of her life.

Mother was a cheerful person, a complete extrovert, yet she had an insatiable interest in mysticism. She loved people, was popular, and was interested in everything from court life and political events to the simple people on her estates. Father was something of a scholar, with a thoughtful, philosophical streak. He delighted in shocking the older ladies with some of his risqué stories at the slightest provocation. He had originally studied to be a lawyer, graduating from the law school of the University of Moscow.

The influence of Pan-Slavism had led to the Turkish War of 1877. Pan-Slavism was really a mystical desire on the part of Russians to unite all Slavic peoples. This, together with the age-old Russian drive to the Mediterranean, comprised the national feelings of Russia, and my father shared them.

He was a lieutenant in the Chevalier Guards—where, incidentally, he became a famous gentleman jockey; Tolstoy's story of Vronsky's famous race in *Anna Karenina* is based upon an actual race ridden by my Father on his famous horse Correggio. During the Turkish War, when his regiment was not called to fight, Father was so furious that he pulled strings to get into the Hussars, who were leaving for the front. He was successful, and he made a fine reputation for himself under enemy fire. Soon he was made aide-de-camp to Grand Duke Nicholas. Later he was attached to the staff of General Skobelev, called the "White General," the outstanding general of the Turkish War, and he wound up as aide-de-camp to Grand Duke Michael, the brother of Alexander II. He was also attached to the armistice commission that negotiated with the Turks when English political pressure halted the Russian advance on Constantinople. Somewhere—I don't know where it is today—he kept a very valuable diary of the whole war.

Father came naturally by his interest in military life. He was the great-grandson of Field Marshal Suvorov, one of the greatest military geniuses of Russian history, whose tactics were still employed by the Reds as late as Korea and Dien Bien Phu. Suvorov had Swedish blood, fought as a common soldier against the Swedes and in East Prussia, restored Poland to Russia, suppressed the revolution of Pugachev in 1775, defeated the Turks, and then drove the French revolutionary armies out of Italy, consistently defeating the young Napoleon—he was the only general who did so. Suvorov lived like a common soldier on campaigns, eating and sleeping with the men. He was opposed to the elaborate uniforms and ceremony that Potemkin was introducing into the Russian army. One of our family stories is that when Potemkin came to visit Suvorov dressed in a magnificent uniform and covered with decorations, Suvorov took one look at him, jumped on a chair, and crowed like a rooster.

After the death of Catherine the Great, some of Suvorov's poems satirizing the new Russian uniforms and tactics incensed Emperor Paul, and Suvorov was disgraced, spied upon, and humiliated. He moved to his estate called Jerichovo, which we inherited, worked in his fields with the peasants, rang the church bell, and sang in the choir. His famous chair was still standing by the window when I lived alone in his house years later.

Father had always prided himself on his business acumen, and, in fact, he was first-rate. When he had charge of Grand Duke Vladimir's household, he saved the Grand Duke a lot of money by introducing business methods and strict accounting. The Grand Dukes headed the different departments of the army and navy; all military purchases passed through departments they headed. Grand Duke Vladimir headed the Russian cavalry.

Here is a typical example of Father's work in the Grand Duke's household. He found employed in the kitchen a big, friendly, ungainly farm boy from near Kiev who wanted to become a chef. Father be-friended him, and made it possible for the boy, whose name was Vassily Yourtchenko, to become an apprentice. And suddenly Vassily turned into a true artist of the kitchen, one of the greatest chefs in Russia. Strangely enough, Vassily was to walk out of Russia with Catherine, my first wife, her children, and myself when the Reds took over. He remained with my family until his death here in New York last year.

My first trip abroad came in my childhood, not long after the coronation of Nicholas II. Father and Mother went with the Grand Duke Vladimir and his Grand Duchess on a kind of state visit to Queen Maria Christina of Spain, the queen mother and regent. King Alfonso XIII of Spain was then only a child, and the children of the Grand Duke were taken along, and so was I.

In Paris we stopped at the Hotel Continental, and from there went to San Sebastian, where I played on the beach. The thing that impressed me most—and I didn't like it—was bathing in the surf. On the beach, there were cabins mounted on big wheels and a man arrived with a horse and drew those little cabins into the breakers. We sat in the cabin and watched the waves rising around us, which alarmed me considerably, and besides, the breakers were cold. There were professional bathers who took care of us children in the surf. They wore leather jackets over their bathing suits, and berets on their heads; they stood with their backs against the waves, holding us by the hands, and broke the force of the breakers before they reached us.

My other memory of San Sebastian is of the Grand Duchess Helen washing my hair. She was then thirteen years old. She asked the Spanish maid to bring her a basin of rain water, because rain water is soft and girls prefer it for washing their hair. But the maid misunderstood her and brought her a basin of water with sugar dissolved in it. When she put it on my head it grew thick and gummy before her astonished eyes. My ringlets stuck together and projected out in all directions. With all the other trials I had had to endure about my hair, this seemed to me to be the final indignity, and I cried.

The Queen of Spain, who was a pleasant, good-natured woman, gave me a Spanish harness for my donkey. The harness was amazing—finely tooled leather with hand-worked buckles, and enormously large woolen pompoms of different colors, which gave it a highly picturesque appearance. I put it on my donkey as soon as we got home, but he had grown too lazy to pull the governess cart, and Mother gave me a little brownish piebald pony, named Sitzovie, which means "Chintz."

Later, while we were staying at the Narishkin's place near Viborg, my cousin Cyril Narishkin and I found a pair of scissors one morning and we chopped off half my ringlets. Mother was having breakfast in bed and Aunt Lila Narishkin was having hers on a tray quietly by the window. When we marched into Mother's bedroom, I was brandishing the curls chopped from one side of my head, and Cyril was brandishing the scissors. There was a most awful scream from Aunt Lila, and Mother almost upset her breakfast tray. But—I was a boy from then on. The rest of my hair, now an unpleasant reminder, was chopped off by a barber who was hurried in from Viborg. Thereafter I was given pants and dressed properly.

Soon I was given a sort of personal servant or bodyguard—what the Russians called a *diadka*, a man who looked after a boy and kept him from getting hurt. Mine was a sailor from the Russian marines named Matthew Troufanov. Matthew began each morning by waking me with the orders of the day. He read them. "Today," he would read, "we will wear whites." And so we did.

We did calisthenics. We went for walks. We ran, rode, and under-went all sorts of exercises designed to make a man of me. Matthew was my valet as well as my bodyguard. He was even responsible for seeing to it that I was properly dressed when we dogtrotted around Czarskoe Selo.

I never had an inkling in advance of any trouble between my father and mother. He loved her, I knew, and to my childish eyes they seemed happy together. And of course I was too young to be aware of any subtle differences between them.

One apparently minor thing may have been significant of Mother's growing unhappiness. Despite her extrovert nature there was that deep mystical streak. She began to go to mediums and belonged to a little group of St. Petersburg society people who held seances and tried to communicate with the other world. They were feverishly serious about it all. They had table rappings in darkened rooms, and even levitation, when tables were said to rise and float in the air.

Father, of course, pooh-poohed it all, and it amused him greatly to talk about it. He could hardly have taken to that sort of thing, any more than I could have accepted the cult of Rasputin that swept the Russian court during the First World War. Still, I can tell fortunes with the cards—good ones.

Father may well have joked too hard, and Mother would get furious. There was an incident during that time that truly caused an uproar, and I'm still not certain that Father with his wild sense of humor didn't actually perpetrate the deed. There was once a seance held at the house of old Countess Kleinmichel, and since meetings there were always good, it may have struck Mother that she just might be able to convert Father to her way of thinking. Certainly it is the only logical explanation for his having been asked at all. Father told me that on his part he had *reluctantly* agreed to participate. I noticed that when he spoke, he had a twinkle in his eye. This particular seance, he told me, had been visited by a specially frivolous ghost. At the height of the seance, when all the lights were out, there was a scream from old Countess Kleinmichel. Father said innocently, "Shall I put on the lights?"

"On *no* condition!" she said. So they sat in silence in the darkness, and they heard her scrambling about. Finally she sighed, and said the lights could be turned on. When they were turned on, Countess Kleinmichel's *moumoutka* as Father put it, was upside down on the top of her head!

A *moumoutka* is a wig, and Countess Kleinmichel was known for wearing one at all times. Father told me that this extremely naughty ghost had apparently snatched off Countess Kleinmichel's *moumoutka* and thrown it into a corner, where she found it somehow in the dark. It was awful that without lights she couldn't tell that she had put it back on wrong side out. Mother never took Father to a seance again.

Yet, I am sure that Mother saw people of the other world. There is no question but that the following is astonishing, particularly since there was a witness other than herself. The group interested in spiritualism made a pact among themselves that the first to die should return to visit the others. One of the group was Capt. Korsakoff. He contracted tuberculosis and was sent off to the Crimea for his health.

Mother was alone one afternoon, having tea in her boudoir in our house at Czarskoe Selo, when the butler came up and said that Capt. Korsakoff was calling. She said, "How extraordinary!" for she knew how ill he was and that he had gone away. Korsakoff came upstairs, the butler announced him, and then Korsakoff vanished, just disappeared before their eyes. Mother learned two days later that Korsakoff had died in the Crimea.

Things may have gotten worse between my parents after the birth of my brother Vladimir, when I was about five years old. I do not know. All I remember is that one night we boarded a boat in St. Petersburg. Mother and I and the baby and the nurses. There was a storm, and I was seasick for the first time in my life.

We sailed through the storm to Stockholm. Mother had sent her yacht there. It was anchored out in the harbor. I was wearing a sailor suit, and one of those flat-topped sailor caps that went with it. A ribbon was given to me on the dock. It was a hatband for my sailor cap, printed with the name of Mother's yacht—*Sayonara*, Japanese for "farewell."

We sailed out of the harbor, into the Baltic, and crossed to England, where we landed at Hull. For some reason we went to London, where we stayed at the Piccadilly Hotel. I remember being bewildered by the traffic, the number of horses and buses, and the attention created by Vlady's nurse, who wore her native Russian costume.

From London we went to the Isle of Wight, where Mother had taken a villa. We were living there when Father arrived. I do not know what happened between them, but Mother suddenly left. Father remained. I asked childish questions, which nobody answered, and then, like a child, I stopped asking questions. In a dim way I understood that I was not to see Mother again.

I was acutely unhappy. Children need the sort of intuitive affection that a mother lavishes on them spontaneously, even though, in my case, Mother's demonstrations of it were sometimes extravagant and spoiled me.

So far as the elementary needs of my childhood went, Miss Lizzie cared for me, trained me, disciplined me, and acted as a mother to me. And she did the same for my new young brother Vladimir. Miss Lizzie was devoted to us, and it was not hard to return her affection. She always told us that she really loved it whenever we got sick, because then she could have us all to herself. I realize now what she did for us. A child needs those little acts of affection that are funny and unexpected, that make a child's dreamworld day. No amount of scrupulous care can contrive such moments—it is a talent inherent in the individual. People either have this facility with children or they don't. Miss Lizzie possessed it, and entered freely into our world; as a result we were protected from the immediate unhappiness of the divorce.

In a divorce I believe the man is almost always at fault. Whatever the specific circumstances, he creates the kind of life in which those circumstances arise. As for a child, the need for affection that he feels when his mother has been separated from him by divorce is likely to become part of his whole psychological make-up and stay with him all his life. His yearning to be loved may easily turn to resentment of the fact that he was not loved enough to be cared for as other children were cared for.

In my own case, though I had been under Mother's close care through the earliest and most critical years, I felt the loss; and my younger brother Vlady felt it more keenly than I. Automatically, when I thought of some of the boys I knew in those early years I said to myself, "People like him"—an unconscious revelation of my own fear that I was not liked. And before Vlady came I felt a kind of envy of the children of Prince Chahovskoy on the floor below us, since they had each other to play with while I was alone in the big rooms upstairs.

Just at this time my childhood sorrows were deepened by the death of my Grandmother Obolensky. She was buried in our family burial ground in St. Sergius Monastery, about fifty miles west of St. Petersburg. A big cross, with a head of Christ, the work of the great sculptor Vasnetzoff, stood in the family plot, and there Grandmother was buried among all the generals, beside her husband and her son Vladimir.

I did not want to go to her funeral, but I had to. I could not explain why I didn't want to go, so it was put down as simple badness on my part and lack of feeling for someone who loved me as deeply as my grandmother had. But I was really distressed.

The sculpture by Antakolsky, in which the head of Christ seems to be part of the living rock, is a great piece of work; perhaps I can explain what I mean about the quality of Vasnetzoff's sculpture. He was one of the most thoughtful of Russian artists. He once carved a magnificent statue of Ivan the Terrible wearing a skullcap, sitting on his throne and leaning on his staff, with a brooding and bitter expression on his features. The statue is now in what was the Museum of Alexander III in St. Petersburg. The original small bust, simply the head and shoulders, went through many vicissitudes. It was taken out of Russia after the Revolution and wound up in my possession in London. It finally came to rest in my son's house in Rhinebeck, New York. A superb piece of characterization in stone, it shows eloquently the sculptor's struggle to understand Ivan, his greatness as an administrator, his brooding malignance, and his cruelty.

While I admire that statue of Ivan the Terrible as a work of art, I still wish someone could have presented as beautifully the side of old Russia that my grandmother's life symbolized—its simplicity, kindliness and unfailing generosity in material things, its sheer adoration of little children, and in any judgment of the character of other human beings its absolute perception.

I believe my parents' divorce was the first case in Russia involving people of their station in life. It caused a sensation. Father did not want Mother to divorce him, but Mother demanded it; they were divorced in 1897, when I was seven years old.

Then Mother suddenly married General de Reutern. He was an exceedingly brilliant young officer, already a general despite his youth, and he was aide-de-camp to the new Emperor Nicholas II. It was an absolute scandal. General de Reutern was forced to resign from the army, and he and Mother left Russia. She bought a villa outside of Naples, and for years they lived there, entirely apart from our Russian way of life

CHAPTER II

To make clear the importance of my grandmother in my childhood perceptions, I should say something about the Obolensky family history. The Obolenskys were solid, substantial people, soldiers and statesmen, not having much to do with the life of the court.

They stemmed from the Viking sea lords who appeared at the beginning of recorded Russian history. They were seafaring robbers who raided the villages near the Baltic, penetrated inland, and finally moved their long, narrow ships on rollers overland on a legendary portage to the rivers, and then sailed down the rivers to the Black Sea and raided Constantinople.

Our family records begin with Rurik, the first real ruler of Russia, in the year 862 A.D. From him the male family line is traced intact to my own grandson. Rurik was a Viking who was asked by the Russians to come in and impose peace on a country town during the incessant wars of petty chieftains. He ruled for nearly two decades as Grand Duke of Kiev and Novgorod, Nijny Novgorod, the oldest Russian trading center, about a hundred miles south of St. Petersburg.

By the next generation the rule of the dynasty reached six hundred miles south. Rurik's son, Igor, became Grand Duke of Kiev, which city was thereafter the capital of Russia for centuries. A bewildering array of Svyatoslavs, Vladimirs, Olegs and others followed, until in the eleventh generation the line produced a saint, Michael, the son of Vsevolod and Maria, who was the daughter of King Casimir of Poland. He was a Christian martyr, tortured to death for his faith. St. Michael was canonized in 1246. His grandson, Constantine, was the first to be named Prince Obolensky.

Ivan the Terrible, two centuries later, began to liquidate the more independent princes. He wiped out the Obolensky family except for one prince. That prince was one of Ivan's leading generals against the Poles and Lithuanians. This solitary survivor of our line, known as the "Silver Prince," happened to be at the Lithuanian front outside Russia when Ivan set about bringing the principalities under the direct control of his government in Moscow. Ivan the Terrible summoned the Silver Prince to Moscow just after Ivan had declared himself czar—meaning Caesar—a title the rulers of Russia had never claimed before. The Silver Prince realized that he would be executed if he returned, and went over to the Lithuanians. He sent his aide, Schibanoff, with a letter to Ivan. The letter stated that he, the Silver Prince, had done many things for Russia, and that he had always been her loyal son. But now, with his family slaughtered needlessly, he could no longer continue his allegiance.

Ivan was incredibly cruel—he had killed his own son with his own hands in a fit of passion. He always carried a huge heavy staff in his hand. Its long steel point was sharpened. He bade Schibanoff come very close and read the letter, and as Schibanoff read, Ivan the Terrible placed the steel point of the staff on the emissary's foot, and slowly pushed it through. Schibanoff calmly went on reading. It is one of the great stories of bravery in Russia; Pushkin wrote a poem about it. When the letter was finished, Ivan ordered Schibanoff to be killed.

That was the sort of story in the family background. The Silver Prince was, at that time, the last of the Obolenskys. He came back into Russia in disguise to the woman he loved, and Ivan's police nearly caught him. His exploits inspired a lot of poems and stories which were in our library in St. Petersburg, and his numerous sons saved the family from extinction.

By my father's time, however, things had changed. The Obolenskys were civilized and cultured, generally distinguished for a sober devotion to public affairs. Grandmother Obolensky's husband, my grandfather Prince Serge Obolensky, was a liberal who enthusiastically cooperated with Emperor Alexander II in freeing the serfs. He cooperated so enthusiastically that he turned over nine-tenths of the best Obolensky land to the government to be applied to the peasant holdings of the freed serfs. This considerably reduced the family fortune, although, of course, it was no expropriation: the government paid a nominal price for the land, and the peasants paid the government for it in very small installments. Yet when I later managed father's farms I was hard put to it to get good production from the residue. That's when I started to study agriculture. I became something of an expert.

In any event, the Obolensky fortune by Grandfather's time was in real estate in St. Petersburg and Moscow, and in landed estates, like the landed estates of England, except that in Russia the estates' values were reduced. Without primogeniture they were being split up between the various male and female children. By my time our estates were still fairly extensive, though, and the Obolenskys were considered to be among the richer families of Russia. Whether one was titled or not made little difference where actual wealth was concerned.

Grandfather Obolensky died in 1882, soon after the assassination of Alexander II. Then Grandmother's second son, my Uncle Vladimir, died while still a young man the year after I was born. And my Uncle Valerian, Father's elder brother, had no children. So every thing conspired to add to my grandmother's interest in me as the principal bearer of the family name.

Not that the name was in danger of dying out. Other branches of the Obolensky family—my father's cousins and uncles—included big families. There was Vladimir Obolensky, who was aide-de-camp to Emperor Alexander III, in charge of his personal household. Each morning he went over with the Emperor the arrangements for the day, and usually remained to lunch with him and the Empress. After Alexander III died in 1894, his cousin, my Uncle

Nicholas became aide-de-camp in charge of the household of the Dowager Empress Marie.

Then there was Uncle Alexis, who was the representative of the Emperor in the Council of the Russian Church. He was the *OberProkurerator*, the so-called "eye of the Emperor." The post had been established by Peter the Great, who wanted a man responsible to the crown to keep an eye on church affairs and report to him. Curiously enough, the Bolsheviks, when they found they could not suppress the Russian Church after the Revolution, restored a similar post and put in a commissar to watch the Church Council, even though they had already removed Church officials known to oppose them. Uncle Alexis, together with Count Witte, wrote the first draft of the Constitution that was granted by the Emperor in 1905.

Uncle Alexander Obolensky, who was like Uncle Alexis in the Council of State, the Czarist equivalent of the House of Lords, was the head of the Conservatory of Music and of the Stiglitz Academy of Art in St. Petersburg, and was generally considered one of the greatest Russian patrons of the arts. Uncle Alexander was married to Anna Polovtzeff, heiress to the fortune of Baron Stiglitz, one of the richest men in Russian history, and she and her husband devoted their fortune to aiding musicians and artists.

Finally, my father's only sister Aunt Vera, married to Count Koutouzoff, had five children, my first cousins. Count Koutouzoff was the grandson of the general who defeated Napoleon, the stolid genius Tolstoy pictured so brilliantly in War and Peace. He later became Grand Marshal to the court of Emperor Alexander III.

The Obolenskys always deferred to the eldest member of the family. When I was young they were a matriarchy, the oldest then being women, like Great-aunt Dolly Obolensky. The ranking member of the family was actually consulted in all matters affecting the family. At luncheons we all sat in order of seniority. Dolly was always at the head of the table. I, as the youngest, was always at the foot. Aunt Dolly seldom went out; she always received. She often had forty or fifty people for lunch on Sundays after church—as many of the family as might come.

Several of the older people at Great-aunt Dolly's were survivors of my grandmother's era, simple and devout, unconcerned about the world beyond their relatives and friends. Their elderly lives revolved around the health and well-being of cousins and nephews, around marriages, the births of infants in different branches of the family, and which nephew was serving in what regiment. Politics and world affairs scarcely touched them.

Yet the more virulent elements of the family had through the years established a tradition that was strongly liberal. A Prince Obolensky was one of the ringleaders in the Decembrist revolt after the death of Alexander I in 1825, which attempted to establish a constitutional monarchy with a federal government based on a parliamentary system. He was an idealist who threw himself whole-heartedly into the struggle when Nicholas I assumed the throne. He was exiled to Siberia, and left a moving account of his ordeal and his faith.

My extremely liberal grandfather Serge Obolensky had perhaps been too enthusiastic a supporter of the reforms of Alexander II for his own financial good. My own father believed in and pressed for a constitutional and parliamentary form of government for Russia, a limited monarchy similar to England's, although, granted, by his time much of the Russian nobility favored such a government. Certainly all of my father's friends and associates did.

My uncle Sasha Sverbeyev went even further. He was a slightly eccentric old statesman, the governor of a district (the equivalent of a state in the American system), an august personage with a beard so long and white that we always called him Uncle Moses. He was one of the handful of idealists in the nobility who had taken the lead years before in aiding the peasant cooperatives that had sprung up spontaneously in the rural districts. These idealistic pioneers provided the money that hired trained technicians and administrators to organize the scattered business cooperatives into national organizations: a great work, and one that was already expanding into an important part of Russian life during my early years. These groups were so successful that they became a real threat to Communist programs later on. They were either taken over or stamped out.

But while these relatives of mine were either interested in liberal reforms or, as some certainly were, entirely indifferent to politics, they were all a part of the upper class of the time, attending court functions as protocol demanded, and all intensely Russian in their outlook. For they were educated, as my father was, when Pan-Slavism dominated Russian life. It was part of their habit of thought. Russia to them embodied the cultural heritage of the Slavic people; in their eyes Russia was the mother country of the Bulgarians, the Serbians, the Slovenes, of any of the Slavic races anywhere in Europe. They thought Russia's mission in the world was to unite them all in a federation of Slavic people.

Big events for us children were the Christmas and New Year's parties where the family assembled. At Easter Miss Lizzie took my cousins and me from house to house to call on relatives and people whom I rarely saw at other times, like the Marquise Paulucci, an elegant cousin of my mother's, born in Russia, who had spent most of her life all over Europe and in Paris in particular. Each house always had a Christmas tree, lovingly decorated. We would come home loaded with loot.

But each present was small, nothing like the lavish gifts that Mother and Father showered on me. Once I got a Cossack riding whip. Another time I got a toy sword. Both seemed magnificent to me, and I was delighted with them. The best presents were around the tree in the huge Youssoupoff palace on the Moika. They were given by my Aunt Zeneide, the mother of my cousins

Nicholas and Felix Youssoupoff. Felix was the one who later shot Rasputin. Aunt Zeneide bought her gifts in Paris, and they were bright and colorful, strange and foreign, useful and highly prized—things like a pocketknife, or a watch, or something equally wonderful and useful. Aunt Zeneide was another startlingly beautiful woman, greatly sought after, widely traveled, famous throughout Europe in her own right, famous also for the charming portrait that the painter Seroff made of her fragile loveliness.

After these visits we would go to Uncle Valerian's apartment in the Foreign Office. He was an absolute expert on foreign affairs. There was no permanent undersecretary of state in Russia, but Uncle Valerian had held the post for practically a lifetime. As a gesture, the government had given him an apartment, and he had his living quarters in one of the Foreign Office buildings. He had filled one entire room with a rare species of canary that he raised as a hobby. He had an old butler named Michael who looked after the birds. When we all came in at Christmas, all his young cousins, nieces and nephews, he would lead us into the canary room where the birds flew around him like pets. Then he would give each boy a ten-ruble gold piece and each girl a five-ruble gold piece. The holiday season always ended with a big party at Uncle Valerian's on New Year's, with everybody present, from the oldest dowager, like Great-aunt Dolly, to the youngest babe in arms.

At the time of the divorce Father was aide-de-camp to Grand Duke Vladimir. Afterward he was "elevated" to the rank of general. He was really "kicked upstairs." As a general he could no longer be an aide-de-camp to a Grand Duke. Then he was allowed to retire from the army.

Retired generals in Russia in those days were usually given some sort of official position. Father was not considered to bear guilt in the divorce, so he was placed in charge of all the institutions for the blind—a job that he was particularly keen to do.

The next year, Father and I visited Grand Duke Michael Nicolaievitch, brother of Alexander II, in Dresden. The Grand Duke was quite old by this time. He was very fond of Father—as head of the Russian artillery bureau he had formerly been Father's superior officer. Michael Nicolaievitch was a very serious-minded man who had a long gray beard and sang in the choir of the Russian Church at Dresden. After the lengthy services he used to call me up to him and give me a piece of holy bread to eat, which I enjoyed enormously because I was so hungry.

My recollection of Father at that time is that he was always personally driving his four-in-hand, which had a hand brake. It was my favorite carriage, because when we rolled along behind those four horses I was allowed, on command, to use the brake.

Father sold our house on the Mohovaya. He didn't want to live where we had lived when Mother was with us. This was one of the clues that showed me later, when I was old enough to understand, how very upset he must have been. We had other houses, seven in all, including property on the Mitninskaya, on the Neva River directly opposite the Winter Palace. Father built a modern apartment house there. It was of French design, modeled on plans drawn for a house in Paris, a good and attractive building. A third of it was kept for our own house, with a separate entrance, our separate stables for twelve horses, and a big coach house.

Most of our property was in the district of Nijny-Novgorod, about two hundred miles east of Moscow. I was seven years old when we began to spend the summer months there, all of us going together: Father, myself, Miss Lizzie and Vlady. We took the day train from the Nicholas Station at St. Petersburg. It was always crowded: whole families, from grandparents to little children, and many friends, gathered there even if people were only going on a short trip, shaking hands, kissing, and shouting good-bye up to the time the train pulled out. The big bell in the station rang once fifteen minutes before the train left, twice five minutes before, and three times just before the train began to move.

St. Petersburg had no suburbs to the east; it was built by Peter the Great, by sheer will power, upon a swamp, and when the city ended swampy ground began. When we looked back we could see the golden dome of the Cathedral of St. Isaac in the center of the city, and the needle of the Admiralty—blue domes, tulip-shaped brass bell towers, everything blue and gold sparkling like jewels against the horizon.

After leaving the swamps the train passed through lovely country, rolling hills, somewhat like Maryland. The railway ran straight to Moscow, the straightest track ever built, supposedly because Nicholas I laid a ruler on the map between the two capitals and said, "That's the way I want it to be."

Near Moscow the land was hilly, with attractive villages every few miles, each with its bulb-domed church. There were islands of woods standing amid the fields, which made it great country for hunting with borzois, the Russian wolfhounds.

The run from Moscow to Nijny was made at night. The cars were international wagons-lits, and as the tracks were broad gauge, the bunks were long. In the middle of the cars there was a pantry in which a samovar always boiled, providing tea at any time, served with hot buns that were delicious. The tea was poured into a glass which was placed in a metal receptacle with a handle. Outside there was nothing to see except the faint streaks of light before sunrise over the top of the dark woods. Then the forest dropped away like a great curtain, and we were in Nijny.

Nijny-Novgorod, or New Town—one of the oldest cities in Russia, stood on the last hill before the flat lands, the green domes of its churches and the gray walls of its castle built up the steep slope, with the towers silhouetted against the sunrise in the east. But once you were in the city, the smell was terrific—stock yards. Tanned hides were at a premium in this great trading center. Beyond Nijny was nothing but space, which the Russians in those days, and perhaps even now, called "the great enemy."

A big white river boat was waiting for us on the Volga, which was about half a mile wide here. Hundreds of paddle-wheel steamers, as ornate as Mississippi River boats, steamed up and down the Volga in those days. They were fast and luxurious, and we cast off and raced downstream with the current, passing log rafts and strings of barges, the whistle roaring sonorously and startling great flocks of water birds. The river flowed almost due east and then south. On the right bank going downstream were high red bluffs, and beyond them rolling hills, villages and farms. On the left bank the land was flat to the horizon and covered with virgin forest. According to Behr's Law, as Father explained it to me, south-flowing rivers, because of the rotation of the earth, undermined their right banks. They swept steadily westward like gigantic scythes, flattening the earth as the fields are laid flat behind the reapers. The Volga had moved to the west over the ages, leaving the land to the east of it as level as a table. Even now, imperceptibly, the river was cutting down those green hills on the right and spreading their earth out flat in the east, and those dark purple-green woods we could see on the far left were growing on land that had been leveled by the river in ancient times.

In the depths of that immense forest that reached to the Arctic on the north and to Siberia on the east there were hundreds and hundreds of miles where no human being had ever been. Here and there were remote colonies of Old Believers, fanatics who held that the Bible had been mistranslated and distorted by the bishops and the Church, and who fled for their faith and believed that the modern world was run by the Antichrist. They maintained their primitive religious faith, sometimes really devout, but more often fanatical and barbarous. Some of them were flagellants, or sects given to Holy Roller transports, and some held darker rites in which people burned themselves to death.

On the right bank of the Volga, which marked the division between inhabited and uninhabited Russia, the country was gay and cheerful, with groves of beeches and oaks standing among cleared fields. At Liskovo, sixty miles or so below Nijny, we left the steamer. Two troikas or carriages drawn by three horses abreast were waiting, and a luggage cart. A steep lull rose directly behind the town. The horses strained up it, then the river and the gloomy forest on the far side of it vanished from sight, and we were in cultivated country with peasant villages scattered here and there, people working in the fields, sheep and cattle grazing, and innumerable birds singing in the groves.

Krasnaya Gorka, which means Red Hill, stood in a large pine-tree park on an eminence overlooking the river Imza. The house was brick, spacious and unpretentious, with nine bedrooms and with the kitchens built separate from the main building. The barns and outbuildings stood about a hundred yards away. There were horses all over the place, thirty or forty in the stables, and several hundred mares. Father was raising horses for army remount. He had heavy horses, Clydesdales and Percherons and Ardennes, and Russian palominos, with black or white tails and a black stripe down the back. He bred two kinds, a light weight for troikas and carriage horses, and a heavy kind for draft horses.

The nearest village was three miles away. Like most Russian villages, its one street was a continuation of the road, with a wattled fence around the collection of houses, a gate at the road, and a sign listing the number of souls in the village. By the old Russian system of enumeration for the purpose of dividing the village land, a soul was a male inhabitant over twelve years of age, women not being counted. There were 120 souls in our village. Inside the gate were the peasant houses, the wells with their long poles that dropped the buckets into the water, and the church with its cross and green cupolas.

The peasants of Russia have always been an enigma to people who don't know them. The word peasant means farmer, a plowman in its literal sense. There is no such stigma attached to the Russian word as there is here in America, where it has become a derogatory expression. The people on our land were very much in the family circle; we knew them all on a face-to-face basis, and they knew us.

The Russian word for peasant is *Crestianin*—a man who is blessed by the sign of the cross, literally speaking. Some peasants were freemen, a proud people who lived with a sword in one hand and the plow in the other, and many of these were a buffer between Russia proper and the Tartar hordes. Some were exceedingly prosperous people, and many of them before the reforms of Alexander had bought themselves out of bondage. And up to this time, many of the less industrious had been bound to the earth, and these were once the serfs.

In my experiences with them the peasants were an exceedingly kindly group of people, and this went for all of Russia. They lived up to their name *Crestianin*. At the same time, in moments of anger or when they were in an irate crowd, they could be cruel. Probably this stemmed from the terrors of the Tartar invasions, for to a vanquished enemy they gave absolutely no quarter. They took death philosophically, as an act of God, and they were at all times deeply religious. They had a fine sense of humor—Russian humor, that is, which is really an acute sense of the ridiculous.

For instance, when Vassily, my old chef, who was a peasant from the Kiev district, had cooked dinner for Prince Vassily Romanoff here in America and Prince Vassily went back to the kitchen afterward to congratulate him, Vassily the chef said, with a profound bow, "Where do we run to now, Your Imperial Highness?"

This is Russian humor, but it also shows the man-to-man relationship that Russians have always had, whether it involves a prince and a peasant, or a duke and his footman, or noblemen of equal rank. I may say that I owe my life to the peasants who took me in and hid me from house to house in the woods somewhere in Russia when my life was in danger from the Bolsheviks.

In the spring, the country around Krasnaya Gorka was dazzlingly green, with lilacs everywhere and masses of lilies of the valley in the woods, and many nightingales. Our property at Krasnaya Gorka consisted of about ten thousand *dessiatines* of land—the Russian unit of land measurement, a little less than three acres—and we owned another property called Jerichovo (Jericho) of about eight thousand *dessiatines* in the district of Vladimir, near Moscow. These two properties contained more than fifty thousand acres, and our land holdings of all kinds came to about sixty thousand.

The Jerichovo property came to us from Field Marshal Suvorov's daughter Natasha. She married Count Nicholas Zouboff, and their granddaughter was my Grandmother Obolensky. Another branch of the Zouboff family, not titled, and not directly related to us, lived in the country, and the son, Peter Zouboff, exactly my age, became my first childhood friend.

When I say that Peter lived in the country in our general area I do not mean that we were close neighbors, though we often visited back and forth. When we went to see the Zouboffs we started early in the morning, when it was still cool, and spent the day on the road through the woods. The Imza, a clear, fast stream, flowed northeasterly to empty into the Sura River, which in turn flowed into the Volga, and the Zouboff land was on the far side of the Sura, some thirty miles from our place.

Midway on our trips we stopped for a picnic and to give the horses a long rest. We crossed the Sura on a little ferry mounted on pontoons, and drawn by ropes that ran through pulleys on the shore. The horses were frightened, the young ones rolling their eyes and threatening to plunge. Then on the far side of the river the road went straight up the steep bank. Only the coachman rode, and we held our breaths while the horses strained and struggled and the coachman shouted until the crest was reached.

Peter Zouboff was the most kindly person I ever knew. Everybody liked him. He was popular with the farm boys, the villagers, the old herdsmen, everybody. He was a round-faced boy with an engaging sense of humor, an amazing memory, a kind of instinctive sense of human relations, and he was always finding things. When we went out together, he invariably turned up with something splendid to eat like a fine cheese that some farmer had given him, or something extra that we could cook ourselves, or he made friends with somebody who fed us or gave us something very interesting to do.

Peter's father was the grand old man of the area, an invalid and a Crimean War veteran who had fought at the siege of Sebastopol. Late in his life he had married Peter's mother, a young woman, very affectionate and beautiful, and their home life was unique in its quiet gentleness and warmth. The old soldier was the leader of the local nobility, yet, as I pointed out before, he was untitled. This may seem to a European or an American a contradiction in terms; nevertheless it was the case.

Peter the Great had once had so much trouble with the princes, counts, boyars and so on, all of whom struggled to take their proper precedence by virtue of their rank, that he did away with all such seniority. Only the Imperial family was exempted; they continued to take precedence. Peter the Great decreed that henceforth there would be no seniority except that of age or of an actual position in the government. It was therefore ability, old age, or nothing. As a result, if, in these pages, landed gentlemen often seem to hold higher positions than princes and counts, Peter the Great, not I, is to be held accountable. Strangely enough, and contrary to what most of the literature of the last forty years had led one to believe, we were quite democratic. And old Zouboff took precedence over every one of the titled families for miles and miles around.

The Zouboffs were all extremely religious. Peter's father had built a church on the estate where everybody, peasants, farmers, herdsmen and the nobility, all came for their devotions. Peter helped with the service in the capacity of an altar boy, as I also did later when I began to visit them. I loved everything about that part of the country.

My whole life changed when Father and I, Miss Lizzie and my young brother Vlady began to spend our summers at Krasnaya Gorka. I no longer had a bodyguard, and soon I had a horse of my own. This was my first taste of true freedom, and there is nothing more exhilarating in the world. I remember when I was first allowed to watch the herd with the country boys. It was the very first time in my life that I had stayed out all night. Peter went with me, and we slept on the edge of the woods with low stars overhead, the cattle grazing on the open land beyond the woods. I am sure there were no wolves, but we imagined we heard them. It was terribly exciting with the big fire going, in which we roasted potatoes.

Our friends were the sons of the villagers. They grew up as I was growing up. One became our coachman, another a gardener around the house, and so on. Peter and I played games with them—principally soldier. And we swam in the Imza, where I learned to swim by holding onto an oar and paddling with one hand.

We cooked our meals outdoors and looked after the horses. The country boys had to work, so we worked too. In the evenings, when their fathers would come back from working in the fields, which were a long way from the village, they turned the horses over to the boys. So the boys and Peter and I fed them and groomed them and then took them to the pasture, which was also some distance away, beside the river. There were no saddles. Each boy just put a halter on one horse, straddled it, and took two or three other horses in tow, and went off to the river. Generally we merely rode there and walked home. But sometimes we were allowed to stay out.

The horses and cattle by the river were in the care of one man, called the *pastookh*, the herdsman. He usually had a fire going, over which he cooked his potatoes and cereal and a few onions; this stew, with his bread, made his meal. There were always a few of his cronies beside his fire. Peter and I liked to go with the boys when they took the horses. They were good fellows, friendly, amiable, polite, religious—simple and good-hearted country boys; as time went on we became personal friends.

In St. Petersburg and Czarskoe Selo, when I wasn't called Paponka or Horse Blanket I was called Your Excellency. Here the boys called me Serge. Out in those great woods and rolling fields there were no absurdities, and if there are moments in men's lives that can be remembered as sheer peace, this was one of mine. We sat around the *pastookh's* fire and listened to the old men reminisce. Mostly they just talked about people who had lived twenty or thirty or forty years before. They remembered everything about them, one thing after another. One man would remember something, and then another would chime in with something else that a particular man had done. When they finished remembering one man, they would start in remembering another. None of the people they remembered had done anything special, but they made it all sound wonderful.

They could also tell ghost stories that gave you goose pimples. Some of them were really mystical; they believed in supernatural agencies the way they believed in the sunrise or crops or anything else. They were afraid to go to certain places nearby, springs or swamps or valleys, because they were unholy. They said that the *nechistay a-sila*, the evil spirit, hovered over them. I had a dog, an English setter called Artur, who often pushed me out of bed at home. One night after we had been listening to the old boys talking like that, I fell asleep, but soon woke up because Artur, beside me, was growling. He was facing out into the night and bristling. Everything was pitch-black outside the circle of the firelight, and I could see two eyes gleaming at me from the darkness. I wasn't at all sure that it wasn't an evil spirit. To a small boy, it's all full of mystery, a thing like that.

Part II

Land Hunger

CHAPTER III

Perhaps the strongest result of those summers in the country was that I came to understand the hunger of the Russian people for land. Every twelve years the land that the peasants had been allotted was redivided among their families. The rural population had steadily increased, so there was less and less land to be distributed. The boys whom I played with at Krasnaya Gorka received only half an acre.

There is a sense of affection in a Russian's feeling about land that is sometimes so wild and powerful it can become one of the compelling elements in his motives and his memories. Even now I am conscious of a kind of wonder mixed in with my recollections of the endless furrows turned up in the spring, an inward excitement at the promise of harvest revealed in those ribbons of earth unfolding behind the plows. When I first saw the black lands of the Ukraine lying level to the horizon, so level, in fact, that the curvature of the earth was visible, the land itself thrilled me in the way one is thrilled by the wonders of nature—just the land, the look and the scent of it, and the knowledge of its richness lying fathoms deep underfoot.

There were hardly any fences in Russia. One field could sometimes reach as far as the eye could see. Our land at Krasnaya Gorka was good, but shallow. In the Ukraine there seemed to be no bottom to the millions of acres of incredibly fertile soil that was barely beginning to be plowed. Layer after layer of black earth was there, and the trick was to plow just a little deeper each spring, a few inches deeper, turning up a little more of the virgin soil to be mixed with soil that had been worked before. Then it was restored as if by magic to the richness of land that had lain fallow since the beginning of time. When I looked at the black Ukrainian earth, I could understand how the peasants felt when they looked at the land owned by the landed gentry of Russia. They coveted it, and their covetousness was inherent in the age-old feeling Russian feeling about the Russian earth.

When Ivan IV established serfdom in Russia, he became instantly "the Terrible." He decreed that people must remain in the district where they were at the time the edict was signed. The decree was no more barbaric than the values of the day, and it was issued for the good of the people. Whole sections of Russia were periodically starving, and everywhere there were famines in which thousands died. These famines came about because the people had always been migratory and made great seasonal movements north and south following the harvests. The princes were actually administrators of districts, and, most important of all, there were popular princes and unpopular ones.

Great hordes would gravitate towards the princes who governed well and were prosperous, leaving the rest of the provinces to starve. Thus in his struggle to subjugate the princes and unify all Russia under Moscow rule, Ivan the Terrible suddenly delivered his famous edict, enforcing his will upon everyone through his dreaded secret police, the *opritchniki*, with flogging and executions. This won him the support of the landowning class if not all the princes, for they had always faced a shortage of labor. But it riveted slavery in Russia for a thousand years.

Thereafter, the peasants remained on the land. Later generations of those who owned the land came to consider people who lived on it their own personal property, and they traded land and peasants among themselves. For army service they merely sent a number of their serfs. The peasants lived in villages, worked some land for themselves, but in the main they toiled for the landowner. There were several types of peasant land tenure, which later enormously complicated the problem of land reform; but the important thing was the landowners belief, centuries old, that people bound to the land were their property, because they considered the land itself and anything upon it to be their own. No wonder the peasants became the most conservative, immobile people on this earth, living as their fathers had lived, and looking longingly at the great expanses of cultivated acreage that were the landed estates.

When Alexander II liberated the serfs in 1861, he did not give or sell the land to the individual farmer. The government bought land from the landed estates, tracts which were near the villages where the serfs had lived and toiled for centuries for the landowners. But these tracts were not split up into farms. Instead, the whole tract was transferred to the village. The village was formed as a permanent community, with the *Mir* holding title to the peasant land and paying the government for the land.

Mir means world. The *Mir* was made up of all able-bodied men above the age of twelve. If there were fifty men-fifty souls-in the village, the land was broken up into fifty parcels. Each man got ten acres. A man with four sons received ten acres for each son, which with his own ten acres, gave him fifty acres. But another man with six daughters and no sons had to feed them all (and pay the installments of the purchase-price to the government) on the meager product of his 10 acres. Every twelve years the land was redistributed to take care of changes in the households, any new souls, women not included. And everyone stayed on the land.

The rural population kept growing. There were fifty million serfs by the time they were liberated. And by the time I began spending summers at Krasnaya Gorka, four decades later, there were seventy-eight million peasants, in 120,000 villages, living off the produce of 120,000 *Mir*-owned communes. It was because the population had increased so fast that my playmates in the country now got only half an acre, while a few years before each boy got several acres as his share.

In each village a few peasants grabbed a bigger share of the communally-owned land, or the most fertile sections, and dominated the others. They loaned money to the poorer peasants and so got control of their allotments. They were called the *Mir-ovyede*, which means *Mir*-eaters, soul-eaters. They were the equivalent of the bosses of a corrupt union, or the ward leaders of an unscrupulous political machine. No peasant had any incentive to improve the communally-owned land toward the end of the twelve-year period because it would be taken from him at the next communal distribution.

This system of land tenure was the great mistake made by Alexander II and his liberal cabinet. Their reforms were a magnificent step forward for Russia, but they, like all idealists, made no provision for human weakness. As a result, they inaugurated a system of landholding for the people that was self-defeating from its inception, due to increasing population, and they established no administrative agency equipped for proper governmental supervision or effective control.

An interesting sidelight was the fear that haunted the prime minister of the time, Loris-Melikoff, who masterminded the reforms. His objective was to satisfy the peasants as long as possible, until Russian industrial expansion would be able to cope with the tremendous increase in their numbers. He feared that if they ever came en masse to the cities, there would be no possible way to handle them. Hence a scheme was evolved to keep them on the land and, meanwhile, to build up Russia's nonexistent industries. In a sense the government was petrified; it didn't go far enough in its reforms, and thereby put off the inevitable and bequeathed the entire fiasco to a later generation—my own.

So when I was young, the most explosive situation on earth was growing up in the Russian countryside. Investment in land was not very profitable. As a rule, farm land returned a profit of only one and a half percent a year. The landed estates were actually shrinking. Fewer people lived and worked on them. Absentee ownership was increasing. Everything conspired to make the peasants want to take the land of the estates which seemed to be in inexhaustible abundance all around them. When the crisis came, the peasants took it. And after they had taken it they were afraid.

Ours was a working farm. Father not only lived there each summer, but went there often at other times of the year. He was constantly investing in blooded stock to improve the quality of the farm animals, buying farm machinery, and helping increase the well-being of the peasants. He was popular, and was elected to the zemstvo, the local self-governing agency, after he left the army.

The zemstvos were one of Russia's genuinely democratic governing institutions. They were established by Alexander II as the first step toward giving Russia a parliamentary government. Delegates were elected by popular vote, the peasants voting for their own candidates. The power of the zemstvos was nebulous. They had authority over everything that was not specifically the province of the central government. In effect, this meant the power of a local zemstvo and the scope of its work depended on the initiative of the delegates. The zemstvos had the power of taxation. Schools, roads, public health, everything of this sort rested on them.

The seventy-eight million peasants still used the old Russian plow, just two sticks of wood with a piece of iron. They could not read or write—unless they were conscripts, for the soldiers were taught to read as part of their military training. There were only one million school children in all Russia, out of a population of one hundred and sixty-five million.

But just about this time the zemstvos began their astonishing growth. Schools were built and teachers trained, and in five years' time the elementary school enrollment jumped to seven million. In our district, where only a few years before no one could read, all the children were being educated. Every village had its school and every other village had its zemstvo headquarters. These were usually just small, square office buildings. Often the zemstvo headquarters, the new school, and the hospital were the only structures in a peasant village except the peasant houses and the church.

The zemstvos bought pedigreed bulls that came from good strains of milking cows, and set up stations where the farmers could bring their cows to be serviced for a fee. The zemstvos also bought stallions abroad and established local stations where the stallions were able to service all the mares of an area; also rams, for sheep that produced a better grade of wool. In our district, because of Father's constant agitation on the subject, the zemstvos began the purchase of farm machinery for the peasants. Even with a good harvest a farmer could not buy new equipment. He could not pay for it until he had collected for the goods he sold. But the zemstvos underwrote a ten- or twenty-year loan. They set up depots all over the district and sold the machinery to the farmers on long-term credit.

So Father found himself in the middle of the most constructive work that was going on in Russia, or perhaps anywhere in Europe. He was very much impressed with the ability of the men who were his fellow delegates: they were forthright, honest, independent, and it was impossible to confuse them about what was going on in the countryside; they knew their own districts better than anyone in the world. At the district and national level, the leaders of the zemstvos were outstanding. The local zemstvos elected delegates from their own ranks to the district zemstvos, and these in turn selected delegates to the all-Russian congress. These national delegates were good speakers and administrators, often lawyers, generally liberal or moderate in their political views, working for a parliamentary government in Russia but aware of the practical work that would be needed to make parliamentary government successful.

The zemstvos had won general good will, so they were able to command the help of the finest educators and technicians in the country, men whose services they could not possibly have paid for. Father was completely convinced that the zemstvos would develop into a form of self-government for Russia. He thought that if I became an agricultural expert and worked in the zemstvos I would have some part of a movement in Russian life that was bound to go on growing, and I could serve my country in the best possible way. That was his purpose in seeing to it that I spent as much time at Krasnaya Gorka as possible—to learn to milk cows, take care of horses, and in fact to do all kinds of farm work, including work with farm machinery.

I remember when I learned to milk cows. They were milked only by milkmaids. Cows are temperamental animals, and ours wouldn't have anything to do with me. Finally the girls made me a sort of apron that I wrapped around my trouser legs like a skirt. That fooled the cows, and they stood quietly while the girls showed me how the job should be done. I got to be a pretty good milker—the most I ever milked at one time was six cows.

Both our estates were subdivided into several farms, half a dozen or more, with a man to head each farm and a manager for each estate. Then there was a lawyer, Mr. Nikolaieff, who handled all the property and looked after Father's interests while we were away, for we were often traveling. When I was a young man and began to go out a great deal. my aunts used to say to me, "You! You think you are popular with ladies. You should have seen your father!"

Father had grown a beard, which, with his penetrating eves, gave him the air of a professor. He was always perfectly dressed. When he came in to say prayers with us, Vlady and me, each evening before our bedtime. he always smelled deliciously of Eau d'Houbigant. He loved the ballet and followed it assiduously. Often when Miss Lizzie and Vlady and I drove out with his horses, the horses would swerve suddenly of their own accord and start down some street from habit, indicating they had often gone there when Father had the carriage. I never knew anybody who lived there.

CHAPTER IV

Our life had settled into a pattern by the time I was ten. Father and Vlady, Miss Lizzie and I left St. Petersburg in May, when everyone always left the city. But one time, instead of going to Czarskoe Selo as we had in the past, we stayed three months at Krasnaya Gorka. Then we spent six weeks or so in France, first visiting Paris, then going on to Deauville. This became the pattern of our summers, except that some summers we visited Biarritz.

The first Americans I ever met turned up on our first trip to France.

They were three boys from Chicago who came every day to the beach at Deauville to play, and had a sort of gang, laying down exactly what each one was to do in whatever games they were playing. In those days some popular Russian toys were made in America. The toys were small glass tubes filled with a colorless fluid, with a small colored glass figure of a man in each. There was a rubber covering over the mouth of the tube, and when this was pressed in different ways, the little figure inside bounced and displayed violent agitation.

They were fine toys, called, for some reason, *Amerikansky-jitels*, which means American residents. The fun consisted in getting several *Amerikansky-jitels* and making them all dance together. During Palm Sunday week, as we called it, the week before Holy Week, there was always a street bazaar where hundreds were sold. As we weren't allowed much spending money, we hoarded it, and we went and bought as many as we could, in great excitement. I suppose some enterprising American manufacturer had sent them over.

I was interested in the three boys at Deauville because I had never known an American. And they were interested in me because they had never known any Russians—certainly none who talked English with a Scottish accent. So we got along all right, and I was allowed to be a part-time member of the gang. Our duties were to annoy couples on the beach in the evenings before bedtime. We would whistle and make disparaging noises at appropriate moments. On several occasions we were chased.

There was quite a large Russian colony in Biarritz, and a number of people had villas and spent much of their time there. Princess Yourievsky, the widow of Emperor Alexander II, and her sister Countess Berg, and Princess Gagarin, and Countess Shouvaloff were all great friends of my father. They were more or less permanent residents abroad, often related, united by common friendships or family, always meeting for lunch and holding dinner parties and bridge parties, for they all played bridge with passion. In his early days Father had been expected to marry Princess Yourievsky's younger sister, who later became Countess Berg. She was a very beautiful lady, and when she was with Father and I appeared he would say, "Come on and click and say *merci* with your heels to someone who is nearly your auntie!" And he would roar with laughter.

In those days Princess Yourievsky was still attended by a staff of twenty or so. Besides the palace that Alexander II had given her in St. Petersburg she had her house in Paris, the Biarritz villa, and, in the very center of Nice, a big three-story villa of gleaming white marble that looked like an old-fashioned town hall converted into an elaborate residence. Dressed in long flowing mauve dresses, very dignified and gracious, she looked exactly like what she was—the widow of one off Russia's greatest rulers. Officially she was addressed as Serene Highness, as were members of the royal family alone. Her story was the strangest I ever came to know intimately.

When Princess Yourievsky was still a young girl of fourteen, living on the estate of her father, Prince Dolgorouky, she met Alexander II, who was at the height of his reputation in Europe as the liberator of the serfs. He was on maneuvers, riding apart with a few officers. He came upon her riding alone, trying to make her pony jump a little ditch. She just couldn't make him jump. The Emperor was highly amused and stopped and teased her about it, which made her furious.

She told him what she thought of both him and her pony at the same time, which amused him more. Later that day Alexander, who had a fine sense of humor, stopped with his staff at her father's house, and she was horrified to discover that she had insulted the Emperor.

Years later, when she was a student at Smolny Institute, the Emperor met her at her graduation exercises. She was eighteen, and somehow he remembered her. By the time she was brought to court, she had grown into a delightful young woman and soon became a court pet; the next year, when she came out, she was made a lady in waiting to the Empress, who was an invalid. Then began the affection between herself and the Emperor. She was accused of being calculating, but it was not true. The Emperor had his eye on her and it was all his doing. There was a tempestuous romance. Nevertheless, the Emperor was greatly agitated, mostly concerned about her, trying for her sake to hide the affair from everyone, even his own secret police. He was then about fifty and she was nineteen. The relationship continued and they eventually had three children.

I could hardly have dreamed that this great figure from the old world, with her stately and elegant manner, would someday become my mother-in-law. Princess Catherine, the youngest daughter of the Emperor and Princess Yourievsky, was tall and good-looking, already a *jeune fille*, reared, like most Russian girls of family, by an English governess. She had studied under De Reszke in Milan, for she had an excellent mezzo soprano voice. She rode to hounds and was a fine horsewoman. Naturally she was very conscious of her position as a daughter of the Emperor, for before his death Alexander II had issued a ukase conferring the perpetual title of Serene Highness on her and her brother and sister.

Her mother, the Princess Yourievsky, on the other hand, lived entirely in the past. Life for her had stopped the day the Nihilists threw the bombs that killed her royal husband and prevented her from becoming Empress of Russia. To her dying day she kept relics of him in a glass case in a large closet behind her bed. While the thought is macabre, it is understandable for a lady so dedicated to the memory of her husband.

In her palace on the Gagarinskaya in St. Petersburg, near the Winter Palace, and throughout all those years when Alexander was alive, Princess Yourievsky had maintained a brilliant salon where the Emperor met informally with his liberal ministers. The disfavor of the hard-minded, anti-liberal Alexander III caused Princess Yourievsky to leave Russia after her husband's death, but she kept up her salon in exile. Then, strangely enough, Nicholas II, while still very young, came to know her and her children, took a liking to them, and, when he became Emperor, conferred property and income on them and caused them to return to Russia. But so much of their life had been spent abroad that France had become home to them, and they were only very rarely in St. Petersburg.

Princess Yourievsky subconsciously expected French people to treat her as the widow of the Emperor of Russia. She always traveled from Paris to Biarritz in her private railway carriage attached to the fast night train, alone except for her dog and her servants. Princess Catherine once told me—many years later—that on one occasion a commercial traveler got into Princess Yourievsky's private car by mistake, and made himself comfortable. The old princess was horrified to discover a stranger sprawled out on her cushions, and imperiously ordered him to leave. He protested that he had bought a ticket. She said she owned the whole car. He thought she was crazy. Finally the matter was straightened out, but it left Princess Yourievsky badly shaken.

Most of the Russian colony at Biarritz was far less formal than Princess Yourievsky. Countess Shouvaloff, for instance, Betsy Bariatinsky before her marriage, was always called Aunt Betsy. Princess Gagarin was the sister-in-law of Count Tolstoy, the curator of the Hermitage and a famous art authority. His sons Ivan and Andre Tolstoy were my closest boyhood friends in St. Petersburg, as Peter Zouboff was in the country. We went to dancing classes together, and on occasions we shared the same tutor.

The problem of finding tutors for Vlady and me caused Father much perplexity. We traveled so much we never went to school. By the time we returned to St. Petersburg from France, the schools that our friends attended had been in session several weeks. The first tutor was a Mr. Nicolle, the son of the Professor of Egyptology at the University of Geneva. He was vague and dreamy, never knew what was going on, and Andre and Ivan Tolstoy and I did awful things to him. We used to surround him by stealth like Indians, each boy armed with a pillow. When Mr. Nicolle's back was turned, one boy let fly with a pillow. He whirled in alarm to see who had thrown it, and then the boy in back of him let fly with another pillow. Mr. Nicolle was a good teacher, but our tricks were too successful; he departed from St. Petersburg, saying we were impossible.

We would never have dared take such liberties with Dr. Chumi, the tutor of the Tolstoy boys. He was a Swiss-German, as strict a disciplinarian as Mr. Nicolle was lenient. After Mr. Nicolle left we had a number of others, of whom I remember little. Then came Dr. Henneberger, a Swiss-German, the chess champion of Switzerland. He lived with us in St. Petersburg. Dr. Henneberger was a chess master who played a match with Aliokhine and nearly won. He was always entered in chess tournaments, and was more bemused about his games than concerned with our studies. He taught us to play chess. I learned four to five openings through the first few moves. But as we were not enough competition to keep him occupied, Dr. Henneberger used to let us blindfold him, and play all of us, the Tolstoy boys and others, simultaneously. He won, of course, but when he was blindfolded he could not win all his games, and that depressed him more.

But the tutor who really influenced me was Dr. Carl Schindler, also Swiss-German, who instilled discipline into me and forced me to study. He was very severe. For several years he remained with us before he became a professor at the University of Berne. He was a typical scholar and teacher, devoted to his work, and he drove the habit of study into me so firmly that I have always been grateful to him.

I studied music, which I loved, but I had no natural gift and I was too lazy to practice. My teacher was quite famous, and afterwards came to America, where I met her again. She told me frankly that I was the worst musician she had ever tried to teach. Perhaps because he loved the ballet himself, Father put me in a dancing class for children. We practiced at the home of the Hartungs, not far from where we lived; Hartung was a friend of Father's and had three small daughters near my age. In addition to the Tolstoy boys, children from other landed families made up the rest of the class. Maestro Ceccetti, the great ballet master who taught Pavlova, was our teacher.

He had been the virtual dictator of the Russian ballet for nearly thirty years, ever since a spectacular debut that had established him overnight. But by this time Ceccetti was passing middle age; he had a shiny shaven head and a chestful of little medals that jingled when he bounced around. He would put us in one position and then in another position, and shout "Now the fifth position!" or some other position which I could never get right. I was always put at the end of the line. It annoyed me very much. I began to regard him as a fussy old bore, no matter how great a dancer he was. On his part, he took a strong dislike to me. "You are so stupid," he said, jumping up and spinning around to show me what he meant, "that you cannot understand it at all." Finally he said he would teach me to waltz. "Walk three paces forward and three paces backward," he said disgustedly, "and then three paces sideways and three paces forward and then three paces backward, and you'll learn it."

Nevertheless, I learned to dance from Ceccetti, not only a little ballet dancing, but dances like the waltz, the polka, the mazurka and the fandango. The whole training made me somewhat more proficient at ballroom dancing than I would have been had I not received it, and I find woven through the story of my life the strains of waltzes with a great many ladies who loved that most graceful of dances. Ceccetti always admonished me about the clumsy way I held my partner. "When you waltz like a gentleman," he said, "it must be that you are presenting a beautiful flower to the audience."

After tutors were dispensed with and my brother and I were enrolled in school in Russia, we did not attend classes. Our teachers came from the school to our house to teach us. The reason was that, as usual, the school term had invariably begun while we were abroad, and the teachers instructed us privately to enable us to catch up.

I never studied in classes with other children until my last years of high school. Yet I was still a student of the school. Four times a year I went to the school building to take my examinations. Three of these were on the work done in the preceding quarter. The last session was the period of final examination on the whole year's work. It began early in May and lasted two weeks. I got good grades, largely because Dr. Schindler had taught me to study, and because, being so far behind at the beginning of each term, I had to cram to catch up. So I got into the habit of keeping at my books, and when my grades became high I wanted to keep them that way.

At about this time Father decided that I should be schooled in the manly art of self-defense. He got some of the other parents interested, and a group was formed of the Tolstoy boys, the Pashkoffs and myself. Once a week we were to be taught boxing and fencing. A Monsieur Loustalou was to instruct us. M. Loustalou was a Gascon and a magnificent braggart. He was small, amazingly agile, and a tremendous fencer. He was fast as lightning on his feet. As regards boxing, he always enjoyed giving us a good punch in the nose. His theory was, and he told us so at every opportunity, that until he broke the nose of each of us we would not be able to endure punishment. In the ring M. Loustalou was a fierce and leaping little man. "Bam!" he would say. "Bam! Bam!" Once, as a result of his theories, I was going around with a nose like a potato.

One day we decided we would get even with him. We had sensed an Achilles heel in the fact that he was always so impeccably dressed and debonair. The Pashkoffs had a large garden around their house. It was wintertime and the garden was filled with gigantic drifts after a heavy snowfall. We had asked M. Loustalou to meet us at the Pashkoffs' to go sliding down the ice hills with us—the great Russian winter sport. When we saw him come down that narrow snow-covered path, we were delighted. The drifts towered to his shoulders. So we all went out to shake his hand, then jumped on him and threw him in a drift. I remember being propelled through the air, but it didn't matter. That day M. Loustalou ate a lot of snow.

For weeks after that we walked around with our noses like potatoes.

CHAPTER V

It was when I was around ten, eleven or twelve, the years between 1900 and 1903, that I turned into a country boy and began to look forward to the end of the May examinations and the return to Krasnaya Gorka. There I rode my horse, and heard about what happened during the winter from the country boys. Or, on visits to the Zouboffs or Peter's visits to me, I roamed around the country with him.

Every afternoon for a long time my brother Vlady and I went riding with General Lazareff, an old soldier who visited Father often and played bezique with him in the evenings. By this time Vlady had also been given a horse, and General Lazareff taught him to ride. Vlady was always bouncing around, exciting his horse, galloping forward and galloping back, to the great irritation of the General, who nicknamed him The Flea.

Peter Zouboff's mother died during these years. His father, who at Sebastopol had won the St. George Cross, the most prized Russian military decoration, was, as I have said, an invalid. Consequently the family depended on Peter's older sister Catherine, much like her mother and as beautiful. Peter had turned into an exceedingly religious boy. When I visited him I always helped him with the service in the church his father had built. We would go without breakfast. Early in the morning we would ring the bell in the steeple. Then Peter would help serve the Mass with the priests, and I would take part. Every detail of the services became fixed in Peter's memory. Wherever he was, he knew each part of any Russian Church service, what psalm was to be sung at what point, sometimes even better than the priests conducting the service. And that religious training, you will see later, helped Peter all his life.

We were all given a good religious training, though not nearly as thorough as Peter's. One of the leading priests of St. Petersburg was my confessor and, in effect, my tutor of religion, coming to the house three times a week. Every Sunday in St. Petersburg we were taken to church. We stood through the whole service, an hour and a half or two hours. During Holy Week we did our devotions and went to church every day. We fasted through the whole period. Maundy Thursday was the service of the Twelve Bibles, a very long service, and then on Good Friday an icon representing Christ being buried was carried from the church and placed in the church sanctuary. On Easter Uncle Valerian always arrived, bringing Easter eggs for the children. On Easter night at twelve o'clock we went to church again, and waited until the time came that symbolized Christ was risen. Then the period of fasting was over and many ornate suppers were given; everyone made the rounds of them—the men in full dress uniform, the ladies wearing rows and rows of precious Easter eggs around their necks.

Life revolved around the family. The tone was mostly devout, with lots of casual, informal social gatherings and occasional big social events. In these years Father became one of the most popular bachelors in St. Petersburg. His chef was one of the best in Russia, and he enjoyed searching in Paris for new recipes to bring home. Father also picked up somewhere an inexhaustible collection of off-color anecdotes, with which he enjoyed shocking my spinster aunts and great-aunts who came each Thursday night to play whist. I myself cannot recollect these stories, except to remember they were just casually funny borderline humor, not so bad they couldn't be told but still not quite proper, so they evoked at once roars of laughter and—after a moment's pause to get the point—protesting cries of "Oh, Platon!" from my great-aunts, which increased the laughter.

Father was one of the municipal councilors of St. Petersburg, an advisory body to assist the mayor, like the city council of an American community. He had also become deeply interested in his work with the blind, in the organization of the Dowager Empress Marie Feodorovna, the mother of Nicholas II, who was honorary head of the societies that looked after blind children. Father had charge of all the schools for blind children, hospitals and orphanages, twenty-one in all.

Radium was discovered in 1898, and because there was a possibility that its rays could help the blind, Father personally financed experiments with it. I was taken to some of the experiments in a darkened room. There was an apparatus with colored lights, and a number of blind people were led in and placed before it while lights of different colors were turned on and their reactions tested. Almost nothing was known of the properties of radium then, except that its rays had to be controlled with the greatest care. It was fantastically expensive to produce, but the fact that the rays penetrated opaque substances gave rise to hope that the blind might conceivably be helped by it. I do not know what the final results of the experiments were, but my recollection is that some of the blind became aware of different colors when they were exposed to radioactivity.

Russian life in those days was simple in a way that people who have not known it at first hand can hardly understand. We lived quietly, with no display whatever. Father gave Vladimir and me five rubles a month spending money—two and a half dollars. That was standard spending-money allowance for boys in our circumstances. It made no difference whether their families could afford to give them that or thousands—they still received five rubles.

We were all cousins—first cousins, second cousins, third cousins; we rarely knew precisely what degree of relationship existed. I finally figured out the Obolenskys, but my cousins the Youssoupoffs were too much for me, and I never knew exactly how my friend Felix Youssoupoff and I were related, except that it was through the Narishkin line. Many of the relatives were as rich as Croesus—for instance, the Youssoupoffs didn't really know how much property they had. It took two months to visit all their estates, and one of their properties included 160 miles of oil land beside the Caspian Sea. But there was still little display, partly as a matter of taste, partly because wealth was in land and real property.

Boys and girls of the St. Petersburg families met at dancing classes on Sundays during the winter. These were really informal dances for young people rather than classes. Christmas was still the major social occasion of our youthful lives, as we went from one relative's house to another. Uncle Valerian's Christmas party became increasingly important, since that annual ten-ruble gold piece—five rubles for those under fifteen—meant a big increase in our spending money.

Uncle Valerian was extremely shy. He had always been in love with my Aunt Zeneide Youssoupoff, and had wanted to marry her. But he could never get up courage to ask her. He was too timorous and unworldly to propose. Yet Aunt Zeneide was very fond of him, and my mother always said that Zeneide would have married him if he had asked her.

The funny thing was that Father, according to my mother, had also fallen in love with Zeneide before he began courting my mother. Then he discovered that his older brother Valerian was secretly interested in Zeneide, so Father retired and left the field to him. But as Valerian never mustered up enough courage to propose, Zeneide married General Youssoupoff, and Father married Mother, and Uncle Valerian never married anyone.

Uncle Sasha Sverbeyev, the one we called Uncle Moses, held a pretty dignified position as governor of a district, but he lived very moderately. He slept in a little room with one bed, that was built in the shape of a boot. We called it The Boot. This was not his design; the room just happened to have been built that way and he never changed it. Except for a lot of wonderful and valuable paintings, literally covering the walls, his apartment was exceedingly modest: a sitting room, a den with a sofa and writing desk, and The Boot.

Uncle Moses always dressed in a frock coat, with his black tie and stiff collar barely visible under his whiskers. He must have been one of the most hospitable men that ever lived. He wanted us all around him, nephews and nieces, young people especially, students and strangers. Every Thursday that he was in St. Petersburg was set aside for a luncheon that lasted all day, and he was hurt and worried if fewer than thirty or forty people appeared. He never served wine or alcohol in any form, but provided lots of fruit punch. The menus for these luncheons varied strictly according to schedule; that is, the same meal was repeated after an interval of Thursdays, and on a Thursday when my cousins and I liked what was being served we attended in a body. The old gentleman was delighted to see us. There were always several complete strangers present.

Uncle Moses' hobby was religion; he spent his spare time, which was considerable, looking up out-of-the-way churches he had never seen before. He was a sort of collector of churches, the way some people are collectors of rare stamps or butterflies. Having visited all the nearby churches and kissed all the icons in them, he was compelled to take longer and longer journeys to churches that were new to him. One story about him was that in a remote province he found a church with an icon on the ceiling. He could not possibly reach it, even with a ladder, and at last satisfied his conscience by getting a mirror, focusing it on the ceiling, and kissing the glass. On these ecclesiastical explorations Uncle Moses met people on the trains or in the churches, and got into long discussions with them about their lives. He made hundreds of friends as he was a sympathetic listener, and he warmly invited them to his Thursday and Sunday luncheons in St. Petersburg. When they arrived a long time afterwards, he had no earthly idea who they were, so he generally sat down beside them to make them welcome, and kept them to himself in animated conversation while he racked his brains trying to figure out who they were and where he had met them before.

During the Russo-Japanese War of 1904 my portrait was painted by a man who subsequently became known as one of the finest artists Russia had produced. He was Philip Maliavin, who was then only at the beginning of his career. Maliavin painted few portraits. He was one of those artists who wouldn't conform—a modernist, an avant-gardist, a perfectionist—and he found in Russian country life a subject that inspired him. Before his time the tradition in painting peasants had been to show them as somber and pathetic. Seroff who was Maliavin's greatest predecessor, painted big canvases of peasants huddled against the winter cold, or peasants being flogged; he looked on the world the way Tolstoy looked on it.

But Maliavin was of peasant stock himself. He was born right after the liberation of the serfs, and showed such promise that he was placed in a monastery to become a priest. There he painted so brilliantly that he was released to become an artist. In his early twenties he painted a masterpiece, "Peasant Women in Red," a great frieze of laughing peasant women in scarlet dresses silhouetted against a sunlit sky, the figures of the women unselfconsciously sensuous and bold. The professors of the Academy were so shocked they not only rejected Maliavin's application for a traveling scholarship but refused to hang his painting. The head of the Academy at last personally ordered it to be hung. Then in the Paris Exhibition of 1900, Maliavin's painting (renamed "The Laugh") became the sensation of that great international fair.

Maliavin made the Russian countryside exciting and colorful. He understood the peasants, their shrewdness and patience, their earthiness, and their hunger for the land. He painted peasant dances, the swirling vivid dresses of the girls covering the whole canvas like the petals of some exotic flower, or little peasant girls, timid and ethereally beautiful.

He painted few portraits. One that became famous was of the liberal statesman Count Witte. When Maliavin returned to Russia after his triumph in Paris, Father somehow persuaded him to paint a portrait of me. He actually painted two. When he finished the first he destroyed it; he said it was too stereotyped. So he painted another on a huge canvas that eventually covered almost the entire wall of our library in St. Petersburg. At that time the Japanese War had me stirred up. I was a great patriot, all the more so because I had had none of the military training that most of the boys were getting and that Father just didn't believe in for children of my age. I had a gray wooden model of a Russian battleship, a replica of one of those doomed warships that were just then steaming to disaster at Tsushima. I was proud of it, and for his second portrait Maliavin painted me with this battleship. I remember him very well; he was a young-looking man with a great deal of dash, very gifted and serious, devoted to his art. He had me dress in a naval uniform—a sailor suit, white shirt and black trousers—holding up the model and admiring it. The work went on and on. This time Maliavin was pleased with the result. But I grew pretty tired holding up that battleship. The painting was made with gigantic strokes of the brush; it was an enormous portrait, and I never liked it.

But I was fascinated with painting. I wanted to paint. I took lessons and learned to sketch a little, studying with one of the professors at the Stiglitz Academy of Art, which Uncle Alexander Obolensky headed. There too I had courses in design, studying periods of furniture, fabrics, and things like that, which eventually became valuable to me. I never fooled myself into believing I had artistic genius—it was merely that I enjoyed painting and liked the company of artists.

When I was about fourteen Father decided the time had come for me to learn the facts of life. He engaged a tutor for me, a young medical student who came to live at our house in St. Petersburg and who talked to me about sex, male and female physiology, birth, reproduction, hygiene, venereal diseases, and life in general.

We became close friends and I was able to talk with him without self-consciousness. But we principally talked politics. He was a revolutionist. He belonged to the Social Democratic Labor Party, then under-ground, and was a full-fledged follower of Karl Marx, convinced that the governmental and economic structure of Russia was doomed through internal contradictions. Since the socialists had to be very secretive and conspiratorial, we talked candidly about sex and whispered in the deepest secrecy about politics and economics. I was appalled to learn that the declining rate of profit under capitalism was going to sweep us all off the face of the earth.

My tutor was a Menshevik, a follower of Plekhanov, one of the Marxists who wanted to ally the Russian labor movement with the reformers and socialists of Europe and to break with the terrorism and political conspiracies of Russian revolutionists. It was just at the time of the split in the Social Democratic Labor Party. Lenin, who wanted, a small conspiratorial party of dedicated revolutionists, had split the party into the majority, the Mensheviks, and the minority, the Bolsheviks. The Bolsheviks were completely routed. The majority had won,, but my tutor was filled with misgivings. I have a vivid memory of his dejection and his prophecy as to what was going to happen. "The Bolsheviks are going to win," he said. "It's an awful thing to say, but I'm sure, the way it is happening. We Mensheviks are theoreticians. The Bolsheviks will take over." He said the Bolsheviks were only a handful, but they were disciplined and organized. "They are stronger, they are ruthless; and mind you," he said earnestly, "if there is any catastrophe there is going to be a terrific socialist movement, and eventually the Bolsheviks will win."

At that time the Bolsheviks had scarcely been heard of. I often thought of that prophecy later on, both of its accuracy and of the fact that matters of that nature were discussed with me at my age. I was awfully upset, I remember.

Then, too, school was getting tough. I was in high school, the Gymnasium. Our schools were modeled on the German system. We studied Russian literature, French, English, science, natural science, geography, law, the history of philosophy, and finally, in the last years, universal history up to modern times, an enormous subject, thoroughly covered. In math we had algebra, trigonometry, geometry, chemistry, higher mathematics and physics. Because of the time I missed on the trips abroad I had to work to keep up; I was leading my class and I wanted to keep ahead. It was always a tremendous relief when the annual examinations were over and we headed back to Krasnaya Gorka.

There was always a new crop of colts. Several hundred mares had produced offspring with good and bad points to be argued about Father's Clydesdales, from the valley of the Clyde in Scotland, had a little too bushy a foot for artillery use, but his Ardennes breed from Belgium made a very good artillery horse. Raising horses for the army was a lucrative thing in those days. Father bought a fine Arab stallion and crossed it with the Russian palominos to produce a good cavalry mount.

Our local cattle were a hardy black-and-white breed. They produced a lot of milk, but it had only two and a half percent butterfat. Father worked to improve the breed, buying selectively and crossing the local cattle with an imported brownish breed whose milk was richer.

He was also interested in reforestation. Under Czarist law a land-owner could cut timber on his estate in proportion to the amount of land he replanted in trees. The growth was calculated in eighty-six-year cycles. If a man planted ten thousand acres in seedlings, he could cut so many thousand feet of full-grown trees elsewhere on his property. So we were systematically taking the less productive land out of cultivation and putting it into woodland.

All these things made country life of absorbing interest. Those ponderous Percherons had foals that were practically square little animals when they were newborn. There is nothing in the world to compare with a big herd of Percherons, massive and dignified, heavy as elephants and proud as lions, unless it is a lot of Percheron colts playing together. Take a hundred of them on a green hillside in the spring and they make a picture that is unforgettable—anyone who ever saw it would remember it and want to see it again.

CHAPTER VI

Our house in St. Petersburg was next door to the headquarters of the Russian secret police. It had formerly been the home of the Prince of Oldenburg, and when the Prince died his widow rented it to the government, which used it for the secret police headquarters. There it stood in the midst of all the houses of our friends, just like another house of the nobility. So far as outward appearance went, it was a little smaller than the others, a neat white residence, not at all conspicuous. But when the Revolution of 1905 began it was the focal point of everything that was going on.

The Revolution began right at our front door. Father Gapon led a demonstration to petition the Emperor on Sunday morning, January 22, 1905. The throng before the Winter Palace, across the Neva from our house, was enormous. The young captains in command of the guard didn't know how to handle it, lost their heads, ordered the troops to fire; at least a hundred people were killed. It was totally unnecessary. Everybody knew it was unnecessary. Then the Revolution started with riots all over Russia.

We were right in the middle of it. After the demonstration the guards, including the crack cavalry regiment of Chevalier Guards, were called out and ranged in front of the Winter Palace. The Chevalier Guards dated from the time of Peter the Great and were the Emperor's bodyguard, recruited entirely from the officer corps in those days. Grand Duke Vladimir was placed in command of the whole St. Petersburg army corps, about three divisions.

The excitement kept on growing, and before long more mobs formed in St. Petersburg and again approached the Winter Palace—threatening mobs this time. An order came through to see to it that Morskaya was to be cleared. Morskaya ran from the Winter Palace through the great Morskaya archway and past the Nevsky Prospect to the Cathedral of St. Isaac, the center of the city. If the soldiers moved against the mob, it was certain that there would be a bloodier riot than the preceding one. My uncle Youssoupoff, Felix's father, was in command of the Chevalier Guards. He was an extraordinarily calm and level-headed man. Instead of ordering the troops to advance, he took his trumpeter with him and rode slowly through Morskaya to the cathedral and back. He was in full uniform and the trumpeter was unarmed. It took a lot of courage to ride through with the mob on both sides. He returned and reported diplomatically that the street was calm; because it was possible to traverse it without interference.

His tremendous self-confidence impressed people and even gave him a certain prestige with the government. A fortnight after the catastrophe before the Winter Palace, Grand Duke Serge was killed by a terrorist in Moscow, and widespread disorders broke out there, suppressed after a couple of weeks of heavy firing. Then General Youssoupoff was made Governor General of Moscow, and handled the difficult situation there with great firmness and skill. Grand Duke Serge was the fourth son of Alexander II, married to Grand Duchess Elizabeth, who was Queen Victoria's granddaughter. After his death she retired from the world and formed an order of nuns of which she was the head, building hospitals and caring for the sick, almost a saint in her selflessness.

When the Revolution of 1905 began, one of the great fears was that the peasants would seize the land of the estates. With Russia's defeat in the Japanese War the authority and prestige of the government had suffered disastrously. The land hunger of the farmers could explode overnight. Houses might be looted and burned as they had been during Pugachev's rebellion more than a century before. In the spring some estates actually were seized and some landowners were killed.

It was not an organized unrest, but was spasmodic and depended on local relations between the peasants and the owners of the landed estates. Where these relations were poor there was looting and burning of houses. Not many were burned. Though there was some slight unrest in the area, our property was not touched. When word reached the government that a district was unstable, a regiment of Cossacks would be sent in. Their appearance generally quieted down the countryside and stronger action was rarely required. A Cossack regiment passed through Krasnaya Gorka, and the people calmed down upon this evidence that the government was alert.

Now Nicholas II issued a manifesto proclaiming a constitutional government. Count Witte and my Uncle Alexis Obolensky drafted the constitution. Curiously enough, when Count Witte began his sensational rise in Russian political life, another uncle of mine, Nicholas Obolensky, was associated with him by current court gossip. Count Witte had emerged in the space of a few years from the obscurity of a job with the Russian railways to become Russian minister of finance. The gossip linked Uncle Nicholas to Count Witte's wife, who was a beautiful, brilliant woman of Jewish descent. She and Nicholas Obolensky had a sort of mutual admiration that went on for years and years. Uncle Nicholas never married, and, whatever the truth of the story, it came to be accepted as an established fact.

The first elections in Russian history were held in the spring of 1906. At the age of fifteen I more or less supported the Constitutional Democrats, who favored a government on the American model, a federal system, with a limited monarchy, whilst Father was a good deal to the right of this. He was one of the people who supported the Emperor unequivocally in the October Manifesto, which granted a. constitution with a parliament of limited powers. I was pleased when, the Constitutional Democrats won the election; they had a majority in the lower house of the Duma. Potemkin's Palace, where we used to skate on a pond in the park, was made into a hall for the Duma. But no sooner had the Duma been called into existence than the government objected to the first speeches, dissolved the assembly, and ordered new elections for the next year. Count Witte's government had fallen, and Peter Stolypin headed the new one.

The whole Stolypin family were second cousins of ours. We saw Stolypin often, both before and after he became the leading Russian statesman. He was a pleasant, intelligent man, very easy to talk to. He enjoyed talking to us youngsters, asking us questions about school, what we were studying and what we thought of it—that sort of thing. Stolypin became known as the Nemesis of the revolutionists, but in those days he was a liberal, a little more conservative than Witte perhaps, but not much. In fact, it was Stolypin who pushed through the agrarian reforms that had only been talked about before. He had barely taken office when a bomb was thrown into his house; he was uninjured, but his little daughter lost her leg in the explosion.

Stolypin knew what the situation in the countryside meant. Despite the terrorists and the agitation in the cities among the industrial workers, he understood that the real Russian problem was land reform and the blind land hunger of the peasants. His great reform was to set up land banks. They were called agronomes. These banks bought land from the landed estates in proportion to the number of villagers in the area who needed land. The land thus purchased was then transferred to individual peasant holdings. The government financed the purchases with long-term loans that ran up to fifty years; the owners received government bonds.

Everything was done energetically, with a full realization of the seriousness of the problem. Government agriculturists came to Krasnaya Gorka and went over our property. We stated we wished to hold so much, as a unified farm, and could sell so much. The land they selected was near the villages, so many acres near one village, so many near another. We gave these selected tracts of land to the government, and under the auspices of the peasant banks these tracts were subdivided into individual farms. The peasant banks then offered the tracts to the farmers, and the more enterprising bought; then banks also financed the building of farmhouse and stables and the purchase of implements for the farms. About nineteen million individually owned farms appeared in Russia as a result—a tremendous increase in the number of farms, and a very great reform.

These were boom years. A terrific prosperity began in Russia after Stolypin's reforms. In an agrarian country two good harvests in a row means prosperity, and except for 1911 there were good harvests right up to the beginning of the First World War in 1914. The two harvests just before the war were as good as any on record. There was a stirring in the Russian countryside that had never been known before. The people were well fed, everyone was becoming educated, self-government was growing through the zemstvos. Of course Stolypin made many enemies. The revolutionists hated him. And Rasputin, who began his rise to power in Russia in 1908, became Stolypin's deadly enemy.

Besides Stolypin's reforms, another factor increased the prosperity of the countryside. The growth of the cooperatives gathered momentum. At the turn of the century there were no more than fifty-six peasant cooperatives in all Russia, and they were aided by only a handful of kindly men like my Uncle Sverbeyev and Prince Galitzin. But within a decade 7,500 peasant cooperatives were established. They did a business of 290,000,000 rubles a year, or about $145,000,000. That was seven percent of the whole retail trade carried on in Russia. This increase was expansion. The peasant population was beginning to buy and sell in the normal fashion rather than living on subsistence farming alone.

The cooperatives were sponsored either by the zemstvos themselves or by the men who led the zemstvos. These men felt they were helping the peasant class enormously, especially by keeping them out of the hands of unscrupulous traders. The producing cooperatives were established first. During Lent a lot of peasants fasted. Products that could, have been sold went to waste. So arose the idea of forming central, agencies for storing and processing or selling the surplus. Milk that wasn't required by the household could be taken to the cooperative and bought by the cooperative with money loaned by the zemstvo, and butter was made of it, or cheese, and so on. The surplus eggs that weren't eaten by the family, vegetables, and whatever else they didn't consume could be disposed of through the good offices of the cooperatives. Between 1906 and 1914 five hundred dairy producers' cooperatives were created, and their number doubled in the first two years of the war. Then the small cooperatives merged. They became a very big business, with their own retail chain-store outlets. When I was eighteen the first big congress of the cooperatives was held in Moscow, to coordinate and organize their work over the whole country; they had become an important factor in the social and economic life of Russia.

One other program contributed to the growing prosperity. During the long winter months the villages were snowed in and there was not much to do. There had always been handicraft industries and local products in the villages; some were known because they turned out fine lace, or pottery, or dolls, or toys, or wooden spoons, or food products like raisins. But it was all done locally, and there was no outlet for the produce except through traveling traders or fairs in the nearest cities. All the peasant women knitted or made coarse linen goods, but the work was done with no guidance. To make better use of the winter months and increase the income of the peasants, the village industries were organized.

Cooperatives of this sort were called *koustary*. They were built on an assembly-line pattern. The method was worked out by the cooperative leaders, who had good engineers to advise them. One product was scissors: during the long evenings one part of the village made one part of a pair of scissors, another part of the village assembled them, a third part of the village sharpened and polished them. So their output was tremendously increased. The same process was used in making wooden spoons. In Russia everyone ate with a wooden spoon, even the Emperor. Some peasant households cut the wood for the spoons. Others shaped the wood roughly, and still others finished the shaping. The untreated spoons were then passed on to the next household, where they were painted in vivid colors, and then to the last group, where they were lacquered. Thus the whole village took part in the work.

The same was true of linen. The goods produced by the peasant women could not be sold in quantity because it varied in quality and design; it wasn't standardized. The central cooperative hired artists to make designs which were distributed, together with specifications and instructions, to the local branches. The local women then produced goods of a high level of quality and a standard design that could be sold in large lots. Laces, shawls and carpets were produced in the same way, the cooperatives providing the households with yarn and thread. Whole areas of Russia were dressed entirely in cloth made by the local peasant women, often very primitive cloth, and the cooperatives provided improved looms and better thread; the result was a better product and more of it. This side of the cooperatives' activity was sponsored by the Czarist Government and encouraged by the zemstvos.

The producers' cooperatives for foodstuffs, in the early days, had been hampered by the local traders and officials. Now they had grown strong enough to take care of themselves. I took a great interest in them because I was going to work in the zemstvos. In our district I came to know the leaders in each village from the time the movement was in its infancy. It was growing in that decade as fast as the schools were growing. It was a wonderful time, hopeful and optimistic, with everything seeming to work together for Russia to promise a great future and the peaceful, evolutionary solution of her problems.

And it was great fun. We skated, skiied, danced, went to parties and amateur theatricals and thought of ourselves as part of a world that was gradually bettering. As boys we were boisterous and loud with each other, and shy with girls. I was in love with Irina Rayevsky, a vivaciously witty blonde beauty, one of several daughters in a prominent St. Petersburg family, who eventually married my old friend Alexander Tolstoy.

My devotion to Irina lasted for years, all through Gymnasium, which in those days was the equivalent of high school and the first college years. But circumstances conspired to keep us apart, except for those Sunday dances and occasional more important social festivities for young people. For one thing, I was cramming hard. In my last three years of Gymnasium I did not go abroad with Father, in order not to miss the first part of each school year. At sixteen and seventeen I went to classes every day in my black student's uniform, and keeping near the top of my class kept me busy. I didn't go out much. But every afternoon I had a couple of hours off in which to take the air. Then we would all rush to the garden of Potemkin's Palace to skate. There were Russian ice hills there, wooden chutes built fifty or sixty feet in the air and covered with a thick sheath of ice; they had a hand-cranked elevator for the toboggans. Wide steps led up to a platform at the top, where you got on a toboggan, and as the ice was like glass you came down at tremendous speed. The gentleman sat in the front of the toboggan and guided the descent with his skates, the lady kneeling behind him with her hands on his shoulders. It was a lot of fun going down. And pretty healthy exercise, because it was out in the open, and you had to climb those hills in order to slide down.

To get from school to the ice hills of Potemkin's Palace in time to take advantage of the two hours required planning. It took most of the free time I had. Either some one of the boys had to get the family horses, or we had to hire a droshky. But none of us were allowed much money; our parents were universally agreed not to spoil us. A droshky cost thirty to forty kopecks, nearly half a ruble. I got ten rubles a month spending money in my last year in high school—about five dollars and a half. My income in Russia was around 75,000 gold rubles a year, about $37,500. With the purchasing power of the ruble then, it might be reckoned the equivalent of several hundred thousand dollars a year. So the seven and a half dollars I got every month wasn't going to put much of a dent in my inheritance. However, as I said before, all the boys got about the same amount, no matter how much or how little money their families had: it was almost as if the families had formed a union.

My Uncle Valerian died in 1908. He did not leave his estate to Father, but to me and my brother Vlady. So I came into property of my own apart from that which I would inherit from Father. However, in courtesy to Father I left its management to him even after I was legally old enough to have it. Vlady agreed to do the same. Father didn't believe in young people having too much money, and I didn't take much, letting it accumulate in the estate. I'm afraid Vlady later on regretted this, as he preferred to live much higher than I. But we were both pretty well trained by Father, and as a result of my training I wasn't extravagant. I had good money sense, but I was more interested in the world and its betterment. Father had always said, "My country first, my family second, and myself third. That's the way to be." Money was very much behind in the running—necessary, but behind. Uncle Valerian's property was in real estate, principally two big apartment houses in St. Petersburg which were very well managed and were big moneymakers—we kept Uncle Valerian's estate manager to handle them.

St. Petersburg society in 1909 was quiet, cultivated, sociable and friendly, and any lavish splurge would have been regarded as bad taste. So the boys my age were all in the same boat—or more often all in the same sleigh—united in a common democracy based on the equality of insufficient spending money. If our range of enjoyments was strictly limited, we made the most of those that were available to us and never regretted the loss of those we knew nothing about. Moreover, since I was nineteen, I could generally count on Father's allowing me a one-horse sleigh and a groom for any really important occasion.

Some of the important occasions were the parties at the Polovtzeffs', who had two big ice hills on the grounds of their place in the Islands. (The Islands were in the estuary of the Neva. On some of them were residences of the Czar and the nobility, on others the homes of the gipsies.) We were often invited there for the afternoons, my cousins and I and all the younger boys. During the day we went down the hills. Toward evening, tea was served in the house. We changed our clothes, and there was a ball—very colorful with flares on the ice hills and the grounds, and the guests made up of girls in society and the young blades from St. Petersburg. We were the younger crowd, the girls who had just come out and the boys still in the later years of school. I had started going there when I was seventeen or eighteen, which was young to be going out, because the Polovtzeffs were related to the Obolenskys.

CHAPTER VII

Mother had returned to Russia. She lived on her estate in Tambov and did not come to St. Petersburg. It seemed very strange to think of her being back, for I had gotten used to not having a mother. And subconsciously I thought of her as being just the same as she had been when she left twelve years before. So I was naturally deeply stirred and excited when I went to see her.

I made the trip alone. Right at the start it seemed something was wrong. I remembered the train to Tambov as speeding like the wind, but now it chugged along like any train. Tambov had turned into an ordinary little city of wooden houses and improved streets. Then came the long trip overland to Ira. I had learned enough about farmland to see that the estate was plainly well managed and prospering. The land was rich. The sheep and cattle grazing on the hills were good stock. And Mother's horses were very fine, trotters and race horses, much different from our heavy-duty, hard-working draft horses at Krasnaya Gorka.

I suppose the hours I had spent in my childhood thinking about Mother, and glamorizing the past when she was with us, left me more deeply shaken than I knew. The house impressed me like a dream house, with its odd checkerboard of colors; it was just the same as I remembered it, but apparently much smaller.

Then I went inside and saw Mother. She seemed much smaller than I remembered her. I was then six feet tall. She was still very good-looking. What amazed me was that she had a low, husky voice; she was Mother and she wasn't Mother. I could see that she did not want to show her feelings, and we sat and talked about all kinds of things; I remember thinking that the lowness of her voice was probably due to the fact that she smoked so much. She lit one cigarette after another, a typical long Russian cigarette that she fancied, part of which had a built-in cardboard cigarette holder. The smell of Turkish tobacco to this day reminds me of her.

It was a weird reunion. I cannot even explain what it was like. I had a sort of numb, frightened feeling. She wasn't my mother any more. We talked about things that didn't matter. After a while she brought in my little half sister and half brother, Olga and Max de Reutern. With them came Max's tutor, Pavel Ivanovitch, a Russian doctor of law, a very pleasant quiet man, somewhat pedantic, but good-humored and with a keen human awareness that made him a quieting influence. He made things much easier, but I had mixed feelings of kinship and strangeness with the children. They had been raised in Italy, and I immediately realized that they looked upon Russia the way I had looked upon France in my childhood.

Mother took me to my room, to let me change and get a bath after my trip. In many ways she did not seem different; she laughed in the same way, and it made me happy to see that she was happy in her life.

After I had changed and rested, Mother introduced me to her husband, which was the most difficult thing. General de Reutern was by now a semi-invalid. His hair and beard were gray; he was stooped and wore dark glasses. He was extremely polite to me, and very amiable, but he looked ill.

The visit never lost its air of strain. Still, Mother and I came to talk a little more easily. It was at this time that we began reminiscing about the past, and she told me the eerie story of the visit of dead Captain Korsakoff. I felt she would not be interested in the butterfat content in the milk of the cows at Krasnaya Gorka, or the delegates to the zemstvos. So we talked mostly about the people we had known in the old days—we were like people who have just become acquainted and discuss friends they have in common. After ten days or so, I went home with a feeling that I was returning to ordinary life from a world of unreality.

At this time Father was giving me more and more work to do in connection with managing the estate. He sent me to Jerichovo to look over the tree-planting that was being done on Field Marshal Suvorov's old estate. The soil there was so thin and unprofitable that the farm was not being worked. Trees were being planted in the fields so Father could cut full-grown timber elsewhere on our land, and I had to go over the acres put into seedlings, to file our request to the government to cut mature trees.

Suvorov's old house was white, with white columns in front, standing in isolation in a deserted countryside. It was well cared for, with Suvorov's famous chair still standing by the window in the parlor. Suvorov himself had preferred to live alone in a cabin. He slept on straw, throwing his coat over it for a bed. Eccentric or not, he was a deeply religious man and built a log cabin church on the estate.

The trees there were flourishing. They were pines, and they grew fast. Pines have always had an odd effect on me, and I was filled with melancholy thoughts. The farm made me gloomy, the dry, barren soil, and the loneliness. There was no one around except the caretaker living somewhere on the premises, and when I went to bed I could not sleep. In the night I kept hearing odd noises, and I got up and opened what I had thought was a closet door and found a flight of rickety steps leading down into the darkness. I didn't bother to investigate, and I barricaded the door. It was a spooky old house, and in the morning I was glad to get away from there.

CHAPTER VIII

We Obolenskys are always very emotional and not too physical in our relationships with girls. Say that things have to be just right. It is just that we put them on a pedestal. I was an idealist. And I always meant to marry someone to whom marriage would be the first love affair of her life, just as for me marriage would be the first love affair of my life. It sounds ridiculous but it was so.

This view of womanhood and love lasted through adolescence and quite a way into my young manhood. Perhaps the answer is in Russia herself. Remember that in Russia we were all given a good religious training. In addition, many of us were idealists in other respects, thinking of reforms to be made and work to be undertaken for the benefit of mankind. We worked keenly for these things. I don't mean we were allergic to the other sex—far from it—but we idealized women. They were something to look forward to. We did not sow even the tamest of wild oats, and we were chaste.

When I was eighteen all St. Petersburg society was rocked by a tragedy that came very close to home.

Felix's brother Nicholas Youssoupoff was several years older than Felix and was extremely good-looking. He had always been interested in the arts, and was an excellent actor, which the family disapproved of.

At the time there were three beautiful sisters who were having a brilliant social success in St. Petersburg; one of them, Countess Marina Heyden, who had just made her debut, was by far the most beautiful. She was much courted, extremely popular, and a great flirt. She became engaged to Baron Manteufel, a lieutenant in the Horse Guards. Then she met Nicholas Youssoupoff, who wanted to marry her. His parents refused to think of it, and Felix tried to dissuade him. Still, she remained engaged to Manteufel and went off to Paris for her trousseau. Nicholas, however, found an excuse to go there, and when Manteufel heard that they had been seen together in various restaurants, he rushed there himself.

There were some stormy scenes in Paris. What happened there I do not know, but Manteufel challenged Nicholas to a duel which was to take place in St. Petersburg.

Almost every influential person in St. Petersburg connected with the Youssoupoffs tried to prevent the duel. On June 22, 1908, Nicholas and Manteufel met in St. Petersburg, with pistols at twenty paces, which was considered terribly close. Nicholas was killed instantly, and Manteufel married the lady. The effect on Aunt Zeneide was awful, and the shock to the court was tremendous. The lady in question had to leave Russia; I don't know what happened to her. But it was terribly hard on the other two sisters who suffered the same fate. The youngest of the two was one of my favorite dancing partners, so it was hard on me.

The tragedy brought Felix up short. He went through a profound religious conversion. Grand Duchess Elizabeth, the sister of the Empress, befriended him. Her husband, Grand Duke Serge, the Governor of Moscow, had been killed by a revolutionary's bomb, and she had become a nun, devoting her life and fortune to the poor. It was she who had a great influence upon Felix's religious outlook.

Rasputin's shadow had already begun to fall across the court. He had appeared at court that year, gaining his hold on the Empress by two uncanny prophecies he made when the Emperor's only son, who was always ill, was thought to be dying. Once Rasputin even wired the Empress, telling her the boy was out of danger and would recover, and a day or so later he was well. The Dowager Empress Marie, Grand Duchess Elizabeth, Aunt Zeneide Youssoupoff and influential ministers like Stolypin protested against the superstitious hold that Rasputin had gained with the Empress, and because Rasputin was known to have interfered with state appointments, and even policy. Their objections were to no avail. The Empress became offended, and all these people were virtually banished from the court.

Felix left for England to study at Oxford.

Father gave me more and more responsibility in taking care of the estates. I was acting as superintendent in some cases while I was still in college. It was in 1909, before I graduated from the Gymnasium, that we began large-scale experiments at Krasnaya Gorka with hybrid corn, bagging the ears with gauze to prevent cross-pollenization, a complicated process because of the varied times at which the different varieties matured. And we were producing a really top-quality wheat. By selective breeding we had increased the butterfat content in the milk of our cows from two and a half to five percent. In the process a distinctive local breed emerged, a brownish breed, very hardy, producing a lot of milk, and milk of increased richness. We invested heavily in farm machinery, and the investment paid.

Sometimes I went to Krasnaya Gorka in the winter. The steamers were no longer running on the Volga because of the ice, and from the estate they had sent out four relays of troikas to Nijny in expectation of my arrival. So at four stations on the banks of Volga, twenty miles apart, three-horse teams were waiting. The Volga was frozen hard as steel, miles of river steamers and barges and rafts tied up along the quays and locked in by extra pilings to prevent their being crushed by the ice. The river lay like a great white valley, with pine branches and poles marking the course that the sleighs were to follow. I had a big gray wolf rug on my lap, and I was wrapped in my elkskin coat and in furs until only my face was exposed. Elkskin coats had fur both inside and outside. The cold, penetrating, icy air stung my face when the horses began to move, but the sleigh was weightless, and they raced, three abreast, jets of vapor streaming from their nostrils. My big white sleigh skimmed over the ice. On one side the bank of the river rose in vast white glacierlike cliffs, and on the other there was nothing but an immense expanse of trees half buried in snow. The cold was intense, but the speed was exhilarating, and in no time we came to the first post station, or first *isba*, a log cabin, where fresh horses were waiting.

There was a samovar there, and pickled cucumbers, and hot fresh bread. We had a cup of tea immediately and warmed up whilst they changed the horses. And when the fresh horses were put in we went out on the Volga again. Sometimes when we raced around a bend of the river we came upon a big convoy, forty or fifty sleighs, hauling merchandise up and down the river to the Black Sea ports.

If there wasn't much snow when I made these winter trips, the troika horses skimmed over the ice, three abreast. They were all sharpshod. But generally the snow was deep, sometimes six feet, as high as the horses' heads. There was a narrow track in the snow down the middle of the Volga, and if the snow was deep, the three horses pulled the sleigh in tandem, one harnessed behind the other, the coachman cracking an enormously long whip over them. Thus we rode to the second isba and its waiting samovar. The lead horses in the relays were the cleverest horses on the farm. Often whole convoys of sleighs hauling merchandise also moved in single file and forty or fifty in a convoy filled the narrow beaten track. When we came upon a convoy, our lead horse pulled off the track, burying himself in snow up to his neck, the other horses following him, to give the convoy room to pass, a maneuver requiring a lot of horse sense, a lot of horsemanship.

The grain was always sold in the winter. Sometimes I made the winter trip to Krasnaya Gorka to sell it. Selling was a formal rite. The grain merchant came to the house and remained three days. No one talked business the first day. I wined and dined him, and we visited—it was a ritual. He knew at what price he would buy. I knew at what price I would sell. The market didn't fluctuate very much—and we both knew the market price. I knew I could sell a pood—forty pounds—for perhaps ninety-eight kopecks, a good price, but we had superlative grain. So we spent a day with food, beverages, vodka, friendly discussion. He enjoyed that—if it hadn't been done, he wouldn't have bought. His feelings would have been hurt; there wouldn't have been any fun in it for him. So on the second day, he would say "Seventy?" or perhaps even "Sixty-eight?"

I'd say, "Well, listen, my dear Peter Timofeevitch, how can I? It is beautiful grain. You know it is beautiful grain. It's worth— it's worth at least a ruble and ten kopecks."

He'd say, "My dear Serge Platonovitch, you're dreaming! You can't expect— You're ridiculous!"

And so we would go on, all day, and generally a third day, perfectly friendly, and both of us knowing how it was going to turn out. Then we would stop, eat, drink and talk again, and finally he would buy at about the market price. If he offered me sixty-eight kopecks to begin with, and I demanded a ruble and ten kopecks, we could expect to settle at close to a ruble for forty pounds.

These were big merchants, who bought grain in large quantities and were perfectly responsible. But the peasants who sold their surplus goods to wandering traders were often up against it. A lot of the traders were unscrupulous; they bought in small quantities at far below the market and they sold goods to the peasants at far above their value. This stimulated the development of the cooperatives.

I graduated from the Gymnasium with honors in 1910, and enrolled in the University of St. Petersburg. In my day the university was located in a long row of red-fronted buildings on Vassiliefsky-Ostroff, only a few blocks along the Neva from our house. The buildings, erected by Peter the Great, were the original administrative offices of the Russian government.

There were more than ten thousand students, both men and women. Tuition was low. Any graduate of the Gymnasium who passed the examination could enter the university. My own course was natural history, mathematics and physics, with a subdivision in agriculture, but almost everyone was studying law. Typically, Russia needed technicians, but the university was producing legal experts. There was a tremendous intellectual stirring at the time; students rushed to the colleges by the thousands, worked their five years at law school, argued and debated, became bright and keen, with aspirations galore, and then graduated and learned there was nothing for them to do. There was no work for them. At best they might get a small government post at a salary.

They resented anyone having money; they resented every injustice and inequality; they resented everything. But they chiefly resented the system that gave them an inadequate means of earning their living after having provided them with the intellectual resources that led them to aspire to a better life. The system made socialists, made revolutionaries. It was the fault of the government, which should have encouraged technical training and fitted them for the work that Russia needed. The failure to produce technicians was one of the greatest mistakes of the old government.

Everyone belonged to debating societies, everyone argued about life, and practically everyone was a revolutionary of some kind or other. I was a truthseeker. Like everyone else I belonged with a little group of earnest companions who studied together. We met once a week to debate and argue about the future of the world—Russia, the human soul, religion, morals, and the meaning of life. We had formal discussions on such questions as: Is it possible to have ideals in the absence of religious faith? There was nothing we didn't discuss.

One of my friends was the son of a well-to-do businessman; another was the son of a railway engineer; a third was the son of a prominent actor. My closest friend, Michailov, was the socialist son of a doctor. He was an interesting character, brought up not in society but in ballet and artistic circles. He was a great idealist; the end of life for him was to serve mankind, so he had dedicated himself to science. He was a bacteriologist. When he finished his medical training, he was going to a plague laboratory. There were secluded hospitals in Russia, generally converted from abandoned forts, where people with contagious diseases were treated, and all the area around them was quarantined. The doctors who served in them were practically martyrs. Once they began to work in them, they took a vow to remain a certain period and were not allowed to leave for fear of spreading the contagion. The majority of them contracted the plague and died with their patients, which is what eventually happened to Michailov.

Another of my college friends, Feodoroff, was just the opposite from Michailov; he was a playwright, loved life, and meant to enjoy everything life had to offer. Ivanoff, the businessman, became an inventor, quite prominent for patents he had taken out; he was always making gadgets even then. Each week one of us read a carefully considered paper of his own composition, after which the whole meeting discussed it with intense concentration and vehemence.

I was about as liberal as possible, though not a socialist, and I was never arrested, though Michailov was. But I was once charged by the police on horseback. The students had taken to booing the police.

There was some kind of a demonstration, and we were looking on—another student and myself—when we saw the mounted police charging toward us. We ran. Before they caught us we saw a tramcar coming, and we jumped into it. The same idea occurred to hundreds of people, and the tram became so crowded people's feet were sticking out the windows. The mounted police swarmed past, swinging their clubs, but being on horseback they couldn't get at the passengers in the tram. In a few seconds the whole street was deserted, except for the crowd jammed in the tramcar. After it was all over, I remember the hundreds of galoshes that were left behind littering the street. One of my friends picked up a brand new pair. As he said, "Well, my own were rather too worn."

Michailov was arrested that night. He found himself in a crowd of students who were taken to jail by the police, and he was locked up with them. I heard of it and appealed to Father. He saw the authorities, explained that Michailov wasn't a dangerous character and not a revolutionist even though he happened to be in their company. Michailov was set free.

We were idealists rather than revolutionaries, but there were a few real revolutionaries among the students, secretly connected with the conspiratorial parties, and in danger of serious trouble. I had no friends among them that I knew of. What we were more conscious of was a type of student not so much revolutionary as destructive. Among Russian intellectuals there was what I considered to be a Karamazov type—a person who consciously distorted whatever another said, twisted and exaggerated it, or drew a conclusion different from what the other had in mind. Such people had no beliefs of their own. They wanted a sense of intellectual superiority, and in even the most casual conversation would give a mocking distortion of something that would otherwise be readily understood. They would hammer away at the point they were making, bringing in basic philosophical questions, or long-range political implications, in a tireless, excited, or sardonic and bitter way.

For instance, if one said that the zemstvos had a promising future because they were breaking new ground, one of the Karamazov-type students might start questioning one about delegate obsessions, and try to show that one placed a supernatural value on the wisdom of a delegate, which, supposing that, multiplied by a hundred delegates, it would mean a decision a hundred times as wise as one man could make. But everyone knew that we meant nothing of the sort. So we avoided such people. They existed apart, bitter, rasping, sarcastic, a peculiarly Russian kind of frustrated and destructive personality. I have always felt Doestoevsky, in drawing his brilliant portraits of characters of this kind, actually encouraged their existence and gave them a sort of intellectual sanction. There were quite a few of them in college, and I mention them now because, after the Bolshevik Revolution, they came into their own, and were skillfully used by the Bolsheviks.

Along with my new college friends, I had the friends I had known since boyhood. Peter Zouboff was in college with me, and was studying law. The Tolstoy brothers, Andre and Ivan, were also in the university at the same time. Peter had grown up as an orphan after his tenth year, but he had developed into a remarkable character. He had an unquestioning moral sense—right was right, and wrong was wrong; it was as simple as that and there was never any compromise. But at the same time Peter had a lively sense of humor; his morality was not stern, but mellowed by his understanding of people and of the deficiencies of human nature, as well as by his ability to see the funny side of people's faults.

There were no organized college sports then. I belonged to a gymnastic society that met three evenings a week for gymnastic exercises, group training like that begun by the sokols in Czechoslovakia. And I fenced with the Italian epee. My studies included botany, chemistry, physics, biology, histology, anatomy—fairly stiff courses. With the work I did on the estate, going out quite a bit, and taking seriously the discussions of the debating society, it was a full life.

CHAPTER IX

My close friend was Sonia Gagarin, and we were generally together at social events, of which there were a good many. One occasion for them was the visit of Don Alfonso and the Infanta of Spain to the Emperor and Empress. Aunt Betsy Shouvaloff gave a ball in honor of the Infanta at her house on the Moika. The house contained an enormous Empire ballroom, with a theater, and there was an amateur theatrical before the ball, in which I was one of the actors. There were many like that, less elaborate or just as elaborate, at the Polovtzeffs and elsewhere. Sonia was a very sweet, very quiet and gentle person. Our family was distantly related to the Gagarin family, and we were on terms of close friendship with them. There were five sons, with Sonia the only daughter.

Prince Gagarin, her father, was a scientist and professor, the president of the faculty of the Polytechnical Institute of St. Petersburg, which he had virtually created. It had become the leading scientific school in Russia, and one of the best in the world. I should have liked to go there, but the requirements for admission were such that only people naturally gifted in mathematics, or those who had studied science from the start, could pass the entrance examinations—I knew I could not.

A student strike took place at the Polytechnical Institute. Prince Gagarin was unjustly accused of harboring revolutionaries in the school—very unjustly accused. He was dismissed from his post by the government. The dismissal aroused great indignation, for the Institute was almost single-handedly Prince Gagarin's creation. The old government has been maligned in many respects, but its ineptitude in such matters was striking. For the result was that all of us students, already restless and dissatisfied, interpreted it as another example of the government's opposition to progress of any kind. I had been moving steadily to the left in my political views, and while my father was tolerant and did not raise any objections, I believe he became seriously concerned about where these views might lead me.

Stolypin had long been under attack by the extreme right, which resisted changes of any sort, and he now broke with the liberals like my father as the Duma became more and more active in army and navy affairs. But I was more than ever convinced that Stolypin's policies were right, the more I learned of agriculture and the more time I spent in the country. Part of this reform provided that if three-quarters of the peasants of a village wished to divide the community-owned land into individual farms, it could be done. The incredible complexities of peasant land tenure made this reform difficult—permanent division of the land for a man with no sons might be a great hardship—yet the difficulties were worked out, and suddenly the peasants accepted the program.

In village after village the land was divided, a popular response that grew to a wave of enthusiasm. Thousands of peasants became individual owners with property of their own overnight. They were filled with new ambition and self-respect. The means for satisfying their land hunger lay right at hand, for they began improving their own land as they had never worked to improve the community-owned parcels.

I should not like to give the impression that I was preoccupied with politics. In the holidays I went to parties on the Islands, where we danced to those wonderful prewar waltzes that came in inexhaustible streams of melody from Vienna. And I began to go on hunting parties in the country.

We coursed with borzois, the great Russian wolfhounds, in fall and winter. Each hunter had his pet breed. My dogs were provided by my cousins, for unfortunately I had barely started this absorbing sport and had none of my own. Some of the borzois were bred for speed-thin, arched, limber dogs, not at all fierce, superlatively fast and intelligent. They were for hunting foxes or other small game. Others were bred for fierceness, for hunting wolves. These would attack wolves or anything else. The best breed was Grand Duke Nicholas's. He had developed an amazing dog, distinguished by a heavy ridgelike bump across the nose.

I remember the first time I ever hunted with borzois was with my cousin Aliosha Obolensky. Aliosha and his brother Sasha were the clowns of the family. They were great mimics, who excelled at twisting their features into grimaces that caricatured the expressions of prominent people, or the solemn mien of some of our elder statesmen. They were the heart and soul of parties and were so famous for being funny that people laughed the moment they saw them, whether they were clowning or not. When I went borzoi-hunting with them, we went out in a sleigh. Foxes or wolves were not afraid of a sleigh—they were afraid of a horseman. The huntsman rode on horseback and tried to drive the quarry toward the sleigh where we had the dogs.

The huntsman was called the *yaeger*; he was a professional who took us miles into the countryside, where unbroken fields of snow lay everywhere around. We hid in the sleigh not far from a grove of trees and waited, each of us holding a pair of borzois. The *yaeger* had already started out with his two borzois on a leash and branched out from us in a big circle half a mile or more across. We in the meantime moved slowly and watched his every action. We held our borzois by their collars. The dogs waited, alert and patient, understanding perfectly what was expected of them. Part of the *yaeger's* art of hunting with borzois depended on his knowing how the game would run. Animals always run the same way, particularly under stress. When the yaeger spotted his quarry, he would move toward it and force it in our direction by maneuvering.

Suddenly there was an echoing cry—*ooluloo!*—from Aliosha and myself. The dogs knew it as a signal. A fox was heading straight toward us. We let loose our hounds. Simultaneously the yaeger freed his, and the four dogs were off through the snow, running silently with great pistonlike movements of their legs, backs arching and straightening with their smoothly synchronized grace and speed. There is nothing on earth to match this gait. We whipped the horses and spun over the snow, but the hounds were a long way ahead. When they got the fox they did not kill him. They took him by the ears and held him down till we arrived.

I became an enthusiast for the sport. The next fall I went out again. I have forgotten the name of the estate where we hunted. It was somewhere near Toula in central Russia. This time it was after the crops had been harvested. The stripped fields spread away in rolling, unfenced hills. This time we went out at dawn, riding little Cossack ponies, with our borzois on leashes looped to our belts. Far out among the low-lying hills were islands of dark trees that are a mark of the central Russian landscape.

Almost all the professional huntsmen were Siberians. Ours rode with his foxhounds into a woods, which was still shadowed in the thin morning light. We posted ourselves at different points where we thought the fox would come out. Coursing with borzois was competitive. One owner of prized dogs pitted his dogs against another owner's team. We were ranged along the hills, quite a distance apart, the men restless and excited—the borzois alone calm and alert. Then, suddenly, when the fox broke cover, the cry—*oolulloo!*—rose from the hunters. It was a signal all the borzois knew. The leashes were slipped and the hounds raced off with their gliding run. We had a wild coursing gallop after them. One pair of dogs got in the lead, and then another, as they converged on the fox, then a last tremendous sprint as the lead dog caught him, rolled him over, and held him helpless by the ears.

A hunt like that always ended with a party. The borzoi hunting season in Russia was like foxhunting in Virginia, a fitting excuse. We went from one country house to another, hunting in the morning and ending with a party in the evening.

Next summer in Krasnaya Gorka when I was shooting a great deal, I went out with a famous professional hunter of the time named Gratchoff, who entertained us with fantastic stories, real and imaginary, whenever we were in the woods. Sitting around the campfires at night he went on and on about apparitions and wonders he had seen. One of these concerned a real *nechistay a-sila* who inhabited the nearby countryside. Driving through the woods one day, Gratchoff said, his horse suddenly stopped before a bridge and would go no further. He got out to investigate, and saw coming up a ravine a colossal animal, literally breathing fire, that passed by in an instant. He swore it was true. It reminded me of the stories the old *pastookh* had told Peter and me in our boyhood. But some of Gratchoff's stories literally made me fearful. I was older now, yet I kept casting glances back into the surrounding gloom.

After these supernatural tales, hunting animals was often an anti-climax. Next winter I killed a big wolf. There wasn't much skill to it. He just came running out of the woods straight toward me, like a huge, savage dog, and I shot him. He was a big brute, and I was proud of him and kept his hide in my room at Oxford.

The year 1911 was a momentous one to me; I passed my twenty-first birthday. Father did not want me in the army. He said that army life in peacetime was not good, and that if war came I should volunteer. So I entirely missed the officer's training from childhood that most boys of the family received. Russia had universal military service, however, and on reaching twenty-one a boy was called up. But if the father was sixty-two when his oldest son was twenty-one, and there were younger sons five years junior to the oldest, then the oldest son was deemed the only breadwinner in the family and received a white card exempting him from military duty. My brother Vladimir was five years younger, so I was automatically excused.

Sonia Gagarin and I became engaged that year. We drifted into our engagement to marry, after a long companionship. We were fond of each other and were the closest of friends. There was a formal announcement. But perhaps the quiet friendship we had known was in itself a sign that the engagement was a mistake.

Father wanted me to study at Oxford before marrying and settling down. His own health was not at all good; his ulcers twice took him to Switzerland for operations—they had turned cancerous. He still entertained, providing his guests with superlative food although he was on a strict diet; he was as fond as ever of his funny stories, and he shocked the old ladies more than ever.

General de Reutern died, and soon I had a revealing glimpse of Father's true feelings beneath his genial and good-natured air. By some arrangement that I never fully understood, I was to see Mother at certain intervals after I reached a certain age. Once when she was in Moscow, and her mourning period was over, I visited her there and took her out to the theater. And, when the play was on, I happened to see Father in the back of the theater watching Mother. The pathos of it suddenly gripped me. While I had known him underneath to be a serious man, he had always appeared light-hearted, absolutely sure of himself, with a bon mot for the old girls and younger ones besides. Now in one instant he had become a pathetic figure. Mother was free again, but I sensed it was useless to try to get Father and her together. It made me want to help, to do what he wanted me to do.

One thing Father particularly wanted was to build a place in the Crimea, near the Youssoupoffs. Felix's father had two properties there, a villa called Koreiz, and a huge palace at Kokos—which means the Blue Eye—where Uncle Felix Youssoupoff had built an exact duplicate of the famous palace of the Crimean khans nearby. So we visited the Youssoupoffs, and Father bought a piece of land and began plans for his villa, first constructing a small cottage on the property.

It was a lovely place in the shadow of the biggest Crimean mountain, Ai Petri, St. Peter. The mountain peak was capped with snow most of the year, while semitropical vegetation flourished at its base. The Crimean coast, the counterpart of the Riviera but gentler in all respects, lay before it bursting with roses and cypress, and the blue waters of the Black Sea stretched away to the horizon. To the north, beyond the mountain slopes, were clean little villages of flat-roofed, white-plastered Tartar houses, each village with its mosque, the natives independent and prosperous Moslem farmers, polite and friendly, their women in purdah, with black veils over their faces that revealed only their eyes.

I was enchanted with the Crimea. Father and I rode all through it. I could not have believed then that in a short time I would be hiding in these same hills, with my life depending on the friendliness of these Tartar farmers and herdsmen.

Father wanted to visit Rome, so we went there in the spring. There we found ourselves among a number of people from St. Petersburg, and we all went about together, visiting, exploring, and going to the races. Irina Rayevsky was there, and Dorothy Radziwill, an American girl, the former Miss Deacon, one of the most famous beauties of Europe, and Maia Koutouzoff, who was married to my cousin Serge. This was an exciting and pleasant time, my first adult glimpse of society outside Russia.

In Rome I came the closest I ever came to fighting a duel. A Rumanian gentleman had made disparaging remarks to me about my cousin Maia, and hothead as I was in those days I demanded satisfaction. Next day when I was told that swords were his choice of weapons I thought I was in for it.

I had stopped boxing when I was fourteen or so, but I had been keeping up the fencing with M. Loustalou. I was rather glad I had. Nevertheless, I thought I might be a little rusty, so I went over and got a few pointers from the Commandatore Greco, the famous Italian fencing master. Rumanians are never to be trusted. Strangely enough, this Rumanian came up and apologized to me the very next day. The duel never came off, but I really had picked up some very neat tricks from the Commandatore, and I could hardly wait to get back to St. Petersburg and try them out on M. Loustalou.

I called him immediately on my return, and he came over that afternoon. I had a few of my friends over to see the fun. There was nothing unusual about this. There were always people dropping in.

We fenced easily for a time, and then I sensed an opportunity. In a flash I had disarmed him, and my friends all cheered.

"*Merde!*" he cried, hopping up and down in rage. "Where did you learn that?"

With perfect swordsman's etiquette I retrieved his epee and handed it back to him across my arm. My friends by this time were hysterical. He seized upon it, and with fierce Gascon spirit "*En garde!*" he cried. "I'll show you, you so-and-so, how a *Gascon* can disarm you!" And he did so three times in quick succession, bowing to the gallery after each. He had wrists like bands of steel. After that, he seemed mollified somewhat, but I know that he smarted for years at the memory of that one afternoon.

The harvest of 1911 had been disappointing; there was famine in some parts of Russia, and the government rushed food to the stricken areas. That winter my cousin Prime Minister Peter Stolypin was assassinated in Kiev before the horrified eyes of Emperor Nicholas. It was at a theater. The Emperor was in the Imperial box, and Stolypin in the orchestra. His assassin, who was a double agent, had entered on a pass from the local police, and sat right beside him. After he was shot, Stolypin stood up, blessed the Emperor, and died.

Despite these shattering events, Russia as a whole was now in better shape. The news of progress was everywhere—a tremendous stirring that went through the whole country and touched all classes of society, including the nobility.

Russian industry was only beginning, but it was growing fast. The textile industry had doubled in size, making Russia the fourth largest producer in the world. Steel and iron production jumped from under a million tons a year in 1900 to nearly five million tons, making Russian production almost equal to that of France. Grain exports were doubling every few years. And plans for the future were flourishing, practical plans, including plans for governmental reform and agrarian reform.

Professor Boris Bakhmetieff was a hydraulic engineer, a very kindly, imaginative and far-sighted man, to whom I later often turned for advice. He had conceived the project of a great dam to be built across the Dnieper River, the same project that the Bolsheviks afterward took credit for. He had drawn up the plans and secured governmental approval to build. The war and then the Revolution stopped it. Professor Bakhmetieff, subsequently a great friend of mine, entered Kerensky's government. He became ambassador to the United States, and, after the Revolution, a professor at Columbia University. His Dnieper dam project was only one of any number of works that were in the making which would have solidified if not transformed the life of Old Russia.

In my own case, I wanted to develop new farm land. Russia's farm land was enormous by European standards, but it was still not large enough, and there was then almost as much Russian territory that was not developed as there was land being cultivated. Ivan the Terrible had tied the people to the land where they were. They had remained there for generations. Even if they were dissatisfied, they still remained there, and looked with longing eyes at the landed estates. On the Lena River was some of the richest land on earth, as good as the land of the Ukraine. It had never been touched. One of my cousins, Count Medem, whom we all called "Papa," and I got together and organized a syndicate of fellows our own age. He eventually wound up in the Fourth Squadron of the Chevalier Guards. We were young men of landed estates, and we financed what were called "walkers"— men who went over the land on foot and studied its quality to report on where we should buy. Land as far away from the big cities as Krasnaya Gorka, which had once been inexpensive, had now grown expensive, and our idea was to move much of our operation to the Lena, the stables especially, and cultivate the land at Krasnaya Gorka that had grown too valuable to be profitably used for pasture.

As quietly as Sonia and I had become engaged, we decided to break our engagement. There was no bitterness about it and we remained friends. I realized that I could not make her happy. Still, it was all a mistake. Yet it was not unusual for the time. We young people were all thinking of great things to be done, working hard, and dedicating ourselves to humanity. Say that we lived for the romance of life as a whole, which was our work, and fondness was magnified out of proper proportion. Yet we enjoyed ourselves at parties on the Islands, sliding down ice hills, coursing with borzois, and in other ways.

And then I went to Oxford.

Part III

A Russian in England

CHAPTER X

Father and I arrived in London in May 1912. He telephoned the Russian Ambassador from our hotel and asked permission to bring me to meet him. Our Ambassador was Count Benckendorff, the senior diplomat at the Court of St. James, who had been in England for many years. His reputation in Russia stood very high because of the tremendous improvement in Russian and British relations. But he had been in England for so long he was practically an Englishman, and one of Felix Youssoupoff's jokes was that Count Benckendorff couldn't speak Russian.

Count Benckendorff's son Paul, who was in the British Horse Guards, was married to Ella Narishkin, the most beautiful of all the beautiful girls who used to assemble at the Narishkin family place in Finland in my long-haired childhood. She was perhaps the most vivid of Mother's remarkable nieces. Despite the celebrated Narishkin-Obolensky divorce, the old Count and my father got along. So we were received. We were taken at once into a big room in our Embassy on Curzon Street, where Count Benckendorff was working at his desk.

It was a strangely formal meeting. Father said his purpose in bringing me to the Count was that he had concluded that Oxford was the place for me, and wanted him to assist me. He said he had explored the matter thoroughly and had concluded that Christ Church College would be best. He explained that I wished to study political economy—poor law and local government. And he hoped that the Count would give me letters and recommendations.

The old Count was amiable. He asked me a few questions, what my grades were, what I had studied, and so on. I had brought my papers with me, and showed him the excellent grades I had got in my baccalaureate exam and the record of my year and a half in agriculture at the University of St. Petersburg. He appeared to be duly impressed. Then he asked me to demonstrate my mastery of French and English, and while he looked a little startled at my Scottish accent, he decided I was fully qualified to go to Oxford. He said he would write a letter and give me an introduction to Reverend Thomas Strong, the Dean of Christ Church College.

With that letter, and my papers. Father and I went to Oxford, where we met the dean. Reverend Strong was a charming man, very sociable and hospitable, but he was, unfortunately, excessively nervous, and I think his jitters gave Father the impression that it was going to be a close shave. In the midst of all his abrupt and agitated expressions, it finally emerged that I should write an application. In a couple of weeks he would be able to give me an answer. Meanwhile, he recommended a Mr. Theodosius, a tutor who had made a profession of helping boys pass their entrance examinations. He drily suggested that Mr. Theodosius just might be helpful to me when I came to take the exam—that is, of course, in case my application were accepted.

On leaving. Father looked pretty grim, but he cheered up after we visited Mr. Theodosius, who had a comfortable, roomy house. This, Mr. Theodosius explained, would become filled with boys as the examination days approached. Father plainly liked .Mr. Theodosius, who was very prim and formal and evidently proud of his connections. He had crammed the finest families of England. It was arranged on the spot that I should live there for three weeks in the fall, studying daily. We then looked over Oxford, but Father was growing restless, and, apparently having decided that Mr. Theodosius could take care of me, we returned to London. Next day, Father departed for the continent to take the cure.

I decided to stay in London on my own until I heard from Reverend Strong. Felix Youssoupoff was then living in a flat in Knightsbridge, just off Belgrave Square, a quietly sumptuous place in the midst of tall old mansions and embassies. Felix had passed his final examinations at Oxford, but had decided to remain. His flat contained a piano, a pet macaw, a dog, modern furniture, black carpets and green silk curtains. A French couple looked after him and cooked. Friends were always dropping in at all hours of the day and night.

Felix introduced me to a lot of people I came to know well. They gathered at his place casually because there was always somebody there. Felix would get out his guitar and sing gipsy songs. He had a pleasant voice—a small voice, by the stentorian standards of Russian singers—but of a very pleasing timbre, and he sang those native songs, of which he knew an astonishing number, with a quiet directness, like a Russian Bing Crosby.

I was very fond of Felix. In his autobiography he has described this as a happy time in his life, saying that "Paul of Serbia, King Manuel of Portugal, Serge Obolensky, Jack Gordon and I were inseparable and went everywhere together." He is right, but he got the time wrong. On that visit I was there only a short time; it was a later occasion that found us together.

On that first visit I was mainly concerned about getting into Oxford. Some of those whom I saw in Knightsbridge I had known in Russia, people like Prince Christopher of Greece, whose country was then the subject of much discussion because of the conflicts that later that October led to the Balkan War against Turkey, with Greece, Bulgaria, Serbia and Montenegro lined up against her. Prince Christopher, who was one of the gayest of Felix's gay companions, later married Nancy Leeds.

Felix took me to my first London party, at Mrs. Hwfa (pronounced Hoover) Williams's. She was very old and slightly deaf and kind as she could be. She had a wonderful sense of humor, but in her old age she looked exactly like Mary, Felix's pet macaw, and later, when she came to Felix's for dinner,

Felix mischievously said, "Mrs. Hwfa, you know there's someone in London who looks just like Mary," and he pointed to the macaw.

"Why! It's me!" Mrs. Hwfa Williams said. She turned straight to me and said, "That naughty gray wolf says I'm like Mary! Isn't he frightful!"

Her house was not in London itself, but about half an hour out, in the general direction of Epsom. It adjoined Coombe Court. Four of us, Felix, myself, Christopher of Greece, and Jack Gordon had all been in the theater, and went there afterwards in Felix's Deloné-Belleville. Anna Pavlova came late, because she had just given a performance. Nellie Melba and the Fokines were there, also Bakst, Diaghileff, Juliet Duff, the Marquis de Cuevas, Lady Allington, Karsavina, Viscountess Curzon, King Manuel of Portugal, and my future mother-in-law, Mrs. John Jacob Astor, later Lady Ribblesdale.

Pavlova was brought in by Bertie Stopford, a great and muscular Englishman with a droll, elephantine sense of humor, who later became a British agent and carried out incredibly dangerous secret missions in Russia after the Bolshevik Revolution. Pavlova was in a gay mood and the party was exceedingly relaxed. She and Bertie and I wound up doing a burlesque fandango. I could vaguely remember the steps from Maestro Ceccetti's teaching, tied my coat tails around me, and with me on one side and Bertie on the other Pavlova scored another theatrical triumph while we provided the comic relief. Anna Pavlova was a great friend of Felix's and I saw her constantly at his flat in Knightsbridge. In fact, we dropped back to Felix's later with her, and Bertie was nowhere to be seen.

Another famous hostess of the time was the Marchioness of Ripon, and through my letters of introduction I met her. Her specialties were social events having anything to do with Russia. She was of Russian descent. After the Napoleonic Wars, the Russian Ambassador to England was Simon Vorontzoff, whose daughter married Lord Pembroke, the eleventh Earl of Pembroke, and Lady Ripon was a descendant of this marriage. She had been several times to court in St. Petersburg, staying the last time with the Grand Duchess Vladimir (Marie Pavlovna the Elder), who was my godmother.

When I met Lady Ripon, she was also Lady de Gray, she was in her middle years, and it was easy to understand the enthusiasm of one of her contemporaries, who wrote in his memoirs: "The most wonderful and beautiful woman, with rare distinction, unconquerable high spirits, and in her youth a joie de vivre and vivacity unimaginable." From my point of view, she was thin and tall and had a beautiful head; she was absolutely brilliant to converse with and spectacular to look at. She entertained at Coombe Court, a beautiful place near Hampton Court Palace, Mrs. Hwfa Williams and a golf course. Her husband, Lord Ripon, or Lord de Gray, from another title, was a collector of rare Chinese porcelain. He was a real connoisseur, polishing and caring for his collection with his own hands. He would fondle and caress a rare item whenever he displayed it to visitors. He was also renowned as the finest shot in England. Lady Ripon herself was a patroness of the arts, and between the two of them they had furnished Coombe Court with exquisite taste. Their house was always filled with artists of all kinds, either painters or, at the moment that I met her, dancers; Nijinsky and Pavlova and Karsavina appeared for lunch or at the garden parties that Lady Ripon gave on Sunday afternoons.

Lady Ripon was the person responsible for bringing the Russian Ballet to London in June 1911. Their first appearance on the eve of the coronation of George V was one of the most sensational successes in theatrical history. It was a great company, with Karsavina and Nijinsky and even my old dancing teacher, Maestro Ceccetti.

Unlike the others, Nijinsky had never been seen there before, and there had never been a dancer like him. People said the air seemed to be his natural habitat, and every jump was a separate ecstasy. Wit and imagination were combined with an amazing grace and incredible virtuosity. His leaps were astounding, and he had a sense of humor. Dancing Schumann's Carnival, for instance, he dramatized a torrential passage of music by abruptly sitting flat on the floor at exactly the instant that a note was struck by the orchestra. The opening night, with *Prince Igor*, *Carnaval*, and *Paganini*, the critics called the most purely artistic performance that the theater had ever seen, and their enthusiasm grew. There were later performances of ballets like *L'après-midi d'un Faun*.

Lady Juliet Duff, the daughter of Lady Ripon, was married to Colonel Robin Duff of the Horse Guards. She was a wonderful stimulus for the younger generation at her mother's parties. She was a tall, attractive girl. She was also a patroness of the arts and carried on the family tradition after the Russian Revolution when she brought the ballet under Diaghileff back to London again, and raised the money to hold it together. I often helped her in this capacity.

I was lucky to have reached England at the height of a fantastic period in British history. Money was plentiful, and trade was flourishing after decades of increasing prosperity. Despite occasional short setbacks, the industrial output of England, France and Germany had been booming. And with her amazing industrial and agricultural growth, Russia now joined them.

Meanwhile the Russian-English Treaty of Friendship, signed in 1910, created the Triple Entente to be poised against the Triple Alliance of Germany, Austria and Italy.

But England was still on top of the world. Currency was coming in to her from everywhere. To be sure, it was being spent in all the great capitals of Europe—in Paris, in Berlin to a lesser extent, and also in Vienna (Austria-Hungary, like Russia, was booming after a series of good harvests). But it was in London that the spending was spectacular. It was in London that the world of wealth and the sense of unpushing easy power was strongest.

From London, that wonderful friendly city—and all cities have their human personalities—the trade lines radiated out to the dominions and colonies, the

Far East, the Near East, Africa and South America. An army of British salesmen, enterprising and ambitious men, were now for the first time facing tough competition from dynamic German newcomers. But people other than the British and including the Germans tended to base their decisions not so much on their own objective situations as on their best guess as to what London was about to do. The hand of London had become an intangible economic factor, almost mythological, a sort of natural resource in itself; and whatever was accepted by London was accepted everywhere.

The city of London, meanwhile, took on an air of massive elegance and leisure all but inconceivable in any later period. The great houses of the aristocracy; the amazing theatrical renaissance; the almost constant round of dinners and balls and garden parties; and the heady excitement of the London season, all had the roots of their very existence buried and fertilized by a veritable golden age of world trade, prosperity seemed unending, and to some it was virtually bottomless.

The social life of England's capital went on in an atmosphere unlike anything that I had ever seen or would ever see again anywhere in the world; I believe I saw the end of it. In those first years of the reign of George V, the mellow grandeur of the Edwardian age of art and conversation persisted, unquenched, uncompromising. In fact it was in full cry.

It must have cost the equivalent of a hundred thousand dollars (£20,000) a year to maintain a London house and the country places that went with having a London house. And only the very richest English landed estates brought in that much. But the great English families, unlike those of Europe generally, who frowned on such practice, and entirely unlike those of Russia, were associated with big business. The people visiting London from the far corners of the earth were often connected by business as well as by family with the leaders of society and fashion.

A second factor that colored London society was that a social class which no longer exists today fused together the worlds of trade, banking and social life. Parts of the royal families, the heads of the smaller principalities of Europe—and some of the Oriental potentates, like the Aga Khan, who was then a young man, or Prince Ranjitsinhji, who emerged as the ruler of a small state in India to become one of the greatest cricket players the world had ever seen—made up a kind of traveling social circuit. Moving amiably from one capital to another, royalty provided occasions for entertainments, and leading financial figures of the world spent money freely. In consequence, the whole flavor of the time compared on the top social plane to golf tournament circuits of today in which champion golfers meet the same people at one course after another. The brilliance of the prewar London theater was another factor that made London preeminent among the world's capitals. I became interested in the theater from the time I arrived.

Felix was then in love with Margery Manners, the daughter of the Duchess of Rutland, the half sister of Lady Diana Manners, who be-came Lady Duff Cooper; Margery, like Diana, had a great interest in the theater.

Margery was of the type of beauty of the American actress Katharine Cornell, dark and vivid, a fine musician as well as a dramatic actress of natural gifts, and she could unquestionably have made a fine career on the stage. But she had already given up whatever ambition she had in that direction. She was in love with Charles Anglesey, who was typical of the Englishmen of the time with business interests all over the globe.

He had taken himself off to British Columbia to develop some big project at that remote outpost of the British Empire, and Margery was patiently awaiting his return. Then they married, and she devoted herself entirely to her family. Meanwhile, Felix was playing his guitar in the late hours of the night, and singing mournful gipsy songs. He said he was turning into Dorian Gray. It was at this time that I visited him. Diana Manners was often there also, a blond girl as striking as her brunette sister, and I began to suspect that, while Margery was in love with Anglesey and Felix was hopelessly in love with Margery, Diana fancied Felix.

While I was living in London, a letter arrived from Reverend Strong saying I was accepted into Christ Church College. He said I was to appear at Oxford at the beginning of the Michaelmas term, early in October. Unfortunately, he added, there were no rooms available in the college and I should have to find digs for myself. Digs, he explained, were rooms outside the college proper. While being delighted in one way, I was a little nervous as to what was in store for me, and I asked Felix, "What is it like?"

"It will be difficult at the beginning," Felix said. "No one pays any attention to you. But after the first term they get accustomed to seeing you around and then you will get to know them. But you just have to wait until they come to you."

However, I was luckier than Felix had been. The reason was Mr. Theodosius and a little matter of finding digs. I returned to Oxford, turned the whole formidable problem over to Mr. Theodosius, and went home to Russia. And in my absence Mr. Theodosius found digs for me with four Balliol students who would not only help steer me through Oxford, but become lifelong friends.

It was a long journey from London to St. Petersburg in those days, and I had only a short time home, but I went. I usually returned via Switzerland and Vienna. Father had established a small account for me in a bank in Berne, and on passing through and seeing my bankers, I made a practice of visiting Dr. Chumi, the tutor of the Tolstoy boys, who was teaching at the University of Berne.

Night life had begun to blossom in St. Petersburg, and the fashionable place to go after parties was the Aquarium, a night club with glass walls behind which were tanks of water in which bright-colored fish darted. A Parisian couple was dancing there, and a girl, Crisise, who also sang, had become a great favorite. From there one went later to visit the gipsies. I was very taken with a gipsy girl named Masha. When I went to the gipsies I would ring up during the day and say that my party would arrive there at one or two o'clock in the morning. The gipsies lived in a village in the Islands, in ordinary houses like all the houses around them. The village was Novaya Derevnya or New Village. We would drive over the Neva and out to the Islands to the particular family where our favorite singers were. There were several famous families of them, or Tabors, in Russia—the Shishkin Tabor, the Massalsky Tabor. The Sadovsky Tabor lived in Moscow. Several famous stars, old women like Varia Panina or Nastia Poliakova, were magnificent. A good many of the first Russian families have gipsy blood in them from marriages of their sons to gipsy girls, like the Galitzin family.

In the gipsy house there was always a big room, nearly empty except for a long table and ordinary wicker chairs. On the opposite side of the room the gipsy women of the family sat, with the men with their guitars behind them. All the gipsy houses had big wine cellars, champagne was brought up, and an evening there cost a lot of money. The oldest gipsy woman, the grandmother or the great-grandmother, sat in the middle, with the soprano on her one hand and the mezzo-soprano on the other, the others accompanying them as a chorus. We just sat in the wicker chairs and listened—but that was enough. They could transcend the barest walls, warm the coldest calculating heart with their wizardry. They were sheer hypnosis.

It was impossible to make an appointment with a gipsy girl. The only way they could leave the household was to marry. The only time one could see them, except when they sang, was to drive out in the afternoon and have tea with the whole family, and then, to marry a gipsy girl was a financial undertaking. One had to pay a ransom of at least twenty or thirty thousand rubles to the Tabor. With good reason our mothers worried whenever we were going to the gipsies, and I'm afraid they worried a great deal. The girls were fascinating. Evenings they sang in a chorus, almost like a choir, each part perfectly trained, they sang fiercely and from the heart. At the afternoon teas they were coolly formal and restrained, but if one of them fell for an admirer, she would sing twice as well when he was present at the party at night, in rapturous and unrestrained melody that broke completely free of the harmonies of the chorus. It was their form of symbolism, and in this way alone could they let us know.

I used to visit Masha at teatime, and I always found her mother exceedingly hospitable with her samovar and fresh bread and marvelous jams. One night I was dragged there by General Polovtzeff and his wife, Mimi. He was always very gay and now runs Monte Carlo. He brought along a whole party including society girls. I never saw Masha in such a rage. She was utterly chill and aloof—and boy did I get it the next day at tea!

At the last moment, as I was packing up, a bit reluctantly, to leave for England, Father suddenly decided that my brother Vladimir would also benefit by some study abroad. Vlady was still in Gymnasium. Father's idea was that he could study English and live with Mr. Theodosius, who had really impressed Father deeply. In that way Vlady would get a good grounding far in advance of his entrance examinations in case he went to Oxford later on. So Vlady and I left together.

This time we went straight through Europe without stopping. We didn't even stay in London.

This was when I discovered how well Mr. Theodosius had done in finding digs for me. I had a bedroom and sitting room on the top floor of a house on High Street, and on the floors below me were the four Balliol men. They were, I was told, all great scholars, since it was necessary to have a brain to be in Balliol at all. I had brought my white bearskin rug and my wolf pelt from Russia with me, and it just happened that when I was standing with my feet planted firmly on the rug Mr. Theodosius introduced me to them by my full title, which raised their eyebrows. When I opened my mouth they looked puzzled. I think they thought I was Scottish. They called me Obo.

One of them was L. G. Brown, a famous rugby player, the captain of the Oxford team, internationally famous even then, for he played for England. He was a year ahead of the others, having entered in 1909. I never even heard his Christian name. Everyone called him L.G. He was a big fellow, never saying much, and he had a silent morning ritual. He used to stamp in and pick John de Salis bodily out of bed. He would lift him up gently with one hand and with tender concern drop him pajamas and all into a cold bath.

John, the second of the four, was a fat, absent-minded boy, the son of Count de Salis, who was a fixture in the British Foreign Office. At the time the Count was Ambassador to the Vatican. His son was called Fat John. He was the worst-dressed person in Oxford, which even then was saying a great deal. His standard habit was a coat of one color, well spotted by refreshment, and trousers of another—anything he happened to find around when he put on his clothes. His socks were unmentionable, and I think he must have been color-blind. He had a mind that instantly retained and synthesized any amount of material.

But Fat John was a genius. He could skim through books, absorbing their contents at a glance, and pass his examinations. The professors all knew he rarely studied. He might attend only one of their lectures during the whole term and the professors were all after him. John never gave them satisfaction. Yet when it came to his own special interest, which was Talleyrand and diplomacy, John de Salis really worked.

The others in the digs were Cuthbert Holmes and Carlo Purcell. They were juniors, like John. Cuthbert was a big, red-headed law student, as steady and sagacious as John de Salis was mercurial, and an officer in the student officer corps. He was our conscience. Carlo Purcell, an Irishman, also studying law, was another character. Perfectly level-headed and with both feet firmly planted on the ground, he had a fey streak of the Irish mystic about him. For instance, he read palms. He read mine so accurately that even today I sometimes start and say, "My God! Carlo was right again." He made a thorough study of it. It was an uncomfortable feeling and very scary. I've never allowed my palms to be read since.

Carlo was a great Irish patriot, and claimed to belong to the Sinn Fein, and when he told his own fortune he said it was simple: soon there was going to be a revolution in Ireland, and it was obvious to him what was going to happen—he was going to be killed. This gloomy prospect did not reduce his high spirits in the slightest. He died all right, and he died in the Irish Guards, but fighting against Germany.

I was overwhelmed by the hospitality of these four students. They took me in and, from the very first meeting on the bearskin rug, treated me as though we had known each other for years. They were helpful in every way, including scholastically.

Passing the responsions under Mr. Theodosius' guidance was not too difficult, but picking up the thread of English instruction in the college itself required some cramming. I felt as I had when we returned from Europe in my early school days. I was always in arrears, but now on a vast scale.

My tutor was Mr. Blunt, a man with enormous eyebrows and a low, earnest voice. At our first meeting he lectured me for a long time in a roundabout fashion, and I had no idea of what he was talking about until it finally dawned on me that he was telling me I could do whatever I wanted to do so long as he didn't know about it.

Almost at once, however, I came in contact with Dr. Gilbert Slater, who taught me poor law and local government. He had the strongest influence upon me of all my college years. Poor law was what we would now call welfare law—the papers in those days were filled with long discussions of reform of the body of poor law. Dr. Slater was the head of Ruskin College. He was a man of great learning and simple good will, with a capacity for exact generalization in summing up complex issues. He had innumerable friends among the reformers of England.

He had only recently taken over the leadership of Ruskin College, and so I studied in what must have been the strongest educational institution in Great Britain. Ruskin College was started in 1899 on Washington's Birthday as a tribute to its American founder. A businessman from the United States, Mr. Walter Vrooman, had put up money for it as a gesture of international friendship, endowing a college with the aim of reducing class conflicts. His idea was that labor leaders, unless they were remarkably gifted people, could not cope with their educated opponents in debates and negotiations or in Parliament, and Ruskin College was to give labor people the same background with respect to labor problems that their opponents in the Conservative Party had with respect to the problems of their constituents. A statement of principles read: "Ruskin College was not established to enable a man to rise out of his class. The hope of the institution is that every man, by raising himself, may help to raise the class to which he belongs."

The college opened with tremendous enthusiasm. It built its own hall on Walton Street, and an immense crowd made up of representatives of millions of trade unionists attended the opening ceremonies. The students were the brainiest of the reformers—Charles Beard, the famous American historian, was one of the first.

But almost at once poor Mr. Vrooman lost his fortune, and Ruskin College found itself not only with no income, but heavily in debt. It sank into complete obscurity, the program deteriorating to a few lectures. Then there was a ghastly sensation, for it developed that the syndicalists had captured control of Ruskin College, and its principal sympathized with them. A group of very tough characters, members of the International Workers of the World, occupied the pleasant building beside the Worcester College gardens, and there they buried themselves turning out inflammatory magazines attacking Oxford, and satirizing its traditions, its students, and everything else.

Of course the result was that they nearly put Ruskin College out of existence. But Dr. Slater wanted to move the school. He believed in its original purpose. For years he fought the people who had gained control of it, until they left to found a labor college in London. Under Dr. Slater's leadership Ruskin College became recognized as an outstanding institution for the study of political economy. Through his efforts its finances were stabilized, and during my first year there another new building was opened, with a small quadrangle faced by a colonnade.

Almost at once Dr. Slater sent me out to see the work the different municipal governments were doing. I went first to Birmingham. It had an aggressive liberal government that had begun large-scale projects in slum clearance and low-cost housing. At that time the big subject among reformers was the garden city. City planners and a few far-sighted architects were designing factories surrounded by parks with separate houses for the workmen, each with its own grounds, to replace the slums of industrialized England.

I realize that a later generation has come to look indulgently on the prewar reformers, considering their work dated and ineffectual, but I am sure that to do so is a serious mistake. The reforms were on a grand scale. Anyone who had gone through slum areas and then through the garden cities that replaced them would have been a singularly callous individual if he was not moved by the transformation of humanity. Mankind is elevated when its people are able to live in good surroundings, and such change was a marvelous thing. Then, of course, the work was only beginning, but the people were overwhelmingly for it. Both the Labor and Liberal parties supported these projects, and the Conservatives did not oppose them. They, too, were fully aware. Their position was not resistance to change or such: they merely insisted that the world as it existed was a pretty good one, and in many respects it was.

After returning from Birmingham, I wrote papers on the subject for Dr. Slater to criticize, and then made a similar trip to Manchester.

Eventually I went all over England under Dr. Slater's direction, studying not only housing, but municipal taxation, county government, and similar subjects. Dr. Slater was well informed about Russia, particularly interested in the zemstvos. Aside from my college studies, we discussed these matters by the hour.

There was one aspect of the British reform movement that impressed me a lot. Even after all parties concerned had agreed on a needed reform, say slum clearance or a housing project, fantastic difficulties remained, and there was rarely a single clear authority. Dozens of agencies and government bureaus were involved. First the approval of one agency had to be secured, and then another and another in a maze of red tape and overlapping jurisdiction. In this respect the Russian zemstvos were fortunate: no other governmental body was engaged in the work they were doing. In several areas—public health for one— they were ahead of the most advanced of English cities, simply granting free medical care to everyone, a solution that the complex British system could not possibly have reached.

At the same time that I was studying the slums and slum clearance, I was seeing another side of English life. Soon after the first term started at Oxford, I was invited by Lady Ripon, together with her nephew Michael Herbert, to Coombe Court. The occasion once again had to do with visiting royalty. There were about forty people at luncheon, including some of the most famous beauties of the last Edwardian days: Lady Mary Curzon; Lady D'Abernon; and Consuelo, the Duchess of Marlborough.

The most spectacular American there was Mrs. John Jacob Astor. She wore very few jewels, was perfectly dressed and had the most astonishing upswept hair. It was prematurely white for her very young face and it had black roots at the nape of the neck. She was stunning, and more than held her own. She was later to become one of the greatest British hostesses, after she had married Lord Ribblesdale.

I was extremely shy in those days. The presence of so many beautiful women made me more so. But seated next to me was a flowerlike young girl, Lady Bridget Colebrook, who performed the great service of putting me at ease. She was exquisite, and dressed in the costume of the time that we can now see in Sargent's portraits, wearing a hat with white swan feathers similar to the one that Pavlova was wearing in Swan Lake, and one that I admired for the setting it provided for her wonderful oval face. Previously, on occasions like this, I had had to force myself to talk, but now I was bowled over by my delight. These scenes—my Oxford digs, the wealth of London, the razing of slums in Birmingham, the beautiful women gathered in an atmosphere of quiet charm at Coombe Court—are among my first impressions of England.

CHAPTER XI

College was absorbing, my Balliol friends could not have been kinder, but still, I was lonely. I was older than the boys of my class. I had nearly finished at the University of St. Petersburg, but I entered Oxford with the class which began in 1912 and planned to graduate in 1916. There were student organizations for everything, however, and I joined the fencing club. There we were almost all foreigners. But the sport I was most at home in was riding, and from the moment I entered Oxford until I left, much of my spare time was spent with the Oxford Drag Hounds.

There were about twenty of us in Oxford who rode to hounds. Two afternoons a week we rented horses from MacPhearson's stable. Fred Lawson was the Master of Foxhounds in my time and took his responsibilities seriously. As members, we dressed in traditional ratcatcher clothes and bowler hats; only the master and whips wore black coats and hunting caps. We kept our hounds by subscription, and several stiff courses with water jumps, posts and rails, and bullfinch fences were dragged before a hunt—that is, dragged with scent for the hounds, there being no foxes. It was good training, although MacPhearson's horses generally had weak forelegs. When you jumped, you knew you were going to come down somewhere.

The first students of my class that I got to know well were those who hunted, Eric Ednam, first of all, and also Oldric Portal, Ronnie Stanyforth and Barney Charlesworth, all Christ Church men. These latter two were later, in the Second World War, A. D. C.s to Lord Allenbrooke.

There were many others who entered Oxford that same year who were not involved in hunting, and I met them by degrees. We all dined in the refectory hall of Christ Church, which was a common meeting ground. Some of the men I met there became close friends of mine. Among them were Bobberty Cranborne, later Lord Salisbury, and Timothy Eden, later Sir Timothy, a gifted writer, the older brother of Anthony Eden.

The Prince of Wales entered Magdalen College at Oxford in October of 1912. The first time I saw him was at a Magdalen College wine, which is similar in some respects, I suppose, to an American college beer party or smoker. His famous tutor, Mr. Hansell, an enormously tall, handsome man who looked like a sort of outdoor Alfred Lord Tennyson, was with him at the time. The Prince seemed to me to be frail and diffident by contrast.

The high point of that evening was Gunstone's celebrated banana trick. Gunstone was the red-faced, bald-headed old scout who served the drinks. "Scouts" at Oxford were really valets. Gunstone's banana trick was to impress King George V as being the damnedest trick that he had ever seen. It was performed for everybody, or at least, as the Prince of Wales observed ironically, "everybody who counted for something."

Old Gunstone, who never did anything without grumbling, was coaxed into locating a banana. Then, muttering about the waste of good refreshment, he poured a little brandy into a bottle and ignited it. He stuffed the end of the banana into the neck of the bottle, leaving a tiny circle of peeled-back banana peel outside the bottle. The burning brandy created a suction that suddenly drew the banana into the bottle with a mighty pop, while the skin fell away, peeled neatly off outside. Old Gunstone, the sea scout, became a hero on the strength of it.

One day Eric Ednam's mother, Lady Dudley, and his sister Honor came to Oxford to visit him, and he brought them over to see me. Lady Dudley was a remarkable woman, serene and kindly, who treated me as if she were my mother. She took an immediate interest. She invited me for the weekend at Whitley Court, as Eric would be there, and also Margery Manners. The trip to Whitley gave me my first glimpse of English country life of the period and it was wonderfully relaxed and pleasant. One small point stuck in my memory. After dinner, instead of finger bowls, a silver dish that Lady Dudley had found in the Orient was passed around. It contained warm water, faintly perfumed by the petals of some exotic white flower that floated in it.

Whitley Court was an enormous Victorian house with wonderful grounds. It had great charm. The first sight that met my eyes was the unmistakable dome of a Russian church. Lord Dudley, Eric's grandfather, had had many connections with Russia. He had brought back to England a lot of Russian art treasures and relics, and he had built the church. It had a golden cupola, like St. Isaac's Cathedral on a small scale.

I learned that Eric's father had been Governor General of Ireland before his three years as Governor General of Australia. He was not present, and by the conversation I gathered that he and Lady Dudley did not get on. Inside, Whitley Court had been furnished in the grandfather's early Victorian manner, which left something to be desired, but Lady Dudley had converted some of the suites, furnishing them with good French furniture. She kept up a superb household for Eric and his sisters, Honor, Dickie and Patsy.

Shortly before the Christmas vacation I was invited by Lady Ripon to Coombe Court to a dinner in honor of Dowager Empress Marie Feodorovna of Russia and Queen Alexandra of England. This was not an invitation, but a kind of command performance, as the Empress, having heard I was in England, expressed a desire to see me. Queen Alexandra was a great friend of Lady Ripon. The Empress, who was, of course, the Queen's sister, was staying with the Queen at Marlborough House. My friend Michael Herbert was also invited.

Michael was at Balliol. The Earl of Pembroke who had married the Russian Ambassador's daughter was Michael's great-grandfather. Michael and I got permission to remain outside the college overnight, and he took me to Coombe Court, with which he was thoroughly familiar, Lady Ripon being his aunt.

Count Mensdorff, the Austrian Ambassador, was present, and Prince Serge Dolgorouky, the aide-de-camp of the Empress. Their Majesties arrived. The royal sisters were of Danish birth. Both had delicately chiseled features, wore their hair in the same fashion, with a high upswept coiffure, dressed very similarly, and had the same grace of manner.

Throughout the decades when Empress Marie Feodorovna had been the wife of Alexander III of Russia and Queen Alexandra the wife of Edward VII of England, these two sisters were considered to be in no small degree responsible for the long European peace. Both were now nearly seventy years old, and they were still much alike, except that the Queen Mother of England was, alas, a shade deafer that evening than the Dowager Empress of Russia. You had to shout a bit. I learned this because after dinner we all took turns talking to them. When I was seated beside the Empress she asked me about my studies at Oxford and expressed her pleasure that I was studying local government. Fathers work with the blind was administered through the Empress Marie Feodorovna's Guardian Organization, a benevolent society which was typical of her widespread activities. And throughout the reign of Nicholas II, my uncle Nicholas Obolensky had been *haufmarschall* of her court. But this was my first meeting with her and I was amazed at how well-informed and up-to-date she was.

Uncle Nicholas had remained in court after Nicholas II became Emperor, but differences developed between the Dowager Empress and the young Empress—differences which came to a head over Rasputin's increasing influence. As he became more arrogant, the old Empress made no secret of her distrust of him—the young Empress stood by Rasputin more firmly.

At Lady Ripon's, Empress Marie Feodorovna asked me questions about Father's health, about my brother's schooling, and discussed the family in general. She kept me conversing with her for some time, a great mark of favor in those days. Finally Their Majesties departed. Michael, Juliet Duff, I and some of the younger guests stayed up awhile and talked; in the morning Michael drove me back to Oxford.

When Christmas vacation came, Vlady and I raced back to St. Petersburg, to the old familiar round of Christmas parties. Vlady had completed his cram course for Gymnasium with Mr. Theodosius, and was in high spirits. After the parties, I made my way out to the Islands to listen to the gipsies and Marsha. Then I returned, a bit reluctantly, to England. This time Vlady remained at home with Father.

My second term at Oxford was so different from the first that it was like entering another school. Quarters were given me in Peckwater Quad, two rooms on the ground floor, and I had a scout, a famous old gentleman named

Haithwaite, to look after me. He was one of the most venerable valets at Oxford at the time, and I knew they were all very choosy!

The bathrooms were across the Quad and around the corner. On frosty mornings we sprinted across the Quad, got a quick bath—a very quick one—and raced back to breakfast. Often I had Paul of Serbia or John de Salis to breakfast with me in my rooms; then, if it was Paul, we would rush off to our lectures. Luncheons were also held in our rooms; our scouts would bring them up from the kitchens. Friends were always visiting Oxford. The college bill of fare was not the very best, but nobody worried much. In the evenings we put on our gowns and went to the dining hall. At five after nine the big bell of Tom Tower rang; the gates were locked, and anyone outside was gated, or restricted.

Afterwards, we worked in our rooms, or we visited. There was always somebody asleep in front of the fireplace in my study, on my white bearskin rug. A kettle, known to my disrespectful friends as the *samovar*, was continually boiling invitingly over the fire, and the room was generally filled with students, ringing with the sound of their arguments and general nonsense. It was hard to study under such conditions, but it was a pleasant existence.

Peckwater Quad was a curious place. It was built of very soft stone and all the fogs and rain had softened it still more. The Quad, as it was called, was literally falling to pieces, but it had a patina of age, and so it had distinction. The Quad was enormous, and its massive buildings were faced with battered columns or half columns running up the crumbling three stories between recessed windows, giving it a look of ruined majesty. It was, bar none, the most dilapidated building in Christ Church College. Rundown as it was, it possessed tremendous charm for its temporary inhabitants; and I'm afraid that we, like our predecessors, all did our share to abuse it further. Under the circumstances, I was often up until two or three in the morning. After my guests left I would start working on the papers that I turned over to Mr. Blunt twice a week.

About this time I was made a member of the Gridiron Club, an eating club to which several of my Balliol and House friends belonged. It was famous for its fine cuisine; and it was a gathering place for members who had been recruited from all colleges. A good place to eat was hard to find, so I was delighted. I joined the Dramatic Society; this was a Christ College group. I played a part in a big production. I was some sort of a friar and my job was to shuffle across the stage wearing a hood and carrying a crooked staff. My hand upon its handle was only part of me that was visible.

When the Prince of Wales entered Oxford, his equerry, Willie Cadogan, of the Tenth Hussars, was with him. He was a keen polo player, as was Captain Maitland Wilson, who was in command of the Officers Training Corps at Oxford. They helped us build up the Oxford polo team. Together they took us on, two different beginners each day, to teach us.

We played at the polo club on Port Meadows. There was no regular team to oppose us, and we played against teams of horse dealers. These were always around trying to sell their ponies. They played well enough, showing off what their ponies could do. The Prince of Wales sometimes appeared, usually playing stick and ball with Willie Cadogan, and occasionally playing polo. I came to know him at this time, for I took to polo, and went out every afternoon. We trained together at stick and ball before playing, just riding along and knocking the ball ahead of us, passing the ball back and forth. One day the Prince stopped by my rooms in Peckwater Quad. He had been visiting someone in "The House," the colloquial term for Christ Church, and came in with Mr. Hansell. His Royal Highness was fascinated by my wolf pelt and bearskin rug and the things that I had brought from Russia, and we talked about his cousin, Mountbatten, who had just been to Russia and had been feted by Father's old regiment, the Chevalier Guards. We also discussed my plans for playing polo and hunting in England.

Bobberty Cranborne and Timothy Eden were not part of the horsy set. Timothy was tall and thin—a shy, retiring, soft-featured young man. He was a hard worker, and didn't have much to do with parties, or with breaking up college, as we used to do on big occasions, or blowing the hunting horns in Peckwater Quad, as we used to do whenever there was an excuse for a college victory celebration. Any celebration was an excuse for starting bonfires. Unwanted furniture provided the fuel. Sometimes a student who had imbibed too freely at the celebration woke up to find that his chairs and table had disappeared. All remaining toilet seats were invariably thrown into the fires—the college was uncomfortable in some respects, especially in cold weather.

Paul of Serbia had rooms in Peckwater Quad just across the way from mine. He arrived at Oxford wrapped in a huge fur coat, attended by a couple of servants, with a chauffeur driving his big Daimler. Paul was usually thought to be the Crown Prince of Serbia, and he never denied it unless directly asked. He was really the nephew of the King, a relationship that led to his becoming Regent for young King Peter before the Second World War. His mother was Princess Demidov San Donato, a title bestowed on the Demidovs by the Pope and hardly recognized in Russia. She had married Prince Karageorgevich of Serbia. Paul and a brother, whom I never knew, were their children.

Paul was not in the slightest interested in sports, but spent his time in art galleries and museums. He had genuine artistic ability in his own right, and knew a great deal about painting and objets d'art. Later, King Alexander of Serbia had Paul build up the Serbian National Museum of Art. Paul's tutor in political economy was also Mr. Blunt. His scout in Peckwater was a ruddy-cheeked, red-nosed old man named Milligan who was, Paul was convinced, drinking up the fine port that he had brought to Oxford. I always agreed with Paul, which made him furious because as I pointed out, it was excellent port.

Paul hated to get up in the morning, but I reminded him that he was at Oxford now. I explained to him that English people loved good sport, that he ought to ride to hounds, and that it was the thing to do—even though it meant getting up at five. At first he took a very dim view of it. But I persuaded him on political grounds, saying that in his position he certainly ought to show the flag. We hired an extremely old horse named Raven for him. Raven was the sort of horse that would stand and turn his head and look at you if you fell off.

One day we went out with the Old Berkshire Hounds. The Master was an elderly gentleman named Mr. Drake, a stickler for fox-hunting proprieties of dress and conduct. It was a very unsuccessful day. We never saw a fox; the scent was cold; and we didn't have a run all morning. Drake was livid. Toward the end of the day, I was riding along with some of the students, and we were contemplating going home. I was the senior Oxford student present. The oldest student was always expected to see to it that the others were dressed properly, behaved as gentlemen should, and so on. We were riding peacefully along a wooded lane, in a cover, when all of a sudden we heard the sound of a horse galloping up behind us. It was a very fast gallop—as if the hounds were in full cry. It was Paul on old Raven galloping furiously up the lane. Raven recognized our horses, as they were all from the same stable, and pulled up sharply beside them. I thought Paul looked a little funny. But there was no time to inquire, for just then I heard another horse galloping hard. And here came Mr. Drake, with his face as red as his pink coat. He shouted that I didn't know how to ride, that I didn't know a hunt from a punting pond and to get out! I was astonished, but I had nothing to say. And I hadn't done a thing, so I didn't get out. After delivering his tirade, Mr. Drake galloped off.

"What in hell happened, Paul?" I asked.

"Well, unfortunately," he said, "Raven started galloping. I just couldn't control him, couldn't control him. I saw Mr. Drake riding along. I knew there wasn't much space between him and that tree. I couldn't stop this horror, and Raven charged straight through it!"

It developed that Paul had caught Mr. Drake's knee as he shot past, and nearly unseated him. The worst of it was that Paul didn't stop and apologize, but disappeared up the lane. Little wonder that old Mr. Drake took off in hot pursuit. Afterwards the story went around Oxford. When Mr. Drake heard who the culprit was and the culprit's background, the old fellow came up to Paul at a party and handsomely apologized.

Paul had a wry sense of humor, and after his auspicious beginning in English sporting life decided he would go on with it. Thereafter, he was always accompanied by a second horseman, who carried an enormous hamper filled with sandwiches, and a bottle of port slung in a container attached to his saddle. After we had been riding for a long time, it dawned on me that Raven was taking Paul over every jump, or trying to take him over, and I said, "You know, Paul, you don't have to jump every fence."

"Oh?" he said, interested.

"Yes," I said. "If you don't want to jump, or your horse doesn't want to, you can go through the gate."

"Really?" he asked.

"Yes, you can take it very easy. Ask your man the best way around." After that, the second horseman often opened the gate for him. Paul still jumped, but if a jump looked too big he went through the gate and enjoyed himself.

I went occasionally on country weekends, to the Salisburys, for instance, with Bobberty Cranborne, where Lord Kitchener was visiting Lord Salisbury, Bobberty's father. I remember we played games, and one time Lord Kitchener was Humpty Dumpty. I went quite often to Coombe Court, and in fact made it a practice to visit there before going home to Russia, and as soon as I returned to England. Through my Oxford friends I came to know quite a number of people. One I greatly admired was Lady Victoria Stanley, the daughter of Lord Derby. Then there was Sheila, the Duchess of Westminster. She invited me to a weekend where Leslie Cheape, the great British polo star, was present. The match with the American team at Meadowbrook was coming up in the near future.

Naturally, Leslie Cheape was my great idol. He was Number One against America in 1912 and 1913, one of the Big Four, a ten-goal handicap man, I believe the player with the highest handicap in those days. He very kindly came to Oxford one day and corrected my game. He showed me what I had to do, and gave me a few tips. My sticks were too whippy, for one thing. I needed a stiffer polo stick. I believe my game improved as a result of his teaching. We became quite good friends.

I must say that I had come to admire the esprit de corps, the unity, of the British people. Everyone was interested in politics, everyone had strong opinions one way or the other on public issues, and yet their differences did not really divide the country. The parliamentary system worked exceedingly well: that is what I thought as a Russian observer. The party in power and the opposition created a satisfactory condition where the ills of the country were freely ventilated and steps taken to correct them. The people felt they had a part in the government. They could voice their feelings at will. I rather envied that condition in England.

All my British friends belonged to the Liberal or Conservative parties. From childhood they were trained to take an interest in politics. If one of their family stood for election, or if one of their friends ran for Parliament, they went out to help them. The girls were especially good, going from door to door and talking with the housewives, doing their best to persuade the voters to vote for their candidate. It was part of their social life. And then the public discussions of politics were remarkably frank—or so it seemed to me. F. E. Smith, later Lord Birkenhead, then a brilliant young politician, good-looking and a gifted speaker, came to Oxford to one of our dinners and spoke about Britain's internal politics and foreign affairs with the utmost freedom and clarity. All these things were of deep interest to a Russian student in Oxford in those days before the war.

I didn't make the Oxford polo team in 1913, but our team of Geoffrey Lees, Barney Charlesworth, Stuart Wortley and Freddie Lawson beat Cambridge 9 to 5. Eights Week came on suddenly at the end of May, with the races between the college eights, crowds of visitors gaily bedecked in blazers and boating regalia sauntering in the meadows or picnicking out in the punts and under the trees beside the towpath—eight long days of ceaseless pleasure. The streets of Oxford were thronged, all the windows open in the summer sun, and all the rooms brightened with flowers as the families of the students visited their sons' friends. Visits took all morning, cricket and polo filled the afternoons, and we had tea on the college barges that floated lazily on the river. Then there were parties and dances every evening to bring the college year to a glorious, if exhausting, conclusion.

CHAPTER XII

Carlo Purcell was coming to Russia to spend the summer with me, but first I planned to spend two or three weeks in London enjoying myself, and I intended to be alone. Felix had become engaged to Princess Irina, the niece of Emperor Nicholas II, and was now living quietly in Russia. The Knightsbridge days were no more. But, before I left Oxford, an alarming letter arrived from St. Petersburg saying that Father was seriously ill. I got in touch with Carlo, and we left for Russia at once. When we reached my home, Father was dying of cancer. The family had already gathered. He died very shortly after I arrived, and was buried in St. Sergius Monastery in the family burial ground beside his brothers. He had been in poor health for such a long time that his death was not really unexpected, yet it was still a great shock, and it was only long afterwards, when the Revolution had begun, that I ceased to feel grief and realized what a blessing it was that he died when he did, because he could never have adjusted himself to the changes that were coming.

I came into full responsibility for the estate. Its management fell to me. Consequently, most of my time was spent with our lawyer, Mr. Nikolaieff. Father left everything in good order; the lawyer had handled things for many years, but there still remained much to be done, especially at Krasnaya Gorka. I will always remember Carlo Purcell's remark when we rode across the country and saw the house on its hill above the Imza; he said in astonishment, "It's like Ireland!"

We had planned a leisurely trip around Russia, but work made it necessary for me to leave Carlo on his own much of the time. However, he learned Russian, made friends everywhere and was fascinated by the country. This was the time I worked with my cousins organizing a syndicate to buy Lena River land.

At this same time I was interested in the purchase of one local zemstvo of a hundred thousand rubles' worth of International Harvester Company farm machinery. The matter was still being discussed when International Harvester salesmen appeared on the scene—a remarkable example of American business enterprise. The orders were placed for grain-sowing machines, binders, reapers, and all kinds of horse-drawn equipment. The interesting result of this transaction was that the value of the produce of the area increased by a million rubles within two years. In other words, so much more was produced that the original 100,000-ruble investment was repaid ten times over after only two harvests. The International Harvester people realized they had a tremendous market. They began to work closely with the zemstvos, doing a whale of a business. They freely granted long-term credits which the zemstvos guaranteed—when the Bolsheviks seized everything, the firm must have lost heavily.

All through the summer I mystified the people around Krasnaya Gorka. Several of my farms were on one of the great cattle roads built by Catherine the Great. Catherine had cleared hundred-yard-wide roads throughout Russia, all converging upon Moscow. They were lined with huge birches and cattle could move lazily on them, grazing as went, and not lose weight. They kept the grass down, and it was fine for polo. So I rode down these huge avenues for miles playing stick and ball. The people really did think I was crazy.

From Krasnaya Gorka, Carlo and I went to Tambov to visit Mother, then returned to St. Petersburg, where I got in some further polo at Prince Belosselsky's place. A group of young fellows from the diplomatic corps played there, including Freddie Cripps, who represented Barclay's Bank in St. Petersburg, and Robb Hudson, the British second secretary. Both were former Oxford polo blues. Count Chaki, the Austro-Hungarian secretary, also played, and during the Revolution he later helped Catherine and me get to the Swiss border.

Carlo and I returned to England before the term started, and I rented a flat at the Albany in London, a group of old buildings made over into bachelor apartments, running through a curved street between Bond and Piccadilly. It was famous then, but it has been torn down long ago. The Albany had a covered court and a garden between the buildings. It was a discreet sort of place, so discreet that Raffles had lived there—and I had Raffles' flat. It had a secret sliding panel in. a closet so I had always a second line of retreat. Women tenants were not allowed, and the occupants of the flats were substantial men much concerned with appearances. My flat consisted of two bedrooms and an oak-paneled living room. I had brought a Russian valet back with me to live there and care for it; and I had a few Russian furnishings.

My Albany flat was more or less a permanent address. I intended to keep it, but in fact I only occupied it a short time, because the First World War intervened. But throughout the war I still held the lease, and my Russian valet lived there and held the fort. I sublet it to Paul of Serbia who used it during the war years. It was not until 1919 that I finally gave it up, having lived there only a few weeks during the five years that it was leased to me.

I acquired a few horses, which I kept at Oxford. This was more or less customary. Eric Ednam also had hunters at Oxford. He had a professional hand with them and managed his stable so inexpensively and efficiently that it cost less than to have had it done by a professional. I stabled my horses with his, left all the bookkeeping to him, and we halved the cost.

I acquired my horses pretty much by accident. Captain Maitland Wilson, later Field Marshal Wilson—known as Mait or sometimes as Jumbo—and Captain William Cadogan of the Tenth Hussars, the Prince of Wales' Equerry—were working hard to help us build up the Oxford polo team. I got my ponies from Sidney Herbert, the older brother of Michael. Sidney, who later became parliamentary secretary to Stanley Baldwin (Michael became a banker with Morgan Grenfell) was recruiting for the Conservative party at Oxford. The Conservatives were on their way back after a long eclipse. They had begun to court the ablest students at Oxford and Cambridge, the best scholars and most promising speakers, young fellows who were on the verge of socialism. These recruits gave strength and impetus to the Conservative party within a few years. Sidney was already an accomplished politician, tactfully arranging meetings between the students and the Conservative leaders. But, as the Prince of Wales said, "Anybody in public life photographed in white breeches and wearing a helmet and carrying a mallet is only storing up trouble for himself." In any event, Sidney had to get rid of his ponies and I took them over.

Their names were Crystal and Little Blue Bags. Little Blue Bags, a white pony, really taught me to play polo. She was slow, but she turned fast, and she had an uncanny instinct. If she saw someone preparing a backhand, she pivoted before I was even aware of it and I found myself with the ball right in front of me. Sometimes she was so unexpected about it that we nearly parted company. Later I bought a third pony, Bullet, my best and fastest. We changed ponies, of course, after each chukker—I naturally contrived to be riding Bullet in the last chukker.

In my work in political economy I had come to know my tutor, Mr. Blunt, quite well. Each week I wrote a paper on the lectures I attended, and he went over it with me. I found him a bit dry, but exceedingly pleasant, an old-fashioned scholar, a real bookworm. Reverend Strong, our dean, who subsequently became Bishop of Ripon, was sociable despite his nervousness. He made a point of bringing together the students and the distinguished visitors to Oxford. Our senior censor was the famous Charles Fisher, one of the biggest men I ever knew. He was terribly nice, but there was no arguing with him. He was later killed on the Indomitable in the Battle of Jutland. John Murray, the junior censor, was another Oxford celebrity, an internationally known scholar and much more lenient than Fisher. And then there was old Carter, who was considered the most snobbish don at Oxford, renowned for his great collection of Queen Anne silver. He was a witty, cynical man and employed rapier like sarcasm to control the mob—ourselves.

There was a marvelous atmosphere about the place. That second year was most pleasant; I couldn't have enjoyed it more. The dean and the dons were interesting men—and friends. Those college friendships will remain with us all our lives. Also, people like John de Salis and Cuthbert Holmes became permanent companions. I met them again and again, in all stages of fortune and misfortune.

In the evenings we put on our gowns and dined in the Hall, the old hall of Christ Church being a medieval showplace of the college. For our table we would buy a big Stilton cheese, and dig into that cheese. I had come to appreciate the merit of cheese and ale during those chill winter evenings at Oxford. For medicinal warmth, it was said, the dons always had extremely fine port—the wine cellar at Christ Church was reputed to be the best in Oxford. They did themselves very well, and we were sure they could never feel very much of the cold.

After dinner we stayed home if we had to work. There were always club meetings. I found the English people reserved. They were extremely pleasant, temperamentally nice and hospitable, yet with a tendency to keep relationships at a formal level. In a club or organization, they seemed to have a habit of watching, of noting how one behaved. I think that the clubs provided them with an excuse for getting together that would have been unnecessary in a people less naturally reserved.

The Oxford clubs existed for every purpose. Many were started each year—drama clubs, language clubs, like the German club, which I joined, and eating clubs like the Gridiron. In the Gridiron were a lot of rugger players, rather a sporting club, which I joined through my Balliol connections, especially John de Salis.

There were so many Oxford clubs they had become a joke, and it was said the only reason most of them existed was to provide the members with a new uniform, the only uniform not being worn by some club or other being checked trousers with evening clothes. But there were exceptions, and the most notable was the Loders Club, which had existed a full century, one of the oldest in Oxford history. The Loders had only twelve members, and I was elected to membership during my second year at Christ Church, as the eleventh member. The twelfth member was still to be elected.

Prior to this, however, I was made a member of the Warrigel Club. The Warrigel was a cricket club, and I had no business to belong to it except that Ronnie Stanyforth, who was captain of the Warrigel cricket team, had had great difficulty one day getting together enough players for the annual game with the Oxford police force cricket team. I was hastily recruited as a new member, though I'd never held a cricket bat in my hands before.

Oddly enough, I had a streak of beginner's luck, and made six runs. I was just starting to fancy myself as a cricketer, when the police put in a bowler who was apparently a googly specialist, that is he put a spin on the ball, like the spin of a billiard ball. When it hit the pitch, the ball took an eccentric leap. I ducked in sheer self-defense, and I was bowled out. I gathered from the aghast expressions of my fellow members of Warrigel that my short career as a cricketer was over.

The Bullingdon Club, which I also joined, comprised all the men who rode to hounds. We cracked whips and had Bullingdon dinners, and everyone got very tight. Our uniform consisted of blue coats with white lapels and brass buttons. Each year the Bullingdon Club played one cricket match with a

Cambridge club, the Athenaeum Club, which I shall come to at the proper time—it was my disastrous last experience on the cricket field.

The Loders Club could perhaps be said to be made up of the same group that belonged to the Bullingdon, but its great age had given it dignity. Lionel Gibbs was President and Ronnie Stanyforth was Secretary. In 1814 the Loders Club was launched as a debating society by Vincent Barrington, Lord Belgrave, and the Marquess of Lothian. They started with a debate about the war of the allies against Napoleon. During the long peace after Napoleon's defeat, the debates were given up and the Loders became a wine club. As a requirement for membership, one had to be a gentleman, a sportsman, and a jolly good fellow—attendance at their dinners was compulsory. In my time the regular members of the Loders included Walter Winchester and Eric Ednam. The club met each Sunday for dinner. On my first Sunday as a member, a bottle of champagne was placed before each of us. I learned that this was the norm, and the bottle was to be finished. We then concluded with a loving cup, a sizable one, into which a bottle of port had been poured. The president of the Loders first drank a toast to the King; the cup went around; next, he drank a toast to fox hunting; and the cup went around again. There were only eleven members at the time. I was the eleventh and junior member. The joke was for nobody else to drink very much, because on the second time around the junior member, the last to receive the cup, was expected to finish it up in one go, without stopping, after which, historically speaking, he had often slid under the table and was usually in poor condition for quite a long time. I had no intention of obliging them and had taken the precaution of drinking some olive oil beforehand. It's an old Russian trick, and it lines the stomach.

Poor Walter Winchester was my next senior member. He had been taken in just ahead of me. As long as I was going to be present, and he always made sure that I would be, he was relatively safe; I had to finish up the cup. Then Bobberty Cranborne was taken into the Loders, and Walter, with two people now below him, breathed a sigh of relief. Now he was certain not to be the last at the table. He never even bothered any more to ask me if I was going. But one Sunday just before dinner Bobberty told me that he was unexpectedly called away and couldn't make it. Taking great care that Walter wouldn't know I too managed an excuse for being absent. With only ten present, it meant all the more for him. I have never seen a man more livid than he was next day. I remember I acted very concerned about him and inquired after his health.

I came to know some of the Indians at Oxford through Prince Amardjit Kapurthala, whom I had grown to like. He later married a Russian, Madame Popoff, the widow of the heir to the greatest Russian tea firm. Popoff's tea in Russia was the equivalent of Lipton's tea in England. And through Kapurthala I came to know the Gaekwar of Baroda, generally called The Gaek. He was a brilliant young Indian rajah who gave promise of becoming another Maharajah Ranjitsinhji, Jam Saheb of Nawanagar. When Indians are good cricketers, they are apt to be superlative, and The Gaek was magnificent. He had a keen eye. His father was the ruler of a rich and populous Indian state, one of the biggest and most important, but there was some obscure mystery about the rulers of Baroda; feuds in the reigning families had virtually wiped them out. The Gaekwar of Baroda who was at Oxford with me looked like an exception because he was such a fine athlete. Just at that time, also, there was a great romance that aroused tremendous interest in England, for his sister Indra married the Maharajah of Cooch Behar, a love match that ran counter to all the traditions of arranged marriages in India, and it caught the fancy of the English public. So the young Gaekwar of Baroda seemed on his way to become as popular as Prince Ranjitsinhji. However, he suddenly began to drink. He left the cricket team. He lost all interest and began to pine away, and the ancient Oriental ill fate of the family seemed to be working even in England.

I went to a number of parties and dances in London. This was the day of the great hostesses, the Duchess of Sutherland, Lady Derby, many of them hostesses for a particular kind of gathering, like Lady Ripon who was known as the hostess for any social event having to do with Russia. There had been a tremendous Russian season in England, with the triumph of the Russian ballet, and a great enthusiasm for everything Russian, increased by the visits at different times of members of the royal family: Grand Duke Michael and Countess Torbi came to live in England. Then the Empress Marie Feodorovna returned to visit her sister Queen Alexandra, and lived at Marlborough House. So there were several occasions for being in London—the first performance of Der Rosenkavalier, which was a triumph, or the opening of Maxim Gorky's play *The Lower Depths*, which was a success of another sort, along with Barrie's *What Every Woman Knows*, *Kismet*, or Melba appearing in *Romeo and Juliet*. There was the annual horse show at Olympia, which the Russian cavalry team always entered and in which it was generally victorious or very near the top. It consisted of my friends, Alexander and Paul Rodzianko of the Chevalier Guards, and Dimitri Ivanenko of the Death Hussars. They won the King Edward Cup three times in a row, and they took the cup back to the regimental mess in St. Petersburg.

There was another reason for occasional trips to London. I mentioned in an earlier chapter of these recollections that my youthful attitude toward the ladies was extremely idealistic, and I really expected not to have a love affair until I married. However, in the gay and carefree England of the years before the First World War, this resolution was subjected to considerable strain. I do not mean there was anything serious about these affairs of mine, or that they were numerous. College meant a lot of work, provided few opportunities for escape, and permission to remain away overnight was fairly difficult to secure. Still, I found it pleasant once in a while to have my Albany flat in London, and I certainly intended to keep it.

The Russian fashion ran its course, and, strange as it may seem, a wave of enthusiasm for everything German swept London before the First World War. German operas and German singers replaced the Russian ballet as the favorites of society. The German Ambassador, Count Lichnowski, was personally popular. He went everywhere, and his box at the Wagnerian operas was always filled with prominent London figures. This enthusiasm for Germany had a very important historical effect. The Kaiser confused the ambassador's popularity with an English feeling for Germany, and felt that England would not go to war against Germany if Germany should attack Belgium and France.

Some of the London hostesses were truly international. Lady Minnie Paget was one of the leaders and she knew everybody. I met Nancy Leeds there, the first American girl I ever knew. Nancy stood out from the crowd of Europeans. Her beauty was fresh and clear and unassuming. I took quite a fancy to her. She was then a young widow and in London with a small son. She was famous for her pearls—a magnificent strand that was considered the finest that had ever been assembled. Nancy caused a stir wherever she went, and I think she wore her pearls just to see if people looked at them or at her. We danced together, and became great friends. She also gave very good parties where she was always surrounded by detectives, because a fortune teller had told her she was going to be killed because of her pearls. I remember telling her for God's sake not to wear them, to put them in a safe. If it made her feel better, she should advertise that she wouldn't wear them any more, fire the detectives and live happily ever after. She didn't follow my advice, but she wasn't killed either.

The following may shed some light on the attitude of royalty in those prewar years. Young Prince Aage of Denmark was the nephew of the Dowager Empress Marie Feodorovna of Russia and of Queen Alexandra of England. He was the eldest son of their brother Waldemar. Aage was a strapping, handsome young fellow, very popular with the ladies, always traveling, a great hunter and sportsman, three years older than I.

The years had passed very pleasantly for Aage, and he had shown no inclination to settle down and marry, which was causing his royal aunts grave concern. Then suddenly Aage fell in love with Countess Calvi de Bergolo, of a famous Italian family. Consequently his aunts were pleased and relieved, even though the bride was not royalty. They wished to show that they really approved of the coming marriage because there was talk that Aage's family in Denmark was so opposed to the match that he could not return to his country.

A dinner was arranged at Coombe Court, where Their Majesties were again present along with ambassadors and a group of younger people, Juliet Duff, Michael Herbert, myself, of the same generation as Aage and his fiancée. It was just before the Christmas vacation of 1913. This meeting with royalty was like my previous encounters, with the difference that after Their Majesties departed, Aage, the Countess de Bergolo, Juliet, Michael and I sat up late talking, and then we all went our different ways.

Aage and Countess de Bergolo departed for Italy, where they were quietly married in Turin a few days later. Aage was not really typical of the traveling members of royalty I have described, and he subsequently had a heroic career with the French Foreign Legion.

I went to Russia for Christmas, stopping at Berne, for Dr. Chumi's wife had died and I wished to see him. In St. Petersburg there was a whole series of brilliant social affairs, the most glamorous in the history of the city. Indeed, the culmination of them, the cotillion given by Count Berchtold, the Austrian Ambassador, was the most glamorous thing of the sort I have ever seen. It was, incidentally, the last ball I ever attended in St. Petersburg. I remember I had an ominous conversation with Count Chaki, the Austrian secretary. I don't remember exactly what it was, but it seemed to be a warning. He was a good friend and our talk gave me a sense of foreboding.

Masses of flowers, imported from the Riviera in the height of the Russian winter, were everywhere. Each lady had a basket of flowers beside her. When we asked one to dance, we presented her with a bouquet, or, if she had too many, a ribbon. The favors to the ladies were extremely valuable. Those for the men were things like fine cigarette cases.

One amusing feature of the party was that there were many dances where the ladies chose their partners. In selecting the man she wished to dance with, each lady pinned a medal on him. So the great question became: how many medals would one get? Or, gloomily, would one get any at all? The best dancers came out beribboned and decorated like great heroes of the ballroom. Count Przezdetsky, of the Uhlans stationed in Warsaw, was the victor and came out with medals all across the front of his uniform and a beaming smile on his face.

As soon as the weather cleared at Oxford we began serious training for the annual polo match with Cambridge. Mait Wilson and Willie Cadogan took us out at every opportunity to play at clubs and against the regiments that had their own teams. It was a lot of fun. We left before lunch, entraining the horses, and playing perhaps forty or fifty miles away. After the game we relaxed, and returned to Oxford in the evening. It may have impeded my college work a bit.

One of these matches was against the Blues, the Second Life Guards, at Daggett, an excellent polo field. Colonel Arthur Penn was a colonel of the Blues; he was a great enthusiast for Oxford polo, and put together scratch teams of subalterns to keep the Oxford polo aspirants in trim. One of the Blues team was Ewan Wallace, the father of young Billy.

Our team included Mait Wilson—Back; Barney Charlesworth—Number Three; Willie Cadogan—Number Two; and I was Number One.

The Blues gave us a splendid dinner afterwards. I can't remember too much, but the mess was wrecked. We played cricket in it, using tennis balls and billiard balls interchangeably. It was highly dangerous. When the dinner was over we staggered off to Paul's Daimler, which he had kindly lent us, and started back to Oxford. There was a frightful rattling. Some of the Blues had tied one of their mess hall armchairs to the car's exhaust. When I saw the Prince of Wales later, he told me that he had just seen his uncle, the Duke of Connaught, who had asked him who those terrible friends of his were who had smashed up his mess. I respectfully suggested to the Prince that the Blues were probably passing the buck and that it couldn't possibly have been anybody less than Paul of Serbia, whose Daimler had personally absconded with an armchair.

After that I occasionally went up to London to parties, which was quieter. During the term it was difficult to get away from Oxford, and life was so pleasant there the inclination to do so was not strong. There was polo every afternoon in the spring, and parties on the river, as well as a great amount of work to be done. There were the Bullingdon dinners, and, once a week, the Loders dinner.

Once or twice I was allowed to go to London for social occasions, once to a Derby House ball, given by Lord and Lady Derby, at which the King and Queen were present. We had to get our knee breeches out for that. The ball was magnificent, a superb pageant, the women wearing their jewels, their tiaras, and their court dress, the men with their decorations of the Garter, the music by Ambrose's band. I was always glad that I had a chance to see that vivid instant of British social life.

Sometimes I went to London at Dr. Slater's suggestion in connection with my studies. He gave me introductions to the Labor M.P.s with whom I discussed questions of poor law and political economy. In those days most of the labor politicians were workingmen—they were union officials who had been elected to political office, and were generally blunt-spoken, independent individuals. Professional labor politicians, like Ramsay MacDonald, were just beginning to be known.

The early summer of 1914 was glorious. Even at the time it was recognized as unique—perfect weather, great crowds, and days given over to youth. Oxford was never more beautiful. Eights Week found the old place radiant under the summer sun, the elms and the ancient chestnuts in full leaf, flowers everywhere, Christ Church Meadow yellow with buttercups. All day long the students and their visiting families thronged the streets. And this time, to our delight, at the evening shindigs we were blessed by an amazing collection of exceedingly attractive girls. I remember our favorites were Stuart-Wortley's sisters; we all agreed they were by far the prettiest of the lot, and all of us made valiant efforts to get them into the punts.

This Eights Week was when I played my second and last game of cricket, in the annual match of the Bullingdon Club against the Athenaeums of Cambridge. We played in our gray bowler hats, naturally. The Cambridge club played in regular cricket attire. They were made of good cricketers and up to now they had always won. Our principal Bullingdon activity was eating, which was much more gentlemanly, but ineffective at this time. Thus, we reasoned that if we gave them a big lunch, and they drank a good deal, it might equalize matters somewhat. At this match I played cricket for the second and last time in my life. The luncheon was a great success. Afterwards, there was no danger of the bowler on either side hitting the wicket.

Also during Eights Week we played a joke on the dons. Nobody was allowed to fish in Mercury, a large fountain in the middle of Tom Quad. This was in the Oxford statutes, because undergraduates had been hungry at one time or other. There were goldfish there. So the Bullingdons and Paul of Serbia and I got some fishing rods and folding chairs and beer bottles. We attached dried herrings to the hooks, immersed them in Mercury just as the boat races ended, and began solemnly to fish. Paul looked terribly mournful. Big Charles Fisher came in from the boat races, leading a great crowd of mothers and fathers, who were immediately fascinated by our spectacle. As the herrings were flying out of the water, Charles stalked quietly up to us, seized Oldric Portal and Barney Charlesworth under their arms and, lifting them from their chairs, carried them, fish dangling from fishing rods and all, silently away. The rest of us evaporated as quickly as we could.

We really trained hard for the Cambridge polo match. Oxford had the edge in these annual encounters. Each Oxford man had a one-goal handicap playing Cambridge. But polo was a tremendously popular sport in those days, with big crowds, and several discussions of one's game by polo experts. Oxford was criticized for playing with routine skill—showing youthful keenness, the critics said, but not with a high enough standard to promise a new generation of fine polo stars.

We trained so hard it became a joke with our friends, and one day shortly before the Cambridge match, at some unearthly inappropriate hour, Bobberty Cranborne, Paul of Serbia and Oldric Portal got bicycles, and awakened the echoes by playing polo in the street. They had been celebrating, and when they were arrested Bobberty declared they needed no lawyer; he would speak in their defense as freeborn Englishmen, with an inborn right to play polo on bicycles. So, during the next days, among all the announcements of royal visits, and marriages and balls, the Court Circular carried this item:

At the Oxford City Police Court yesterday, Lord Cranborne, Prince Paul of Serbia, and Mr. Oldric Spencer Portal, undergraduate members of Christ Church, were summoned for playing polo on bicycles in Merton-Street. The offense having been proved, Lord Cranborne said he did not think they had annoyed any of the residents, but had merely entertained them. The defendants were each fined half a crown and costs.

In the boat races, Magdalen College triumphed over the Christ Church College eight by inches, after a magnificent race. That left the final race between Magdalen and University. And everyone made the most of it—a huge crowd, the river jammed with barges, the flags drooping in a lazy wind. And as the two crews swept under the bridges and toward the finish at almost a dead heat, "keeping pace with them along the tow-path," reported the *London Times*, gravely, "came crowds of undergraduates—among them the Prince of Wales—encouraging their college boats with revolver shot and rattle and wild yell." That pretty well pictures the spirit of Oxford in May 1914.

The Cambridge polo game was the last event of the year. It took place at Hurlingham, the leading British polo club, just outside of London, a few days after college ended. The weekend before the game was the hundredth anniversary of the Loders Club. There was a big dinner at the Ritz in London on Saturday night, June 20, 1914, with all the old members assembled—the Duke of Buccleuch, Lord Dartmouth, Lord Halifax, Lord Howe, Lord Galway, Lord Seymour, Lord Gordon-Lennox, about fifty in all, along with the twelve of us who were still in Oxford, and the occasion was noteworthy both because so many prominent people were there, and because so few Oxford clubs lasted that long.

Lord Rosebery, the Hector of the Conservatives, the former prime minister and the adviser of innumerable British governments, was the guest of honor, as it was the fiftieth anniversary of the day he had become a member, as well as the hundredth anniversary of the club. Also a guest of honor was Lord Chaplin, who had been a member in Rosebery's time, and was one of the colorful figures of English sporting life, a great organizer, riding hard to hounds, and playing cricket well, and climaxing his sporting career by winning the Derby. Three generations of the Scott family were present: Walter Winchester, in college with me, his father Lord Dalkeith, and the old Duke of Buccleuch. The old man, the son of the benefactor of the novelist Sir Walter Scott, was the greatest landowner of Britain.

It was a marvelous occasion for a visitor from Russia. I felt that I had never before seen at close hand something so inherently English. They were all sporting people, great horsemen and riders to hounds, good-hearted, cheerful, enjoying themselves simply, and fully convinced that the Loders Club would last another hundred years just as it was then.

Lord Rosebery made an amazing speech. He was probably the most experienced statesman in the world, and he spoke from a depth of experience as he told us what the political line-up of Europe was. We cannot say that we were not told that war was close. The terrific naval race between Germany and England was in itself a sign of the coming storm. So Lord Rosebery addressed his remarks to us younger members. I remember his words about the importance of traditions in troubled times—though, compared to the present, the troubles of the past were scarcely worth worrying about. He said that he was sure we—the members of the Loders Club—in the time of peril that was coming, would live up to our traditions as gentlemen, sportsmen, and jolly good fellows.

I didn't get to stay in London and celebrate, because I had to ship my ponies to Hurlingham. Cambridge had much better ponies than we had. The Cambridge team was strong, and things looked pretty tough. But Cambridge University closed a few days before Oxford. The Cambridge team went to London, and had time for the pleasures of the capital after a hard year at college, whereas we shipped our ponies to Hurlingham, and arrived there the day before the match.

The grand old man of polo, the Marquis of Villavieja, who was always promoting matches and presenting cups, got together a test match on Sunday consisting of himself, Philip Sassoon, and two others, to play us and give us a chance to get accustomed to the field. Hurlingham was a very popular place then, with matches constantly—things like the match for the Villavieja Century Cup, the old men against the young, the terms being that the combined ages of the old men had to be more than two hundred years, and the combined ages of the young had to be less than one hundred years. So there was a big, good-natured crowd and we had no opportunity for London sightseeing before the game. And *that* was fortunate. There was another match on Monday at Hurlingham, when we played Cambridge, a match between the Old Cantabs and the Cavalry Club for the Champion Cup, with serious polo enthusiasts present, what the papers in those days called "well-known people," meaning society figures, sporting celebrities, and royalty. The weather was perfect, the grounds beautiful, and a high wind was stirring the chestnut trees beyond the field. But we could not score a goal. I was too nervous. I was Number One for Oxford, with Leslie Melville, Barney Charlesworth and Hobson, the back, making up the team. Number One for Cambridge was an American, Marshall Field; he and I were the only foreigners on the teams.

It was nightmarish. I couldn't get the ball in, time and again putting it just past. Cambridge outrode us. But their eyes were off. I think it was because they had been in London longer than we had. That ball was passed to me as Number One a dozen times, with nothing in the way, and I missed. I remember Barney Charlesworth riding up to me after one miss like that and shouting "My God, Serge, get it in there!"

We hadn't scored in the first two chukkers. In the third I was on Bullet, and we had to start doing something. I got the first one in, and another right after it. We began scoring right and left just at the end as the Cambridge team weakened psychologically. From then on it was a debacle. The final score was nineteen to one, a terrific margin, and I won my half-blue for Oxford. I'm sorry to say that polo rated only a half-blue.

Our victory celebration began the moment we left the field in triumph. We were really at the top of the river. But the Cambridge old' grads were furious. Perhaps we had run up too high a score for it to be altogether sporting, for the last goals had been like shooting sitting ducks. Anyway, the Old Cantabs were

Hurlingham Club champions. They challenged us then and there to a match the next day, and in our overconfidence we accepted.

Then we went out to celebrate—June 22 and the morning of the 23rd. We had a tremendous celebration, and hangovers on the same epic scale. I doubt if Barney Charlesworth, our captain, had a wink of sleep by the time we got back on our ponies the next day. At least he looked pea-green, and it was an open question for a long time whether he would be able to stay on that pony. So the Old Cantabs rode all around us all afternoon, scored at will, and made us look like beginners. It was a very chastened Oxford polo team that rode off the field only one day after its triumph. I remember one Cambridge old boy rode up to us after the game and said gravely, "We had to do it, boys. We had to avenge it."

And that led us to the next day, June 24, 1914—which was destined to be remembered. For it was on that day that the Archduke Francis Ferdinand rode into the little city of Sarajevo in an obscure part of the kingdom of Serbia that was ruled by Paul's uncle, and met his death at the hands of an assassin. There was a shock, of course, and a great alarm throughout the world, but not so great as later generations might imagine. We were much too preoccupied with polo and things like that. I stayed in London for a while, continuing the celebration of our victory over Cambridge, and then I departed, a bit reluctantly, for Russia.

I expected to be back at Oxford the next fall. I realize it is generally said now that much in that prewar life foreshadowed the stupendous holocaust that was coming. In one sense the war was not unexpected. Certainly there was much that was disquieting in the pleasant prewar world I have been remembering—the unrest in Russia, despite Russia's real progress, stemming from the land hunger of the peasants; the fear caused by Germany's industrial might, coupled with the unprecedented growth of German arms and sea power.

But even if we sensed the war was coming we had no concept whatever of its terrible scope. When I think back on what my years in England gave me, it seems to me that Oxford contributed reality to my education, a sense of what the world actually was and that progress was possible within the society that existed. In Russia my idealism was visionary and impractical, as was that of the reformers among my friends. We had an emotional desire to do something in the great cause of humanity, but we did not have a concrete image in our minds of the society we lived in, and so we lacked a confident knowledge of what could be done or how it might be done. Consequently many of the reformers in Russia turned toward thoughts of revolution, a sweeping and violent overturn, or they became disillusioned and cynical about progress of any kind.

But in prewar England I found that the hope of progress was recognized and accepted in all sides of society. The aspirations I had felt in Russia as something that had to be fought for were accepted, and even sympathized with;

but at the same time there was a steady consciousness of how society actually operated, and how men thought and acted, hammered home all the time, until it became a part of one's state of mind. But the purpose was not to destroy our youthful dreams of a new world which would give the best that was possible to everyone. The purpose was to harness these nebulous hopes to reality. The great quality of that prewar life was its hopeful and forward-looking spirit. I saw two sides of England, the social life, and the work that was being done in clearing slums and improving the lot of the average man. Tremendous work was being done. The plans for the future were even more inspiring. The garden city of the future seemed a realizable goal that could be reached in our own lifetime, replacing the grime of industry and the misery of the poverty-ridden areas. We really felt that a new world was coming into being, a groping for a better life for everyone. And most serious-minded people shared this feeling regardless of what political party or social class they belonged to. We thought the world was gradually bettering.

I realize also that it now sounds unrealistic when I write of seeing the English slums as a student at Oxford, and English social life as a guest at great English houses. But that was the exaggerated quality of the world we lived in. It was then not strange or unusual in the slightest. The prewar world made a considerable contribution to civilization—a long period of European peace, a great advance in science, in art, and in education and technology, but I believe that its greatest creation was a spirit of hopefulness and belief in progress that went all the way through it.

What impressed me was that the state of mind among the reformers of England was similar to that of the truth-seekers I had known at the University of St. Petersburg, but in England their thinking was connected with practical work rather than with abstract ideas. Their hopes for the future, and faith in progress, were to be found everywhere; and their beliefs survived the years of war that were coming. And so strongly was I imbued with these beliefs of theirs that, once I had returned to Russia, I knew that, as far as I was personally concerned, these beliefs would endure. To date they have lived through a war and a revolution, and yet another war, and they still survive. To that extent, at least, the lessons that I learned from Englishmen were lasting; and if they taught me nothing else, they taught me not to make a fuss about it.

PART IV

HORSES IN WAR

CHAPTER XIII

In August 2, 1914, there was a wedding reception not far from Krasnaya Gorka. One of the Demidov girls was marrying. Her fiancé was a pleasant young fellow. There was something nice about the romance that inspired good will, and we all attended. I drove over in my troika. While we were there the father of the bride burst in, saying, "Germany has declared war."

I said goodbye, got my troika, and rode home to Krasnaya Gorka, reaching there that night. Driving through those rolling hills I had plenty to think about. Six weeks had passed since our polo victory and the assassination of the Archduke. Only ten days before the Austrian government had presented its ultimatum to Serbia, including demands which would have destroyed Serbia's independence. And yet Serbia accepted most of these demands, only asking that the rest be submitted for arbitration by the great powers. So the ultimatum expired, Austria declared war on Serbia; Emperor Nicholas ordered the Russian army mobilized; Germany delivered an ultimatum to Russia ordering the mobilization stopped; and Nicholas II replied by asking that the quarrel of Austria and Serbia be submitted to The Hague Tribunal. The twenty-four hours of the German ultimatum expired. Germany declared war.

Russian troops were already on their way to the frontier. I left my beloved Krasnaya Gorka early the next morning, the last time, with one exception, that I ever saw it. I drove to Liskovo, caught the steamer to Nijny, and the train to St. Petersburg. The people on deck, in the carriages, were in an uproar. Russia was as aroused as the United States after Pearl Harbor. There was not the slightest question of moral responsibility for the war. Immediately after the German declaration, France informed Germany that she was bound by treaty obligations to come to Russia's aid in any unprovoked war.

The German reaction was to declare war on France. That was August 3, the day I reached St. Petersburg. There I ran into trouble. I signed up as of August 3, 1914, but nobody wanted me in the army. I had no military training. No one even wanted to see me. I had to plead to be taken in. Then it was discovered that I had a grave physical defect—I had high arches. The army doctors took a sober view of high arches; a man with them couldn't march. I was horror stricken; high arches seemed to me the worst thing that could happen to a man, and I thought I was doomed to be shunned by mankind—forced to live as a hermit, because of my insteps.

However, my cousin Serge Koutouzoff was placed in charge of recruiting. He was the son of my father's sister Vera, and was made the head of all the recruiting stations in St. Petersburg. I got in to see him, and told him about my arches. From his headquarters I went to another cousin, Colonel Levshin, an officer of the Chevalier Guards, in command of the contingent in the barracks. I said, "I want to join the regiment as a buck private. Will you arrange it?"

The Chevalier Guards was Father's old regiment; otherwise it could not have been done. He replied, "I'll send a telegram to the regiment. But they are at the front, probably in action. It's not going to be easy."

I had to wait two weeks. The Chevalier Guards were in action, one of the strangest actions in the annals of warfare. You see, the Russian mobilization required forty-five days, because of the great distances and the few railroads, while Austria and Germany mobilized completely in fifteen days. The German war plan called for a lightning invasion of France through Belgium, in terrific strength, to knock France out of the war before Russia could mobilize. Our treaty with France called for an invasion of Germany to force the Germans to withdraw troops from the western front. And we invaded Germany, though it was known at the time that the invasion could not succeed; we took the offensive to make the Germans pull troops out of France.

The First and Second Guards, including the Chevalier Guards, had been ordered from St. Petersburg by express echelons to the frontier.

That was why there was no regiment there when I tried to join it. These crack cavalry regiments of Russia, were followed by freshly mobilized regiments of the army—and that was the tragedy. They weren't regular regiments. These new infantry regiments following up the cavalry advance were formed about cadres chopped out of every regular regiment, because of the disastrous slowness of our mobilization. Every regular company therefore sent so many officers, junior officers and noncoms to form the cadres of the new regiments. No sane company commander in a situation like that sends his best men. But worse still, these new regiments had no cohesion, and very little stability. They were well-equipped, hastily mobilized units who had only a couple of days of training together before they went into action, and were really green reserve regiments even though they contained a nucleus of regular army material.

These were the infantry troops following the cavalry advance into East Prussia. To the west of them, regular army units were pushing from Poland. As shaky as it was, our advance took the Germans by surprise. They never expected Russia to get in as fast as that, and, fortunately, there were only their lines of frontier guards falling back. But the Germans had been planning a long time. The farmhouses of East Prussia near the frontier were of stone and brick, built like forts. Their windows were like embrasures for rifles and machine guns. They were so solid that they could withstand heavy pounding from artillery. And all the fields were surrounded by barbed wire fences. The famous Schlieffen war plan provided that no German troops were to be withdrawn from the western front, no matter how far into Germany the Russian troops advanced, until France was won. So barbed wire and machine guns and reservists were counted on to delay the Russian offensive. They never expected we would push as hard as we did.

Major General Prince Dolgorouky, our commander, crossed the frontier at Verjbolova with the whole regiment of the Chevalier Guards. He deployed the regiment with the four squadrons in line abreast, and they crossed that way. There was only meager resistance. Twenty or thirty miles over the border, approaching the town of Gumbinnen, the regiment came to three separate roads. Every Guards regiment was commanded by a general, with a colonel his second in command. The colonel suggested that the regiment deploy. "Not at all," said Dolgorouky. "We'll charge." So each squadron charged down a separate road—fantastic—and all converged into the public square at Gumbinnen together. They advanced so fast there was no time for shopkeepers to close their stores. German headquarters were in a building on the square. A German officer was leading a little dog across it when the Russian cavalry galloped in. A machine gun on the roof started firing. The officer and his dog ducked inside.

Dolgorouky sent sappers in, and they planted a big charge of dynamite and blew the place up, the officer, his dog, and everything. Then the regiment moved on.

On that first advance, the Chevalier Guards pushed up to Königsberg, a hundred and fifty miles or so into Germany. Hindenburg was called to command the German army, with Ludendorff his chief of staff, and six army corps were detached from the western front and rushed to East Prussia. The lack of those six corps in the hammer of the Schlieffen plan was of decisive influence in the First Battle of the Marne that stopped the German advance into France.

But they were also of decisive importance on the eastern front. At the battle of Tannenberg, from August 23 to 29, the Russian Second Army, in the south, was surrounded and crushed, losing 92,000 prisoners, and General Samsonoff, after giving the order to retreat, was last seen riding into the confusion of his retreating troops. His fate was never known, but he was said to have shot himself. Hindenburg immediately moved against the Russian First Army, which was holding a sixty-mile line from the Baltic near Konigsberg southward into Poland, in the battle of the Masurian Lakes, early in September.

Back in St. Petersburg, Colonel Levshin received a telegram reading, I will be glad to accept Serge Obolensky into the regiment," signed "Dolgorouky."

There were no horses available for new troopers. I had to buy my own. Then I ran across Colonel Alexander Rodzianko, an officer of the Guards, the brother of Paul Rodzianko, whose team had won the King Edward Cup. Alexander was as famous a horseman as Paul. He had a great bay hunter in the stables which he sold to me for a thousand rubles (five hundred dollars), a fine animal named Rolf. All the horses of the Chevalier Guards were bays, those of the Hussars, gray. I was told to send Rolf to the marching or relief squadron, which was being formed in a nearby village and to report there.

No sooner did I get there than we were loaded into boxcars, eight horses and eight men to each. The horses were tied with their heads toward the middle of the car, and we slept on hay between them. After four days of this, we rode off under the orders of one of our sergeants.

Then, we were in Warsaw. We spent the night in the barracks of His Majesty's Uhlans. They were completely empty. The battle of the Masurian Lakes had by now turned into the second Russian disaster; the front held, but the Germans went between the lakes, rolling back the Russian left flank. In the south, however, the main Russian attack against Austria was successful. Hindenburg started a push into Poland with a small force, trying to help Austria and force the Russians to detach troops from the Austrian front. This offensive of Hindenburg's came within twelve miles of Warsaw, which was why we were being thrown in. Later, the Germans suddenly retreated, devastating the country as they gave it up, and the line was again on the border between Germany and Poland.

After one night in the Uhlan barracks, we rode back to the train. Lieutenant Drisen, a man whom I had known with Mother and Prince Machiabelli in Rome, a regular officer of the Chevalier Guards, was in the officers' coach at the end of the train. He was returning to his squadron, the one that was destined to be my own. We traveled overnight and again slept on the hay between the horses. We finally detrained next morning in the north, not far from Suvalki, which was then in the hands of the Germans. We were at regimental headquarters, and I was assigned then and there to Lieutenant Drisen's squadron, Her Majesty's squadron, Squadron Number One of the Chevalier Guards. It was a crack squadron, and I learned later that they had been all but wiped out in a single engagement.

At this time I received my first military instruction from the squadron sergeant major, Ivan Blajevitch. He was imposing. He weighed two hundred and fifty pounds, was six feet three and a half, and wore an enormous handlebar mustache that he pulled irascibly. He had a deep baritone voice that could be heard two miles away.

He looked me over critically and gave me a highly juicy talk on discipline. His vocabulary was a sheer delight, his way of putting things was a sergeant major's poetry. He tried me out to see if I knew left from right, told me how to address officers and particularly himself, briefed me on protocol, the care of my horse and my carbine, gave me a wooden spoon to stick in my boot, and told me to get the hell out of there and eat.

I learned later that I had gotten off pretty easily with Ivan Blajevitch. He had huge feet which he placed squarely on troopers' behinds when he was irritated. He was loved by them, however, and his nickname was Batko or Little Father.

He rode a monumental horse called Tiger, which got double rations for obvious reasons. But Ivan Blajevitch was a superb administrator, a great spirit on the firing line, and a hilarious one.

Once later on when we were in reserve, some of our fellows found some beehives. As they scooped out the honey, they were thoughtless in the way that they handled the bees, which went for them. As they galloped back in full retreat, Ivan Blajevitch was disgusted at the sight of their red and swollen faces, which, he shouted, "is quite like another part of your anatomies!" His rage at their disfigurement was punctuated by a selection of words that were choice and to the point.

When I became an officer, Ivan was one of my great standbys. That night Lieutenant Drisen passed by me and stopped to exchange greetings. He was in a fine humor and delighted at the prospect of going into action on the morrow. "It will be my first taste of it!" he said. It was raining steadily next morning. We wore our gray cavalry coats of a very heavy fabric, but they were not water-repellent. They became soaked and heavier and were always damp. We formed up at dawn, and we moved off into pinewood country.

All of a sudden we ran into the Germans. We dismounted immediately and skirmished at close range, acting as mounted infantry, or rather, dismounted cavalry. Time and time again, we mounted, advanced, dismounted again in skirmishing lines with the horses sent to the rear. The Germans were retreating.

That night I learned that Lieutenant Drisen had been killed; his older brother, in the same squadron, was given his body to take home.

The next day it was still raining. We kept on going into the woods, and we took a bridge. Then we mounted and deployed. There was a report that a column of Germans was passing on a big road, retreating, and General Skoropatsky, brigade commander, decided to launch a parallel attack on them. We rode out of woods to the crest of a long hilly slope that led down to the road, the horses were again sent back, and we deployed to where we could easily see their trucks lurching along the road.

Just at that moment I was ordered out of there. The Colonel wanted to see me. My old friend Andre Tolstoy, the son of the curator of The Hermitage, was also a volunteer. Neither one of us had had any military training whatsoever. Almost everyone we knew was an officer, including Andre's brother Ivan, who was also in the Chevalier Guards; but Andre was, like myself, a private. Colonel Miklashevsky assigned the two of us to act as orderlies or dispatch riders. He was second in command of the regiment.

He went in with the four squadrons deployed on foot, advancing across a valley. Our objective was, of course, the road on which the Germans were retreating. Miklashevsky ordered us to stay out of sight on horseback behind his command post. We were to take orders to the squadrons on the firing line. Miklashevsky had established his command just behind a village. There were woods on a hill behind us, and flat ground in front with trees and little clumps of brush, and then the big road where a German convoy was under way before us.

But what we did *not* know was that the main part of the convoy had already passed through. We had bumped into the tail end of it. So, instead of trucks and light infantry, we ran into the German rear guard—a couple of battalions of infantry and some artillery, both heavy and light.

There was a priest for the Chevalier Guards and a priest for the Horse Guards. They always followed the regiments, and in combat they would administer last rites. They wore cassocks at all times and rode in them.

Father Scherbakovsky, of the Chevalier Guards, was a famous character. He was dark, thin to the point of emaciation, exceedingly pious, and very brave. In the Russo-Japanese War he had covered himself with glory. With a detachment of surrounded Siberian troops, wounded, he had bolstered up their courage, and, unarmed, had personally led their breakthrough charge holding up his cross in his hand. He was, however, known for his lack of humor. Father Nicholas of the Horse Guards, on the other hand, was blond, equally pious, and inclined to portliness. Together they made a marvelous combination.

I remember we were standing behind the houses, Andre and I, awaiting orders. We were screened from the enemy. All of a sudden we saw the two priests and their orderlies ride onto a little hillock fifty yards behind us. They dismounted and placed themselves beside a post and rail, obviously very much interested in the battle. They had a perfect view of the enemy far below them. As it turned out, the enemy had a pretty good view of them. Suddenly there was the sound of a heavy howitzer shell that seemed to be coming right at us. It passed over our heads and landed very close to the good Fathers. To my utter amazement, Father Nicholas made a magnificent leap. He took off light as a feather, perhaps aided somewhat by the explosion itself, and dropped majestically onto the opposite side of the post and rail. Our Father Scherbakovsky followed suit.

Needless to say, they rushed to their horses and with their cassocks billowing behind them in the wind, galloped off before the next salvos, which fell unpleasantly close to us. We weren't pleased that such godly folk had unleashed a holocaust upon us. That was my first experience with shellfire. The horses were nervous, but Andre and I, I am glad to say, took it in our stride.

They hit some of our artillery horses, and we sustained some casualties. General Skoropatsky climbed onto the roof of the house in front of us and saw a battalion of their infantry deploying, and immediately he sent me down there to recall our two most advanced squadrons which were now in danger of being enveloped. I rode in through their fire. I got the order to the first squadron, which was my own, and then I had to get to number three. In the third squadron, which was in grave straits now, was an old friend of mine, Alexander Timashev, whom we had called Sandrik as boys in St. Petersburg. That day I provided him with one of his favorite stories.

I was determined to do everything right, despite the artillery barrage. He says that I galloped up, white-faced, and saluted. "Your Excellency!" I said. That was all right, but then I recognized him. "Sandrik!" I yelled over the pandemonium, "the commanding officer of the regiment orders you to get the hell out of here! Back to your horses!" As he pointed out later on, they were very unhappy there and were not displeased to get the order, no matter how presented. So we started to retire. All of us were in full view of the enemy. We lost more horses when a shell killed several of them pulling a caisson. I was riding past, and I saw the dead horses. One horse, still standing, had its leg torn off. The soldier who had been riding it was dead. He had fallen to the ground. The horse was screaming. Without orders I couldn't stop to shoot it, and although I knew that the caisson would fall into German hands, we were under orders and had to get out fast.

But General Dolgorouky himself, who had notoriously poor eyesight, somehow saw it from a long distance for him. He galloped up to us, ordered a troop of our men to dismount, unharness the dead horses under fire, harness our own horses to the caisson, and draw it off. I went over and shot the wounded horse, poor thing. I went back to Dolgorouky, and we stood stock still on horseback, in full view of the Germans, until it was hauled away.

Dolgorouky, myopic or no, was brave, sometimes ridiculously so. When he had first led the regiment into East Prussia, he had refused to let the Chevalier Guards lie down under fire. By the lesson of British troops versus the Indians and the American militia, he was two hundred years behind the times. He insisted that everyone should stand up, shouting, "The Chevalier Guards do not lie down!" So these great troops, none of them less than six feet tall, went in as if they were on parade. (I was the smallest man in my squadron when I got there, and I was six feet three.) Six of our best officers were killed as a result. Luckily for me, I was in St. Petersburg then. Eventually the troops began to lie down anyway. We still had silver epaulettes. Whenever we lay down in a skirmish line the epaulettes were highly visible, but no one took them off.

Dolgorouky used to place his riding crop perpendicularly against his eye whenever he knew Germans were about. Apparently it helped him to see better. If he did see them, he would cry, "Germans!" pointing in their direction with his crop. "Attack immediately!" He was terribly impatient.

There was always a terrific rivalry between the Horse Guards and the Chevalier Guards. Dolgorouky was the Chevalier Guards commander. He was always suspicious of the Horse Guards, since he couldn't see, and particularly of Major Wrangel—and with very good reason. (Wrangel was the famous White general who later fought the Reds in southern Russia.)

The Chevalier Guards consisted of four squadrons and the Horse Guards of four squadrons. Her Majesty's Squadron, to which, luckily once more, I only later belonged, was the First Squadron, Chevalier Guards. The Third Squadron,

Horse Guards was commanded by Major Wrangel. The Dolgorouky-Wrangel rivalry dated from the very beginning of the war and the Battle of Insterburg.

At the village of Kauscher a German battery was firing at the cavalry brigade. Prince Eristoff, then the Cavalry Brigade artillery commander, had spotted it just behind the brow of a long hill. He had gotten up on the top of a barn and was plastering the battery and its supporting battalion with shrapnel. The battalion was dug in alongside the battery in a potato field. Dolgorouky, whose proportions were generous, insisted on climbing up onto the flat top of the barn where Eristoff was. Peter Baranoff, the adjutant, and Dolgorouky's trumpeter had a terrible time heaving him up onto the roof. Finally he made it. As soon as he stood up next to Eristoff, he put his crop against his eye. "*Je les vois!*" he yelled. "Tell Lazareff to attack!" He loved to charge his cavalry. Lazareff was the squadron commander of Her Majesty's Squadron, Number One, his reserve. Meanwhile, Dolgorouky ordered Numbers Two, Three, and Four Squadrons to dismount and attack the battalion and provide cover, and Eristoff went on coolly plastering the battery with his artillery as Lazareff charged. "Je les vois" or not, Dolgorouky had been too blind to notice the barbed-wire fence that was surrounding the battery. As a result, Her Majesty's Squadron came to a dead halt before the battery and were chopped to pieces by direct artillery fire, losing thirty percent. They had no choice but to dismount, abandon their horses, what was left of them, and prepare to cut the wire alongside the three squadrons that were crawling up. Michael Lazareff was wounded in that operation; a shell burst under his horse. He was the son of old General Lazareff, my father's close friend, who had taught Vlady and me to ride. His sister later became Mrs. Amory Blaine, the wife of the American businessman, and Lazareff himself died in Chicago only a few years back. Eristoff saved the situation by a direct hit on the battery, silencing it, and then turned his attentions to the potato field and the German infantry. Meanwhile, the wire was cut, rolled back, and the slow advance to the battery began.

Wrangel, who had been watching nearby, saw his moment. The wire was gone, so on his own initiative he ordered his Third Squadron Horse Guards to charge, and they went in under heavy small-arms fire from German infantry and took the battery right from under Dolgorouky's nose. There wasn't a thing he could do about it with no more cavalry in reserve and the horses of the dismounted squadrons to the rear.

Wrangel dragged the battery back to his own regiment with his own horses, and of course it was a great triumph for the Horse Guards. They got the credit.

Wrangel had the instinct of generalship. He had good judgment, and seemed to sense the proper time for everything. So did Eristoff. It really was Eristoff who deserved the praise that day.

Dolgorouky never forgave Wrangel, however. When the caisson was being drawn off, he stood in the open the whole time to make sure that it really was done. "If I don't do it," he growled to me, "I know what will happen. Wrangel will come along and take it!"

When we fell back after the attack on the German convoy we went into pine woods. Our function was to move always ahead and draw out the Germans. Then we fell back and the infantry moved in. We went into action either on foot, as dismounted cavalry, or in day-and-night cavalry patrols, sometimes we established cavalry outposts, and if anything ever happened we were called up to plug the gap. The rain was almost constant. As a private, I took care of my own horse. Coming in at night, pretty tired, we still had to unsaddle and groom and feed our mounts.

We were almost always in the woods. The first major action in which I took part was in the woods, the Woods of Augustoff operation. Augustoff was fought over in the very first battles of the war. It was taken and retaken by both the Russians and the Germans. We moved in again, and took the town in the middle of the night. By this time the weather had turned cold in addition to the rain, and during that night the rain turned to ice. The town was a mass of ruins, and we left the horses in the middle of a square.

And there, suddenly, in that dismal place, Peter Zouboff as usual turned up with something. He was also a volunteer and a private. That night he found a bakery. Siberian infantry troops were not far away, and Peter with his usual resourcefulness had located their bakery, with a good-natured old Siberian baker at work during the night. They had taken over the local bakery and had lots of hot rye bread coming out of the ovens. They also had hot tea. It was nice and warm there, and we spent the night in it in relays, some of us staying with the horses while the others warmed up in the bakery.

The battle of Łódz was in the making, sometimes called the most remarkable battle of the war. When Hindenburg retreated into Germany after his hasty offensive toward Warsaw, he moved his whole army north, around Posen, and mounted a new offensive to strike at the Russian right flank as it advanced into Germany. The Germans were still trying to compel the Russian high command to detach troops from the Austrian front, where the Austrians were growing desperate; but in this they failed. There was a sort of lull while these preparations were going on. As we moved into East Prussia we got out of the woods and into cultivated country, flat, made of marshes that had been drained, with small farms, each with its own windmill. As we went on, we noticed that the arms of the windmills seemed to be locked in fixed positions, no matter what wind was blowing. One windmill was visible from the next, and their arms set like semaphores as we went on.

CHAPTER XIV

There were six of us volunteers in the Chevalier Guard regiment.

As I said, I was in the first squadron. Peter Zouboff was in the second, with Pleske, an old friend of ours, much older than the rest of us, very vulgar, and a fine pianist. He had once been a court chamberlain, and that is what he was called. He had passed his military examinations, but instead of going into the army went into civil service, and then when the war came volunteered, and was made a corporal. Andre Tolstoy was my friend from childhood; we were raised together; but there was another Tolstoy in the regiment who was also a volunteer. We called him Cubic, because he was square. He was in the third squadron, and Andre Tolstoy was in the fourth.

They assigned us all to be dispatch riders. They thought it better to use the more educated young soldiers as liaison officers, because in battle there was no time to write a dispatch. The two Tolstoys, Zouboff and I were with Colonel Miklashevsky, while Pleske and another volunteer named Chicherin were with Prince Dolgorouky. We were under the direct command of the adjutant, Captain Peter Baranoff, who subsequently became a teacher of Russian at the Berlitz School in New York.

At night, when we went into bivouac, we took turns. The squadrons were usually quartered in different villages, one or two squadrons to a village, with the staff of the regiment quartered with one of the squadrons. Two or more miles or so might be between the villages. At night we were often awakened and told to ride to the squadron commander, and tell him to be saddled by a certain hour, and rendezvous at a certain place. Since we had to ride so often at night, we got to know the various squadron leaders' characteristics very well, and of course, as we woke them up all the time, they came to look upon us as their mortal enemies.

My squadron leader in the first squadron was Major Kossikovsky. He was a sour-looking individual, but underneath he was really very pleasant. He had a truly forbidding expression. He was a doctor of laws, a great disciplinarian and very efficient, and we had to be very careful of our demeanor. Saluting, and reporting the orders in the most accurate manner, was essential with Major Kossikovsky. But first we were at liberty to shake him.

Number Two squadron was commanded by Prince Gagarin, always called Toka Gagarin. He was an effervescent man, with a great heart by day, and kind; but he hated to be waked up. He called us his tormentors, and against him we had to take elaborate precautions. First we would cough. He would pretend he didn't hear us. Then we would walk noisily or hum, and we would see him barely opening one eye, pretending he didn't see us. We would also see one hand reaching stealthily toward a boot, and he would open one eye suddenly, and before we could deliver the order, he would throw the boot. As we ducked, we would be respectfully saying that His Excellency was please to be ready at half-past four with the squadron lined up. "Never have I heard of such idiotic orders," he would cry in anguish. "Number Two squadron is always ready at half-past three!" And he would roll over and go back to sleep. His executive, who slept next to him, Captain Bibikoff, always took it in, and he got everything ready.

Number Three squadron was no problem. It was by all odds the best disciplined, always in first class shape, and it was only necessary to look smart to avoid trouble with its young commander, Major Panteleieff. But sometimes after riding in the mud and snow it was impossible to look smart, and we always tried to scrape some of the mud off before we went in and saluted. The commander of Number Four squadron was Major Zvegintsoff, married to one of my Obolensky cousins. He was brilliant, also a doctor of laws and an able officer, but his hatred of being awakened at night verged on the pathological. He vented his rage in slow-spoken and bitterly sarcastic remarks. There was no ducking, or anything like that, but we heard things said about the various officers of the regiment we never dared repeat!

Whenever the regiment was in the firing line, we had to ride up and down the ranks to the various squadron leaders with their orders: advance, retreat, change positions, or whatever it was. Often we had to ride through enemy fire.

Once the Germans were deploying in front of us. They had cavalry, artillery, and infantry. Her Majesty's Squadron was the only squadron left in reserve. We had the standards of both the Chevalier Guards and the Horse Guards with us. So Prince Dolgorouky put us at the base of a railway embankment, dismounted, and in full view of the enemy Baron Knoring—Tanka, we used to call him—went up the embankment with his binoculars. He was a captain—and immense around the middle. He called down, "I see a battery riding out."

Dolgorouky never moved.

"They're stopping. They're turning the guns around."

Dolgorouky did not appear to hear.

"They're pointing it at *us!*"

We still stood there, but we watched the expression on Dolgorouky's face. Suddenly Tanka said, "They're preparing to fire!" and scrambled down the embankment toward his horse.

Dolgorouky still stood as if nothing was happening. The first salvo went right over us. We stood and waited, holding our horses. The next fell just short of us. We were bracketed. We all looked at Dolgorouky, who was utterly impervious.

Miklashevsky was the man who gave the order, "To horse." We mounted like lightning. "To the rear, gallop, march!" he cried, and we shot out of there. The salvo landed right where we had been.

After riding back about a quarter of a mile, we stopped again. There was a knoll, where we weren't so exposed, and there Dolgorouky and some officers gathered, and talked in a slow conversational fashion. They flicked dust off their uniforms, looked at the ground, maybe kicked a pebble, like a group of hunters gossiping together. German cavalry, artillery, and infantry was outflanking us on the right. So the discussion went on, and finally they decided that we would fall back at this time. We took the standards, and retreated at a trot.

The Chevalier Guards was the Empress Marie's Regiment. She was the honorary chief of the regiment, which was why the first squadron bore the name of Her Majesty's Squadron. We took the standards back pretty fast, while the squadron retreated more slowly behind us. The Germans were coming swiftly around us on the right. But after we had gone back about three miles, we came on the vanguard of the Siberian infantry that was moving up. We were delighted to see them.

That was our function—to go in ahead and draw the Germans out.

Once we drew them out there wasn't much we could do. And sometimes, like today, we drew out a hornets' nest. As cavalry, we had little stability. We could strike, but then we did not have enough strength to offer effective resistance. Every third soldier had to hold the horses. As the squadron consisted of one hundred and twenty men, there were only eighty in action, and once, during the bad days, we were down to fifty men.

The rain had continued to fall so steadily that it became a factor in world history. It made the front a quagmire, and things came to a standstill. I had developed a fearful cough, and suddenly the doctors sent me to St. Petersburg. They thought I had tuberculosis. I did not, but exposure in the weeks of constant movement had left me very weak.

I arrived home entirely unexpectedly. Mother had a house on the Galernaya, and I went there immediately. She was overjoyed to see me. As I went in, my sister Olga was rolling bandages with a friend of hers, Princess Mira Koudasheff. They were both eighteen, and it was their coming out year, unfortunately for them. Everyone was working for the Red Cross; Mother was working in Grand Duchess Marie's section, Grand Duchess Marie the Elder, who had at the front her own trains and Red Cross detachments which she had personally organized. Mira Koudasheff after the Revolution became Mrs. Norman Armour, the wife of the American diplomat.

We had a few pleasant evenings at home. A few wounded officers, and young people training, came in while the girls rolled bandages. Someone played the piano. It wasn't anything spectacular, but it was peace, and it was a relief after East Prussia. Vlady was still at home. He had joined the Horse Guards as a volunteer, and was assigned to the third squadron, where his commanding officer was Peter Benckendorff, the husband of Ella Narishkin, Wrangel having moved up. Benckendorff had been badly wounded, hit in the right shoulder by a dumdum bullet, but he was recovering in St. Petersburg; and Vlady, instead of being ordered directly to the regiment, was sent to the Emperor Nicholas Cavalry Academy.

I went through a rigorous treatment every day at the hospital. So there was no social life then, except for those pleasant evenings at home. In addition, I was a private, and privates, in the army of those days, were not permitted to ride in automobiles. We could only travel in droshkies or sleighs. The test for tuberculosis was negative, and after a couple of weeks I returned to the front.

The defeats of Tannenberg and the Masurian Lakes had not broken Russian morale in the slightest. On the contrary, they were overshadowed by the victory over Austria, for the Austrians were driven back with the loss of 250,000 dead and wounded and 100,000 prisoners, of their 900,000 men in Galicia. They had left behind them in their retreat their greatest fortress, Przemysl, with 100,000 men bottled up inside, and certain to fall when action was resumed in the spring. There was a tremendous exhilaration in the great upsurge of patriotism that now united the country. Russian mobilization was at last complete. The Germans had been stopped in France; and while our casualties were very heavy, the determination of the people gave a promise of victory that had never been felt during the war with Japan. And the building up of our industry and the expansion of agriculture that had been pushed through was now beginning to pay off.

The one dark spot was the problem of supply. The armies were so huge that all our surplus was going to the front. The railroads could not handle it. The narrow muddy roads were jammed with slow-moving wagons, and we eventually broke down in Russia simply because the strain was too great for an agricultural country. When we all went into the war, neither England, France, nor Russia had any conception of mobilizing industry for war. Everyone thought that the terrible engines of destruction simply meant that the war could only last two months at most. Only the Germans had carefully thought it out and mobilized their industry. German armament and munitions made every German division as strong as a Russian division and a half. We had, however, far better cavalry, no less than sixty-four regular cavalry and Cossack divisions, of which thirty-five had been formed since the war began, and the mud helped us. No agricultural country could have supported an army as huge as ours. Everything was going to the front. At the end, Russia had twelve million men under arms.

While I was in St. Petersburg, the regiment was moved to Radom, beyond Warsaw. What happened was this: Hindenburg pulled out the army that was opposing the Russian advance into Germany from western Poland, organized a new army, and within ten days was preparing to strike from the north while our army was still pushing ahead in Germany, groping for the German force that had disappeared. Hindenburg was prepared to strike the Russian line from the north perhaps fifty miles behind the most advanced Russian troops, developing this movement from Cracow, on the way to Łódz. We were thrown into what was called the Petrokoff-Radom Operation, a phase of what the Allied history books call the Battle of Łódz, when I rejoined the regiment.

I can't possibly describe accurately all the engagements we were in, but I will attempt to recount some that I consider the most exciting.

On November 10, 1914, Hindenburg ordered an advance of the whole regrouped German Army on an eighty-five-mile front. The weather had turned very cold. The temperature fell to ten degrees above zero. And still there was no snow. The rains fell during the day, and at night icy winds glazed everything in a sheathing of ice. On November 15, the Germans struck the main body of the Russian First Army about fifty miles due west of Warsaw, and we were driven back somewhat, but held. Part of the German army then contained the Russian First Army, while the bulk of it swung to the south, and, on November 17, was on the flank of the Russian Second Army, twenty-five miles south. The breakthrough was an accomplished fact.

We marched over to Petrokoff and were in the battles around there, falling back slowly toward Radom. That was where the Germans began shelling us with the big shells that we called *chemodans*, or suitcases. They were so big and slow that we could see them coming. I developed a splitting headache from shell shock, and ran a high fever. While in that condition, I was ordered to ride orders over to General Arsenieff in the front line, our most brilliant cavalry general of the time. Shells were falling all along the road I had to travel, so I galloped parallel to it, within a hundred yards of the road itself. It was highly unpleasant, until I had ridden through a village. I really thought my head would burst. At the far side I ran into the General, and delivered to him the orders to retreat. He just said, "Yes. Thank you very much. I am actually doing it."

The General and I then rode back over the same course that I had taken to reach him, while the chemodans kept pulverizing the road nearby. The difference was that the General walked his horse the entire stretch, and I had to walk beside him.

We were on the flank of the rear-guard action of the Second Army. Our cavalry was used heavily as a stopgap. Besides, Grand Duke Nicholas Nikolaievitch, in supreme command of all the Russian armies, was an old cavalryman. He had reorganized and reformed the Russian cavalry, using as models the cavalry in the American Civil War. We fought according to the precepts and examples of Jeb Stuart and Nathan Bedford Forrest. It was a war of movement, sometimes very fast movement. One German army corps had penetrated the Russian lines and was far to the rear of the Russian Second Army, nearly twenty miles back. A single Siberian division of first-rank troops, going to the aid of the First Army, unexpectedly met this isolated German corps. The division was enveloped and annihilated, but did great damage. At the same time, the German corps was surrounded on three sides. We fought against their dwindling pocket near Cracow. Our infantry lines closed, skirmished, and then closed behind the Germans. Finally, the German corps that had been trapped was miraculously set free. They were actually surrendering, when some damn-fool general of ours marched the wrong way and opened the gap instead of closing it. It was a bitterly cold and starry night when I carried the dispatches telling our headquarters that the Germans were retreating and escaping. I remember crying with anger on that ride. They lost 35,000 men, but our losses were heavy too. It was the biggest blunder of that campaign.

During the Petrokoff period of our fighting, I galloped from the staff to the new commander of the regiment, Colonel Prince Eristoff, who was directing the artillery fire himself. Dolgorouky had been promoted and transferred. Eristoff was magnificent, a clear thinker and militarily sound; and he saved rather than expended his troops. He was an old artilleryman, and he still liked to fire his own artillery, which he did with great precision. Also, he had infallible sense as to where someone might be expected to be. The Austrians were firing back at us, and I had to gallop to him and back to the staff several times. I tried to time it between salvos of the Austrian artillery. I took a few minutes for the shells to come over. I stopped behind a house and leaned against the wall. Rolf got so used to it he automatically leaned against a house when we stopped. By the end of the day, when he heard the Austrian batteries fire he would stop of his own accord after a minute or so and lean up against the wall of a house. Then the shell would burst over us, shrapnel. There would be a little while before the next, and in that pause we would gallop on again. I have said that the horse became accustomed to it. That is not quite exact. Horses grow more familiar with the sounds, and less nervous, but they never become accustomed to it, and under machine-gun fire especially they lose their heads and just have to gallop.

I was awarded the Cross of St. George, the first of three I received, second, third and fourth class. It was given to me for riding under fire with dispatches that got the squadron out of a pickle. In my experience, most of the things you did weren't seen or noticed, or weren't reported, and you didn't think you really deserved the award for the particular occasion for which it was given. There wasn't much ceremony about it. We were just lined up one day, and our names called out. It was raining hard.

Soon all of us dispatch riders were being trained by Colonel Eristoff—whenever there was any time for training. He would ride along, side by side with Miklashevsky, and we rode along behind them. Suddenly he would bark out "Obolensky! Two miles back we passed a house, and there was a woman in the doorway. What was the color of her dress?" Or at night if a light flashed somewhere, I had to snap out at once, "One hundred yards," or whatever my estimate of the distance was. He wanted me to notice everything. He said a soldier always had to be on the alert, and be aware of the little signs, for you could sometimes tell by the way people acted if the enemy was not far away.

Especially on patrol, he said, it was extremely important. "It might even save your life!" His dictums actually have saved my life since then on many occasions.

After the Battle of Lódz, there was a static condition that lasted until nearly spring. We were in winter quarters at Mariampol on the borders of East Prussia. We were taken out of there for the Petrokoff operation, and afterward returned there by train. The Germans weren't pushing, and we weren't pushing. Then the Germans temporarily decided to halt operations on the western front and concentrate everything in the east in a great offensive, coordinated with an offensive of the Austrians in the south. Today this is known as the Winter Battle. Heavy snow had fallen, followed by a thaw that left the country a morass. We had cavalry outposts. Sometimes we could hardly reach them. The horses sank to their bellies in the quagmire. That's how we lived, like worms. After a while we even looked like them.

The Germans masked their offensive with a feint in the direction of Warsaw. On January 31, 1915, they used poison gas for the first time in warfare, throwing 18,000 shells against the trenches northwest of Warsaw. The Russian high command, strangely, did not even report it to the Allies. Moreover, the German movement was only a feint, and immediately after that there was a blizzard that buried everything under two feet of snow. In the midst of the blizzard, while the soldiers of the Russian army were clearing snow from their trenches, the main German attack rolled over the Russian Tenth Army, on whose right flank we were. That was on February 8, and the battle went on until February 21. There was a sudden thaw on February 14 that melted the snow and flooded everything. Our left flank was turned, and the whole Tenth Army trapped, but the Germans could not advance or retreat even if they had wanted to. This battle, too, is put down as one of the most remarkable in history because of the terrible suffering of the men in the bad weather. The Tenth Army was finally destroyed, with 100,000 men killed and 110,000 taken prisoner, though Hindenburg considered the battle a failure because the Germans could not follow up their advantage against us.

When the land dried up, the Germans started pushing us again. It was their infantry against our cavalry.

CHAPTER XV

Then there began a cavalryman's paradise, a form of warfare that will never come again. We began the slow retreat from the Niemen to the Dvina, from May until October, 1915, for about 250 miles. This was the big German invasion of Russia. Amazingly enough, our side of the war on that great front was fought with just cavalry screens. It was an astonishingly slow retreat, and sometimes half a squadron of us might be left far behind the enemy lines. This was the most interesting period of the whole war to me, because it was entirely cavalry warfare. We had our patrols, first in the pinewood, undeveloped country before we reached the Niemen, and later in more prosperous rolling country, with lots of beautiful lakes and farms and small islands of trees. The lakes were very dangerous, for you could get trapped against them.

It was our job to slow down the German advance as much as we could, because there wasn't enough infantry to fill in a solid front from the Baltic to the Black Sea. We had very little ammunition, especially artillery shells, and we had to watch our step. So there were islands of infantry, and between them there was always a gap, sometimes as much as fifty miles. When trouble developed, the cavalry was thrown in to fill those gaps in a constantly fluctuating form of warfare.

The Germans did not have enough men for a permanent front either and they were using their cavalry primarily against us. I think that we probably had done too good a job. Far ahead of us, on patrol, rode two men called *dozors*, like scouts—there were front *dozors*, side, and back *dozors*. Whenever a troop of us (twenty-five men) rode up to a village or a farm, the two in front would gallop up, and gallop back, and try to draw German fire to see if the village or farm was occupied. Generally the Germans tried to let us ride in and then started shooting. But there was usually some nervous fellow in their unit who fired too soon and so we found out where they were. They were generally better informed about our movements. They had a few planes, Fokkers, I think. Sometimes they would fly low and try to throw a stick of grenades at us from the cockpit. There was no bombing, but to avoid being spotted we hid in the islands of trees. After they began to machine gun us, we would move at night.

In the first major battles of the war, Russia had lost a million rifles. We retreated and retreated, until the ammunition started coming in, but during the retreat we had only a couple of caissons of shells per gun, and possibly a couple of hundred cartridges per man.

At the beginning of our retreat we were deployed as a screen in front of our old fortress of Kovno. The fort was considered strong by the Germans, and they approached it cautiously. It wasn't strong at all. To our horror, when we were ordered to make our stand there, there weren't any first-line troops. Reservists of the second order, and home guard units who were armed with Crimean War rifles were thrown in to stem the tide. The Russian army did not have either enough ammunition or troops to fight on an entire front that ran 800 miles southeast from the Baltic.

The first skirmish, I remember, was again in the pinewoods. I was my troop's second sergeant. I was with my troop sergeant Bolshakoff and a squad. Our cavalry troop was the equivalent of a platoon in the American army, about twenty-four men. We had a machine gun. We were deployed in skirmishing lines on the edges of a clearing in the woods. Beyond the clearing was a village, Olita, occupied by the Germans, to which we had advanced, made contact, then pulled back. They were shooting everything at us, and we were shooting at them from behind the roots of big trees. We couldn't waste any of our precious artillery, so we had to try to hold with our machine guns. We were under heavy machine-gun and rifle fire.

I was on the extreme right with a machine gun and three men, and Bolshakoff yelled to me that the root of the tree he was behind was too small; he was going to make a run to me. At that moment the Germans began shelling us. Their machine-gun fire started as he ran. A shell had burst in the tree directly over us. As he fell and partially covered me, his hand across my shoulder, there was a terrific crash. When I came to, there was a dead silence. I felt something wet on my cheek and realized that it was blood. Then I saw what had happened; Bolshakoff had been hit by a shell fragment that would have hit me if he had not fallen upon me at that moment. He was badly wounded. The machine-gun crew was dead. I remembered that you must never leave a weapon in the hands of the enemy. I got Bolshakoff over my shoulder and retreated, dragging the machine gun behind me by one of its legs. After about half a mile through the woods I came upon some of the men of the second squadron. They took over, and we went back to our horses and reformed. We found out that a German battalion was attacking, and a company was moving to outflank us, so we were ordered to retreat.

I got the second St. George Cross for that day, but the shell shock from that blast put me out of action. I could not keep food down, so I was evacuated to St. Petersburg.

During the Kovno episode, Paul Benckendorff, the son of the old Count, had been in command of the squadron on our left. Paul was older than I, a major at that time. He was trying to make out where the German forces were. His trumpeter begged him to take cover, but he would not, then a bullet hit him right in the heart. I escorted his body home, and I also took back a number of the wounded.

For three weeks I was in the hospital in St. Petersburg. They did some fantastic things to me, putting me in an electronic cage. It did the trick. It was while I was on leave this time that I made my last trip to the gipsies. I had moved heaven and earth to get back to the regiment, which I had heard was in action. There was a party just before I returned to the front. I rang up in the afternoon and said we would be out that night—I still had that same feeling for Masha Shishkin I had before, though I never saw her except at these parties, for there was no longer time enough to pay those afternoon calls for tea. With us on this evening was a young officer from the Chevalier Guards. Everything went as it had before; we sat at the long bare table in our wicker chairs, and drank champagne and listened; but suddenly Masha began to sing with that ardent and unrestrained rapture of the gipsy girls, and she was not singing to me—she was plainly singing to the young officer who was with me. I went back to the front. I had been convinced that we'd be doing a lot of fighting in trenches. In St. Petersburg I had found two Very pistols and the flares to go with them. I knew we didn't have any in the squadron, and I thought the pistols might come in handy. I bought them.

In those days when one went on leave, one's horses were left at the convoy of the second order, a supply depot in the deep rear and an evacuation station for the wounded. So when I returned, I went there immediately to pick up my horses and to find out the position of the regiment at that time.

It so happened that the commanding officer of the Chevalier Guard convoy of the second order was my bon vivant cousin Aliosha Obolensky. His equally gay comrade was Peter Dolgorouky, a very distant cousin of the General and totally unlike him. Peter was the Horse Guards commander of the convoy of the second order. They were both lieutenants, and both rotund. They always managed to set up shop in the best house that they could find. The particular house that they quartered in when I returned from leave was a fine one with a porch and a rose garden in front which was enclosed by little bushes. And here it was that Peter and Aliosha gave Tanka Knoring, myself and a couple of officers a magnificent dinner. Tanka was on his way home. He was bigger than ever, and now, against all regulations, he was affecting an immense beard which he parted in the center.

Something, however, must have been wrong with the food, because Tanka and another officer began to look uncomfortable at table. They suddenly got up and disappeared. Dinner ended shortly, and I suggested that we ought to try out my Very pistols; so Peter, Aliosha and myself and the others all trooped out onto the porch. I loaded, pointed toward a star, and fired. There was a frightful explosion, and I was left with the handle of the pistol in my hand. The barrel with its blazing charge screamed off into the night, pinwheeling straight into the rose garden. The ghostly white light of the flare revealed to us the imposing figure of Tanka Knoring, who was in the process of crouching behind a bush. The flare was heading straight at him. I will never forget the stunned expression on his bearded face as he was eagled himself backwards on the ground. Never have I heard such cries of indignation!

In July 1915, I was promoted to sergeant major, the highest non-commissioned rank, a wonderful thing for me, for I no longer had to carry a carbine. That carbine slung over my back and bouncing and into evasive action and spread hitting me on the shoulder blades when I galloped was a terrible burden to carry. Almost at once, however, I was promoted to second lieutenant in the field, and I commanded a troop.

This was during the big retreat. We were going to stop on the eastern fringe of a big woods, and the Germans were advancing through those woods. It was my troop's tour of duty on patrol. I was ordered to take my whole troop, twenty-five men, with machine guns, to penetrate the woods, stay three days, watch the Germans advance, count them up, and then rejoin the division that would be slowly retreating.

We moved at night. And we moved not by roads, but by compass. It was a moonlit night, and we started by skirting the woods in the shadow of the trees. We rode twenty to thirty miles from where we left the regiment. There we hid in the woods and watched. We counted them. The weather was good, we were comfortable, and it was great fun. Then, about half a mile away, I saw Bavarian cavalry riding past, with their standards, the Shwere Reiters, and the Cheveaux Legers, the Bavarian Uhlans.

I had two friends in that regiment. They were brothers, Arco-Valle by name, two German boys whom I had met at Mrs. Hwfa Williams's, charming fellows. Luigi was a great sportsman, who used to hunt in England. The younger, Nando, began playing polo, and bought Little Blue Bags from me when I made the Oxford varsity—she wasn't fast enough for the varsity match.

They rode in beautiful formation, wonderfully mounted. It was interesting to see them. The time came to go back. We knew exactly where we were, and rode straight back by compass toward where we hoped our own lines would be. We rode in double columns of twos, each horse right on the tail of the horse ahead, through the woods. We didn't know where the division was. We hoped it was where we left it, but we didn't know.

Suddenly the men in the lead stopped. There was an opening in the woods, and a squad of German cavalry in formation by a little hut beyond a potato field, a dismounted German officer talking to them. They were about four hundred yards away. I charged. We broke out of the woods, and I remember beating Rolf with the flat of my saber to urge him on, past two frightened women digging potatoes in the field. The Germans jumped on their horses and galloped off, dropping their lances and their rifles as they fled. We were gaining on them when a large squadron of their cavalry appeared, so we halted and rode back, picking up their lances with their black-and-white pennants, and some carbines. The Germans were deploying behind us, so we galloped east by compass and came to a road running directly toward our lines. In about fifteen miles the whole wooded area ended, and we came to the rolling countryside where we had left the regiment. A German patrol appeared simultaneously on our left and it was a question of being shot at by our own outposts who had immediately engaged them. Luckily, it was the second squadron of the Chevalier Guards, who had sharp eyes. They were on a hillock beyond the woods. It was lucky because the Germans would have cut us off in another few minutes.

We had some food with the second squadron. We had no casualties, but one horse was wounded. It was amazing; a bullet had gone clear through it, below the spine, but not touching anything vital, and the animal moved as if nothing had happened. I found out where the staff division was, and rode back to report. We were behind our own lines. The men asked permission to unfurl the German flags we had picked up. They were very proud of having captured them. So I gave them permission since we were behind our own lines. We rode to headquarters in columns of twos, without outriders, which was customary in friendly territory. As we swung down the hill toward the village where the staff of the division was quartered, our German lance pennants made a gay display. Suddenly I saw a horseman dash back into the village at full gallop. Immediately there was terrific activity at headquarters. An officer appeared, gesticulating, and men raced out into skirmish positions. Somebody in the troop muttered, "Typical staff officer!"

I was surprised, and I halted the patrol. I sent my orderly Makaroff ahead, and watched him enter the village. He came back with an officer. He galloped back with a long and gloomy face. "The Chief of Staff of the Division, sir! That's who we saw, and he's damn mad." So we sauntered down the hill to take our punishment. He gave me hell. He said, "I'll have you broken! German flags, indeed! I had a machine gun on you! I damn near fired!" I sat there, and when it was all over I apologized. Then I rode behind him into the village. There he said, "I'm going to report you. I was on my way to your regiment for dinner. I'm late. General Skoropatsky is dining there tonight. You will report there; and I will report you to your commander."

I saluted. "Yes, sir."

"Now!—And bring your troop!"

"Yes, *sir!*" And he rode off to dinner.

But I had to make out my report. The troop then rode over to the village where the staff of the regiment was. The very first thing whom we saw there as we rode in was the majestic figure of Ivan Blajevitch before his campfire. He didn't say a word, but beamed at us. He'd obviously heard everything. Before long he would be sitting there beaming as before but with a dozen German lances stuck into the ground in a halo around him, while his voice boomed approval for the General's ears. By the time I got there they were all having dinner, General Skoropatsky with them. Skoropatsky said curtly, "Come in." I asked permission to report. I said I had just returned from my patrol duties. Prince Eristoff, our commander, who used to train me in observation, said, "I hear you've behaved badly."

"Yes, sir," I said.

"I'm told you unfurled German flags and were nearly shot up." After a moment he went on, "I give you a very severe reprimand here. I do not want my men shot up by our own soldiers." Then he got up from the table, and said "Come along." He took me into the other room. There he admitted, "My dear boy, if I had done what you've done, I'd have unfurled the flags."

There was another cavalry charge about the same time. This was what we called a lava. This was a maximum effort on our part, a maneuver initiated by Genghis Khan. Old Prince Lieven was in command of the squadron's Number One Troop when we came to our objective, a village that was held by German infantry. There was a long slope down toward the village, and woods behind it. Major Kossikovsky's idea was for Lieven to approach by the left flank. We would approach from the right and center. If possible, Lieven would charge right in without dismounting, and at the same time we would charge down the hill into the village.

We saw Lieven dismount, fire, mount, and charge. So Kossikovsky said, "In open front—charge!" We were unleashed onto the village, about a mile down the hill. We were deployed in two gigantic lines, the first with lances, the second with sabers. It was a beautiful sight, I must say, swooping down on the village from the brow of the hill. Once you charge you let the horses out, and there is no stopping. We charged right into the village and out the other side, but by the time we got there Lieven's troops had already swept it clean, and he was now chasing the Germans into the woods.

Afterwards, Lieven told me a story. As he had come through, an officer ran out of the last house, started to mount, and fired at Lieven. Lieven killed him with his saber, right through his helmet. "I killed him," he said. "Terrible."

Lieven was an old man, a very gallant old soldier. He still had blood on his sword when he was speaking about it. He dismounted then and went into the house. The officer he had killed had fixed it up, with pictures of his family on his desk. Lieven felt terribly about it. He took the German's things and sent them to his widow, with a letter saying he was sorry. It was still a gentleman's war.

Meanwhile, we bypassed the town of Vilna. One Saturday afternoon we were pulled back in reserve, and the staff stopped in a Russian monastery, and all the officers were invited to lunch the next day after church. It was one of the saints' days on which a special service is held.

The service went off, and we all adjourned to the refectory. The conversation drifted from war to the beauty of the monastery, and our General complimented the Bishop on the choir's wonderful singing.

Just then a voice piped up. It was Lieutenant Peter Zouboff. He was very much afraid, he said, that the choir had sung the wrong psalm for that particular saint's day.

Immediately there was consternation. The General turned beet red and began to splutter. The Bishop insisted it could not possibly be so. There was a general ecclesiastical stir amongst all the monks. But Peter was absolutely certain. He said so again.

There was nothing else for it. The Bishop sent for the Holy Books then and there, and after a careful investigation and much argument, to the consternation of the Bishop and the clergy, Lieutenant Peter Zouboff, Chevalier Guards, was right.

Needless to say, his fellow officers were not inclined to forget this one, and he was forever known in the regiment to officers and men alike as "our bishop."

The third cavalry charge I was in came on my birthday, the third of October in 1915. I came back from a patrol where I had stayed out four or five successive days with my troop. It was a deep reconnaissance patrol, and it was successful; there were no casualties, and after four days we rejoined and went back behind our lines. For the first time in a while we were put in reserve and thought we could relax. We got our beds out. Mother had sent me some wine for my birthday. We had a feast. I had a folding rubber bathtub and got a bath. I even had hot water, such a luxury. Then I shaved. I put on clean clothes, and I felt marvelous. After a bit of conversation, I undressed, went to bed, and, my God, almost as soon as I had gone to sleep: "Saddle!"

Apparently a division commander of infantry needed a cavalry squadron to charge through his lines to the German trenches and create confusion prior to his attack.

I was at the tail end of the squadron, with the fourth troop. We rode through woods, early in the morning, nodding in the saddle. I had no idea that within moments we would be charging through our own infantry over the German trenches. I felt the pace of the column picking up. It went faster and faster. Ahead of us, as we broke out of the woods, the men were lining up and charging. There was no time for us to form, so when we broke out of the woods, we charged after them. I think they should have waited. I didn't even know where we were charging. We galloped into a farm. I remember jumping a fence there, and the horse falling. I thought he had been shot. "Not so good," I thought, but he had only slipped. Suddenly we saw our infantry line, and our first troops sailing right over the German trenches. The Germans there lifted their hands and rushed out surrendering. The cavalry kept right on going. I learned later that they had run into staggered machine guns. But even so, we lost only about ten men out of a hundred. So far as we were concerned, the recall sounded just after we reached the German trenches. During the confusion the infantry division commander attacked and attained his objectives.

My leave came in October, after six months at the front. This was my first leave as an officer. I went out a great deal, and I gave a few parties at my place, and went to the gipsies a lot, after the parties, or with groups of my cousins and friends. A wartime fast set had grown up in St. Petersburg, a lot of society ladies, young divorcees, very different from what had existed before—the younger, gayer crowd that exists in every capital, but that had previously been somewhat blanketed by the heavy tone of the older St. Petersburg society. They were a glamorous set, these sophisticated young women.

My leaves went by with amazing speed. There were quite a few things to be seen to about the estate. Mr. Nikolaieff handled all the details while I was in the army, but Father's lawyer was now an elderly man and his health was bad, so there were many things he wanted to discuss with me. I have said that almost all the Obolensky property was in land, and so it was, but gradually over the years we acquired interests in other businesses, some of which were important for one reason or another. For example, one of my great uncles, years before, after a visit to Venice, tried to introduce Venetian glass blowers into Russia. He hired some skilled artisans to come to Russia. The local sand was inferior, so the project failed. But subsequently a prosperous business grew out of it, manufacturing windowpanes. In much the same fashion we acquired control of a textile factory. This had grown into a substantial business, so much so that I was compelled, before the war, to familiarize myself with textile manufacturing, fabrics, looms, costs, and so on. Now, Mr. Nikolaieff knew nothing whatsoever about manufacturing. He did not want to have anything to do with it. The result was that I had to deal directly with the Moscow lawyer who was the manager for the textile firm. I saw a good deal of him, liked him, and came to trust him. I also knew him and his wife socially. She was a prominent figure in theatrical circles and very beautiful. Their friendship eventually saved my own life, and the lives of many others as well during the Revolution.

Countess Kleinmichel was the lady whose *moumoutka* had been snatched off by a ghost. She was a famous and somewhat eccentric lady, extremely shrewd, but concealing her shrewdness under an air of extreme polish and astuteness. She owned a mortgage on some of our property, including the apartment building we lived in. She held a famous international salon. She was a great friend of Father's, a great wit and a bluestocking. She surrounded herself with literary people, and she possessed a huge library of all things visible and invisible. We knew her spiritual attributes. The Countess Kleinmichel had a game leg, did not go out, and kept in touch with everything through her literary friends and spiritual controls. When I heard from Mr. Nikolaieff about the mortgage, I had it paid without thinking anything about it. To my astonishment

Countess Kleinmichel was deeply hurt. She said that Platon had always let her own the mortgage. She liked the mortgage. To humor her, we restored it precisely as it had been through Father's lifetime, with payments to be made by us at periodic intervals. She certainly did not want the mortgage for financial reasons, as she was very wealthy.

During the Revolution she had an uncanny perception of what was happening. When all the big houses were looted, and the people in them imprisoned or killed, she was not touched. She simply closed all the shutters, locked the doors, and had a printed notice put up on her doorway:

> *No Trespassing! Property of the St. Petersburg Soviet! Countess Kleinmichel has been imprisoned in Peter and Paul Fortress, and this property has been requisitioned by the People's Government.*

Then Countess Kleinmichel lived quietly inside without being disturbed, while she made her preparations for getting out of Russia. Many years later, in Paris, I found her very ill and poor, and until the end of her life I continued the regular payments on the mortgage she held on our St. Petersburg property, though we knew we would never see it again.

The important matter of my first leave, however, was entertainment. And during this leave as an officer I gave some parties at my house. Some of the gipsies came to sing, like Smirnova, or composers like Delazary with their guitars. Mother was living in her own place across the Neva, near St. Isaac's cathedral. I was quite alone on the Mitninskaya except for the family servants. Some of the officers of my regiment were also on leave. Often some old friends, like General Marsengo, the Italian military attaché, Grand Duke Boris and Grand Duke Dimitri, and some young ladies, like Dolly Radziwill and Maia Koutouzoff, were the guests. We had a band (Goulesko's gipsy orchestra was my favorite), we danced, and before the fortnight was over my parties had become rather famous.

Occasionally, I gave a party for the gayer groups. A great favorite in St. Petersburg at the time was Nastia Naturchitza. Nastia was an artist's model. She had a benefactor, an elderly man of wealth, who kept her in great style in an elaborate house, where she lived with a girl friend called Forell, of her own age. She looked like Anita Colby. She dressed beautifully, and each afternoon the two of them appeared in her sleigh and were seen on the street behind two magnificent horses. The old benefactor was never around then.

I met Nastia Naturchitza at a party almost as soon as I came home on leave, and I began to see her off and on. I remember one evening when I was at her apartment the doorbell rang. There was an uproar in the hall and a maid with a very long face announced Nastia's benefactor. I had to beat a hasty retreat out the back door.

One evening Nastia and Forell came to one of my gay parties. There were also a number of beauties of somewhat the same type as Nastia, we had a band, some gipsy singers, and a few of my officer friends. One of the Italian secretaries was there also. Italy had come into the war on the Allied side in 1915, and we celebrated to the limit—in the Russian way. I had the feeling that our Italian ally was having difficulty with our Russian toasts. I thought nothing more of it, until he vanished. We looked all over for him, but couldn't find him. The party was a late one, and about eight-thirty in the morning I took Nastia and Forell home in a taxi and sat between the two girls. To my horror, we passed Mother going to work at the Red Cross. She gave no sign of recognition, but I put my hands over my face just to make sure.

When I went back to the house I decided to take a bath and get some sleep. Father had had a big red marble bathtub built into the wall, lower than the floor, and I had just put figured Indian cotton curtains before it. I was about to turn on the water when I saw a pair of shoes sticking out from under the curtains. It was our vanished Italian guest. I roused him, had my bath and gave him breakfast, and he went off somewhat revived.

That afternoon, after I'd slept, I thought I ought to go to tea with Mother. I took my huge Tartar coachman, one-eyed Ivan, with his racing trotter and we drove off like the wind. We crossed the two bridges, passed the Cathedral and arrived at Mother's house just as she was leaving for the Red Cross again—she worked very hard over there. Mother didn't even appear to notice me, but she put her hands over her face and walked out to her car.

Dolly Radziwill asked me to have lunch with her at Donons, the fashionable restaurant of the day, to meet Princess Murat and M. Chambrun, then the first secretary of the French legation. This was the time that Rasputin was in full glory, and conversation was largely about him: he was opposed to the war; his conduct was scandalous; and he was surrounded by second-rate people; he was a spy; he was evil. They asked me questions about the front, and then Marie Murat suddenly said, "You can't guess what I am doing. I'm painting Rasputin's portrait."

We were dumfounded.

"What kind of a man is he?" I asked.

"He's a stupid peasant," she said. Then she hesitated. "He really has terrific magnetism. His eyes are extraordinary. I feel I'll be hypnotized if I'm not careful. But there must be somebody behind him as a master mind. He's too stupid for that."

Princess Murat was a sophisticated, intelligent woman, not in the slightest superstitious or susceptible. "You know me," she went on, "and I think I'm pretty well able to take care of myself. But he does have hypnotic powers. I do feel it when he looks at me."

It must have been in this period that Felix Youssoupoff decided to kill Rasputin. He has written his own account of those days, and I will not try to retell it, except to show how things appeared to me. First of all, I could not imagine Felix cold-bloodedly carrying out a murder plot. He was not in any way a conspirator or a killer. On the contrary, he was too generous and too kind, a man with a great heart, fundamentally religious and deeply mystical. He left England before taking his degree at Oxford. His fiancée, Princess Irina, the daughter of Grand Duke Alexander, was the only daughter in a family with six sons, and they were opposed to him. In time he won them over, and they became his friends.

The marriage was a great social event, and Felix and his bride went to Egypt and the Holy Land on their honeymoon.

At the start of the war, soon after their return, they were in Berlin. The Kaiser personally ordered their arrest. Through the assistance of the Spanish Ambassador they were promised a place to live if they would agree to take no part in the war; they refused, and were sent without escort to Copenhagen, menaced and insulted by hostile crowds, and from there reached Russia.

Felix was in the Corps des Pages, the equivalent of West Point, which had adopted an accelerated training course. He and Princess Irina lived in the Youssoupoff house in the Moika, where their daughter was born. Rasputin, who opposed the war, had become so influential that he was now able to intervene in the affairs of government departments, secure the dismissal of unfriendly officials, and the appointments of obscure and undistinguished people who surrounded him. Felix had first met Rasputin in the time of his own religious conversion after Nicholas Youssoupoff's death. Felix had distrusted him and began to watch him. Felix was himself then in good favor at court—the whole Imperial family was present at the baptism of his daughter, with the Emperor her godfather—but Rasputin's influence with the Empress was so powerful that it was dangerous to express opposition to him, and he was rarely even called by his own name in conversation, being referred to as The Unmentionable.

In the summer of 1915 the head of the Holy Synod of the Russian Church told the Emperor he could not continue in office unless Rasputin's interference in church affairs was ended. Rasputin left the capital for a month. He returned in greater favor than ever. Felix then concluded that an intolerable situation would continue as long as Rasputin lived. He spoke of it to Princess Irina and she agreed. Felix then approached several friends who hated Rasputin, but found they were terrified of his power. Grand Duke Dimitri, however, agreed, and brought into the plot a wounded officer he trusted, Captain Soukhotin.

Felix then went to a member of the Duma, Pourichkevitch, who had courageously attacked Rasputin in a speech, and Pourichkevitch joined them. They decided that Felix should cultivate Rasputin's friendship, under the guise of seeking mental healing from his supposed powers, that Rasputin should be lured into a basement apartment of the Youssoupoff palace and killed there, from which place his body could be disposed of in the Neva without implicating the conspirators.

I knew nothing of these matters at the time, and did not see Felix on this leave from the front. Bertie Stopford, the genial Englishman with whom I accompanied Pavlova in the fandango, was in St. Petersburg at the time, as a diplomatic courier of the British Embassy. We called him the Messenger Boy. His position was really more important than his official status suggested, because of his English and Russian connections; the Emperor had taken a liking to him, and he personally carried messages from the Emperor of Russia to the King of England, and from the King to the Emperor. Bertie subsequently published a book about these days, though he did not put his name to it, a book made up of his diaries and his letters to Lady Ripon and Lady Juliet Duff. In this volume he describes a visit of mine to him the day before I returned to the front—November 2, 1915. He wrote to Juliet Duff that I was older and more serious—"The war has changed him, as it has all of us."

I suppose I was serious, but it had nothing to do with events as such. I had fallen in love, Maia Koutouzoff was securing a divorce from Serge Koutouzoff. They were separated, and the divorce was going through. I had been greatly impressed by her dark, reserved beauty ever since I first came to know her well, which was on one visit to Rome in 1911 before going to Oxford. And I soon found myself in the first really serious love of my life. We went out quite a bit. Nothing happened; I did not then speak of how I felt. The situation was complicated. She was divorcing Serge—they had two children—and she was being courted by Captain Dubassoff, an officer of the Chevalier Guards, who wanted to marry her. Serge was my cousin, and Dubassoff was an officer with a higher rank than mine in my own regiment. He was even in my squadron. So I was troubled, and I suppose I did seem older and more serious to Bertie Stopford.

CHAPTER XVI

I spent the rest of the winter of 1915-1916 on the Dvina. The regiment was then moved to the southern front, to aid in the offensives of General Brusiloff, who afterwards went over to the Bolsheviks.

We were pleased. The Germans we had fought were awfully good troops. The Austrians in the south were easier. Timed with the Allied offensive in the battle of the Somme, the Russian high command agreed to launch a major attack—really a series of offensives—that lasted throughout the summer of 1916. There was real trench warfare there, like that on the western front. For the first time we had enough heavy artillery and ammunition, and Brusiloff attacked on June 3 and 4, 1916, on a 300-mile front, with, at first, startling success; we took some 300,000 prisoners. The cavalry had little part in this, for the country being fought over was a maze of trenches, swamps, and barbed wire. In July another massive offensive was launched, but the Germans once again had brought over troops from the western front, troops that they now could ill afford—fifteen divisions—and the progress was slower. These vast offensives accomplished their purpose; they moved the front twenty or thirty miles nearer the Austrian border; they cost the enemy, especially the Austrians, very great losses, no less than 450,000 prisoners being taken.

But Russia at home was stripped to mount the offensives. Our casualties were very large. Russia lost 2,700,000 soldiers killed in the war, forty percent of all Allied casualties. All the other fronts had been cleaned out to provide men, and especially to provide guns; and all our resources went into preparing for the heavy artillery, which, as in the battles on the western front, preceded the attack. The terrible losses undermined home morale; and as food shortages increased in the cities—for everything was going to the front to support the colossal armies that were being created—discontent was growing.

In the late summer of 1916, after the Brusiloff offensive, we were moved to the trenches on the Stohod River front. The Stohod rises in the Ukraine and flows almost due north 125 miles to empty into the Pripet River in the Pripet Marshes. The marshes were huge, and filled with quicksand. The cavalry had to be forgotten. We were put in the trenches. We were used as fillers between amazingly thick concentrations of infantry. There had been so many attacks back and forth between the trenches that the swamp was filled with the dead of both armies. Whole companies had charged into quicksand and had gone down. Still above the sand one could see the tops of their bayonets. It was a macabre field, and the sand made it horrifying. As a result, the trenches were not dug into the ground. They were built up over the swamp.

We would be given perhaps a mile of trenches, with the infantry on both sides of us. We put out our outposts, on foot. We sneaked our patrols out, on our bellies, much aware of the quicksand. And so were the Germans they had brought down to face us. They had some planes there and tried to bomb the horses. We put them in the islands of woods well behind the lines, the characteristic groves found in the Ukraine, where the supply wagons were also hidden. And at night these planes would drop flares. The planes were slow, and often flew very low, but we had nothing to use against them. Finally we put a light gun on a tripod, so it could shoot into the air, and a gunner actually downed a plane.

In our own unit there was no deterioration of morale. I still had my own horse, Rolf, and the twenty-four men of my troop who had been together from the start had become an efficient fighting force. We were sometimes sent back into reserve between movements from one sector to another. There were large expanses of land, completely uncultivated, and we hunted partridges there. Several of us rode in a long line, until we lifted a covey. The birds flew fast and low, and as soon as we lifted them we galloped, so that as soon as they came down we lifted them again. After three or four times, we could pick them up with our hands.

While we were on the Stohod my brother Vlady appeared. He was in the first squadron of the Horse Guards, His Majesty's Squadron, and had become a good officer, cool as a cucumber. He was stationed next door to my squadron. I went over to have lunch with him. It was a sunny day, a beautiful day, and I stupidly forgot my gas mask. I had lunch with Vlady and one of the Gagarins. While we were eating, the Germans began shelling us with gas. I went straight for home—but over the top. It would have taken too long to go around, and of the two chances I was taking, it was better not to take a chance on being gassed.

Soon we were in reserve behind the town of Proskourov in the Ukraine near the border of Rumania. Russia was massing cavalry corps for a raid behind the German lines. The front there was static, and the plan was to make a break through with a very large cavalry force.

It was a plan that never took place. Why it was not carried out I do not know. I do know that being in reserve made those winter months the pleasantest of the war. We were quartered in a small Ukrainian town, in a typical clean little cottage with white stucco walls, very warm and cheerful, with beautiful stoves, window boxes filled with geraniums, and chintz curtains. The winter was one of fine weather, with lots of snow. The townspeople enjoyed having us there; we went to the local cinema, to the amateur theatricals; and to a charity ball where we danced with the local girls. And at parties we danced to an old gramophone. The rest of the time we trained our men, and kept them occupied with regimental drills.

For days and days nothing at all happened. We still expected there would be an attempted breakthrough with cavalry. The arrival of a huge body of Don Cossacks livened things up, briefly. I have never seen such magnificent soldiers. They were fantastic-looking, handsome men, wearing their hair long on one side and combed back and up to offset their canted *papahas* or Cossack hats. They were wild as bandits, with a Mephistophelian look to them, and great horsemen. But then they, too, were put in the trenches as replacements for infantry. They were massed around us, three full divisions.

I bought another horse at Proskourov, with a marvelous gait that gave one a perfect ride, but he was half-blind in one eye. A beautiful charger, he shied only because of the speck on his eye; and I got him reasonably as a result of that one defect. We still had fine horses, but I made the mistake of using my new horse in a regimental parade. This was always an intricate performance. When each individual troop within the squadron wheeled on a pivot, their officer, in front of his troop, had to wheel with them. My charger could only wheel in one direction—the wrong one. As each troop wheeled, it left a small gap between it and the next. I was supposed to ride through this gap, but my horse always refused to, so I had to gallop all the way around, and balled up everything. The worst dressing-down I ever received in my military career came as a result. I have never seen anyone as angry as my squadron leader Kossikovsky was then. I consoled myself with the thought that it had only been a dress rehearsal. The Czar was coming and they were sprucing us all up.

That night we had a family meeting and talked over old times. Aliosha Obolensky and I had been appointed squadron censors. We had to read all the mail. A lot of the men were our friends, some were related to us, and we knew the families and the girls with whom they corresponded. Aliosha would pick up a letter addressed to somebody we knew, some pretty girl; he would hem and haw, shake his head, and pretend to throw it aside without opening it, saying we could not possibly let such inflammatory information pass. When he had to black out something that really was militarily revealing he would, of course, do so; but if the letter was to one of our friends, he would write in a wholly fictitious account of why he had removed it, usually a long account of some imaginary misadventure of the unfortunate letter writer, such as my sorry experience with my one-eyed horse.

The day after our family reunion was the day of the Emperor's review of the Guards Brigade. We had hoped for good weather, but it was dismal and raining. I had another horse, a captured gray Arab, which I had bought from the squadron. Captured horses were sold and the money went to the men who had captured them. But for the review I borrowed Captain Stroukoff's bay gelding, which he couldn't ride. It was a beautiful horse, but difficult.

The Emperor arrived. My squadron had been ordered to be the guard of honor. Kossikovsky had mercifully gone on leave, so Prince Lieven was in command. First we were reviewed on foot by General Ivanoff, who was then commander in chief of the sector. As we stood at attention we saw a wild-looking Cossack marching solemnly behind General Ivanoff. Astonishingly, to me, at least, it was my cousin Sasha Obolensky, the brother of Aliosha. He had got himself assigned to a Cossack regiment, and had been made an aide-de-camp of General Ivanoff. I couldn't believe my eyes.

As Sasha passed by us, he turned on one of those famous facial caricatures of his, stretching his long features into a perfect parody of a dignified old general reviewing his troops, and I could feel the whole squadron struggling to keep a straight face.

Then the real review began, before His Majesty. My horse behaved, but Tanka Knoring had an Irish hunter with a white face, a good animal, but with a short tail. It had been cut in the Irish style. By regulations, all horses ridden at reviews had to have long tails. Also, Knoring, due to his great tummy, had inadvertently disfigured the horse up front: one cavalry exercise of ours was to ride by a stout pole and cut it down with a sword. Tanka had not been able to lean out as far as the rest of us to swing his saber. It was a matter of center of gravity. As a result, Tanka had accidentally cut his horse's ear off. He had been much distressed, but he had cleverly kept the ear, and had had it preserved. On great occasions like the Emperor's visit, he fastened it back onto the horse, like an earring. It had two little screws. And, also for such occasions, he had bought a false horse tail, which he would fasten over his Irish hunter's short stump of a tail.

The review was splendid, but just as our squadron was passing in review, Tanka ran into difficulties. He was on my right. We were on the extreme left flank, passing in a column of squadrons, all in one long line. On the command I turned eyes right for the Emperor, and I saw Knoring salute. At that instant one screw of his horse's ear slipped off. The ear saluted, too, and then the strings that tied up the tail slipped, at exactly the same moment, so that just as our line passed by the Emperor, a horse's tail was being dragged along the ground.

I had really fallen in love with Maia Koutouzoff. What with the war, I was even more serious. It was serious on Dubassoff's part also. He was my superior, and what is more, he was an officer in my squadron, and I liked him. Now, to complicate things even further, while we were at the front, Maia suddenly arrived. She had gotten herself attached as a Red Cross nurse to a mobile hospital that followed the brigade. I could have throttled her. Things got more complicated than ever, and they continued to get worse, for Maia's divorce from my cousin and great friend Serge Koutouzoff had not yet gone through. It was a very sticky situation.

I could have throttled Mother, too. I think she was thrilled by the whole situation. She had talked to Maia, told her that I was in love with her, but I had never said a word to Mother about my feelings. She even urged Maia to marry me. In some respects Mother was an extremely naughty girl. She wrote to me, telling me what she had done, and saying that she believed Maia would accept when I proposed. I didn't know what to say. In the Chevalier Guards we were supposed to take to our colonel any problem that might reflect on the honor of any officer of the regiment. I finally went to the colonel, Miklashevsky, and told him the whole story. I did not know what my own conduct should be. I gave him Mother's letter, and my answer to her telling her the whole thing was ridiculous.

He said, "Let me sleep on it"—a word of advice in itself that I have always followed. Since then I've never made a big decision without "sleeping on it."

The next day he called me in and said, "As I see it, anything you do will put you in a troubled situation. She is still married to your cousin; the divorce hasn't yet been granted. Not only will she be involved, but your cousin, and another officer of the regiment as well. I do not see how there can be any solution that will not make your situation more difficult. I think you ought to forget it."

I took his advice.

My leave after six months of duty came just then, and it was extended beyond the usual month. I was coughing a great deal then. I went to St. Petersburg, but almost at once the doctors sent me to Yalta. They said I needed the air of the Crimea; that I was badly run-down, and that I had never really recovered from the effects of exposure in East Prussia. With its resulting pleurisy, they feared I was developing tuberculosis.

I was in Yalta about two months. I lived at the Hotel Europa, and reported for tests at the hospital every other day. The tests showed that I did not have tuberculosis, but treatments continued to build up my strength and to correct the dry pleurisy. I was ordered to exercise. I rode in the hills around Yalta on Tartar ponies that I hired. Prince Abamelek, an uncle of Paul of Serbia, was living at the Europa; he was the husband of Paul's Aunt Mohina, who left Paul her fortune. Abamelek was one of the shrewdest businessmen of Russia, a famous international financier of the day. He was tremendously well informed, receiving information from all over the world. I saw him every day, and we talked about Paul, and he told me exactly what was going on in other countries.

The belle of Yalta at the time was Mme. Popoff, the wife of the owner of Russia's biggest tea company. Her husband was in the Caucasus. She was very wealthy, and gave great parties. At them I saw some distant relatives of mine, the Narishkin family connection. The father had been an ambassador at one of the European capitals, I forget which one. They had two daughters, attractive as the girls of the Narishkin family seem always to have been. The younger wrote poetry, and later published an account of these days, in which I appear as one Prince Orlinsky. The older, Natalie, was a tall girl, very reserved. We arranged paper chases on horseback, the whole group of us, a very pleasant and carefree recreation.

I had no further correspondence with Maia, who married Dubassoff after her divorce from Serge. I tried to put her out of my mind. Three days before my leave was up, I wandered into a street bazaar, where things were being sold for the benefit of some war relief organization. I saw a beautiful lady selling things in one of the booths. She was Princess Catherine Yourievsky, the youngest child of Alexander II and Princess Yourievsky—or Princess Catherine Yourievsky Bariatinsky, as she was now, for she was the widow of Prince Alexander Bariatinsky.

We began to talk. I had not seen her since childhood, when Father and I visited Princess Yourievsky at Biarritz. We remembered each other, and she asked me to come to a concert that afternoon where she was singing. I went. She had a wonderful voice, and sang Russian ballads with a simplicity and sincerity that moved me. The First World War was different from the Second. When we were at the front in those days we were in combat almost daily, while in the Second World War there were long periods of preparation followed by relatively brief and intensive action. When we were on leave therefore in the First World War, every hour was immeasurably valuable. The law of averages then was so terribly against us. I was deeply impressed by Princess Catherine's singing at the time of our meeting—that was all. In my boyhood she had appeared a glamorous figure to me as the daughter of Alexander II, and that day the extraordinary poignancy of her voice, and the mood I was in, touched me as I have been touched few times in my life.

Catherine was now a young widow with two sons. Her deceased husband, Prince Bariatinsky, came of a famous Russian family. For twenty or thirty years, early in the nineteenth century, the Caucasus had never been conquered by Russia, until Field Marshal Bariatinsky finally accomplished it. The Caucasians were led by a famous native imam or chief, Shamyl, who fought continuously for decades, and defeated every force the government sent against him. Field Marshal Bariatinsky chased Shamyl on the last campaign for three years, into that wilderness of towering mountains, finally surrounding him in a high stronghold in the very center of the ranges. So Shamyl at last became a prisoner, and Field Marshal Bariatinsky was given enormous lands in the Ukraine. These were put into sugar—the family fortune came from sugar lands and sugar refineries.

The Prince Bariatinsky who married Catherine was the grandson of the old Field Marshal. He had a big allowance, and he became widely known because of a long drawn-out love affair with the famous opera singer Lina Cavalieri. She was internationally famous, singing in America, in Russia, all over Europe, with Bariatinsky often in her company. He gave her presents, including a tremendous collaret of emeralds. The affair finally ran its course, and Bariatinsky married Catherine.

After their marriage, Cavalieri suddenly reappeared in Bariatinsky's life. Catherine was a very clever woman. She thought Bariatinsky might go back to Cavalieri, and to forestall it, she decided to make friends with her. She cultivated the friendship of the opera singer, even wearing her hair as Cavalieri did, with tresses wrapped around, very becoming on her. The three of them were often seen together in Paris, at the opera, the theater and similar occasions. Once as they prepared to go out together Catherine admired the emeralds that Cavalieri was wearing. The singer gave her a startled look. After a moment she took off the collaret and placed it around Catherine's throat. "I really have no right to them," she said. "They are yours." They were the Bariatinsky family jewels that he had given her.

Prince Bariatinsky died in Venice in 1911. Catherine was appointed sole guardian and trustee of the two boys by the Emperor, and they lived in their estate in Ivanovskoe in the district of Kursk, in southern Russia, an enormous place. Or they lived in Italy or Bavaria, where Catherine also had villas, for they had spent much time abroad before the war.

Catherine's accompanist at her concerts was a young, frail-looking pianist, Dimitri Tiomkin, later a very successful composer of musical scores in Hollywood. He was highly nervous at the time, and extraordinarily shy. Catherine lived at Yalta with several members of her former husband's family, including the elder Princess Bariatinsky, and a number of friends, among them a branch of the Demidov family, a sister and two brothers, who were visiting her.

I saw her again after her concert. My leave was nearly up. Just before I returned to the front, we went riding in the hills above Yalta. There I asked her to marry me. We did not become engaged then, but we agreed to write, and she said she would give me her answer in the fall.

As I was leaving Yalta, Natalie Narishkin came to me with a little icon to keep me safe, and as she gave it to me, she kissed me. Suddenly I realized that there had been an impending romance right there before me, and I had been unaware of it. I ought to have known better. She was a very attractive girl. But possibly it was just as well.

I returned to the front. Catherine and I corresponded constantly. When my next leave came, I went first to St. Petersburg, got Ignatie, my butler, and went to Krasnaya Gorka with him. Ignatie and I drove to Mme. Demidov's as we passed through Nijny. I had heard her son was missing in action. I got there at twilight. I rang the bell in the dark hall, and after a long pause Mme. Demidov herself came to the door. It was very painful; she thought I was her son who had come home, and it was terrible to have to tell her the news I had of him after her momentary joy when she thought he had returned. The others of the household came, and we tried to calm her.

I was amazed at the transformation that had taken place in a few years. Little trees that I could remember being planted in my childhood were now so tall that I could just reach the tops by holding my rifle at arm's length over my head. Ignatie and I went through the things I wanted to take to St. Petersburg. One thing I have regretted that we did not save. One of the family retainers in the old days had been a primitive artist. While Natasha Suvorov—Countess Zouboff—was still alive, he had painted a quaint but very good family portrait of her with all her children, grandchildren and great-grandchildren crowded into the canvas, forty people in all, with my father as a small boy shown in the corner of the picture. But we left it behind, and it has disappeared.

Krasnaya Gorka was depressing. The horses were gone. All resources were going into the raising of foodstuffs, and there were not enough people to keep the estate up. All the young fellows I had played with as a boy were at the front. The house had the empty air of an unwanted place that has not been lived in. I left Ignatie there to transport some things to St. Petersburg, and the next morning started for Kursk to see Catherine. I remember taking a last look at Krasnaya Gorka in the early morning, the hill, the house, the stables, the ring of trees in the park of pines, and the Imza flowing under the early-morning mist that hung over it. It was a place that I loved. I think I realized then that I was never in my life going to see it again.

I went straight to Catherine's estate at Ivanovskoe, traveling by train to Kursk, then to the station of Kolontaievka, and a drive of several hours to the estate. Old Field Marshal Bariatinsky had ended his days in beautiful surroundings, a big country house, with white columns, surrounded by a park which in turn surrounded a blue lake. An immense avenue of trees led to a fountain, with the house beyond it Catherine put me into rooms that had a kind of history of their own. They were nicely furnished, with French furniture, and overlooked the lake. And they were the rooms that Shamyl had occupied after Bariatinsky captured him. For the old Field Marshal and the native chief had fought each other for so long and had chased each other around the mountains of the Caucasus for so many years that they had come to admire each other, and even to feel a sort of personal friendship. So when Shamyl was made a captive he was placed in Field Marshal Bariatinsky's custody. And together they both lived out their last days on the estate, wandering around the grounds, talking over their battles, their mistakes, and joshing each other. Shamyl had shown such amazing generalship with his tiny forces that he had become a world hero. Both their tactics are being studied very carefully by the Reds.

It was a romantic setting and it boded well. Catherine and I became engaged, deciding to marry in the fall, and to keep our engagement secret. She wrote to the Emperor, and told him she was going to marry me. He was at the front; he was very conscientious and concerned for the troops. Grand Duke Nicholas Nikolaievitch had been relieved, and the Emperor was commanding in person. He sent her a courier with a necklace of aquamarines, his favorite gems. Then we set the date for our wedding, in October, if I could get away.

Meanwhile, those of us who had been promoted in the field were assigned to the cavalry school in St. Petersburg to take our examinations as officers. I reported there, got leave to be married, and went back to Yalta. The regiment was then in reserve, with no action planned.

In the Russian ceremony, both the bride and the bridegroom have someone to represent their parents if their own parents are dead or cannot be present—

what the Russians call the seated mother and father. Catherine's seated mother was Princess Bariatinsky, an aunt of her first husband. She asked the Emperor to be her seated father, but he was still at the front. He sent, as his proxy, an old and greatly respected marshal of the court, Baron Fredericks, a venerated figure then. Mother came to Yalta in time for the wedding on October 9, 1916 at the Russian cathedral in Yalta: so I had no seated mother but Mother herself, and for the life of me I cannot remember who my seated father was.

In the marriage ceremonies of the Russian Church a crown is held over the heads of both the bride and bridegroom throughout the long service. The crowns were heavy. Consequently several ushers were necessary; half a dozen, lining up behind both the bride and bride-groom, held up the crowns in relays. Then they marched three times around the altar. My brother Vlady was my best man, and the ushers who held the crowns over us were officers of my regiment, together with my half brother Max de Reutern, and Catherine's oldest son Andre.

Grand Duke Alexander sent us a car to start us on a very brief honeymoon. We drove over the hills to Sympheropol, stopping for tea at the palace of the Crimean khans at Bakchisray, with its famous fountain of a hundred tears. We then caught the train to St. Petersburg, where we lived at my house while I prepared for my officer's examinations at the cavalry academy, or as it was then called, the Nikolaevsky Cavalry School, the school for cavalry officers. But I was also given an additional assignment: to take care of the remount station at Luga, where the wounded horses were treated, and I rented a house there so that we could live near the post.

The crisis had begun. Food riots started in the late fall. People were beginning to complain. The Emperor personally was at the Stavka or Headquarters at the front. There had never been a close contact between the Emperor and the people. The Empress wanted a quiet family life, and saw few people. She was ill, her son was an invalid, and she had limited the Czar more and more to a single small clique. The Emperor was straightforward, honest and simple, with the same desire for a quiet existence. As a result, they had come to know only a handful of their subjects, which wasn't good, basically, because you have to give in order to get. And you have to have someone's confidence to gain vital information. Not only was the atmosphere of the court itself suspicious and strained, but outside the court circles it seemed that everything we did was known to the Germans. There were those who said Rasputin was a spy. He wasn't, but there was a group who got him drunk and pumped him.

Felix Youssoupoff and his fellow conspirators were now ready to carry out their plan to kill Rasputin. They had taken in one other member, a physician, to work with Grand Duke Dimitri, Captain Soukhotin and Pourichkevitch, the Duma member; they had decided to poison Rasputin with cyanide of potassium. Felix had been cultivating his friendship with Rasputin for months, and had come to believe that Rasputin was the very devil incarnate.

They decided to kill Rasputin in a basement apartment of the Youssoupoff Palace, remodeled from a wine cellar. Rasputin wanted to get to know a well-known young lady. Felix lured him there under the pretext of meeting her. She was really far away in the country. When Rasputin found that she was not present he became suspicious. But Felix explained that she was entertaining elsewhere, and would join them when her guests left.

The only guests at Felix's were the other conspirators, who were waiting to carry out Rasputin's body and drop it under the ice of the Neva—it was now the end of December 1916. They were also to provide an alibi, and one of them, wearing Rasputin's coat, was to pretend to be Rasputin returning home.

While they waited for the lady, Felix tried to persuade Rasputin to leave St. Petersburg and the court. He felt he had to give him a chance. Rasputin dismissed the thought. At last Felix, about two in the morning, gave Rasputin the first glass of poisoned wine. Not having much experience in poisoning people, the conspirators bungled it. They put in too much cyanide, or the poison they had prepared long in advance had lost its strength, but in any event it didn't work.

Rasputin became uncomfortable, and Felix pressed the second glass on him, which Rasputin drank, but still he did not die. Felix then diverted his attention to a crucifix on the wall, and while Rasputin was looking at it, he shot him in the back. The others then prepared to take the body to the car. But when they went back to the basement room Rasputin had vanished. He had made his way up the stairs, and out into the courtyard. There the member of the Duma shot him twice, and he fell on the doorstep. But the shots had aroused the neighborhood; the police came. They left after explanations that a dog had gone mad and had been shot. I think the conspirators were let go because of the prominence of the people who were present.

Rasputin's body was wrapped in window curtains and taken to Grand Duke Dimitri's car, driven to the Islands, and dropped from a bridge. The whole business was so bungled that one of Rasputin's galoshes was left on the ice.

After Rasputin's disappearance became known, suspicion immediately fixed on Felix. All sorts of rumors flew around St. Petersburg on New Year's Day 1917, the day after the killing, I telephoned Felix and asked him what was going on. He was quite calm, and said everything was going to be all right. But he was arrested, and exiled to the Youssoupoff estate at Rakitnoye, in the center of Russia. Grand Duke Dimitri was exiled to Persia, and would live at Teheran.

As a result of war-weariness, the authority of the government had been severely challenged. The Austrian army was in poor shape. In fact, the whole Austrian Empire was ready to collapse. Meanwhile, we were preparing for one last big offensive, and we felt that it would do the trick. The morale of the country at home was another story. After the war, it became known that the German high command reckoned that a new Russian offensive was one of the greatest dangers that they faced.

Meanwhile, there was no action from the Russian government of any kind. When Bertie Stopford saw the Emperor after Rasputin's death, he told me that he found Nicholas II drawn and white, sitting very still in church, looking straight before him. Only once did he glance up when the sun came out and lit up the dome of the church.

Rasputin was buried at Czarskoe Selo. The Emperor and Empress attended his funeral. Thereafter, all effective leadership from the court ended. The Emperor had been at the front most of the time, with the Empress making the political decisions, based on Rasputin's advice. With Rasputin's death even that sort of action ceased. Prime Minister Stunner, who was Rasputin's puppet, was afraid to face the Duma. So fifty-seven days passed between Rasputin's death and the beginning of the Revolution in March. Meanwhile, the Emperor returned to the front. Bernard Pares, the English historian of Russia, who was in the British Embassy at St. Petersburg at the time, concluded that the immediate cause of the overthrow of the Romanoff Dynasty was the death of Rasputin.

But the real crux of the matter lay in the lack of transport and supply to the cities. When the food riots began in St. Petersburg on March 8, the police tried to suppress them; there was shooting, and the soldiers joined the mobs. On Sunday, March 11, the whole city was taken over by demonstrators, joined by more troops. Rodzianko, the president of the Duma, urgently wired the Emperor at the front to appoint a prime minister who had the confidence of the country. But the Emperor did not reply. He did order General Ivanoff to St. Petersburg to suppress the disorders, but the troops could not get through to the capital. So on March 14 the Provisional Committee of the Duma established the Provisional Government, with Kerensky at its head, a moderate socialist regime. It all happened that quickly.

When the Emperor held a conference with his generals he found them unanimously in agreement that he should abdicate. He did so, firmly urging the continuation of the war in one of the great and moving addresses of history.

Catherine and I arrived at St. Petersburg by train when the Prince Lvov-Kerensky temporary government came into power. Because the house next door was headquarters of the Czarist secret police, the Kerensky revolutionaries were convinced that there was a secret passage connecting our house with it. Actually there was no such thing. Yet they repeatedly searched the place, looking for this passage. These searchers were armed civilians, accompanied by a man with a search warrant. I surrendered my luger, as they were also looking for firearms.

Their leader began to order us around roughly. One of the soldiers stopped him. "No, comrade," he said, "I know who she is," indicating Catherine. Alexander II was still venerated as the liberator of the serfs, and as his daughter, Catherine was often given a measure of respect by the people at a time when the others generally were being brutally treated, insulted, and killed. Sometimes the visits were pretty rough, but in those first days outright murder was less common than it became.

Meanwhile, the war was still officially going on. The front, however, was inactive. Catherine's two boys were in the Crimea. The only thing to do was to try to get back to them. The Chevalier Guards were practically disbanded. I still had excruciating headaches from shell shock. I filed medical affidavits with the regiment, certifying that I was ill, and was ordered to the medical authorities in Yalta. I arranged to get Miss Lizzie Arthur back to Scotland through Finland. The staff remained in our house in St. Petersburg, the old butler and the maids. Catherine and I had lunch with Bertie Stopford early in April, just before leaving. He was in bad shape, with rheumatism that affected his hands; and I see now that he noted in his diary: "Serge Obolensky is and looks ill."

We made the trip without being molested, though the trains were jammed with soldiers demobilizing themselves. Catherine's house in Yalta was the Mordvinov Palace, overlooking the city, a Crimean landmark surrounded by a magnificent park. The Crimea was still peaceful. The Tartar regiments remained loyal, and the Tartar Republic, when it was set up, was a constitutional government with a president, a moderate socialist, elected by popular vote. Around Yalta itself a number of people had come down from the north. The Dowager Empress Marie Feodorovna was living nearby with her daughter Grand Duchess Xenia, who was Felix's mother-in-law. Grand Duke Nicholas was at Dulber, his brother's estate, with Prince Leuchtenberg. Princess Orloff, the Bariatinskys and others were in Yalta proper, and Felix and Princess Irina were at Koreiz. More and more refugees assembled.

I was trying to get my strength back, and I did a lot of riding into the country. I came to know some of the Tartar villagers, and I liked them. The farmers on the slopes of the mountains behind Yalta had good land, farmed it carefully, and were self-respecting people who had built a high standard of life for themselves. They owned their own land. The country was beautiful at that time of the year, wild cherry trees and crabapple trees in bloom, lilacs everywhere, the weather calm and sunny. It reminded me of my childhood days, right in this region.

Just as then, roses were blooming everywhere, a marvelous expanse of fragrance and color.

The Tartars were inherently amiable and polite and apparently had no real grievances except their enmity for the Greek settlers in the Crimea. If the Greeks were on one side in any question, the Tartars were on the other. They invited me to eat with them, and we sat on the floor with our legs crossed, around the big dish of meat and rice, which we ate with our hands, after which we were expected to belch loudly to show our appreciation. A towel was then passed around, and we wiped our hands on it, after which dried fruits and coffee were served. I learned a few words of Turkish, and was shown over the farms and the vineyards; they were first-rate. The towns were picturesque: white-walled houses, with blue, green or maroon trim.

I met a famous portrait painter, Sorine, at Olga Orloff's, and he wanted to paint my portrait. He told me later that it was because he thought I was a specific type of Imperial Guard Russian officer, and that type would soon be extinct. Sorine was one of the intellectuals who had first sympathized with the Revolution. He was a leftist originally, a revolutionist; he drew away from the Revolution when he saw where it was heading. He was a very successful artist, well-known and popular. I told him I couldn't afford his prices, as he charged a lot. A thing—he appeared a few days later, and said he would paint me for nothing, because he wanted to record me. He said he would even loan me some money if I needed it. I didn't need it, but I thought that an unbelievably kind answer. He required about thirty sittings to complete my portrait. We talked while he painted. We found that we thought alike about life, politics, everything, and, in fact, Sorine became my closest and most valued friend, someone I knew I could count on no matter what happened, as he knew he could count on me.

Meanwhile, there had been rumors that Russia was planning to mount a final offensive against the Germans. Kerensky was behind it, and he was trying to get the army back into shape. Germany was so interested in destroying the Russian army that it was acting through revolutionary groups to create dissension. Thereby the Germans made the cardinal error of meddling in the politics of another nation to gain short-term ends. At the moment the objectives of the Bolsheviks and the German high command coincided, and from Switzerland the Germans shipped Lenin and other revolutionaries secretly into Russia in a sealed train.

In the north, the Provisional Government under Kerensky was steadily losing ground. It was a matter of time before the Bolshevik seizure of power in October. Yet it kept its pledge to elect a constituent assembly. This took place. But any elected government of a permanent nature such as this was something that the Bolsheviks could not abide, and it was a matter of days before they seized power in October. Then the Baltic fleet mutinied, and the sailors battled their officers; but the Black Sea fleet, for the time being, was still loyal. The strongest adherents of the Kerensky Government were in the south. The Tartar regiments were anti-Bolshevik. The Crimean Tartar regiment, a cavalry regiment which still had discipline, had come back from the front and was stationed intact at Livadia, the palace where the Emperor had liked to spend part of each winter.

In these months of crisis it is generally overlooked that the zemstvos provided Russia with a measure of self-government in the absence of any other authority. Only the historical accident of the Bolshevik minority having control of the soldiers and sailors in St. Petersburg and the support of the industrial workers, only eight million or so in all Russia, enabled them to break up the democratic government that was coming into being.

I had never thought of myself as anything but a liberal, a progressive, and wanted the people to have the best break they could possibly get, under the law. The Czar had abdicated. Where was I now to turn? But I hated any kind of aggression. The audacity of the Bolsheviks in overthrowing the legal government, and the atrocities of the ensuing Red terror, made me feel more strongly than ever the hatred of oppression that was my birthright.

Besides, the heart of the problem was the land hunger of the Russian peasants, and the Bolsheviks had no real solution for it. Even more than their demand to end the war, the action of the peasants in seizing the estates was decisive. So powerful was this movement that the Bolsheviks for a time could only side with it, though they did not favor breaking up the estates into small farms and feared any agricultural economy based on individual ownership. Above all, they feared the emergence of a class of farmers, each owning his own farm, but they had to support a movement that would have swept them into oblivion if they had opposed it.

After Alexander II's reforms, the landed estates had been left about ten percent of Russia's cultivated lands. The interesting thing was that this ten percent produced all the agricultural produce that went into export and almost all the food that went to feed the cities. Furthermore, the value of the ruble was inextricably tied to the favorable balance of payments that was derived from agricultural export; and this, in turn, was wholly dependent upon the landed ten percent. Peasant farming was largely subsistence farming. Seizing this land and breaking it up into small farms would merely expand the area of subsistence farming, as the Bolsheviks discovered when the peasants took it over. The immediate result was that the already meager food supply to the cities was cut off and prices of food soared. With the virtual elimination of the export market, the value of the ruble dropped like a stone.

The Kerensky government had been a government by men who at least knew the economic facts of life. They understood that confiscating the landed estates would not solve Russia's food problem if it merely extended the area of subsistence farming, yet they had no solution further than a division of the land in a parliamentary way, a legitimate way. Many of us were for anything of a parliamentary nature, so we had voted for them. It was a scholarly government, a government of intellectuals, idealistic, mildly socialist, but it was weak because it was built on talk and disinclined to fight for its constitutional rights.

During the summer months of the Kerensky regime, all the important Bolsheviks including Lenin, Trotsky, Stalin and others were living in St.

Petersburg in the villa of the ballerina Kchcsinskaya, which they had commandeered.

A large group of officers loyal to the Kerensky government and under the instructions of that government had been sworn to secrecy about a certain planned operation. No one person knew more than two or three others in the plan. Code messages and methods of identification were established. An entire chain of command was formed that would disseminate signals and hold all personnel in readiness. At a certain signal, the entire group was to descend on the Kchcsinskaya villa, surround it, and apprehend the Bolsheviks. They were to be taken dead or alive. A certain night was earmarked for the attack. The all-in-readiness and favorable signals came back early that evening, and these seasoned and well-disciplined men were on the alert for orders from the government to go ahead. They waited and waited. Signals were sent back: "May we move in and apprehend?" For hours the government could not make up its mind.

The *apprehend* signal was *never* given that night, and, finally, it was actually countermanded by the government with the statement that the operation was temporarily called off. The signal was never given again or any time. The Kerensky government had lost its nerve; and, as a result, the entire history of the world was irrevocably changed. Or perhaps, as S. Melgunoff says, with reference to the Kerensky regime's sending the abdicated Czar off to Siberia: "All this moves one to conclude that the Government feared much more the restoration movement, rather than the Bolshevik coup d'etat."

Whatever the reason, the entire incident remains as a clear warning, what can happen to a government, like Kerensky's, whose members are afraid to shoot to defend their parliamentary system or fight for their constitution. After all, it was only a Bolshevik minority that took over St. Petersburg with mob violence. This minority then consolidated in the north and then did the same thing over again in Moscow, and so on throughout the cities of Russia. After that there was no stopping them. It was a brilliant technique; and it was once again employed in Bagdad not so long ago.

After the Bolsheviks had been in power for some time, they took drastic steps to save the economy. They told the peasants that of course the land is yours, but now you will work for the government so many days a week. This was enforced, government cooperatives were established, and the peasants realized too late that they had been taken in. By then they didn't even have the land. They had the choice of returning to the days of Ivan the Terrible or fighting. Many fought for their rights, and the Bolshevik government liquidated hundreds of thousands of these people in the great "liquidation of the kulaks."

Back in the Crimea, our little group met, sifted the news, and made such plans as we could. For most people the great problem was getting possessions—money, jewelry and valuables—out of their homes in the north. Felix Youssoupoff made three trips to St. Petersburg after the Revolution.

Once he got two Rembrandts, "The Man in the Large Hat," and "The Woman with the Fan," from the family collection, cut them out of their frames, rolled them up, and took them on the train to the Crimea. Another time, while the Bolsheviks were boasting in the newspapers that they had imprisoned Felix in Peter and Paul Fortress, Felix made his way to the Youssoupoff Palace on the Moika with no other disguise than his turned-up coat collar. He secured the most valuable of the Youssoupoff diamonds, and took them as far as Moscow, but there he was forced to hide them, and concealed them under the stairs of his Moscow house. I can say it, because they have been found.

One morning, out of the blue, Bertie Stopford suddenly appeared at the Mordvinov Palace, and lived with us for a time. He was now extremely nervous. Every day he took out a little green cloth, and on that he laid out a deck of tarot cards. His fortune was coming out awfully badly for him. He said that something awful was going to happen every day—he was certain he was going to be killed by the Bolsheviks.

What he was doing was going into Russia and carrying out jewels and money. He carried out millions of dollars' worth. When the Grand Duchess Marie fled to the Caucasus at the beginning of the Revolution, she left cash and all her jewels in the safe in her palace in St. Petersburg. She was getting short of cash. In disguise Grand Duke Boris and Bertie got into her palace on the Neva with the help of a caretaker who remained loyal. They made their way to the Grand Duchess' bedroom, to the secret safe she had told them about, and took out all the jewels and the money.

But then there was nothing they could do with it. Bertie took the cash to the British Embassy. He was a diplomatic courier, so he stuffed the jewels in a suitcase and carried them to London, where he deposited them in a safe deposit box in the Grand Duchess' name. Then he went back to St. Petersburg, picked up some of the money, and made his way across Russia, through the Revolution itself, and delivered it to the Grand Duchess in the Caucasus. He made three trips across Russia that way. He helped innumerable people, and carried Mother's jewels out for her. I have a feeling also that he was doing a lot more on the side. He knew a little Russian, but he was a complete Englishman in appearance, and if he had been apprehended anywhere he could not possibly have brazened it out. Then, jumpy and nervous, he came to us in the Crimea, and stayed there.

I had seen General Wrangel often, as he was married to a cousin of mine. We had been, of course, in the same brigade. When Sorine finished my portrait, he gave an exhibition of his work, with the painting included. General Wrangel saw it. So he learned that I was in Yalta, and called me up; we met and talked. He had been asked to take command of the troops of the Tartar Republic. The government seemed to be moderate socialist, of the Kerensky type, but he had misgivings about it. I volunteered to go to Sympheropol, fifty-five miles away, where this Tartar force had formed, to find out.

I went home and broke the news to Catherine, and we had our first quarrel. She did not want me to go; but she finally agreed, and in the morning I started out in the general direction of Sympheropol by bus, the only way I could get there. It was late when I finally arrived. I went to the headquarters of the Tartars. There was an old friend there, Alexander Dumbadze. He had just received news that two destroyers were in the process of bombarding Yalta. The fleet at Sebastopol had mutinied and gone over to the Bolsheviks. I was immediately fearful about Catherine and the boys, and sorry I had left them. I had to try to get to them.

The Tartar cavalry units stationed at Livadia had been ordered to get into position to cut the road to Sympheropol. The newly appointed prime minister of the Tartar Republic was on his way to Yalta, and young Gregory Dumbadze was going with the prime minister. They offered me a lift, to take me back as close to Yalta as I could get, and I quickly accepted.

The Tartars proclaimed a holy war against the Bolsheviks. In every village the mullahs were exhorting the faithful. And the faithful were coming out with flintlock guns and God only knows what. It was the most amazing collection of obsolete weapons I have ever seen. Sympheropol is in the center of the Crimea. We climbed up steep hills, and at the top of the pass, we could see the sea far below and Aloushta, a small Tartar resort town near Yalta.

We saw the lights of four cars slowly climbing up the road from the sea. The Tartars put up a road block and lay in wait to ambush them. It was fascinating—completely primitive warfare, a road block with flintlock guns. The cars happened to be the cars of friends. Their occupants told us that Yalta was completely in the hands of the Bolsheviks: that was all they had been able to learn. I tried not to think about Catherine, but I had a sick feeling in my stomach.

We made the last part of the trip down to the coast and came to a halt at the village of Nikita, about five miles before Yalta itself. There we found Tartar cavalry outposts and the Tartar squadron leader. With them we moved down to the sea through the rose gardens of the Massandra Palace.

We were now organized. By this time we had a number of officers, White officers, who were serving as soldiers in the ranks. I was given command of the Tartar militia, with all their queer weapons. Our effective strength consisted of the squadron of Tartar cavalry, a battalion of infantry made up of White officers and ordinary troopers, and me with the militia. And as we had expected, the Reds attacked. We put up road blocks, and in the night a car came along, with some Red sailors and a commissar in it. We captured them, and the commissar, a tough-looking individual, begged me for mercy. He groveled on his knees; it was a disgusting sight. I couldn't bring myself to kill him, so I sent him back. It was a mistake. After having debased himself in this fashion, he wanted revenge for the humiliation, and became notorious for his cruelty in the area.

Yalta lies in a cup-shaped depression, like a huge natural stadium facing the water. The roads switch back up the slopes; the town lies along the water at the base of the crescent; and on a hill in Yalta itself is the Massandra Palace and its famous rose gardens where I had so often played as a child. During the night the Reds attacked through the rose gardens of Massandra, a lot of fighting went on around the palace and in the gardens themselves. The Red forces were sailors from the fleet, and freed convicts from Yalta to whom they had given arms. I remember, during a lull in the engagement the next morning, walking through the rose gardens with my men. The shock to me was overwhelming, seeing the corpses of the Reds hanging on the wires that supported the rosebushes. It was a lovely sunny day, I had played there on just such days as this many years before. Nothing is more sickening than the total destruction of a childhood memory.

We organized as well as we could, and I became a kind of chief of staff. A plan of attack was worked out, a pretty good one, and it went off like clockwork. We were going to take Yalta itself in the early hours of the morning. The infantry force made up largely of White officers was in the center, with the Tartar cavalry squadron attacking on the left flank. I was to take my Tartar militiamen and go around through the hills, several miles around, and attack from the right flank, to the rear of the Reds who by then would be up against the officer units and the Tartar cavalry.

We had already put out outposts for the night. We called them in and set out at once. About three in the morning we came to the town of Ai Vasil. We formed in front of the mosque, the mullah exhorted the faithful, and more recruits joined us.

My group had one machine gun. I mounted it on the slope above Yalta on the east, and used it to cover the men as they moved down the hill just as the main attack was launched from the west. We took Yalta. The Reds retreated to the jetty where the two destroyers were moored. Everything went well on our part of the operation, except that my company of irregulars sort of dribbled away after coming down the hill. I was accompanied by one brave old Tartar, who never left my side. The two of us made our way across Yalta to join the rest of the White force. We came to the house of Prince Scherbatoff, a relative of the Bariatinskys. He gave us breakfast, the Tartar and myself, the first food we had had in twelve hours. I tried to find out about Catherine, but nobody knew.

When we left, the son of the household, a thirteen-year-old boy, Cyril, started to come with us. I said, "Not now—you're too young." He was greatly depressed. From there on the Tartar and I hurried across Yalta. In the distance we saw some of the Tartars from the cavalry squadron. We went to join them. By this time I had collected about ten of my men who had gotten dispersed after coming down the hill, and we started across a street toward the Tartar cavalrymen. Somebody yelled "Stop!"

We stopped. A young musician, a cellist, Michael Arens, came running from a house. He, along with Tiomkin, used to accompany my wife's singing. He said, "Don't cross that street! There's a Bolshevik machine gun pointed at you!"

Red sailors from the fleet had concealed a gun beyond the intersection. It swept the whole street; in another moment we would have all been killed. Quickly we moved to outflank them, and they retreated toward the jetty. More of my Tartars were beginning to come together again, some of them bringing prisoners. We herded the prisoners together, looking for a place to lock them up. They thought they were going to be shot directly, and fell on their knees, begging for mercy. It was terrible to see how these men, who were so ruthless when they were winning, became abject and terror-stricken when they were beaten. We were in front of the house of an old general I had come to know. I had no intention of having the prisoners shot, but we were undecided as to where to send them. I finally sent them back to our jump-off point, the village of Ai Vasil.

The old general had witnessed the whole episode. He ran out of the house, blessed me with the sign of the cross, and said, "My son, remember: Mercy, mercy, mercy!" I have never forgotten it; it still rings in my ears.

I was trying to get to the Mordvinov Palace, for I did not know what had happened to Catherine and the boys. We made our way carefully up the slope, but the Reds had vanished. The house was a shambles. My portrait, a picture of which is on the back of this book, was hanging behind shattered glass, with bullet holes through it. A shell had gone through the window, and only a few feathers were left of our canaries. All my personal belongings had been taken.

I rushed to Yalta where I finally heard that Catherine was safe. She was hiding with friends in a house in the northern part of the town with the daughter of General Dumbadze. That part of town was still in the hands of the Reds. It was toward Livadia. My Tartar and I decided to try to get through to her. We made our way there by back streets.

There was a brief, hurried meeting with Catherine. When the fighting had begun, Sorine had realized she would have no way of getting out of the Mordvinov Palace, and had gone there in the night to guide her out. The boys were now with the Scherbatoffs. This whole part of town was crawling with Reds. I wanted to get her behind our lines, but I did not know whether she could get back safely with us. We were marked men. She would have a better chance alone. I told her so. I said we would go first, to try out the way. "Now listen," I said, "after we leave, you wait fifteen minutes, then if you don't hear shooting, you come down this street with your dog. Otherwise, stay where you are. I'll get in touch with you after a while, no matter how long. Don't worry." I kissed her. I really thought it was good-by.

The Tartar and I started down the main street toward Yalta. We came upon two men with rifles facing the other way, looking down upon Yalta. We were walking in the middle of the street. They challenged us, saying, "Who are you?"

I said, "We're Whites."

They shot, and ran for cover. We shot back. They missed, and I think we missed. The Tartar and I vaulted over a low stone wall. Funny things have always happened to me at the worst moments. This time I landed on somebody. It was Uncle Kostia, the plump gipsy guitar player who had accompanied Nura Massalsky at our parties. He had heard shooting and wanted to take a peek. I realized then that we were in his garden. I have never in my life seen such a frightened and astonished face. I laughed and slapped him on the back and told him couldn't wait. Just then the Reds fired a blast at us. It was like a Keystone comedy. He ducked and the Tartar and I vaulted over a wall at the bottom of his garden, into a back alley; and luckily we got back without any further excitement to our own lines. The next time I saw Uncle Kostia was in London, when we had a gipsy party at Felix Youssoupoff's several years later. We had many things to tell each other.

In the street I met Peter Dolgorouky. He wore a felt hat, dark suit, a waterproof coat, high buttoned boots, gloves and a fine cane. I immediately remembered the Very pistol episode after his and Aliosha's dinner. Peter was a retiring, kindly individual who wouldn't hurt a fly and right now he only volunteered because I told him to. Peter obviously wasn't a fighting officer. He was married, had two children, and liked a quiet life. I was amazed at his acceptance. He said, "If you don't mind, I'll just go tell my wife." In two minutes he had, and he came along just as he was, cane and all.

We came upon a number of Tartars of our detachment, and I stretched out beside them. I realized then that they had no commander. They literally didn't know what to do. A ragged column of Red sailors was approaching across a field. So I took command, and ordered in Turkish, "Hold fire, until my command."

The sailors approached. "Open fire!" I said. That was about all the Turkish I knew, but it was enough. The sailors immediately fled back to their jetty, leaving behind a number of killed and wounded.

At our headquarters in Yalta, the mayor and a delegation of Yalta citizens assembled. The Reds had threatened to bombard Yalta unless we withdrew, and the mayor asked us please to leave. So we decided to withdraw to the perimeter of the hills. We ringed Yalta with outposts in the woods for a couple of miles in depth. During the afternoon another Red destroyer arrived, and threw shells in our direction. A Red plane circled, and dropped a few small bombs. Then a messenger arrived from Ai Vasil, with news that sailors from the Red garrison at Sebastopol had fought the Tartars at the field of Balaklava, where the famous Charge of the Light Brigade had taken place in the Crimean

War. The Tartars were beaten, and Symphreopol itself had been taken over by the Reds.

And so the handwriting was on the wall. The Tartar government disbanded, and operated in hiding. There was nothing we could do except take to the hills, and either become guerrillas, or make our way out as best we could. A small group of us decided to take to the hills and become guerrillas.

There was no use for me to go to Catherine. Besides, the Reds now held Yalta, and it would be suicide to try to get through their lines. And Catherine was safer as long as she was not associated with me in any way. She was in good hands and by now would be disguised. I, on the other hand, had a price on my head. I had received word that Sorine's portrait of me had been stuck up in a meeting hall in Yalta with an inscription underneath:

> Serge Obolensky
> Wanted
> Dead or Alive

I was gratified to hear that the price they were willing to pay for me was high.

Sorine, however, for more reasons than one, had bribed a Red guard at the meeting hall and for three rubles took it down. He rolled it up, and when the Germans took over the Crimea later on, he took it out of Russia under his arm. It is now in my apartment in New York. Its bullet holes are still in evidence.

Part V

The Reign of Terror

CHAPTER XVII

It was the middle of January 1918 when the reign of terror started in Yalta itself. The jetty extends far out into the bay, visible from all parts of the town on its terraced slopes. There the Bolsheviks slaughtered fifty officers, first torturing some of them, including Alexander Dumbadze. His brother Grisha, as a result, turned into the scourge of the Reds. The officers, some dead and some alive, were thrown into the bay, with stones attached to their feet. The water of the bay off Yalta is very clear. For a long time afterward, on a sunny day, the corpses were visible under the water, waving their hands with the currents.

One of them was a relative of mine, Prince Mestchersky, who had tried to be neutral. All he wanted was to live quietly in Yalta and not take sides. They killed him, smashed his face in, and threw him into the bay. He was of my build, and I learned later that they had mistaken him for me. When the fighting ended in Yalta, the Bolsheviks boasted of their victory, and listed me as one of the White officers who had been killed. That is why I was on the Bolshevik registers as officially dead. It was a great help, because they weren't looking for me after that. Still, I knew that I had to stay away from Catherine and the boys. I learned that as a result of Mestchersky's death, my friends and the boys now thought me dead as well, and this was the safest thing for them, and me. Knowledge is a dangerous thing if there is ever an interrogation.

The northern slopes of the Crimean Mountains are capped with snow except in the summertime. We were living in this snow belt, for there were Tartar huts up there where the sheep were grazed in the summer. The winter was cold, and my cough returned. We were obliged to keep fires going. They were enough to give us away. But for some time we were not disturbed. A wounded Siberian officer joined us. He had been wounded eighteen times, and, though in weakened condition, he was still full of fight. Bit by bit, others came into the mountains. On our first raid we ambushed the Reds on the road from Yalta to Sympheropol. We felled trees across it, and intercepted their cars during the night. We took our captives to the Tartar government, which was still in existence, though in hiding. There they were probably shot.

We went on several raids, and were fed by the Tartars, who brought us food by donkeys. We still had a little money, but it was running out, and we tried to get papers, for it was difficult to hide in a wilderness. Everyone knows you are there. It is much easier to hide in a big city where at least there is anonymity.

In the meantime, we raided. On one raid I had volunteered to lead the attack. We were deployed and moving up when suddenly the whine of several bullets came from behind me. Somehow, they missed. I dropped to the ground and took up the rear as the men advanced. Obviously the Reds had infiltrated our group, or some of our men were in sympathy with them. And I thought, "My God, why am I doing this?" Clearly it was useless, absolutely useless if the men were beginning to feel that way. I realized then that Russia would have to go through a blood bath, for her people no longer realized what liberty meant, and they did not understand. It could only be after terrific pain and hardship that they would be able to comprehend that the Bolshevik government was not the government they wanted. In the meantime, it was useless to fight for them. And I decided to try to get the family out of the Crimea and out of Russia.

It was about this time that we learned that the Czar had been taken to Siberia. Many of the men wanted to fight things out and go to rescue him.

The Siberian officer had by now recovered, and led a raiding party, returning with a coat which I recognized as mine. He told me that he had found it on a Red guard. The Communist had been stopped, because, frankly, he looked a little too smartly dressed. What's more, the Siberian officer had found my name sewn in the lining. The Communist said he had bought it in a pawnshop, but questioning revealed that he had obviously been looting. The Siberian officer had had him shot.

We looked at the coat. There was the label: Davis, London, and my name sewn on the inner pocket.

I asked the Siberian, "Was there anything else?"

"A watch," he said. "Can you describe it?"

"Gold," I said, "and with 'Andre' or 'Buddy' engraved on it."

He nodded, drew out a gold wristwatch, and gave it to me. When Catherine and I had become engaged, I had given each of her boys a watch. "Andre" was engraved on the back of one, "Buddy" on the other. I turned the watch over in my hand and there was the word "Andre." Nothing has ever frightened me more. Nothing has ever made me feel more helpless. I was certain that something terrible had happened.

I reached in my pocket to pay him for it. "Keep it," the Siberian officer said, and walked away. Only later I found out that the watch had been left behind by Andre when they had fled from the Mordvinov.

Through friends most of the men had got false papers, and had left. Only six of us remained, Peter Dolgorouky and I among them. I had no papers of any kind, and wore my uniform under my rough Tartar clothes. Peter had no papers, no uniform, except the extraordinary clothes that he had worn on joining up with us. These were now in an advanced stage of disrepair. Peter was unbelievable, and he kept our spirits up. We were all in reasonable disguise. The only concession to any subterfuge that Peter had allowed was a tiny Tartar sheepskin cap that sat ridiculously on the balding top of his head. Meanwhile, the high button boots and the waterproof were his standard uniform, disintegrated or not. I'm sure that if he had had a razor handy, he would have done credit to Lloyd's bank, and shaved. We hid our weapons after every raid, but some of us kept concealed daggers on our persons. There was nothing in the hut to give us away. The Reds were organizing a dragnet over the Crimean hills, going from one hut to the next.

Early one morning they broke into our hut. Two men stood in the doorway, pointing rifles at us, and five guarded the hut outside. Six of them were Tartars, luckily under the command of a Greek corporal. Four of the Tartars had previously been with us. Perhaps this helped. They searched us haphazardly and found nothing. Then they ordered us outside. I realized then that the Tartars had probably gone over to the Reds to save their skins. The Greek was the Red, and he looked uncomfortable being suddenly alone amongst so many of the historic enemies of the Crimean Greeks. I asked him where he was taking us.

He muttered, "To Kokos." The Crimean soviet had established headquarters in the palace that Felix Youssoupoff's father had built. Being well-known, we were certain to be shot as soon as we arrived. But Kokos was a good twenty-five miles away. The distance, the friendliness of the Tartars, and the fact that our weapons had not been found gave us a dim hope.

In the Crimea the mountains rise straight up from the sea. The Crimea is the counterpart of the French Riviera and much more beautiful. Ai Petri's snow-covered peak looms in the background. Our guerrilla raids had been down by the sea on the mountain's southern slope. A good road, used by motorcars, went through the pass of Ai Petri. The pass was very high, requiring careful driving. The trip even then took several hours. On the opposite side of the pass, the road dropped down into the valley of Kokos.

In other words, we had lived on the north side, in the empty Tartar huts, and raided the south side. We knew the country. And soon we were approaching the big road that led to the pass. There we would find Bolsheviks passing by in their cars and trucks. Once we reached this road we would be finished. Meanwhile, the pine trees got ominously smaller as we climbed, and soon we would be visible from the road. The Greek corporal was in advance. Then came his two Tartars followed by us six prisoners, while the four Tartars who had been with us brought up the rear. We worked out a plan as we went along, by occasional words and sign language. We were to stop, summon the corporal, and, when we had them all together, offer them everything we had to let us go. Of course, if they refused, we would have to jump them. But we hoped that at least the four Tartars who had served with us would not shoot.

And so we stopped. The Greek must have sensed the undercurrent when we made our offer. I realized then that we really had a chance, and, more important, I saw Peter Dolgorouky ready to throw himself on the Greek if he refused. The humor of it touched me, and I had a hard time to keep from laughing. I have never seen such a fierce determination on a kindly man's face. We gave the Greek the gold watch I had given Andre, and all the money that we had. Strangely enough, he then warned us to stay away from certain paths that he knew were being combed by patrols that would be tougher than his had been. We scurried off while the patrol was dividing the loot. We moved fast because we were afraid the corporal would start shooting. Under cover of the trees we put a good half-hour between us and the patrol. Then we climbed to get to a trail that led to the southern side. I was coughing a great deal, and it slowed me down. At the timber line, where the trees and the vegetation ended, we would have been exposed to view from the road, so we decided to wait until dark. From there we peered down on the road and the valley of Kokos, and watched the northern slopes being searched.

As the night fell, we moved. Several miles to the east from the big road we expected to pick up the trail—just a goat path, really. We knew it well. It would be marked by poles in the snow at regular intervals. But snow began to fall. The snow turned into a storm, and we couldn't find the markers. After hours of wandering, the snow abated, and we realized that we had been going in a huge circle. Then all of a sudden the wind scattered the clouds over the peaks, and we could see the polestar. From it we got our bearings, as we often had on night patrols with the cavalry, and we headed south and then east. To our great relief, we found the path with poles. We hurried down it out of the snow line and into the concealment of the woods, where we slept.

Next morning we decided that it would be wiser to break up into groups of twos, and not attract attention to ourselves.

My companion was Captain Alekseev of the Tartar regiment. We were both dressed as Tartars. I had a bedraggled Tartar coat, and carried a canvas bag with my cavalry boots in it. We both had beards and fur caps, but his disguise was better than mine. Also, I wore Tartar sandals, and the stones had cut my feet so that I limped. By this time I had none of the elasticity of the Tartars.

We made our way by paths, avoiding the roads. However, we came to a narrow gorge, and a waterfall, where there was no way across except by a bridge. A party of men and women and children were walking in the same direction, and we straggled along behind them. They looked pretty tough, but in a crowd we had a better chance to get across the bridge unnoticed. They seemed to pay no attention to us.

After crossing the bridge, we dropped back, as if we were merely wandering along. At a bend in the path we came up close behind them. We heard them say something Like "Suspicious characters!" One man said "Never mind, there's a post at the foot of the hill."

That was enough for us. We left the path, and ran across a field. A hedgelike fence ran parallel to the road on the other side of the field. On the far side of this hedge we ducked down, and hurried on until we were ahead of the party we had followed. We figured that a patrol would not be looking ahead, if the people said the stragglers were behind them.

There was another curious thing here, a sort of upper path running along the ridge of the Crimean hills. It, too, ran parallel with the road, and it seemed little used. Nevertheless, we went along it cautiously. We were approaching Yalta now. I did not dare go near the Mordvinov Palace, nor the villas of any of my friends. We had been nearly two months in the mountains, and all we knew was that we were being hunted. The path led us around Yalta, toward the outskirts. And when I got my bearings, I remembered a place there. In a cottage nearby lived a retired artisan whom we had known in St. Petersburg. He was an old-timer whose identity and trade I shall have to conceal, for he was well-known, and some of his family may still be alive. I shall call him Ivan. Shall we say that he made the boots for the cavalry officers in the old days, and knew everyone, a fine craftsman. I had known him since childhood. Father took me to his shop when I got my first pair of riding boots. There had always been horsemen around there, for the old man would also work on saddles and such as a favor to his friends and customers. He still worked a little, and had in fact repaired my boots while we were in Yalta. I thought I could trust him. In any event, we had to take a chance. His house was on the outskirts, and again we waited until dark. Then I said to Alekseev, "If I don't whistle, don't approach."

Through the window I saw the old shoemaker putting logs on the fire. I watched him for some time, and decided he was alone. I opened the door and walked in. Quick as a flash he picked up a piece of wood and brandished it. "Get out!" he cried.

I said, "Ivan, it's me—Serge." I had completely forgotten how I looked. Finally he said, "I thought you were dead." He came cautiously up, still holding the piece of wood in readiness, and examined me. I have never seen anyone's expression run through so many changes so fast. Then he grabbed me and embraced me. He had heard about my body on the jetty. Once again I knew I was indebted to poor Boris Mestchersky.

I went outside, whistled, and Alekseev came in. Ivan fed us, heated a bath for us, and fixed up two mattresses in the garret. We were completely exhausted. The mattresses in the garret were so well hidden that even if there had been a raid we were not likely to be found.

When we were rested, Ivan brought me a basin filled with red wine. He told me to soak my hands in it. My hands were still soft, and the first thing the Bolsheviks did at control points was to look at the hands of the people who passed through. If one's hands were soft, one was likely to be shot. The alcohol in the wine cracked the outer skin. Then Ivan brought dirt into the garret, and we rubbed dirt into my hands until they looked cracked and calloused.

Ivan was a Ukrainian, and a mighty shrewd one. He said Alekseev would not be much of a problem to disguise. He had mobile and expressive features, flexible as putty. All that would be required would be to dye his hair and fit him up with different clothes, which he did. Then Ivan could find him a laboring job. But my case was different. He looked at me and shook his head.

My features have always been stiff and inflexible, except, of course, for my nose—thanks to M. Loustalou. In the Crimea by this time they had come to be well-known. The safest disguise for anyone in those days, Ivan said, was that of a workman holding a job somewhere until he could build up a new identity for himself. "But with you I don't dare do it."

"Why not?" I asked, and then I had a coughing fit.

"People would recognize you. Bah! With a cough like that, you can only be an intellectual!"

For my part, I still thought I looked pretty good. My hair had grown long, and I had quite a long beard. And I had a greasy mustache, growing down over my mouth, very unpleasant, but I had had to let it grow to conceal my mouth.

"Whoever heard of a Tartar with a red beard?" Ivan scoffed. I hadn't thought of that. He produced a pair of dark spectacles, and disdainfully placed them on my nose. They completely changed my appearance, as I had never worn spectacles. "You see?" Ivan said. "You have one chance. You must be a revolutionary intellectual."

A tubercular Moscow student Ivan had known had recently died, and from a friend he secured the dead man's passport. I suppose my cough had given him the idea. We worked that whole evening folding and creasing it, erasing the registration of death. It was not too good, but it was the best we could do. Finally, Ivan suggested that we squash a tomato over that page.

"Why not?" I said.

But not until Ivan had found some new clothes for me could he be satisfied. And he produced these too. They hung on me grotesquely.

So indeed I was a student with tuberculosis who, before the Revolution, had come to the Crimea for his health, and in a matter of hours I had taken on a different aspect, different smell, different face, and now I had a different name. I cannot give it, even now, for some of the people involved may still be alive.

Ivan was getting nervous. Reluctantly he said, "You can't stay here tonight. Or anywhere, or they'll catch you. For the moment you must sleep outside. Go to the Tartar cemetery and rest. I'll meet you there."

It may have been because he had had trouble getting the passport. Or perhaps he sensed that a raid was brewing. Ukrainians have a way of knowing things. A raid at this moment would be fatal to everyone, since I now held the passport of a man who had been known in the neighborhood, and that man had died.

When Alekseev and I entered Yalta that night we saw cars passing, filled with drunken sailors. The sailors were covered with bracelets and jewels. They were raiding and looting. What the Reds were perpetrating there was really beyond description, except in studies of abnormal psychology. Because the Reds had found so little support among the folk of the Crimea, the revolutionists at Sebastopol had opened all the jails, had taken the convicts into the fleet, given them uniforms and used them to terrorize the population. It was not a pleasant atmosphere. I remember seeing the lights on in the villa of a friend of mine, but I resisted a powerful temptation to go inside. In times of direst stress there is a compulsive desire just to end the strain. But deepest of all, Alekseev and I had the instinct for survival, and we kept on. We walked about a quarter of a mile to the cemetery. There we spent the night between two tombstones.

The cemetery was an old Tartar burial ground, not with crosses marking the graves, but with headstones. It was extremely cold, and I had a hard time stifling my cough. Before dawn, Ivan came to the cemetery. He told Alekseev that he had a job for him as a bricklayer and he was to go to a certain place before it got light. "Now you come with me," he said to me, and he led me five or six miles into the country. He said he was taking me to a small sanitarium for tubercular patients. "In case we are stopped and questioned," he said, "I have already talked to the woman who runs it. I have confided in her, but I have not told her your name. She has agreed to take you in."

Then he laughed. "It might even help your cough."

All this seemed plausible to me, and I thought that we really could get away with it, even if we were picked up and questioned. But this time, of course, we met no one.

When we got there, the sanitarium was dark. Ivan knocked, and almost immediately a woman, wearing a nurse's uniform, opened the door. She whispered that she had a cot prepared for me, in a small room. We went there, making no noise, and when the door closed she turned up the light. She said, "Oh, my God, I know you!"

After a moment she added, in an ordinary tone of voice, "I'll do it. But that's the worst disguise possible."

At that point Ivan left, God bless him, with a wink. I suppose he didn't want to give her a chance to change her mind. There never was a man the like of him.

She put me straight to bed, telling me what I must do to be a patient, that if I ever had to walk anywhere, as she suspected I might, I had to walk with a stoop. She then told me how to cough, which wasn't hard. I was fearfully ill, you see. She thought they could barely save my life—in more ways than one. "You've got to get out of the Crimea," she said suddenly. "You're a white elephant here—everybody knows you." She seemed to think a minute. "I have a doctor friend who will help us."

The one thing in my favor was that I was supposed to be dead, and the Bolsheviks had been boasting everywhere of killing me. So there would be no alarm out for me. And there was a good chance that I would not be recognized, so long as there was no inquiry into my past or how I came to be there. The important thing was to keep me out of trouble of any kind.

In the morning, Mme. Petroff, the woman who ran the sanitarium, went to her doctor friend to get a certificate from him, stating that I was critically ill with tuberculosis. She then went to the police, to register my new name, saying

I was dying. But presently she came back to the sanitarium, tired and depressed. She said, "I have to go to the police. There is a man there. You must be registered. I'm going to have to spend some money."

I said, "I haven't any."

There was a pause; then she said, "Well, I'll get it. You can pay me when you can."

I told her I did not know when, if ever, I could pay her. She said, "Life is more important than money."

She raised money somewhere; and from her doctor friend, who never came near me, she got a certificate stating I was extremely ill with tuberculosis. Then she went to the police. Luckily, the police official was an old-timer.

He looked at the passport, and said "This is no good. I think I understand what you're doing. I'll register the whole thing. Come back in three days and say you've lost the passport. I'll issue new papers. I'll need a photograph."

In this way I would get authentic papers, bearing my own physical characteristics and photograph, instead of the blurred old papers liable to arouse suspicions because so much was illegible. Mme. Petroff took a photograph of me. As soon as she had developed it and taken it to the police things moved very fast. One of the nurses in the hospital was a young girl, only eighteen or nineteen years old, quiet and level-headed. I liked her, and it was quite mutual. Mme. Petroff confided in her to the extent of saying that I was an officer under a false name who had to be saved, and asked her if she would take a patient through to Moscow. I would be the patient. The nurse agreed. She knew that she would certainly have been killed if we were discovered.

Quarters were secured for me in Moscow. Mme. Petroff had a cousin there, and the cousin was married to a man who had a job under the Bolsheviks. He had been the manager of a railway maintenance plant in the old days. When the industries were nationalized, and the national syndicate formed, he had been kept on as a technician—what the Bolsheviks called a works expert. He was told that I was to live there until I recovered enough and got a chance to go on to my family in Estonia.

We went to Sebastopol in an old four-horse carriage, which was at that time the least conspicuous means of transport. There were no cars available. There was the nurse, myself, and a Bolshevik soldier who had fought against me and who was recovering from his wounds and now was being sent back to his home in Moscow. He knew nothing about it, but Mme. Petroff realized he would provide an excellent cover. He was asked to volunteer to help take a desperately sick invalid—myself—to Moscow. He would be provided transportation and a fee. It was amazing. My nurse was instructed to give me injections at periodic intervals. I was given one just before we left.

The very night we left was the St. Bartholomew's Eve of Sebastopol. The local revolutionary committee had raided a great many houses occupied by former officers; and all their occupants, including the women and children, servants, and even dogs, were killed and their corpses dumped into the streets. When we arrived, bodies were strewn everywhere. We went directly to the station, where a train was waiting on the tracks. Because of the nurse and her charge and the wounded soldier, who arranged everything conscientiously, we were put in a four-berth compartment. I was placed in an upper berth.

I supposed I was drugged, or was given something to induce fever, for the whole experience was dazed and dreamlike. The compartment filled up with soldiers and sailors. It was a rough and tedious trip; some of the windows were broken, and the train was constantly starting and stopping. The men were talking about what had been happening. And then they began talking about me. It was a weird sensation, listening to them. Some of them had fought at Yalta against troops I had led. They talked about what they did, and what I was supposed to have done. Then they described graphically how I had been tortured and shot and my body thrown into the bay.

While it is nice to be remembered by your enemies for the damages you have served up to them, the strangest part of it all was that, as I listened to them, it did not seem to be me that they were talking about. In my torpor I had really become the person I was supposed to be. I no longer existed in my own identity. I had no sense of fear whatever, for in my drugged state I really thought I was a student who had become ill and was going home, not an officer in hiding under a disguise. There was one small point that hung in my consciousness. The men talking about me pronounced my name differently. People educated as I was, and raised in St. Petersburg, spoke an academic Russian, somewhat swallowing the syllables. I had a different accent from most Russian speech, just as the English that is spoken, in Boston, Massachusetts, has a somewhat different flavor from the English spoken in other parts of the United States, or anywhere else in the world for that matter. Our St. Petersburg pronunciation of the name Obolensky was "Ah-bah-len-skee," while the soldiers and sailors in our compartment used the pronunciation "Oh-boh-lyen-skih." There would have been a dangerous difference had I been compelled to say my own name.

But of this there was no likelihood, thanks to Mme. Petroff. Meanwhile, the trip went on and on. It took three days. Whenever I had to go to the toilet the wounded Bolshevik pushed his way through the crowd in the aisle to get me there. I really had grown so weak I could hardly walk. He was by now deeply concerned about me. He got me food, and he did a hundred things to help the nurse take care of me. I thanked him from the bottom of my heart when we reached the end of our long journey.

At Moscow he went on his way, and my little nurse and I got into a droshky. She had never been in Moscow before and she was fascinated. We went immediately to the home of the works expert, where they received us warmly. I doubt that he ever suspected that we were not what we were supposed to be. He talked volubly. He was trying to keep the plant going efficiently. He was still earning a good salary. And then the nurse said that she had to start back. There was a train, and she must start back.

I had been provided with a few rubles; I could not let her go without doing something for her—no matter how little or ridiculous. So I went out and bought her a little brooch with a red cross on it, one that would be safe for her to wear. The army nurses all wore little red crosses. I came back and took her to the train, and then I gave it to her. I'll never forget her. As the train began to move, her eyes were filled with tears. Only then did I see how fond we had become. She said, "This is the cross I will always have to carry. God bless you."

It was only after she left, and I had gone back to the house, that I realized with a start that she must have come to love me, that that was what love meant. And I was moved as I have been moved few times in my life. I said a prayer of thanks and I asked God to watch over her and keep her safe.

My hosts fed me well, and I began taking walks near the house to build up my strength. I was exhausted. Gradually, the walks grew longer and it wasn't too long before I felt myself again. So I stooped a little less, though the hard racking cough I had perfected remained. Actually, I still did have a cough— one not nearly as violent or persistent as I made out—and I made the most of it.

I was still a marked man. I never walked to places where I might be noticed. It was necessary to be careful, to be cautious about going into any unfamiliar area, to avoid trouble of any kind. Above all, I must avoid any place where I had been known before. I must not be picked up for questioning.

I saw Trotsky on one of my walks. He rode past in a gigantic limousine; he passed very close to me. Big cars with the big Communists in them were always racing by, and once I believe I saw Lenin. There were other Reds still alive at that time who were prominent, like Kamenev. But they have been forgotten.

In Moscow the atmosphere of terror was growing day by day. The police, the fire department, and everything else, of course, had been taken over by the Bolsheviks and the Red Guards. No one knew who was reporting what or whom. In those days it was just pretty much everybody for himself, keep quiet, and stay out of anything. It was only the beginning, but it was already horrible.

On one of my walks I saw someone I thought I recognized. I followed him. Of all the lucky chances I had in that period, this was the most fortunate. The man in front of me was the manager of the small textile firm that we had owned. I was certain I could trust him.

I did not dare approach him in the street, and it seemed to me he would never stop walking. Then he went into a courtyard, and passed through it into a smaller courtyard. There was a small apartment house on one side, and he went in and started up the stairs. I hurried after him and climbed the stairs behind him. No one was around.

"Feodor Alexandrovitch!" I called.

He stopped. He looked frightened.

I took off my hat. "Don't you know who I am?"

An expression of disbelief and then relief swept over his features.

"Come in," he said. "Come in quickly."

And then it all began. He couldn't wait to talk to me. He was laughing and crying all at the same time, shaking me by the shoulders. He had heard I was dead. There had even been a funeral service for me. "Maria!" he called. "Come see what the Lord has brought us back!"

Maria, his wife, was a former ballerina of the Imperial ballet. Today, she taught ballet. She knew everyone in artistic and theatrical circles. She welcomed me as if she was my own mother. Feodor and she insisted that I come to live with them. I warned them about my status with the Bolsheviks. But they laughed and said. "Why, you've become a myth. You don't exist!" They thought this was terribly funny! As it turned out, I didn't actually stay with them. A friend of hers, a retired dancer, had a garret room in the courtyard nearby. I told my friend the works expert that I was leaving for my family in Estonia. I also became Feodor's secretary in our now nationalized textile firm.

When the Bolsheviks first came into power they had closed down on all bank accounts. Our estate had had several accounts in different banks, the equivalent of a hundred thousand dollars in the account of textile works, a general estate account of another hundred thousand, and twenty to fifty thousand in my personal account. The Bolsheviks confiscated it all, putting everything that they thought belonged to me in the government account, and allowing a limit of ten thousand rubles over all the accounts. But as there was no capital to operate with, the businesses had collapsed. Their produce, however, was essential, so adjustments had to be made to keep them operating. I was just one small case. The Bolsheviks abolished private ownership of property, transferred the factories to the state, took over the banks, and then closed the banks in favor of a single state bank. As a result, life came to a standstill. Society literally ceased to function; for there had to be trade, and business, and credit in some fashion or another. People worked, or tried to work. They went to offices and factories. My friend Feodor and I went to the office of the textile firm every morning. It was mainly a matter of going through the motions. The factory only ran whenever material could be secured. But there was a great demand for clothes. So we were favored. The state itself wasn't paying too much attention to the decrees where we were concerned.

Meanwhile, all sorts of ingenious ways were being devised to get money credited to the account of a former property owner or to a business firm that had been expropriated. Certain small funds were left credited to the individual's private accounts, but the bulk went to the business account that he owned. It was dangerous if not suicidal to make any direct withdrawal. It was debits and credits that we worked with—nothing more. But everything was in such confusion that it was difficult for the Bolsheviks to keep track of the money.

The various accounts that had been taken over by the government were in a state of chaos. It was possible for a bank official, or even a bank clerk, to transfer money from individual or firm accounts to the government, but in so doing, credit much less than the correct amount to the government account, leaving an enormous surplus of as-yet-uncredited cash unaccounted for. By making a deal with the clerk or the official, an individual could get part of his own money back in this fashion. That way some people got a lot of money, the bank officials in particular. But it wasn't easy.

My friend Feodor was not a suspected character. The factory was now really producing goods, and through influence it was easy to build up a cash surplus. So I was able to get some money, pay Mme. Petroff in Yalta, and send a present to the little nurse who had taken me to Moscow. When I was hired by the factory, it was highly familiar work, and I fitted into the office as if I had been connected with the company a long time.

By now a little information was filtering back into Moscow. People were beginning to come through from Yalta. Under the treaty of Brest-Litovsk, in March 1918, all of western Russia passed into German hands, and the Ukraine became a separate state under my old commander, General Skoropatsky, who, however, could not have held it without the support of the Germans.

This anti-Communist regime in the Ukraine increased the chances of getting out of Russia and provided a base for counterrevolutionaries. At the same time, the Bolsheviks became absolutely ruthless. Anyone they even suspected of opposing them was taken out and shot. Every time we met there was another report of someone we knew who had been killed. There was no relaxation whatever in the atmosphere of horror. It was hard to realize that the Bolsheviks now just killed anyone—anyone at all—for any reason, or for no reason. We of the underground rarely discussed these things. Whenever we met, we acted as if there was no problem. We laughed together, and we lived. Only as we were leaving, someone might say, "So-and-so has been killed." After a while this was commonplace. The list of people I knew who took no part in the political struggles, and nevertheless were killed, runs into hundreds of names—professors, doctors, musicians, not to speak of those who died as a result of experiences they were forced to undergo. Many of these people were caught, I feel, simply because they had not taken sides. They were lulled into a false sense of security. I had fought, and I had my wits about me at all times.

At that time the attack on the priests was under way. The churches were still open, but thousands of priests were being killed. The people still continued to go to church, and the priests kept on saying masses. In times of stress, people pray. And how they prayed in Russia throughout this time. They packed the churches. Only the Communists themselves did not dare go, and people too closely affiliated with the Bolsheviks to risk being seen by them in any act of prayer. Many of the latter were people like myself with jobs in industry. I assure you I rarely went to church during this time.

The Communists then began their antireligious propaganda. There is a belief in Russia that saints don't deteriorate corporeally after death. They exhumed the bodies of the saints, and forced thousands to march past their decayed remains. Then they put God himself on trial, showing He was guilty. And they had embalmed Lenin, their saint, who would not decay. But it still made no difference. The churches were jammed more than ever. They were unable to destroy the people's faith. Finally the Bolsheviks gave up, and their antireligious propaganda dwindled away. The Bolsheviks have since tried to neutralize the church, infiltrating it, putting in their priests, but can they ever be sure of them? Masses are said on a quid pro quo basis. You the Church do something for us, and we allow you to sing so many thousand masses in a year. The Church survived. What really mattered was the Russian people who wouldn't give it up. Everybody was afraid of the terror, but they went to church.

I heard from travelers who trickled back from Yalta that Catherine and the boys were safe, and living separately. The Germans were pushing toward the Crimea, but could one wait? The Germans were showing signs of weakening in the west. The boys were in a sort of protective custody, and I can't elucidate. It might even have been possible with pressure from abroad to get the children out, but I felt it best to start taking steps rather than wait for chance or fate. It would now be easier for Catherine herself to come to Moscow and temporarily leave the children safely where they were. Accordingly, Feodor and I began making arrangements to get her back to Moscow. It would be the first step toward getting us all out of Russia in the north.

One sight that impressed me during the time was the slipshod appearance of the guards around the Kremlin. They were Red guards, of course, and among them were toughs in civilian clothes, bristling with pistols. They had a look about them that made it impossible for one to mistake them for anything except what they were—demobilized soldiers. Their clothes were scraps and patches of all kinds of uniforms.

Like its new constabulary corps, Moscow had become shabby in appearance. Many of its little shops were boarded up. The buildings had a ragged look. A couple of the big department stores were still open, but the prices were so high that few people could buy in them, and it was impossible to live on the meager rations sold in government shops. The black market was enormous, and it existed openly, even in the streets. Here, too, the prices were extraordinarily high, but we bought there in order to live. We could get eggs and vegetables, some meat once in a while—juicy tidbits like the lower part of a horse's leg, for example. A large group of Chinese laborers had been living in Russia, and some of these had been hired by the Bolsheviks as mercenary troops. Many of these people were now merchants. A story was going around that the meat they sold was the flesh of the people who had been killed.

Meanwhile, I went to the office, saw people in connection with the textile firm's affairs, and carried out the instructions of the manager. But there was one unfortunate result of my disguise: When I had been an officer, I had often struck up acquaintances with young women, exceedingly good-looking girls in many cases, like Nastia Naturchitza for example. Some of them had been birds of fine plumage. Now that I had long hair and black spectacles and a beard, ladies of that caliber never even glanced at me. Even mousy secretarial types in the firm didn't seem to know that I existed.

An entirely different type of woman now became unpleasantly friendly. These were great strapping ladies, much older than I was, and often bigger, with hearty back-slapping manners. I couldn't understand it. They would come right up and joke with me, but they wouldn't stop there. Somehow I attracted them. It sometimes became awkward, for it was not advisable for me to be scrutinized too closely; and from my point of view, despite my fake black glasses, I had extremely good eyesight, which was the worst thing of all. One afternoon Feodor sent me to an office to talk to another official, but no one was there except his stenographer. She was a fierce, red-headed woman of gigantic proportions, and immediately she became excessively hospitable. She smiled horribly, and told me not to worry because her boss wouldn't be back until tomorrow. I gulped and then she grabbed me. I had to figure out a way to extricate myself and fast. So I gave her a hefty pinch which made her giggle. It was an unpleasant sound, but it took her mind away just for the second that I needed. I'll never forget her cry of rage as I ran out of there.

The theaters were all open. I never heard more theatrical talk than at that time. The old ballet dancer in whose apartment I lived was always entertaining other artists. I learned that Maria, Feodor's wife, had just choreographed a ballet that was being put on by the national ballet. She was angry about having to put in lots of Bolshevik propaganda. The older dancer and his friends then talked about what was happening to the ballet: the company now had its commissar, and this was typical of the theater in general. Insignificant extras and dancers were often the commissars. They made life impossible for the others, especially if they had prima ballerina or premier danseur aspirations themselves. They denounced people, and pushed up their own friends, including themselves. Mostly they were washouts. It had nothing to do with artistic ability. The quality of performances dropped, but the ballet still went on. I also learned that even in those days artists, writers, dancers, actors, musicians, all were considered the salt of the earth. Since they were creative spirits, they were adulated by the government and they were given high salaries, extra rations and everything else that went along with privilege.

I went to a few performances. It would have seemed strange if I had not, in view of my friendship with Feodor and Maria. I saw her ballet and several others, and I went to a play or two. Once, I saw the comedian Balieff, and I found it surprising that he went as far as he did in making wisecracks about the

Bolsheviks and the conditions—very careful cracks, yet unmistakable. He was extremely popular. Once in the theater I sat in the row next to a man I had known in the old days; he did not recognize me.

One of the trying aspects of that time was the sudden rise of the Karamazov type of Russian intellectual I had known in my college days. Under the old society these embittered individuals were just avoided, as far as possible, because they were rude or provocative and tiresome. But now they were incredibly dangerous. They flourished under the Bolsheviks. They were glib and quick, and they knew politics. The atmosphere of terror that made everyone afraid to speak up gave them a field day. Many of them became Bolshevik agents. They would wander around trying to provoke arguments, twisting the most casual remark into something that had a political meaning. Nothing could be done except to suffer in comparative silence. Not too silent, though! That also would be held against one.

I came to realize that my own way of living was like acting a part on stage. After a time, it ceased to be acting. I was by now completely divorced from my former self. Once, while I was visiting Feodor and Maria for dinner, an old lady arrived from Yalta. She was of the old school, but I was introduced by my fictitious name. As we were drinking tea, she talked about what had happened there. The terror there had gone on for nearly six months. Since we had had only a few hundred men at the battle of Yalta, and the Reds several thousand, there were all sorts of legends about what we had done, and about our guerrilla activities as well. Because I was thought to have been killed, exploits were attributed to me, great exaggerations of what had really happened. I sat there and listened objectively to a romantic account of a life and a death my own. I had no sense of any connection with myself.

Two days later, I walked right into a group of soldiers who had served with me. I had a moment of real panic. They did not recognize me. I passed through them, trying not to hurry so fast as to call attention to myself. But the strangest meeting of this sort was when I bumped into Captain Alekseev. It was really astonishing. He was sitting behind the wheel of a big car in a crowded Moscow street. He just opened the door and said "Get in." I jumped in beside him, and he drove around the block. We talked for just a few minutes; then he let me out and went back to where he was waiting for someone. He was now repairing automobiles. A lot of cars that were wrecked or had broken down during the war and the Revolution were being rehabilitated. He took parts of one and fitted them into another, and so got a lot of automobiles working, acquiring a good position as a master mechanic and an organizer of used auto parts distribution. We wished each other "Good luck," and I never saw him again.

I lived in Moscow in disguise for a total of seven months. After about two months Catherine joined me. By now she was a schoolteacher. She taught French. Catherine was amazing. She was so good in her disguise that when her heart troubled her—she had a heart condition brought on by asthma—she had learned how to conceal it lest it give away her identity. She was afraid that she was being used by the Bolsheviks to lead them to me, and had covered her tracks so brilliantly that Feodor and his contacts in the Crimea had the greatest difficulty in reaching her.

When the Reds took the Mordvinov Palace in Yalta, they did not kill her because through her they could set up an ambush. They planned to wait for me and my friends to return, and she was the bait. She had waited upstairs throughout the battle of Yalta, hoping to be able to warn me away. The Reds, however, were driven from the Mordvinov Palace during the battle, and, as I have said, Sorine arrived that night and got her out. After she had stayed a long while with the sister of Gregory Dumbadze, where I last saw her, the Dumbadze family could keep her no longer. It was getting dangerous. One of her close friends took her in and hid her; but her friend's husband protested it was too risky. She was saved by one of her former servants. They dressed her as a nursemaid, gave her a child to carry in her arms, and got her to a farm, where she scrubbed floors, did farm work and cooked.

There it was that my friends located her. One day a woman stopped by at the farm, spoke some code words to her in French, and offered Catherine a job. Catherine said nothing at first, pretending not to understand; and the woman said, "*He* wants it that way." The woman gave Catherine a scrap of paper with an address, and walked away. This woman was my little nurse.

Heart condition or no, Catherine walked twenty miles to the address, a boarding house. There she was given papers; she was to be a French teacher who had been caught in the Crimea by the war. She gave French lessons and helped around the house, a perfect imitation of an impoverished and helpless lady of good family with resources. Quite a bit of organization was necessary before she could get to Moscow. She too traveled with a Bolshevik soldier who had made a lucrative business of taking refugees through to Moscow, asked no questions, was well paid, and apparently genuinely friendly. All went well until Sebastopol. There a big group of soldiers boarded the train, and among them Catherine recognized two soldiers who had been in the first raid on the Mordvinov Palace. She became convinced the whole thing was a trap to lead the Bolsheviks to me and to my friends. Thereafter it was a nightmare that only ended when she slipped away from her Bolshevik escort in Moscow. There was a curfew, and Moscow nighttime was unsavory. She reached Feodor's house on her own and at night, having finally bribed a reluctant droshky driver with a fantastic price the equivalent of seventy-five dollars, to take her there.

We were not to know each other. She was employed as an office worker by the textile firm. I busied myself at my work, and when the weather cleared I planted vegetables and had a garden in a patch of cleared ground beside a church where we lived. That garden gave me hours of relief, and its vegetables supplemented our food supply.

A big trade delegation was going to Kiev in the Ukraine to negotiate an exchange of commodities. I was attached to that delegation as a textile expert, and Catherine as an office worker and translator. We were to follow by train to Kiev as two workers joining this delegation. All seemed well, when the whole escape was nearly destroyed from an unexpected source. This time it was my young and unthinking brother, Vlady.

When the funeral had been held for me in St. Petersburg, Mother had refused to go to it. She had never believed that I was dead. However, some time later Vlady had returned to St. Petersburg. He knew nothing about what was going on; and he thought me dead. There were still some property rights, as I have said, those pertaining to real estate, and he was an heir. He filed in the courts the required notice of my death.

Up until that moment I was not legally dead. The bank officials had been happy to comply, and substantial funds were being transferred to the surplus firm account, some of it going to me. Then the bank officials notified Feodor in the textile plant of Vlady's action in St. Petersburg. They could no longer transfer funds. Vlady's court action had to be stopped at all costs, or our whole plan of escape would fall through. Whatever happened, we needed twenty thousand rubles. So Feodor hurriedly left for St. Petersburg, saw Mother, and got Mother to tell Vlady to drop the action because I was alive. Vlady stopped it and sent me the twenty thousand rubles. It took money to escape from Russia in those days. Vlady got out of Russia, went to Switzerland, and then to Paris. I never saw him for seven years, though at one time we both lived in Paris without either knowing the other was nearby. Mother's jewels, as I have said, were gotten out by Bertie Stopford; then she escaped to Finland, where she lived under General Mannerheim's anti-Bolshevik government, playing a great part in drumming up support for General Yudenich's White army.

Catherine, throughout our escape operation, was as cool as a cucumber. We were just a team following the others, going to Kiev to negotiate for the exchange of goods that the Bolsheviks needed. We even had papers from the Bolsheviks. Everything was arranged ahead of time. In Moscow, as part of the official delegation to the Ukraine, we got on the train. The first stop was St. Petersburg, where we had a few hours. The control points at the stations were frightening. You went through them before you got on the train, and when you got off. The secret police were everywhere. It was impossible not to feel nervous. The police were ugly-looking people, and they watched everyone. But because everyone was so nervous at these points, one's particular nervousness aroused no suspicion.

At St. Petersburg I could not go to my house, but a messenger picked up a suitcase for me there, with some of my clothes. We were placed in a small reserved compartment, and for a day and a night we rode in style to the German border at Pskov. The train was jammed with returning German prisoners who had been released. They were quiet and subdued.

We got to Pskov early in the morning. Here was the final control point and we were passed through. Then the train began to move, and in two minutes we were across the border in German-occupied territory. As we entered the station, a German brass band began to play in honor of the returning prisoners. The German soldiers, who had been extremely cautious throughout, now dug out army caps and parts of German army uniforms and proudly revealed themselves. After that, we boarded a new train and whizzed south across the German-occupied countryside to Kiev. From there, in more amenable Austrian-held territory we could direct operations to extricate the children.

Prince and Princess Anatole Bariatinsky, he was Catherine's brother-in-law by her first marriage, had an apartment in Kiev. We went there the day we arrived, and they put us up. The Austrians and Ukrainians who occupied the city were polite, but we had the feeling that the place was a volcano. I told Catherine there was no time to be lost. However, I couldn't resist shaving my beard and coming out of my disguise. And so did Catherine.

I went the next day to see General Skoropatsky. At our last meeting he had been present where Eristoff had publicly given me hell for displaying my captured German pennants. Now he was the nominal head of the Ukraine, which would have been overrun by the Bolsheviks in no time had it not been for the Austrian troops and the treaty of Brest-Litovsk. General Skoropatsky received me gravely. He gave the required official permission for Catherine's boys, Andre and Buddy, to cross into the Ukraine from Yalta, with their governess and servants. Yalta had just been taken over by the Germans, and now it was a matter of official travel permits.

While we were waiting for them, word came of a new Bolshevik butchery. At Ekaterinburg in Siberia, the abdicated Emperor, the Empress and their five children, Olga, Tatiana, Marie, Anastasia and the little Czarevitch Alexis were slaughtered. Along with them was Prince Dolgorouky (not the General), an old friend of Father's; Dr. Botkin, physician; a young lady friend of mine, Miss Gendrikoff, a lady in waiting; and the children's old nurse. The order came direct from Lenin. Admiral Kolchak's White contingent in Siberia was a few miles away. The butcher was Youroffsky, who was subsequently killed by one of our officers.

The murder of the Imperial Family took place on July 16, 1918. The next day other members of the family, including Grand Duchess Elizabeth, the pious nun who had so influenced Felix's life, were thrown down a mine shaft. She had been a major threat to the Bolsheviks. After all, she was a holy woman, who had given up absolutely everything for the poor, and the people loved her. They had found it necessary to send her to Siberia as well. When the Whites moved in and threw the Reds out of Ekaterinburg, there was some fantastic evidence of her heroism. She had survived the fall down the shaft. With her legs and arms broken, she had laid out all the others, tearing her clothes to bandage them. She had died, however, by the time Kolchak's troops arrived, in peace, after having performed one last triumphant act of mercy.

The news reached Kiev a few days later. We had a Mass sung for their memory at that time. There was a large group of refugees in Kiev, including several officers of the Chevalier Guards.

The murder of the Emperor had occurred during the anti-Communist uprising at Yaroslavl, which came within an ace of succeeding. It also took place just as the large Czech detachment of war prisoners, which had been armed by the Kerensky government to fight against the Germans, had neutralized the whole of the eastern part of the trans-Siberian railway. In the meantime, the anti-Bolshevik socialist republic had been established in Siberia, and Yudenich was moving in in the north.

After the Mass, we held a meeting of officers of the Chevalier Guards. And it was decided to activate the regiment. General Denikin's movement was forming in the south with the help of the Allies. The idea was to establish contact with Yudenich in the north and Kolchak in Siberia and to gradually squeeze the Bolsheviks into oblivion. We were asked individually if we wanted to rejoin.

This was a hard decision for me to make. At that moment there seemed a better chance than there had ever been to overthrow the Bolsheviks. But everything was so mixed up; everything was fluctuating. Russia was beaten. The Ukraine and the eastern areas were surrendered. The Germans had won. The Allies, not to be outdone, were interesting themselves in Russia, and at the same time the German and Austrian troops were coming under Communist influence. The symptoms of increasing disorder could be felt at Kiev. Skoropatsky was not at all popular. He knew it, and it was a shock to the Russian refugees that he had not attended the memorial service when word was received of the Emperor's death. I had walked a good deal in the streets of Kiev, partly from relief at being able to move about freely. Everywhere among the common people I had sensed sympathy for the Reds. I was even beginning to feel apprehensive that Catherine and I had come out of our disguise.

Even so, it was Catherine and the children that made up my mind. So I said I could not go with Denikin's army. From the time I heard bullets coming from behind me in the Crimean hills, I knew that Russia wasn't prepared to support an anti-Bolshevik movement. It is often thought in the United States that the White armies planned to restore the monarchy. This was not true; we all, generally speaking, supported a constitutional, democratic government against dictatorship of the Bolsheviks. But for the time being the difference meant little to the Russian peasants. They had taken the land; the Bolsheviks had merely to say "Here come the Whites to take the land back," and the peasants became more afraid of the Whites than of the Bolsheviks. And the White movement stupidly took no steps to counteract the propaganda. Doubtless some of those who supported the Whites hoped to regain their estates. I know that I, personally, did not; I thought the only hope was to save Russia, at whatever cost.

I gave my reasons. I said I wished to God I could believe in the White movement, but I was sure it could not succeed until Russia had learned by bitter experience. So they said, "Everyone has to do what he feels."

I'm sure that if I had not been married to Catherine I would have felt differently. But after the experiences in Yalta, and the months in disguise in Moscow, I could not leave her. Her children were coming from the Crimea. I was helping her raise what money she could for them by selling their property in the Ukraine for which she was the trustee. We were able to transfer a substantial amount of money to Switzerland, nothing compared to the intrinsic value of the Bariatinsky property in the Ukraine, but enough to provide a start in life. A great deal more was raised and arrangements were completed for it to be transferred, but through the negligence of the local agent in Kiev it was allowed to remain in the Ukraine until Skoropatsky's government fell, and all funds were confiscated.

We were in Kiev nearly three months. We all lived together in the Bariatinsky flat; Prince and Princess Bariatinsky, ourselves, and Baby Bariatinsky, who later married an Englishman and wrote a book about those days. Prince Bariatinsky's butler, Joseph, was from Monte Carlo, and Joseph's wife did the cooking. Joseph subsequently retired in Monte Carlo, having acquired a considerable fortune.

The Austrian legation in Kiev was housed in the apartment upstairs. The charge d'affaires was my old polo-playing companion Count Chaki, who had been in the Embassy in St. Petersburg. Through him I applied for permission to go to Vienna as our first step toward reaching Switzerland.

More and more refugees were arriving. Catherine and I found an apartment, which we filled with odds and ends of furniture. I spent my time working on the transfer of Catherine's property. My cousin Dimitri Obolensky arrived, and then Aliosha whom I hadn't seen since his convoy of the second order days. Aliosha was three years older than I, and was married to Princess Luba Troubetzkoy, who now as Princess Obolensky runs a ladies' shop on Park Avenue in New York.

Aliosha's real interest had always been music. He had a tremendous bass voice, untrained as yet, and eventually he became a well-known opera singer and concert artist, and a great friend of Chaliapin. But in those days he had only sung in choirs, and his instrument was the violin. Aliosha had showed so much promise in his childhood that Uncle Alexander, my father's younger brother, gave him a Stradivarius. Aliosha had his Stradivarius with him when he reached Kiev. It was all that he escaped with, and his wife had a single string of pearls.

In the fall, about September, Catherine's boys arrived in Kiev, with their governess, Miss Lily Pickens. With the help of Skoropatsky's permits, they had taken the boat to Odessa, then gone by rail to Kiev. With them was Catherine's coachman, an Englishman called Albert Stanard. But what was most surprising was that the chef, Vassily Yourtchenko, was with them also. I have told how Father, when he managed Grand Duke Vladimir's household as aide-de-camp, befriended a young apprentice chef in the Grand Duke's kitchen. That was Vassily, a big, awkward, exceedingly loyal man. Since then he had been highly successful, and eventually became the chef of the Bariatinskys, from whom he came to Catherine.

When he reached Kiev and learned that we were leaving Russia, he begged me to take him along. "The Princess has to eat well," he said simply, "and I know what to prepare for her."

"You're too expensive, Vassily," I said, chuckling. "Things aren't the same any more."

"I will do it more cheaply than it could be done by anyone," he said. After a moment of reflection he added, "And it will be better."

He did as he claimed, providing extraordinarily fine food for less than what ordinary food would have cost if anyone else had prepared it. Meanwhile, we arranged through Chaki that the boys, Catherine, Vassily and I should go to Austria. But Miss Lily and Albert the coachman were English, and Austria and England were still at war. They could not go through.

In the meantime, however, the French had taken Odessa from the Germans. So we got Miss Lily and Albert to that city, where the French passed them through their lines, and they eventually reached England. But now our own chances did not look so good. The atmosphere in Kiev grew worse as the situation in Germany weakened. The German support of General Skoropatsky wobbled. Chaki came through with our permits just in time. If the Germans and Austrians moved out, we would be in another Red slaughter. We were passed through to Vienna just before the Austrian control of the Ukraine collapsed. In fact, we got to Vienna as another revolution, the Austrian revolution, began. In another couple of days, even Chaki's permits would have been empty scraps of paper.

In Vienna everything was quiet, on the surface. We were met by Alfred Potocki, an old friend from English days with Felix and Paul, who entertained us; and we lived at Mme. Sacher's, where Father and I had always stayed when we passed through. Mme. Sacher, too, seemed unchanged—the same determined face, the same gray hair and tight-fitting collar, with the black apron over a voluminous skirt, and the same big bunch of jangling keys on a chain that I could remember from childhood. The food was still good. The hotel was unchanged, very small, a few rooms around a courtyard, the famous restaurant, private dining rooms with Hungarian Tzigane music.

Our Austrian friends were delighted to see us. Countess Liechtenstein—Maritza Liechtenstein, of the family whose castle dominated the tiny country of that name—feted us, as much as that could be done under the difficult conditions of the time. The youngest son of old Count Mensdorff, the former Austro-Hungarian Ambassador to England, entertained us also; and Alfred, for the sake of the boys, took us to the Imperial Austrian stables, where we saw the fantastic array of gilt coaches. Everything had been kept in first-class condition despite the war. The equitation school was flourishing, and we saw the famous white Lippizan horses go through their astonishing routine with the same prewar precision.

But we could sense the revolution coming hourly, as one can sense the coming of a tornado. One could feel the tension build. I felt it while walking the streets—something different in the air. Perhaps it was the change in the attitude of the officers, as though they were constantly on guard. There was an argument behind scenes in the hotel. The waiters had a wage complaint. They refused to serve. Mme. Sacher had her own ways of dealing with things. "Who is the spokesman?" she said, and a waiter slipped forward. He was a new man and shifty-looking.

"Ahah!" she cried. She slapped his face, turned him around, kicked his behind, and said to all the rest, "Tonight we go talk things over. Without *him!*" Then she ordered them all back to work, and they returned.

Next day the Austrian front was collapsing. The troops were running. A few days later when I was in the street I saw a mob forming. I saw the police and the soldiers edging out of its way, as I had seen them doing in Russia a year before. I rushed back to Catherine and said, "Now is the time to get out of here."

We took what we had, and caught a train for the Swiss border, which was jammed with soldiers. At the frontier we were stopped. I had no legal identity. So far as the records went, I was still a Soviet textile expert. But of course with my hair and beard trimmed neatly—I had returned to my mustache. The picture on my Soviet pass didn't even it. Besides, we looked rather shabby, and shabbiness was often revolutionary in those days. The Swiss took a dim view.

Dr. Chumi at the University of Bern was the only person I could think of who could establish my identity. I wired him from the border post, saying, "I must be recognized by you."

The old professor came there the next day. When I met him in the office he looked at me questioningly. Then his face lit up; he recognized me. We talked for a few minutes, and he established my identity positively as Serge Obolensky. The Swiss government accepted his identification.

We all passed over the frontier, the two boys, Vassily the chef, Catherine and I, and the next day the Italian front collapsed and the Austrian revolution began in earnest.

I shall never forget those first few moments in an uncorrupted land. It was one of the most exhilarating sensations I have ever known, just to look upon peaceful fields, the quiet streets and houses of Switzerland, and its solid people going about their daily business. Catherine and I stared open-mouthed at this beautiful, orderly country. It was unbelievable to us, all the more so because we were ourselves again.

Part VI

Exiles

CHAPTER XVIII

The Bernerhof in Bern was one of the diplomatic centers of the world. The diplomats of the belligerent countries lived, ate, and met there. They were all watching each other. The hotel was a center of intrigue, of constant diplomatic struggle. Discussions of one kind or another were going on between the belligerents all the time. The diplomats all knew each other, met constantly, and, when they came into the dining room, passed each other and did not speak. I was told there were spies and counterspies of every nation there. I didn't notice any.

We were just a refugee family without papers. But I was very lucky to find that my cousin, Mika Bibikoff was in Bern as charge d'affaires of the Kerensky government, and he naturally knew the whole of the diplomatic corps. And then there was another piece of good fortune. The consul general of Russia under the Kerensky government had been the consul general of the Imperial government before. He was a Mr. A. Onou, who had been in the ministry of foreign affairs, and had worked for years under my Uncle Valerian. The Swiss government had refused to recognize the Bolshevik regime. Between them they were able to get passports for all of us. As I had my own bank account in the bank at Bern, and Catherine had been able to transfer her money to Switzerland, we were able to move around, and received permission to reside in Switzerland.

We wanted to begin knitting the broken threads of life into a new pattern. Catherine's boys had gone to school irregularly ever since the war began, and the first problem was to start their education. But the diplomatic struggles that centered in Bern made it hardly the place to start living a peaceful life, or to begin school. I remember walking up toward one of the mountains one evening soon after our arrival, and coming to a pavilion, a sort of shelter. Inside it was a sign:

"THE RUSSIAN REVOLUTION BEGAN HERE"

It was a place that Lenin had frequented during his exile in Switzerland.

We went to Lausanne, where we stayed in the Savoy Hotel. It seemed more than comfortable after years away from anything of the sort, a big, old-fashioned hotel surrounded by gardens and tennis courts. At night we gathered in the lounge or on the terrace, overlooking a wild ravine beyond which lay a magnificent panorama of the Alps and the lake. Around in the wicker chairs, like so many portraits of ancestors, were stately widows, countesses, marquises, each with some impoverished kinswoman of advanced years to help care for her.

Grand Duchess Helen of Russia—then Princess Nicholas of Greece who only died two years ago—with Prince Nicholas and their three daughters were at the hotel. And there too was the Grand Duchess Anastasia Mikhailovna, the mother of Crown Princess Cecilia of Mecklenburg-Schwerin. She was a charming old lady, most gracious, who had had many admirers in her early years, including the Kaiser. As she felt herself to be Russian, she had lived in Switzerland during the war, not wanting to live in Germany while Germany and Russia were at war. A relative of mine was there also, the Marquise Paulucci, who was a cousin of Mother's. In my very early childhood, Miss Lizzie used to take me to visit her and her mother at Easter and Christmas. Paulucci, who was an officer of the Chevalier Guards, had married a Russian, and their daughter was an elegant product of Paris. She lived most of the time in the Ritz in Paris or in Switzerland, and had a great deal of money invested abroad. Consequently, unlike most Russians of the time, she was not worried as far as her income and livelihood were concerned.

As for Grand Duchess Helen and Prince Nicholas, they were in an uncomfortable situation with people from the Allied countries, where many of their friends lived, because the Queen of Greece was Kaiser Wilhelm's sister, and Greece had preserved her neutrality with great difficulty. Their lives were principally taken up with their children, then small girls, Olga, Wolly and Marina, the future Duchess of Kent.

At night, as I say, we all gathered in the hotel lounge after dinner and played parlor games. Catherine's boys were now in the Ecole Nouvelle in Lausanne. By an odd coincidence, as we were preparing their schooling I heard that my old tutor, Mr. Nicolle, had become a prominent Swiss educator. He was a professor of archaeology at the University of Geneva across the lake, where his father was a famous authority of ancient Egyptian art. We called on him. He and his father gave a luncheon for Catherine and me. Mr. Nicolle had married an extremely wealthy woman, and the lunch was impressive. He entertained us with anecdotes of the misbehavior of the Tolstoy boys and myself when he had been our unfortunate tutor in his early years of hardship.

Over Christmas, Catherine and I went to Gstad to ski and stayed there a month. Coming down from the mountain one evening I found a group of Russian officers, in uniform, at the hotel. Tanka Knoring, Serge Rodzianko and two of the Chihatchoff brothers from the Chevalier Guards had not only gotten out of Russia, but were still in their uniforms. They were on their way to different places. Tanka was going to Finland, where he became a Finnish citizen. Serge had a job training horses on a Canadian ranch; and the Chihatchoffs, shortening their name to Chercheff, settled in England—but we had one great day tobogganing down the slides before we separated to meet our respective destinies. Tanka was, of course, our anchor man.

Catherine and I were waiting to hear when, if ever, the French government was going to give us permission to enter France. We had applied for permits to visit Princess Yourievsky in Nice. Anything involving so much red tape meant endless delays and frustration, questions, papers, more proofs of identity. So we simply waited, enjoying being in a country that was rolling with prosperity.

During the winter the mountains were sparkling with the frost in the air, and the hotel was very gay. Sofieka Roidi, the lady in waiting of Grand Duchess Helen, wanted me to read her fortune. Carlo Purcell and Bertie Stopford had both been such fanatical fortune tellers that I had a pretty good idea of the various ways it was done with cards, tea leaves, and the lines in the palms of a hand. I took Sofieka's delicate little hand in my own, determined to find for her the happiest future I could think of. It seemed to me likely that the biggest problem that absorbed her was obvious, and so I said gravely, "I see, Sofieka, that you are going to marry." She was pleased to hear it, quite willing to believe it, and she was so charming that I had no doubt that the world cataclysm would indeed become overwhelming if some enterprising youth did not claim her. I went confidently on, prophesying a most happy marriage, a tall, blond husband—I had already learned she secretly aspired to a blond husband—travel, dances, parties, and as many good things in life as I dared foresee in the times we lived through.

"When am I going to marry?" she asked, looking at her own life line.

"Very soon."

"And will I have any children?"

"Yes."

"How many?"

"Two."

At this point something warned me that the future was appearing too rosy, and it was not a good game to deceive these young people about their hazardous futures. "But I see trouble, too."

"What is it?"

"I see a divorce. You will part from your first husband. . . . She looked so pained that I added hastily, "But you will marry again, just as happily."

Political changes were beginning to happen fast, but for most of us there was nothing to do but to be patient and wait. The Armistice scarcely changed our lives. We read about it in the paper. But later I heard that Sofieka, in the heady excitement of those first days of peace, met at St. Moritz a handsome young Hollander who had taken advantage of the Armistice to get in the siding that four years of war had deprived him of. They fell in love. They became engaged. Then, life having been speeded up, they married, and went on to a happy future in The Netherlands that I would hardly have dared prophesy. Still later I met her in Europe, and she had two children. Ten years later I met her again. "Yes," she said, without my asking. "I'm getting a divorce. And I'm marrying again."

Then one fine winter day the permission arrived. Catherine was overwhelmed with anxiety lest something else go wrong. I pointed out to her that, having crossed all of Russia in disguise, it was not likely that we would meet with any difficulty in the peaceful confines of a friendly country. Catherine had a temperament that was magnificent in adversity, but it was the petty annoyance of everyday life that she could never cope with. So we hurried to our train, and there, by God, in our very compartment, sat the old Grand Duchess Anastasia Mikhailovna, with all her luggage, and her personal maid. That is how we traveled to the French frontier.

"Madame," I said, "I trust that your permit is in order."

"Permit?" she said. "What is that?" This was the end of that conversation.

We found out later that the Grand Duchess was actually traveling under her Russian passport as the aunt of the late Emperor Nicholas. Tactfully, she made no mention of her German connection. She told us she had heard we were going to Catherine's mother. She had decided to come along, and that was that.

Catherine was very disturbed. She drew me aside and said, "I hope they won't stop me because of that."

At the border, there was no mistaking it, something was brewing. Various civil authorities had gathered on the platform. They were throwing their hands about wildly and arguing. They held a long consultation, and at last, obviously selecting the bravest of them, came in and tried to persuade the Grand Duchess to get off the train. She wouldn't budge. "I am going to see my cousin, Princess Yourievsky," she said, and, pointing to me, "There is her son-in-law. They all have permits, and I am traveling with them." I thought the French handled it very well, by the simple expedient of giving her a two-week permit.

At Nice I had my first meeting with Princess Yourievsky as her son-in-law. She was a truly astonishing woman. She was at least seventy then, but did not show it. She hardly appeared to be more than forty, but she was not well. Her only son, Catherine's brother, had died shortly before the war; most of her contemporaries were gone; and she now lived completely in the past, the Bolshevik Revolution scarcely seeming real to her. She still had a little money—a lot of money, in fact, by our modern standards—which she was spending as lavishly as ever.

She took an immediate liking to me and told me so. I do not know what her relations with Catherine's first husband, Prince Bariatinsky, had been, but in my case she could not have been nicer. She was extremely intelligent, very gracious, but her life had stopped with the death of the Emperor. She had cut off her hair at that time. She always wore the same type of mauve dress. She kept fine horses, and drove daily, no matter how she felt, to a small villa in the hills where all her pet dogs were buried. She still maintained her salon, and she had the graves of the dogs carefully tended—little friends who had provided her with companionship in her long exile.

She couldn't sleep. So I used to come in to her room in the evenings and talk with her until late at night. It was a fascinating time. I put questions to her about her salon, the reign of the Emperor, and what Alexander II was aiming at, his reforms, and what his ministers were like, and the background of the changes in Russia that Alexander was putting through. She loved to talk of those days.

Actually my own hero in the ranks of the Russian Emperors was not Alexander II, but his grandfather, Alexander I. One of the great problems that preoccupied the imagination of the Russians of my generation was the question of whether Alexander I had really died in 1825. I was one of those who believed that he had not. Alexander I came back from Paris after the defeat of Napoleon with the world at his feet. It's a very interesting thing, and quite revealing of our Russian mental processes, that Alexander I really believed that Napoleon had duped him. He had hero-worshiped Napoleon. And as Napoleon had been one of those men who did not always keep his word, Alexander I interpreted Napoleon's double cross after the Treaty of Tilsit as a personal slight. He resented the fact that Napoleon had gotten the better of him by promising him something that he didn't do and had no intention of doing. From that point on, he decided to destroy Napoleon. It became his purpose in life.

When the Allies met in Paris, Alexander I was a young man, in his early thirties, and in spite of what the history books relate, I believe that he had much more to say about what was to be done than the English or the Austrians. All the works that have been devoted to Waterloo, and the escape from Elba, have obscured the fact that Napoleon was really destroyed in Russia, and that it was Alexander I who destroyed him. Napoleon's escape from Elba, and the Hundred Days, were the last hopeless efforts in a war that was already lost, and Napoleon's second defeat at Waterloo gave the British an authority in the peace that followed which they had not had after Napoleon's defeat in Russia.

The great moment of Alexander's life occurred when he entered Paris after Napoleon's Russian debacle. He was the master of Europe. And when he went back to Russia, St. Petersburg must have become very dull. So he conceived his great plans for liberalizing Russia, plans that he was never able to achieve. He grew embittered with his discoveries of plots and intrigues against him; he grew increasingly mystical; and in the little city of Taganrog, on the Sea of Azov, far from his capital, he fell ill and died. His remains were sent back to the burial place of the Czars.

But the great question was, did he really die? Someone who closely resembled him in stature died about the same time. The Emperor had often expressed a wish to retire to a monastery, and become a hermit. And a little later a holy man appeared in Siberia—someone who looked like Alexander I, who lived in a monastery in a very secluded place and won the respect of the people who came on pilgrimages to be blessed by him. A legend grew that this holy man was Alexander. Now, the problem in Russia was this: So long as an Emperor was alive, it did not matter if another claimant had been crowned and been blessed by the Church as the Emperor. He was still no Emperor. The first was still the ruler of Russia. If Alexander I had retired to the monastery, what was the position of the Emperors who came after him? Of Nicholas I with his period of reaction, and the building of the Russian military machine that came to disaster in the Crimean War? Of Alexander II who came into power at the end of the war, and began the great program of domestic reform? Of Alexander III who became Emperor in the midst of the terror and chaos that came on the day the Nihilists threw the bombs that killed Princess Yourievsky's husband?

Were they really Emperors of Russia? The peasants to a great extent believed the story that Alexander I didn't die at Taganrog. Many of them made pilgrimages to Siberia to be blessed by the holy man they believed was the real Emperor. One curious thing gave me a kind of family interest in this ancient Russian mystery. Uncle Vladimir, my father's brother who died when I was little more than an infant, was aide-de-camp to Alexander III, and a man the Emperor trusted and liked. He was in the court when word was received of the death of the holy man in Siberia. And with word of his death came a sealed box of papers, to be opened only by the Emperor himself. Among them was a gold cross with a particle of wood from the True Cross, which only the sons of the Emperors of Russia were given, handed on from generation to generation.

Whatever the meaning of the gift and the papers, the Emperor spent the whole night reading the letters and burning them all, one by one. So Uncle Vladimir said. Because the mystery was being discussed, Emperor Alexander III decided to open the casket of Alexander I, and see if there was a body there. The story was that he opened it, and saw the body, but an alabaster mask covered the head. He ordered it closed again, saying, "I cannot go any further."

After the Revolution, the Bolsheviks opened the tomb. It was empty. The body was an effigy, with the mask for the face. So again the question of whether Alexander I had really died at Taganrog was something that Russians were thinking about.

And as Princess Yourievsky and I talked in the winter evenings in her Mediterranean villa, I asked her about Alexander II, and what his opinions had been on these matters. Once I asked her point-blank: "What did the Emperor tell you about the holy man in Siberia? Was he Alexander I, or not?"

She smiled, and said very pleasantly, "It was merely someone who looked very much like the Emperor."

There was one point about that story that impressed me tremendously, and which I had never heard pointed out. Vagrant tramps who went to Siberia in those days received twenty lashes before being exiled. If the Emperor had become a holy man, and had consciously planned to retire from the world and his throne, he also must have deliberately planned to be a vagrant and must have endured those twenty lashes before he set out.

From the time in Paris after Napoleon's defeat, when the young Emperor of Russia had really come as close to being the ruler of the world as anyone, to the time when he was tied to a stake somewhere on the road to exile, being flogged by one of his own officers of his own kingdom—that formed a picture in my imagination that haunted me then, and has interested me all my life. Princess Yourievsky, while she told me of many things beyond what our records show of Alexander II's personal life and opinions, had nothing to say on this question. I was disappointed in her answer, and tried to get her to say more, but she merely repeated that the holy man who was thought to be Alexander I was someone who looked like the Emperor.

CHAPTER XIX

I have never liked to gamble. It is not that I have any prejudice against it, or that I disapprove, or have lost heavily. It is just that I never held the cards, or never had a run of luck, and it is tiring. However, in Nice at some time or other everyone gambles, and one night I stopped at the Casino and placed the money I had on the table. I had around two hundred francs, perhaps the equivalent of thirty-five dollars as the franc was then valued.

It was amazing. I couldn't lose. I played the red and the black, and my two hundred francs became four hundred and then eight hundred and then sixteen hundred. Then I began to play more seriously. I made quite a lot of money on those two hundred francs. A crowd gathered. The regulars began collecting around me and following my bets. Anything I put them on came out. I went off with quite a lot of money, about twenty thousand francs. The next morning I bought a car, a Peugeot, a pretty good car for those days, which cost me the equivalent of several thousand dollars. With it Catherine and I spent a lovely month driving around the south of France and loafing in the winter sunshine.

It was a very strange time, that period immediately after the war. We heard all sorts of stories about what had happened, but we really knew very little about where anyone was, and who was safe, or dead.

I had rented my old flat in the Albany in London to Paul of Serbia, and I heard that he still occupied it. The fates of my Oxford friends were entirely unknown to me. The last Englishman I had seen was Bertie Stopford who had managed to get out of Russia with his brief case loaded with jewels. Being completely separated from everyone I had known made me uncomfortable; I wanted to find work of some sort that would bring me back into the main stream of life.

Catherine's own plans for the future were simple. She wanted to follow the ambition she had always held, to become a concert singer. Artistically her voice was lovely, a contralto; she had beautiful high notes and a marvelous mezzo voice. She tried it, but eventually the strain on her heart of singing professionally was too much for her. She had a first mild heart attack. She had no choice but to stop. But the poignancy of her singing was remarkable, perhaps for that very reason, and when she gave her first concert in London in December of 1919 the London Times said, I think quite accurately, "The Princess, who possesses a mezzo voice of considerable charm and quality, was heard to advantage in Russian ballads."

Mme. Litvin, the most famous Russian singer of the time, was in Nice. She befriended Catherine, helped her and assisted with her training. They became great friends. Early in the morning the villa resounded with the incessant trills and runs and high notes repeated over and over in the music room.

I still wanted a job. I recognized that I might have trouble getting one. My training was in agriculture and in estate management, and there was no opening in Nice. Time was passing, the armies were being demobilized, jobs were scarce, and the areas of unrest were spreading. The outlook was daily growing worse. I told Catherine I'd better go to Paris and try. One morning I sold the car, took all the money I raised on it, and went. Catherine stayed in Nice and continued with her voice lessons. Meanwhile, I thought I might find something to do dealing with agricultural machinery, which I had practical experience in operating.

On my first morning in Paris I bumped into John de Salis. What was even stranger was that John was well-groomed, although he had little choice, being in the uniform of a British officer. He had even grown thinner; and I might not have recognized him if we had not come face to face; I suppose I had changed as much.

We greeted each other with the usual expressions of astonishment that follow the meetings of people who have never expected to see each other again. He said, "Well, my God, old boy, what are you doing here?"—things like that. I said I was going to the Ritz to register. He said, "Clever boy! But don't stay there. It is expensive. Come over to the flat. Cuthbert and I have an apartment."

I thought I could not possibly have heard him rightly. People were passing by in the fresh Paris morning, and the phantasmagoric quality of the meeting was intensified because I was remembering a dream I had when I first joined the regiment in East Prussia—I had been dreaming that I was in the Ritz in Paris when I was sleeping in a school that had been shelled, and was awakened by someone slapping a pair of gloves across my face. "I thought you said Cuthbert," I said confusedly. "You mean Cuthbert Holmes?"

"Yes," John said. "We have our digs over here a ways."

It was exactly like going to our digs on High Street in Oxford. I thought that every moment we would run into Carlo Purcell and L. G. Brown, and then I would wake up. John seemed different, more serious and older; not quite the same person I had known. He told me that I had lost some weight and probably my sense of humor. I said, "Yes, and I've grown taller." This was such an unexpected remark, even to myself, that he began to chuckle; but the fact was, for some obscure physiological reason, I kept on growing until I was twenty-five years old. During adolescence I had grown like a weed to just under six feet tall; then my height continued to increase slowly until I measured six feet three inches or so, though I was no heavier than I had been before.

"Well, don't worry about it," John said heartily, as I explained the circumstances. My theory was that cavalry training had been partly responsible. He explained to me that he and Cuthbert were assigned to duties at the peace conference. Then he told me that Cuthbert had done very well indeed. He had served throughout the war with him in the Irish Guards, and was now a major, and a most important individual these days. Carlo Purcell was dead. He and L. G. Brown went into the Irish Guards in 1916. L. G. rose through the ranks to Lieutenant Colonel, and died of wounds in France in a base hospital just before the end of the war. At the outbreak of the war, Carlo was killed in action.

As for himself, John explained, with his familiar absent-minded air, and his puckish humor, he was just a sort of footman at the peace conference, running errands and ghost-writing speeches. He had got into the war at the start, and was assigned to special duty in the Balkans. His father, old Count de Salis, the diplomat, was as irritated with him as ever. John's family was originally Swiss. If I remember rightly, it had been, way back, an Irish-English family that migrated to Switzerland; then John's father returned to England, married a Belgian princess, and became a fixture in the Foreign Office. It was a Catholic family, and John's brothers followed the family traditions, but John himself was the complete black sheep, the old Count strongly disapproving of his unconventional behavior and, even more, of his careless dress. In any event, the De Salis family still owned property in Switzerland. They had a villa in Maloja Pass. Because John was so often in his father's bad graces, he was kept on short funds, given as little money as possible, with the result that he had to live in Maloja Pass for long periods of time.

Cuthbert was not at the apartment, but busied amongst books and papers was a tall, handsome girl, Irene Boyle, one of the secretaries of the British delegation at the peace conference. On the tables and on the floor, scattered everywhere around the rooms, even in the loo, were the works of Napoleon and Talleyrand. They were opened at various places and underscored, with objects placed on the books to mark the passages John wanted. Each pile represented some speech that John was writing. He explained to me that no Englishman had ever written better than himself on European affairs. "After all, dear Serge," he said, "it's hopeless to try to improve on the words of Napoleon's astute minister of foreign affairs!" Therefore, whenever an important address had to be delivered by the British statesman he served, John merely clipped appropriate paragraphs from Talleyrand, translated them, and presented them to the statesman concerned as Britain's considered opinion on the problems before the peace conference. "Here! Look," he said. "Lloyd George said this yesterday. It all fits him perfectly!"

John, however, talked about it much too much. It wasn't long before they fired him.

Meanwhile he was serving as military secretary to Lord Derby, who was one of the prominent members of the British delegation. I moved into a spare room with John and Cuthbert, and began malting my contribution to world peace by going to a lot of parties and luncheons. This sounds facetious, but in fact there were social gatherings constantly. Miss Boyle, who was always called Boylie, and the other young women of the delegation were required to be present at these functions and needed escorts. Boylie was a great waltzer, and we often danced together. There were many young Englishwomen in Paris at that time: Lord Hardinge's daughter, I remember; and Victoria Stanley, Lord Derby's daughter, who was already a widow, her husband, Neil Primrose, having been killed in action in Mesopotamia.

In our more serious moments, John, Cuthbert and I talked about what had happened to our mutual friends during the war. I learned that there were many of them I would never see again. Those who had survived had, in general, covered themselves with glory. They were now going on with their education, or were remaking the careers the war had interrupted. Bobberty Cranborne married Betty Cavendish during the war. He was a distinguished lieutenant of the Grenadier Guards. Eric Ednam was a lieutenant in the Tenth Hussars, a cavalryman who served throughout the war. Just about that time, in March of 1919, he was marrying Rosemary Levenson-Gower. Timothy Eden was now Sir Timothy—he had succeeded his father in 1915, while he was a German prisoner—he had been confined for the first two years of the war. That sort of thing occupied us by the hour.

We also talked about the Crimea, and about the Russian Revolution. The peace conference was being criticized for failing to aid the different White armies. Grand Duke Alexander, the father of Irina Youssoupoff, had made his way to France to appeal to the heads of the Allied governments, but Clemenceau would not receive him, and he was not even permitted to enter England. I myself could not take an optimistic view of the prospects for the White armies, with or without Allied aid. So long as the Russian peasants feared that the coming of the Whites meant the return of the land to the landowner, they would not support the Whites, no matter how greatly they feared the Bolsheviks. The result was that the White armies, after their initial successes, bogged down in country where they had no support, and where they could not possibly get support so long as the peasants believed they meant to take back the land. In the south, Denikin's army was already pushing up from the Crimea, and making good progress. The worst of it was that by and large, the Allies still did not take the Bolsheviks seriously, and expected they would be overthrown. The brilliant military successes of Denikin and Yudenich and others, operating with small and inadequately equipped forces, and really dependent on superb generalship and the self-sacrifice of their troops, inadvertently contributed to Europe's conviction that the Bolsheviks were weak, and could not maintain power.

John de Salis was keenly interested. He had a lightning perception of what was involved. He quoted to me Talleyrand, who had always maintained that a parliamentary government was the right one and who felt that his duty, when the French Revolution and the reign of Napoleon made parliamentary government impossible, was to try to remain in office and moderate the policies of the dictator as much as he could until democracy could be established. The long-range result of these talks with John was that he departed for the Crimea to serve as a British military observer with Denikin's army. I briefed him with everything I knew about the terrain, the personalities and the military prospects and the political situations involved.

I was still trying to get a job. About the end of April I decided I could remain in Paris no longer, and bought a ticket to London. Just before leaving I met Nancy Leeds. Nancy was then the fiancée of Prince Christopher of Greece, and had a beautiful house in Rome near the Colosseum. She asked me if I would chaperon her son, young Billy Leeds, who was then about sixteen, back across the Channel to return him to school in England. I said certainly I'd do it. So we went off, and Billy and I had a big lunch on the Blue Train.

"Do you want to eat that much, Billy?" I asked. He was tucking it in at a tremendous rate. "The weather's not so good."

"Oh," said Billy, "I'm a good sailor. Nothing gets me."

It was Saturday evening, April 27, 1919. We got on the Channel boat in sullen weather. From the polar regions seventy-mile-an-hour winds swept across the British Isles. They struck the Channel at about seven o'clock in the evening. A blinding snow accompanied the storm, covering England with a couple of feet of snow. Conditions, said the British authorities later, were exceptional. Our boat stood on its beam-ends and corkscrewed. I was horribly ill, but young Bill Leeds spent the entire night in the men's room. When we got into Dover the next day, I told him he'd better have a gigantic breakfast like his lunch the day before.

I stayed at the Ritz in London. My flat at the Albany was rented in turn from Paul of Serbia to my old friend Jean de Ribes, who was the third attaché at the French Embassy, and he came to my rescue and put me up. Now how does one go about looking for a job in a line of work for which one has no professional experience? I talked over the prospects with everybody I knew. Jean was not very practical, and couldn't advise me. He was Count de Ribes, one of the most wonderful snobs that ever lived, terribly funny about it, and admittedly impossible. He was in love with Marie Antoinette, which was not very fruitful for him. He had her slipper in a little glass case and he carried this with him always, spending all his time studying about her and collecting things related to her. Anybody less noble was almost outside the pale to him. When he met Walter Dalkeith at a party he drew me aside and asked anxiously, "This Buccleuch, who is he? Does one know him?" I explained as well as I could that Walter was the Duke of Buccleuch, and then I added, "It is believed that one of his ancestors was an illegitimate child of Charles II." That made Walter all right with Jean. He placed his monocle in his eye, beaming, and from then on he and Walter were on the best of terms.

Anyone with that outlook on the world couldn't be expected to be of much help in finding a job. I saw Bobberty Cranborne, whose parents, Lord and Lady

Salisbury, very kindly asked me to come and live with them. Their house was next door to the Ritz itself, and I occupied a small room on the top floor for a couple of weeks until I explored the chances of doing something with agricultural machinery. Then Emerald Cunard, when she heard of my problem, said she would bring me together with Sir Basil Zaharoff, who would certainly be able to find something for me to do.

At that time Sir Basil Zaharoff was still generally viewed as Europe's man of mystery. He was Greek by birth and believed to be the richest man in the world. He had a large bloc of Vickers, the munitions firm, which in turn owned an unknown number of British enterprises of all kinds. Emerald prepared one of her famous luncheons.

Emerald's luncheons were an institution. She made a practice of getting together people of different political parties, or of opposing views on current questions, surrounding them with interested spectators which for them she realized was important. At the termination of the luncheon, she would call upon them to express their opinions on the most controversial matter of the moment. I recollect at one of these luncheons I attended, Sean Leslie and the Chancellor of the Exchequer, Sir Robert Horne, at the height of differences over the Irish question, faced each other over the table while Emerald asked questions whose answers, if made public, would have provided sizzling political material for the partisans of both sides. I must say they carried it off very adroitly, tactfully appearing to appreciate their hostess' interest and avoiding fisticuffs; and eventually both sought a solid haven, steering the discussion to the subject of the influence of Catholicism in Irish history. These luncheons at Emerald's were great fun. I always enjoyed them.

The luncheon with Sir Basil Zaharoff was but another of Emerald's strokes of kindly genius. Sir Basil was elderly, thin, with a gray goatee, very soft-spoken, gentle, and concerned. What's more, he looked like the richest man in the world. With him was the Bourbon princess, the Duchess of Parma, who accompanied him everywhere. His enemies asserted that he kept her with him as a symbol of his power. He had come from humble beginnings. He was most friendly, and when we met he shook my hand for a long time, looking at me keenly. "I give you my handshake," he said. "It brings people hick." During the lunch he expressed interest in the talk of Russia, and told me about his early life in Odessa; and before it was over Emerald found an opportunity to explain that I was looking for a job. Zaharoff gave me an introduction to Sir Francis Barker, who was president of Vickers and of a number of its subsidiary companies.

Sir Francis was also president of the British-Russian Club. He was in the news at that time, because of speeches he had been making, in his capacity as president, on the dangers of Bolshevism. He received me most cordially, and told me of Vickers' plans for reorganizing from its wartime expansion to the perspectives of peace. The upshot of our talk was that I was to become attached to one of Vickers' subsidiary firms, manufacturing grain-handling machinery, the Robert Boby Company. The firm also made machinery for breweries. I went through the Boby factory to see for myself the manufacture of our equipment, and I went to the office each day by tube, and studied the various prospects in the British Isles who might be inclined to purchase our equipment for conveying the produce of the field up an inclined conveyor, into a silo, or grain into elevators, or into the vats of breweries and distilleries.

CHAPTER XX

All through the period of escape from Russia, hiding in Moscow, and all the rest of it, my health had remained good, generally speaking, at least in the sense that after periods of starvation and hardship I bounced back immediately with no more treatment required than a few good meals and a few days' rest. But now that I felt myself to be safe, all the accumulated disorders of five years of unbroken strain came to a head. Their principal effect was headache, the aftermath of the shell shock, and in consequence I lived quietly during these first months in London.

While I searched for a house for Catherine I lived part of the time with Felix Youssoupoff at his Knightsbridge flat, which he had kept ever since he arrived in England a decade earlier, after his brother's death. To me it was perhaps the most colorful place in London. When Felix and Irina were on their honeymoon in Egypt and Jerusalem, Felix had acquired a slim Abyssinian servant named Tesphé who wore a tarboosh and added an exotic quality to surroundings which were already pretty much that way.

Tesphé was an extraordinary man. He was well educated and, of all things, was a member of the Eastern Orthodox Church. He had committed some crime or other in his native land, and fled to Jerusalem. While he was in hiding there, Felix and Princess Irina had passed by in a kind of religious procession that the Greek Orthodox colony in Jerusalem had organized, and Tesphé ran through the crowd, threw himself at their feet, and begged them to take him with them to save his life.

Felix did so. Despite Princess Irina's disapproval, he smuggled Tesphé out, became attached to him, and kept him with him always. Tesphé was devoted to him. He was intelligent, very well-informed, completely fearless, and utterly loyal to Felix. He had lived in the Youssoupoff palace in St. Petersburg, and stayed with Felix throughout the years of war, following Felix into exile when Felix was sent to the Caucasus after Rasputin's murder. He remained when the Soviets took over the job of guarding Felix in his imprisonment, when he was daily threatened with death, and he stayed with his master after the Germans came to the Crimea, leaving with him when Felix was taken out with the Dowager Empress on the British dreadnought Marlborough after the Armistice. Now Tesphé was the principal functionary of Felix's establishment at 15 Parkside Street in Knightsbridge.

In spite of Felix's own account of the murder of Rasputin, in which he took full responsibility and described how he had personally committed the crime, I came to believe that it must have been Tesphé who had prepared the poisoned drinks that were given to the mad monk. I had the feeling that it was really Tesphé who finally finished him off. Felix was such a gentle soul that I could not picture him coldbloodedly acting as he described himself acting. On the other hand, Tesphé would have done anything for him, and while Felix's position made him immune from prosecution by the ordinary authorities, Tesphé would have been executed outright. So I suspected that Tesphé had done the job at Felix's request, and Felix had taken the responsibility to save him.

At any rate, with Tesphé, Felix, Irina and others including a bizarre array of gipsies, and myself, we were a crowded household. The Russian evenings began almost as in the old days. Diana Manners was still among the group, and so were others of her generation—Eileen Sutherland, the Duchess of Sutherland; Freda Ward, a cousin of Eric Ednam's; Sheila Loughborough, who was Freda's close friend; Terence Phillips, whose family had owned the two big department stores in Russia, in both St. Petersburg and Moscow, and who spoke Russian fluently. And there were others, varied people interested in hearing the Russian gipsy songs: Juliet Duff, who loved our parties; Mrs. Hwfa Williams and her friends from artistic circles—even a few Russians.

I remember the evening after I had been hired by Sir Francis Barker. I came in filled with elation, and there, playing the guitar for one of the gipsy singers, was Uncle Kotia, whom I had last seen when I landed on top of him at Yalta. He grinned when he saw me and went right on playing his guitar.

It may have been that night that Felix was robbed. For we had made it an excuse for a big party, celebrating our escape from the Bolsheviks. Uncle Kotia was an excellent guitar player. He was a short, fat, round man, with a ready smile and a great store of songs. He also by now had a dressmaking shop and was prospering. It was all very pleasant, and only friends were there, but when it ended, Felix discovered a packet of gems was missing.

Felix had managed to get quite a bit of property out of Russia, besides the two Rembrandts. Most of the Youssoupoff jewels were still under the stairs of the house in Moscow, but Felix had smuggled out many smaller stones, and had about a hundred diamonds in his Knightsbridge flat. They were not tremendously valuable, but were still worth many thousands of pounds, both Cape and Brazilian diamonds of varied value and quality. They were all loose stones, having been taken out of their settings. Preparing to put them in safe deposit, Felix had divided them into packets, ranged roughly according to size and value, with many jewels in each. Then he placed all the packets in a single envelope, and locked them in a drawer. Among them was a string of very valuable black pearls.

Felix place was so crowded in those days that I slept in the sitting room on a bed couch. Vassily, our chef, had arrived, and cooked for us. Both Felix and I had begun to lose our hair, and we had a barber who came in regularly and massaged our scalps. Vassily watched the barber carefully and presently drew me aside and said it was a waste of money—he could do that for nothing, as a part of his regular duties. So he massaged our scalps. Felix said, "He always makes me feel he's pounding a cutlet."

Felix had been occupied with his hair on Monday, and there was a party at the flat that night. The jewels in his desk disappeared; nothing else was taken. For some reason the story got exaggerated into a rumor that the stones were part of the Russian crown jewels. It became so much a topic of discussion that a week or so later Scotland Yard issued a formal announcement: "The diamonds reported as having been stolen were the absolute property of Prince Felix Youssoupoff himself. They had been in the family for many years, and had nothing whatsoever to do with the late Czar's jewels."[1]

The police got nowhere, and we all were suspects. The thief had to be one of the staff, or one of us, me, or another guest, or one of the people at the party. So Felix began by a process of elimination to figure out who it must be. He analyzed each of us, and the exact events and placement of people at the party. By and by he decided in his own mind who it must have been. Then he gave another party, and had his suspect there. When the party was well along, he asked the man he thought guilty to come into the room where the desk was. He sat him down where the thief must have sat when he opened the drawer. The man began to sweat. Felix opened the drawer and pointed inside. Then he walked away. And after a time the packet of jewels was replaced in the desk drawer. Felix did not bring charges against him.

This was a time when much confusion was being caused by strange figures who appeared, on the international scene. The Bolsheviks were constantly claiming that members of the nobility had come over to their ranks. In truth, I knew of only one of our friends and associates who joined them, a member of the staff of the Foreign Office who remained at his post. The others escaped, or were dead or in prison. But a fairly important Bolshevik functionary adopted the name of Prince Michael Obolensky, and actually served as a Bolshevik emissary to Poland—or more exactly went to Poland as ambassador, but Marshal Pilsudski refused to receive him. And another commissar took the name of Obolensky, one of the group that fell into disfavor because of more liberal inclinations in the early days of the Soviet government.

In London itself there was a strange character who went by the name of Prince Serge Obolensky, or Prince Michael Obolensky. He was my age, claimed to have lived in St. Petersburg, and to have served in the British army during the war with the rank of major, a disguise he kept up successfully until, in the middle of 1921, he was arrested for I don't know what. In the investigation following his arrest, the police announced that he had actually served through the war with the British army, as a private, under the name of Wellesley; but he then claimed to have been in an insane asylum throughout the war, and dropped out of sight.

---

[1] *London Times*, October 18, 1919.

He crossed my path early, but I did not know it. Sir Francis and Lady Barker had been very kind; I was at their home for dinner on a few occasions, and we came to know each other. My work took me to English cities in connection with grain-moving equipment being installed at docks. While I was away, Lady Barker was told that Prince Serge Obolensky was calling. She told the butler to show Serge in. When he came in she found Prince Serge Obolensky, a short, thin, nervous individual, very well-dressed, wearing a monocle, and speaking with a broad English accent and, simultaneously, with a pronounced foreign intonation.

"I beg your pardon," said Lady Barker, "I thought the butler said Serge Obolensky."

"I am Prince Serge Obolensky," said this apparition.

"But there must be some mistake; Serge only recently left here."

"That is my brother," he said.

"Your brother! But Serge didn't say his brother was here!"

"It is a Russian custom. We do not speak of family things."

Nonplused, Lady Barker murmured, "Isn't it strange? . . . But I thought you said you were Serge."

"I am Serge."

"But his name is Serge!"

"We are both named Serge. It is an old Russian custom to give brothers the same name."

Lady Barker excused herself. She thought the stranger looked pale and hungry. After thinking it over she gave him ten pounds, saying she understood the hardships of being a refugee, and he hurriedly left.

I heard of him directly a little later when I got a bill for a substantial amount from a tailor. I never had debts in England. At Oxford I ran a few bills, the tailor, and expenses of the horses, which the estate automatically took care of, but I actually spent little money in those days, and the people I knew were not extravagant as a matter of taste. So the quite unexpected bill for clothing was a shocker. I was put to enormous trouble. The stranger claimed to have been to Eton and Oxford, at Magdalen College. For a time I was kept busy writing to the president of Magdalen College, answering protests about bogus claims affecting that ancient institution. And friends of friends of mine were often reporting odd things about Serge Obolensky. People who have never experienced anything like this can hardly imagine how mystifying it is; I had to spend hours at Scotland Yard helping track down the impostor. He was believed to have been born somewhere in the Bronx or Brooklyn.

The police were catching up with him. The mysterious stranger left the country. He went to Paris, where he became Lord Wellesley. Jerry Wellesley, later the Duke of Wellington, was soon puzzled to find himself charged with ten pounds for some shirts he had supposedly bought in Paris, and the wheels of justice began to revolve again. Meanwhile the "Prince" had again become Prince Serge Obolensky and turned up in New York.

There he made a hit. He loved Broadway, and came to know an extraordinary number of chorus girls, as he claimed to have been sent over by the Prince of Wales to select appropriate companions for his forthcoming American tour. He went to Newport and Long Island parties, an adroit, picturesque figure, colorful and entertaining, with more gall than anyone I ever heard of. I finally came face to face with him years later. It was at a party given by Joan Payson—Jock Whitney's sister—and he was not in the least abashed, merely fixing his monocle in his eye, and drawling, "Prince Serge Obolensky? ... I believe we are related!" But that story belongs later in this account.

The release from the tension of the war years had an unfortunate effect on many people. I often thought of Bertie Stopford, who had taken greater risks for a longer period of time than almost anyone I knew, a cheerful, hearty, healthy individual who really enjoyed facing incalculable dangers from the Bolsheviks. Somehow he had miraculously escaped, but then, safe in London, with everything in the world to live for, an almost Proustian climax ended his career—or anticlimax, for there seemed nothing for him to do. He was bored and restless and the world of peace had become a prolonged waste of time whose dullness caused him infinite trouble as he struggled against it.

He had been an unfailing friend to all of us in any hour of need, but he lost his bearings with the ending of the tension he had lived under. One of the most normal, happy-go-lucky, good-natured people I have ever known, he went to jail as the result of an unfortunate episode in Hyde Park, revealing a side of his character in the pitiless blaze of tabloid publicity that no one could have suspected of him. He served a year in jail. On the day he was released from prison, Juliet Duff and I met him and went to his apartment for tea. We felt it was the least we could do for someone who had done so much for our friends in Russia. It was a painful occasion. Bertie had braved the gunmen of the Cheka without a moment's hesitation, but the censure of his supposed friends was too much. He told us so. It was tragic, and we knew then he had to go away. Soon after he left for the Continent. He never returned.

With my new job, and what I hoped were good prospects for the future, I leased a house in Hyde Park Terrace, on Hill Street, and went to Nice to fetch Catherine. I found it a terrific uphill job, dealing with grain-handling equipment. I traveled over the country to see people, and while there were some big orders for such equipment from the docks, from the big grain elevators, or municipalities, these big contracts were not easy to get.

Catherine began to sing professionally almost as soon as she arrived.

She had already given concerts in Nice. Melba helped her. King Manuel of Portugal, who had lived in England after a coup d'etat in his kingdom in 1910, was living at his country place near London; he was an accomplished musician, and accompanied Catherine when she sang for small groups of our friends.

This was either at our house on Hill Street, or at King Manuel's house in Richmond. Nancy Leeds then gave a large dinner for Catherine, and asked her to sing professionally for her guests, a wonderfully nice gesture. Nancy knew we were hard-pressed for funds. By means of these gatherings, Catherine became known to London musical circles.

Finally, on December 3, 1919, the time came for Catherine's professional debut in England. It was sponsored by Mrs. William Corey at her home at Connaught Place, and it was a critical success.

About the time that she was becoming known, Prince Alexis Obolensky, my cousin Aliosha, the son of Father's brother Alexander, began his career as a musician. Aliosha had sold his Stradivarius when he reached France, and organized a group of Russian singers including Nina Kosshetz. They became sensationally popular in Paris almost overnight. Melba heard him. She decided he had a great future if his voice could be trained—even at this late date. The director of her Australian opera company then took Aliosha in hand and began to train him at a farm outside of Paris. Aliosha said it was heartbreaking. He could only reach A-flat. After that, he could go on only by mighty effort and concentration, but while he was straining to reach those high notes, his facial expressions were so funny that people laughed. "This was a terrible discovery!" he said. "The rest of me was loyal, but my voice had become a Bolshevik!"

He struggled with it all and won. Later, as is well known, he became one of the opera stars in Melba's great company, singing half a dozen leading opera roles with her, and accompanying her on her final around-the-world tour. After Melba retired, he became a concert artist in the United States, and eminent as a teacher in the Damrosch Foundation—later the Juilliard School—in New York. He had not at that time appeared in London. Unfortunately, his London debut, which was a triumph, came almost simultaneously with one of Catherine's concerts, her biggest to date. I'm afraid she was eclipsed. She could have been a sensation, but her heart was too much of a handicap. And besides, Aliosha was great. Catherine had been much aided by the patronage of social figures, but Aliosha's first appearance was a truly brilliant event in both musical and social terms. The list of those present was headed by Queen Alexandra, and Aliosha's concert was sponsored by the Duchess of Rutland, the mother of Margery and Diana Manners.

For a long time things had not been going well with Catherine and me. We had been forced to live apart much of the time. Her friends were different from mine, and for the most part older. I had little in common with most of them. She was, remember, fifteen years older than I was. The English people I knew were generally interested in sports, and Catherine's musical circles contained no sporting people. Even if she had wished to, her heart would not have permitted her to exercise.

It was true that I did not take part in sporting life as I had in an earlier period. Polo was out of the question. For one thing, I felt it was callous for me to do something like that. Too many people had died. Too many were still in travail. Besides, it was now far too expensive for me, and for that matter had become too expensive for many wealthy people. Indeed, the sport never recovered the popularity it had had before the war. Nor could I afford to ride to hounds.

But I had a very good friend in Tommy Bouch, who was the Master of the Belvoir (pronounced Beaver) hounds. He owned a string of forty hunters at Woolthorp, near Belvoir, the castle of the Rutlands. And Tommy always invited me to come and hunt with him, and lent me horses. It was his father who had built the Firth of Forth Bridge, remembered for its collapse as a train passed over it. Tommy was a poet, and his book, *Storms in Teacups*, has a wonderful tribute to the Belvoir hounds and the joy of riding out over the Belvoir vale in the morning. We had some fine hunts on an eleven-mile point. I was always grateful to him for introducing me to that dramatic Belvoir country, steep hills, dark vales, secluded woods like the islands of trees in Russia, and the magical Vale of Belvoir. But Belvoir itself, to my thinking, was an astonishing edifice. It was a Victorian castle, of all things, and even then showed all the signs of being a white elephant.

I must here say something about my wife Catherine, which will make abundantly clear why we had chosen to live apart. Our marriage had been one of wartime delusion, of a short, sharp romantic attachment sought by both of us in a tiny moment of desperate calm. The absence of shellfire was in itself hypnotic, and in the long run the match had measured up to what it was—infatuation. Almost immediately after our escape from Russia, it was evident that our marriage was an impossible one. It was, as I have said before, a mistake, and that was that. I was of the school that said, "There is no point in going on for the sake of mere appearance." She was opposed to this. I was of the school that said, "After a while the hypocrisy will be desperate for both of us." She felt that didn't matter. She believed in the union being kept apparent to others above all else. It was a noble approach, but by and by she realized what such a course entailed.

We were destined to search out different paths. Catherine herself becoming a Catholic at this time; and her confessor, an astonishing man, actually advised her to initiate steps toward a separation. From that point on we were free to seek our own ways. We were then, in all respects except in name, apart. I have always regarded her with the greatest warmth and admiration, for she had the courage of a lioness, and there was not anything in the world that I would not have done for her to help her in her illness, and to aid her in her considerable artistic interests. We were, had been, and always would be friends.

Edward, the Prince of Wales, was just setting out on the first of the good-will tours throughout the British Empire that occupied him for several years. I met him again through such friends of mine as the Francises, the Wards, the Sutherlands, the Loughboroughs and others. Both the Prince of Wales and his younger brother, Prince Albert, liked dancing. They danced a lot at the big parties, and they mingled freely. They were exceedingly kind to me. The two princes favored a group of attractive young people. They made up a younger set that went about together much of the time, and I went out with them. The Prince of Wales and Prince Albert were very amused by Sheila Loughborough. In particular, the Prince of Wales was fascinated by Freda Ward, who, I suspect, came to have a profound effect upon his life. I can well understand it. Freda's tremendous steadiness in all things, her will of iron, was tempered by a tremendous sense of humor. She dressed with a delicate taste, a rather fragile one, and she always reminded me of an exquisite little bird, so sharp and quick were her features and her movements. Whenever she and Sheila got together, a literal panic of laughter always ensued.

Sheila, however, was a lazy lady. Her entire appearance was languorous. Her every gesture was dreamlike, as placid as an inland sea. She had golden, flowing hair that swayed gently as she walked, and she had the most beautiful skin I think I've ever seen. She dressed softly and with simplicity, and one could hardly suspect the fertile imagination that was always bubbling within. For underneath, Sheila was pixyish and she adored a good prank. All of a sudden the most astonishing remarks would pop out of her.

As Sorine once said to me, "You know, I'd just love to paint her, but I can't."

"Why not?" I asked.

"Because she's Puck. She's got one of those beautiful but incredible putty faces—impossible to put on canvas."

Freda was the wife of Dudley Ward, one of the Liberal whips in the House of Commons. Loughborough, Sheila's husband, I'm afraid enjoyed good cheer a bit better than some. He generally preferred to go his own way, and he didn't always turn up at the various festivities. At the time I thought he just couldn't keep up the pace, which was understandable, for it was also difficult for me. I had to be at the office the next morning.

Some of these young people were habitues of Felix Youssoupoff's fantastic menage, and during this period I came to like Sheila immensely. Michael Herbert was also in our group, and Freda favored him in those days, and there were many others. It was an unusual clan; and many of the men, like Dudley Ward, were really high up in British politics despite their youth. Their conversation was enlightening, and well-informed.

I came to realize what close friends Sheila and Freda were. They were truly inseparable. I had met the Wards before. In fact it was through the Wards that I met the Loughboroughs. They took me to a fancy-dress affair one evening, and I was smitten by Lady Loughborough almost immediately. The competition, however, was frightful! She was always surrounded by a number of admiring cavaliers, including the Prince of Wales and Prince Albert. Ali McIntosh was another of her swains, Captain Alistair McIntosh, always a riot, and that evening he was in our party. I'll never forget his costume, particularly his too-tight tights, which he continually cursed at because it was so painful for him to sit down. Ali had chosen to be Romeo that night, a furious one, and his costumer had bequeathed him an outlandish beret with a chewed-up feather which he referred to as "my wretched tickler." He was going to give his costumer blue hell in the morning.

That evening I found out about Sheila. She said she was from Australia. Her father, Mr. Chisholm, I gathered, was extremely well-to-do. He had built up a business called Yearling Sales and in fact he was known throughout Australia as "Mr. Yearling Sales," whatever that meant. I assumed that he was closely associated with racing. He had set up his two sons on ranches of their own, the older with a sheep ranch in Queensland, and the younger with a cattle ranch on the other side of the continent in New South Wales. I found out from Ali that they really were the historic family of Australia, similar to the great families in America.

In Cairo during the very first days of the war, almost on the date of her sixteenth birthday, Sheila had married young Lord Loughborough, the son of the Earl of Rosslyn. He was well-known, an officer of the Coldstream Guards who became one of the first officers of the newly formed Armored Car Division, at the very beginning of modern mechanized warfare. Sheila had two charming children, and in spite of her own tender years was a devoted mother who fitted gracefully into London society without losing for an instant her abundant gaiety and charm. Loughborough on the other hand, like many who were ruined by the war, found the mere state of postwar living boring, and he drank more than he probably should.

Contrary to reports of that time and the impression that it seems to have left with succeeding generations, it was not an era of loose morality, devil-may-careness or anything of the sort. Rumors that one slept with anybody one wished to, raised Cain in a manner that rivaled the last years of Marie Antoinette or the earlier court of Le Roi Soleil, could not have been further from the truth. People were just so damned happy, happy to be free of bloodshed, happy not to have to wait for the next day's casualty list, happy to be happy, happy not to have to cry, that they set about their various pursuits of happiness in as constructive a manner as was afforded them. In general, they had a whale of a time, were keenly appreciative of a good party, refused to be bored by anything, and consumed quantities of cheer—which I may say served the worthwhile purpose of bolstering the British economy. I am glad to say that I was part of all this, and I saw nothing wrong with the age-old adage that begins "When in Rome. . ."

The above is representative of the approach of the younger crowd around the Prince of Wales and Prince Albert at that time. We had convivial days, and no one can begrudge them. Everybody had been through so much. Everybody was long of temper and inclined to understanding, except the clergy. As a result, this was really the gayest social period I have ever known. The lingering traces of Edwardian grandeur had thrown a mellow light over English social life before the war, touching every part of it with easy enchantment; but postwar London society was brilliant, flashy and shimmering, always a spectacle. It was as if a whole highly civilized people had refused to sink into despair. They literally disowned the frightful cost of the war; they made make believe with a vengeance, in high spirits, remarkable good humor, considerable cheer, and were always in good taste.

London society of that day consisted of several sets, and there were very often a number of parties on the same evening during the season, which was exhausting, but fun. The greatest parties were always Lord Derby's and the Duke of Sutherland's. The King and Queen were often present; the panoply was unbelievable. The women wore their tiaras, and every scrap of jewelry they owned. The men wore their decorations, and the result was a pageantry of a sort that is rarely seen today. I must say I liked the outward beauty and glamor of these occasions, which the irrepressible British have always managed so well.

But there was one aspect of the time which Englishmen and particularly English ladies found unmanageable, and I suspect that things are much the same today. The Latin temperament is something which most English people have always found difficult to fathom in all sorts of ways. At the time, there was a famous Latin character in London who turned up at all the parties. He was a ladies' man of the first water and many of the ladies that I knew had had near-disastrous experiences with him. At dances he was always trying to get them in a corner. He was a "pouncer," they said. His name was Foulouetta, and he wore a monocle that would drop from his eye in his frequent moments of appreciation of the gentle sex. Whenever Foulouetta was known to be invited somewhere, the ladies all took to wearing heavy bloomers with strong elastic edges, or so they said. It was a great source of amusement amongst the group. "Oh my God!" one of them would cry as the unfortunate man came in the door, his monocle dangling in approbation rom its string, "I've forgot my anti-Foulouettas!" When one of the ladies of the group took a trip over to Paris she went to a dinner, and Foulouetta himself turned up as her dinner partner. Nor, as she said, had she had the foresight to wear her anti-Foulouettas.

She told us later, "I'll never cry anti-Foulouetta again."

In the early part of 1920 the Prince of Wales set out on his second goodwill tour, this one to Australia. The publicity generated by his trip gave me an idea that it might possibly be a good thing for me to try my luck there. As an Australian herself, Sheila Loughborough talked to me about the country, which seemed to offer a promising future—or would have offered a promising future, except that I did not know a soul in that entire continent. But just at that time her parents, who lived in Sydney, wanted her to return with her children to visit them. She had not been home since the war. Sheila made arrangements to leave on a certain date. The passage to Australia in those days was such a lengthy one that the visit had to last at least a year. Loughborough said he was going through India to join Sheila and the family later on, after they reached Sydney.

This gave me an idea of trying out Australia. Machinery that I was finding hard to sell in England and on the Continent might well be in demand in thriving Australia. As to whether I might settle there permanently—I didn't know. I wanted to look it over, to see how it would work, but I thought from all I had heard there was a magnificent opportunity there. I knew no one in Australia, aside from Sheila's formidable family—her father who was a famous horseman, and her two very operative ranching brothers.

I got the approval of the firm without any trouble. Australia's economy was expanding. They were interested in Australian volume. They sent a cable to their Sydney agent, Henriques and Company, arranging that I was to work for them. Then the financial arrangements were straightened out, and the coast was clear.

The next thing was that I had to broach the subject to Catherine. We were almost completely apart by this time. She was often in France with her mother, and she was now singing professionally a good deal, and making money from her concerts and phonograph records. I left her all that there was in the house, and signed over to her all the money I could. The only thing I took with me to Australia was Father's personal rings, which were heirlooms. Later on, one of Catherine's bitter relatives wrote a book about the family that described how "her young husband, caught up in the mad glitter of London society, abandoned the unhappy Princess and dashed off to Australia with a fashionable married woman." The reference stung me deeply, and it was ludicrous under the circumstances. I was a friend to Catherine, as she was to me. We simply wanted the best for each other, and we had finally agreed that the best was to be apart. Our interests by now were hopelessly divergent.

The P. and O. Line's *Malwa* had already sailed from England on September 24, with Sheila and her retinue of children, nanny and maid, and childhood friends, many of whom were aboard. I learned that the ship was to lay over in Marseilles for a considerable period, and many passengers arranged to board her there. So my tickets were booked through by train across France. On that train there were so many passengers destined for the *Malwa* that we were practically a boat train all the way. It was very gay, and I was delighted, until I found myself on the *Malwa* sharing a cabin with an aged Catholic prelate. He was a Monseigneur, who at first regarded me with absent-minded benevolence. I must say he put a considerable damper on proceedings. Also in the cabin was a young Australian who turned out to be a salesman for Lipton's tea, and at first he was more chagrined than I.

But while lack of money had forced me to share a cabin with these two fine gentlemen, I got to like them tremendously. They turned out to be highly entertaining. The Monseigneur was a man of considerable parts. He was on his way to look over an Australian diocese, which as he put it, was in a state of evil flux due to irresponsible Protestant inroads. "A disgrace!" he would say. "Heresy!" And he would laugh. Meanwhile, the salesman was bubbling over with projects for persuading the Australians to drink gallons of tea. He was going to cut in on the liquor market; tea was better for them, he said. By the end of our six-weeks voyage I knew a lot about the problems of the Catholic Church in Australia, and also quite a bit about selling tea.

I drily suggested that my machinery could increase the production of grain, which in turn would immeasurably aid in the production of spirits. I told them I had no sympathy with either of them: I was Russian Orthodox. If they had ever tried to sell grain-handling machinery, they would learn what it meant to handle a commodity that was really hard to move—religion and tea were nothing. Where was buyer resistance in their fields? We kept that sort of thing up all through the voyage.

I had never been out of Europe before, so this trip was a great adventure for me. I could hardly believe that I was on my way to the East, which I had heard so much about throughout my childhood. At the prospect of Australia and its great tracts of land, I was filled with a tremendous sense of exhilaration. I felt the stir of Russia in me again—soil and land.

The weather was wonderful. The passengers were interesting, vivid people. They were Australian businessmen, merchants, wool buyers, and engineers. There was a sprinkling of Indian civil servants and British army officers on their way to India. At an earlier period I might have put them down as highly conventional people, but then I thought they were the most colorful human beings who could be found anywhere. We played deck games, discussed books, and the conversation was well-informed, enlightening and I learned a great deal. But the nights were enchanting! The captain, who had invited Sheila and me to sit at his table, was a dear old gentleman with a delicious sense of humor. He was an old sea dog who had been on the Australian run for years and had known many of his Australian passengers since the time they were small children, Sheila included. He seemed to regard us all as members of a far-flung family who had gathered for a family reunion. There was a genuine heartfulness about the old man and his little ship. The Australians were strong, tough, dynamic. I was enjoying every moment of their company. The old order, I thought, was done for me for the rest of my life.

Our first stop was Port Said. I remember so vividly even now the thrill when we sighted the harbor and took on the pilot, the warm air, the fragrance, the sense of the tropics, the Egyptian fishing boats with their colored sails, and the naked little boys in small canoes begging for coins and diving into the clear water to pick them up when they were thrown over the rail.

We had twelve hours in Port Said, as the *Malwa* was going to coal. The passengers were warned to close all portholes, as the coal permeated all the pores of the ship and lay like a film over the deck. Two lighters arrived, carrying hundreds of natives, who wore loincloths and bore small baskets; the natives proceeded to fill these small baskets with coal and to carry them to the ship by hand, to the accompaniment of a weird chant that must have come from time immemorial—a perpetual chain of human beings, singing, carrying, yet covered with coal dust so completely you could only see their eyes as night began to fall. The ship had grown blacker and blacker.

A group of us went ashore and took an open carriage to a restaurant near the beach. It was a night of Egyptian darkness modified by stars that seemed to lie a short distance over the rooftops. The lights of the harbor, the quiet sea, the dim outlines of the fishing fleet, the sense of the past and the mystery of the future, made the night memorable beyond any I had ever known. One funny thing happened. There was a fortuneteller who told fortunes in the sand. He made marks in the sand and by interpreting them foretold the future. As we wandered past there, I remember a kind of fright I felt when he looked up; his eyes had a fierce, holding intensity. He made a few scratches in the sand, and some of it trickled through his fingers. He told me in a matter-of-fact way that I would be coming back through Port Said in about a year and I remember I was irritated.

It was very late when Sheila and I returned to the ship. We reached the gangway, but then realized that the heat on board was going to be unbearable, because all the portholes would be closed. So we decided to spend the night wandering through the city until daylight came and with it the time for the ship to sail. I had grown very attached to Sheila by this time. She was then, is still, and always has been a true and helpful friend. We watched the dawn come up upon the shimmering harbor, and I realized that I was in love.

I was struck with the hidden animosity the natives showed when the bright hours of civilization gave way to the Oriental night. So long as the crowds were about, and the lights on, they swarmed about, and tried to sell us anything they had; but as soon as these hours had passed and they saw we were not buying, they sulked, and said things which, despite their untranslatable nature, were plainly profane insults. I remember wondering how long Great Britain would be able to keep this up, this thin film of white control over the Eastern abyss.

The battleship Centurion was anchored in the harbor. That symbol of British might was still unchallenged. It had lasted for so long that generations of Orientals had come to think of it as eternal. Only the British navy held the East, controlled it, and enabled the white man to develop trade and commerce. If anything happened to break its hold, I sensed that it would be difficult for white men to exist in those regions. To a far greater extent than any of my English friends, I thought that that hold was already broken and only the fact that the people of the East, and the English alike, did not realize it, kept life going on as it had gone on before. The sullen people who watched Sheila and me from the side streets and the doorways needed only to realize that the ancient controls were gone, and whole continents would pass from the control of the white man. Even then I felt that soon on no street in the Eastern world would it be possible for two people to pass as we were passing then, any more than it would have been possible for us to walk through the streets of Yalta.

We watched the Oriental sunrise and then returned sadly to the ship. The next day the *Malwa* steamed through the Suez Canal, always an unforgettable experience, the ships passing each other a few feet apart, great convoys going through, British troop ships, officers in their scarlet mess jackets on deck to watch us. On the shore beyond the canal there were camels and Arabs passing in the shadow of the gray steel vessels, an extraordinary picture of the ancient world and the modern world existing side by side. At night the chatter of the jackals followed the ship through the dunes.

Suez itself I remember as less impressive than Port Said, with the forlornness of an outpost, a symbol in its drabness of the point where the color of the Orient, and its novelty, departed, and beyond which lay the harder world of deserts and jungles. I suppose it was old-fashioned, and something out of the prewar world, that sightseeing preoccupied us; it sounds intolerably dull to a younger generation, but in fact it was thrilling. Bazaars, mosques, native foods and things like that took up our time. We reveled in the glories of the Straits of Babel-man-deb and the passage into the Indian Ocean, with a stop at the harbor of Aden, and the sight of the feluccas, with their red sails and inevitably the little boys retrieving pennies, but this time from shark-infested waters.

There was one curious routine about the trip. As it was so hot, people slept on deck. And the rule was, all ladies below after 11:00 P.M. It didn't matter how or with whom, but below was an order. I consoled myself with the thought that in the good old days men and women had to sleep on deck, women on the port side, men on the other!

The innocent high spirits of the time were exemplified in a practical joke, one of many, which the Australian girls on board played on the purser. He was very nice, but singularly stuffy. Sheila put a notice on the bulletin board saying the *Malwa* would heave to at noon to permit passengers to bathe in the Red Sea. Why this shark-infested prospect should have seemed so inviting I cannot say, but according to the announcement the gentlemen would bathe over the starboard side of the *Malwa*, and the ladies on the port side, and bathing suits for both men and women were readily available at the purser's office. The girls then gathered near the purser, and chatted with him, when to his bewilderment many passengers started arriving and tried to rent bathing suits. He was still perplexed about the whole business when we came to Bombay and often referred to it with an air of mystification, saying nothing of the sort had ever happened before.

Loughie Loughborough met Sheila at the pier and we all put up at the Taj Mahal Hotel. The place was swarming with Indian boys who slept on the doorstep of each room, with one in the room itself working the fan over the bed. And that startled me. I counted three boys to each room. It gave me a sense of the immense human resources of the East, as vast and inexhaustible as the land resources of Russia had seemed to me in my childhood.

We dined that night at the Yacht Club, Loughborough and Sheila and I and a young English couple. He was A.D.C. to the Governor, and one of Loughborough's old friends. Loughie was charming that evening and he seemed improved by his trip.

I have intimated certain things about Loughie before, and I had better clear up any misconceptions that may have arisen. Loughie had really had a liquor problem, and he knew it. It was almost beyond his control. The war had done it to him, a war in which he had thoroughly distinguished himself. But the situation had become a difficult one for Sheila, so much so that Loughborough's own family decided to send him off on a business trip to India, visiting the governors and officials. In a sense, it was a separation—a trial one. That evening in Bombay, Sheila and he seemed on the best of terms. I was terribly happy to see this. Sheila and I talked about it later. The next morning, Loughborough saw Sheila off and I felt very sorry for them. The *Malwa* pulled away, and he stood there, bareheaded in the sun, until we could see him no more.

The next part of the trip was singularly subdued. Sheila, I knew, felt things very deeply. But, mercifully, there was a dance on board the night before we reached Colombo and long before we arrived the air was fragrant with the scent of flowers sweeping over the sea. It seemed like a new lease on life and we laughed again. The dance was a gay one; we all went to bed late, and the *Malwa* anchored while we slept.

Late the next morning I opened my eyes, and saw what I thought was a devil, with a dark face and steel horns, peering over me in my berth. My immediate reaction was to feel that I was already in another world and not in a good one either. I opened my eyes a couple more times and saw it was a native trying to convince me that I ought to take a sight-seeing trip in Ceylon. All the natives wore sarongs with jackets, and wore their hair long, holding it in place with combs on both sides of the head, and as the combs had horns it gave them a weird and satanical look.

So we all went ashore and I had my first ride in a rickshaw. The *Malwa*, which ate coal like a glutton, was taking on coal again, and we were not going to sail for twenty-eight hours. Once more we had a lot of time and spent the day and the night in the wonderland of the Indian Ocean.

Business life in Ceylon began at four in the morning and came to a complete standstill at seven in the morning. Other times it was so hot that work was impossible. The offices reopened at four o'clock in the afternoon and closed again at eight or nine. The air was saturated with the delicious odor of nutmeg flowers. We rode out in the evening from the Galeface Hotel, one of the best in the world. It had long been the favorite hotel of Russian tea merchants and all the signs were in both Russian and English. On the beach, we watched fishermen come through the surf in their outriggers. Their boats came in and beached at terrific speed, like surfboards; it was fascinating to watch them, with their bulging sails, skimming the breakers.

There was obviously no such thing as air conditioning in those days; I was wet with perspiration whenever I moved. Here, too, at night boys sat behind one's bed, pulling strings that moved two large fans suspended from the ceiling. In Ceylon there were even more boys for each room than there were in India—four or five, and perhaps an attendant as well, for each room in the hotel. Each boy had a special function. They slept in relays on the doormat, or in the room itself, and while they seemed totally oblivious to what was going on they gave the visitor no privacy whatever. I know they displeased Sheila immensely.

One of the mornings in Ceylon I called up an old friend of Oxford days, whom I'd met during the Bullingdon-Athenaeum cricket match. He was now an A.D.C. to the Governor. One of his Ceylonese boys answered the phone.

"Could you give me Major So-and-So?" I asked.

"Sorry," he said. "Major is out. Would you speak to Major's lady?" "Certainly," I said.

He went away for a moment. "Sorry," he said. "Major's lady not now either. Major's lady on thunder box."

Needless to say, I never did reach them, and I realized that there was a certain inconvenience in having servants in the Orient.

A group of us rode in rickshaws to one of the ancient temples, the name of which I have forgotten. The road wound through tropical woodlands and rice paddies, under palm trees, and around mountain heights, through astonishingly beautiful country, with placid elephants by the roadside, and immense butterflies fluttering over lantana flowers and hedges of scarlet hibiscus. And that was the end of it. The *Malwa* was ready to sail. Coaling was over. The twenty-eight hours of enchantment had come to an end. When we returned to the ship, the film of coal dust was being scrubbed from the deck and the crew members bore that curious look of half-pain that one sees early in the morning on the features of a charwoman scrubbing a hall when one comes in from a party. Shipboard life started over; we again assembled at the captain's table for dinner. And he told us exciting stories of his previous voyages through these waters. I'm afraid this time we listened with profound regret, on my part at least, that we had not missed his boat.

CHAPTER XXI

The *Malwa* made its first Australian landfall at Perth, where we all went ashore, and I played golf on the Perth course beside the Swan River. I had a sense of something important happening to me. It was the first time I had ever put foot on Australian earth. But all I recollect of it was that it was exceedingly dry, and the fairways of the golf course were of bunch grass. Sometimes the lies were terrible. Yet it was a good course and Perth was an attractive little city. It was already warm midsummer weather in October—the trip took six weeks—and plainly going to be scorching hot, the scenery a gray-brown haze of burnt grass broken by the odd blue shade of the gum trees.

From Adelaide, a brief stop in a big important commercial town, we sailed along the underside of the continent to Melbourne. We got there the day before the running of the Melbourne Cup, the greatest race of the whole continent. Sheila's father, Harry Chisholm, was one of the stewards of the Australian Jockey Club. All anyone could talk of was the race. Australia had produced one of her wonder horses, Poitrel, believed by all good Australians to be the greatest race horse in history, except for a preceding Australian wonder horse, Carbine, which had broken all records twenty years before.

Poitrel was carrying 140 pounds, more than any horse except Carbine had ever carried. The race was two miles. Poitrel was a six-year-old, undefeated as a three-year-old, four-year-old, and five-year-old. For four seasons he had stunned Australian racing fans by coming from far behind and winning in the last two furlongs—not once by a fluke, but again and again, in every race—and now the age of the horse, the weight carried, and the huge field, with a score or more entries, brought the betting to a feverish pitch.

Mr. Chisholm and his wife met Sheila at the pier and took us all straight to the Flemington Racecourse, the most lavish institution of its sort I had ever seen. All Australia was present. I met innumerable officials, including Lord and Lady Foster—he was the new Governor General—as well as a host of young Australian women who were knockouts. My spirits lifted correspondingly. It seemed almost as if my introduction to Australia was to everyone, all at once. That day all Australians seemed to me to be millionaires, wearing their gray top hats and spending money more freely than I had ever seen it spent. The equerry to the Governor General, Ken Digby, and his wife Patsy, who was the mother of the present Mrs. Randolph Churchill, were among the party that assembled at the big luncheon given by Sheila's father at the Jockey Club Restaurant. Ken Digby had been phenomenally lucky in his betting throughout the race meeting. He had been raking in loot, adding to the impression I was receiving that all Australia was rich. I was convinced that I alone was poor. I could afford to bet only a pound on Poitrel at eight to one to watch him come from behind in the last seconds and win by half a length.

We had, of course, come around Australia to Melbourne from the west and south, and the *Malwa* now steamed around the southeast corner of the continent and up the coast to Sydney. Sheila's parents joined the *Malwa* for this north eastward leg of the trip. We arrived in the Australian midsummer, a beautiful November morning, with the two huge headlands, a mile apart, that mark the entrance of Sydney Harbor opening before us like a gigantic gate. It was very early and the sun rose behind us. As we passed between these headlands, the sea grew as still as a lake, and the immense harbor, with its bays and inlets and tree-crowned headlands, looked to me to be what my Australian fellow passengers said it was—the most beautiful harbor on earth.

At the very least it seemed an auspicious beginning. Sheila's father had arranged temporary membership for me at the old Union Club on Bligh Street, the most attractive of the Australian clubs, and quarters that compared very favorably with those of London. I was told that the whole business community lunched there. The idea was for me to launch my business career without stirring from the club. I was a little alarmed by Australia's routine. And, in fact, the routine of business life in Australia in 1920 and 1921 required that I should get up at 6:30! Being British trained, that seemed inhumanly early to start the business day. But a younger member, a Mr. Hargrove, made a 7:30 appointment with me and I did as he suggested. He was waiting in his car in the fresh morning sunlight, and we drove through wide, pleasant streets to Bondi beach, seven miles or so away, a fifteen-minute drive. It was completely wild, that beach. The only structures were to were from which lookouts watched for sharks. But the beach was packed with people. Beyond the expanse of white sand, all of Sydney, it seemed, was riding in the early-morning surf. This was the way the business day began, with a swim in that tremendous surf before breakfast. It was also where I first learned to shoot the breakers. Then Hargrove and I breakfasted together at the club and went to his office at 8:45.

I had a desk already assigned me at the office of Henriques and Company. Correspondence having already been exchanged, I was expected to set to work at once. I put in an appearance there and went to my second appointment. With great good fortune, on my very first day I secured an order. And it was a sizable one. It seemed wise to me not to become too elated, but to take it in my stride. So I returned to the office, trying to keep my face from beaming. I met my friend Hargrove, who again took me swimming for lunch. Afterward, I went back to work at Henriques and Company until a quarter to five, when all business ceased. It was hard work, but a full and wholesome life, filled with athletics. Ever since, I have considered that the secret. It's also one of the reasons why today I am a yoga. Exercise, if it does nothing else, keeps one in gentle disposition. That evening I drove out some distance to a country club for a round of golf with Sheila and some friends, and remained for dinner at the club.

This was the standard routine of Australia in those days—good business practice. However, the pattern was changing before my eyes. Between the time I began to dream of a future in Australia and the time I actually arrived there, the economy of the country crashed just as it did in the United States in 1929. The feverish flush of betting on the Melbourne Cup and my luck in getting a good order on my first day at work obscured the crisis. The new Labor government of New South Wales had suddenly established a minimum wage far above that established anywhere else in the world. The shock to industry was not a gradual one. They had no time to assimilate; they had no time to adjust. It was just a bomb and they could not profitably operate. Immediately after I arrived in Australia the Broken Hill steel works, the biggest in the country, closed down. They said they just couldn't meet the requirements and the workers went on strike. The president of the firm happened to be a member of the club and asked me if I'd like to visit the works. He said right now it wasn't what it should be, but it might give me some ideas. He said sadly that they ordinarily employed about five thousand men, but now had only a skeleton crew. I naturally jumped at the chance and we wandered through towering empty buildings, mile upon mile of them, with huge Bessemer furnaces, unlit and untended.

Living on the nearby beaches, or on farms, in tents, shacks or in any kind of shelter, were the strikers. And they were obviously enjoying themselves. The weather was so mild and life was so easy that there was no incentive for them to terminate the strike. It was almost possible to live directly off the country, since fish and game were plentiful. They had no intention of going back to work so long as the weather remained good; they said so. And this was a disaster, for when steel production ceases, everything ceases, and so it was with Australia.

Living at the Union Club was Willy Kelly, a cheerful, gnomelike, middle-aged politician, who had been minister of home affairs for Australia in the early years of the War. Willy was a brilliant statesman whose active political career had ended a year or so before because of a serious illness. Still in his early forties, he had been twenty years in politics, having been elected to the Australian House of Representatives from New South Wales when he was only twenty-five. During his first year he created a political sensation by revealing some propaganda he had uncovered that was being circulated by the Navy League of Germany, calling for Germany's expansion in the Pacific with the ultimate aim of taking over Australia. That was in 1904. He woke up Australia, and thereafter his political stock in trade was the German menace. His persistent warnings which were beginning to be scoffed at were finally vindicated in 1914.

But Willy was the sort of politician who was more effective in loyal opposition than in office, and I think he realized this. He used to say, "Serge, I always prefer to be a voice crying in the wilderness." His wife had died, or they were separated, and he had decided to retire and spend the rest of his life traveling. Meanwhile, he loved to play chess. I still possess a handsome chess set he gave me as a memento of those relaxed Australian evenings. Most Russians played chess, and while I was no expert, Dr. Henneberger, the tutor who had taught us chess when we should have been learning arithmetic, had drilled us well in fundamentals and Willy and I were about evenly matched. After a game, we talked about the world of politics.

Essentially, my fond hopes for an Australian future depended on political connections. The kind of business I was in was dependent largely upon state and municipal contracts. In this neither Sheila's family nor my friends in England could help me. Besides, they were now all out of office in both places. People like Willy could help me, and did. The new voluntary wheat pool program was still being worked out. He explained to me the government's plans. These included the building of massive grain elevators, and once they got under way my company would be in a most favorable position to supply the machinery for cleaning and transporting the wheat.

Grain comes from the fields with dust, pebbles and chaff intermixed with the grains; our equipment for cleaning it was superlative, glistening with nickel, almost hand-fabricated; and destined to last for generations, like a Rolls-Royce car. It was expensive machinery, Willy thought, but it was worth it, for once the installation was made there were no further expenses. And the high cost was partially met by the lower import duty that we paid. After all, our American competitors paid a duty of forty-four percent. We paid only nineteen percent. Willy said that through channels he would see what he could do. He thought that as soon as Australian politics became at all stabilized, I could reasonably expect to become hellishly prosperous.

Through the Chisholms I met most of the people who befriended me in Australia—they were unbelievably hospitable. I found myself going to various dinners and parties. Practically every day I played golf or tennis with someone at the country club. After work, I would board a tram which took me there. It went right around the harbor and it was the most beautiful tram ride in the world. Telford Simpson, a cousin of the Chisholms, and his wife, or Sheila and some of my friends from the club made up our foursomes.

It was a pleasant, easy life. Then there were the periods of the races. Sydney, like Melbourne, had luxurious race tracks and during the meets there were a lot of big, very gay dinners and parties. I have seldom seen such lavishness anywhere. People did what they wanted, strike or no. They weren't concerned with self-conscious European attitudes at all. A charming family, the Littles, contributed greatly to my fun. There were four of them, mother and father, and two charming daughters. I took a shine to the younger, Molly, a great beauty, until Sheila explained to me that Molly was to marry her brother, Roy Chisholm. I felt that she had explained this fact to me with rather more point than usual, and I couldn't help chuckling. "And besides," she said, "if you're good and you behave, he's going to ask you to his ranch. But I'll come, too!"

All through this we played a highly unorthodox game of bridge. Mina, the mother of the family, was a real character, but I was nevertheless always amazed that her generally reserved husband, when he lost, would roundly accuse his wife of having sneaked a glance at her cards. She was always completely unruffled, and used to say, "One peep is worth two finesses." The Littles were conservative, absolutely genuine, courteous, and kind.

There was also a distinguished bachelor, Theo Marks, a fine architect, who built the great Australian race tracks. He was a brawny charmer who struck home to a lady's heart after a few moments of conversation. Foulouetta's ways could not compare to Theo's, and while I am not thinking of Theo in the following context, I do feel that I should take a moment to warn the ladies of America and England and the Continent about Australian men. In my days in Sydney, I gained an ever-increasing respect for their method of operations. I shall not divulge their secrets. I shall not break their trust, but I have satisfied my conscience in so issuing my warning, lest the ladies be surprised with their defenses down. And I assure you, during the Second World War, I gave my U.S. paratroop boys a few fatherly tips when I heard that the Aussies were around!

The most colorful people in all Australia were the famous Walker twins. George and Monty were the Sydney jesters of all time. Every visitor to Sydney in those days was asked two questions: "Have you seen our harbor or do you know the Walker twins?" The twins lived across the bay and I was often invited there for Sunday. I played golf with them on their aunt's garden course, which wound through trees and flower borders. It was a beautiful putting course and the Walker twins always liked to get ladies over to their aunt's to try out their putting. The twins were absolutely identical. They threw consternation into the ranks of Sydney's eligible young ladies by their remarkable similarity. The twins watched out for each other; and often, it was rumored, when one twin got bored with a girl, he would get his brother, who could only be delighted since the groundwork had already been laid, to substitute for him. Thus the young lady, all unknowing, would be furious once she found out, if she ever did. It was one of their many jokes upon humanity. In fact, they were never completely happy without a joke being played on someone somewhere. If you ever had a girl that you were attentive to you could be sure that the Walker twins would be waiting for their opportunity. You didn't have a chance since they were always in cahoots and worked in shifts. One would divert your attention for a second, and the other would disappear with your girl. Then they would vanish for a while and reappear delighted with themselves. They had a wonderful sense of humor.

I am glad to say that Monty's son, Jimmy Walker, is following in the family tradition. Years later, when I was running the Sherry-Netherland Hotel, he arrived in New York with a letter from his father. I got my son Ivan to help show him around town. Ivan reported to me that he thought Jimmy needed no help whatsoever. Apparently, Jimmy had wanted to see the Empire State Building. On going there, while they were waiting for the elevator to the tower, Jimmy Walker began questioning the proud elevator starter of the highest building in the world:

Q. "How high is this building?"
A. "Our building is twelve hundred and fifty feet high, sir."
Q. "How high did you say?"
A. "I said it was twelve hundred and fifty feet. It's the highest in the world."
Q. "You say it's twelve hundred and fifty feet?" (doubtfully)
A. "Yeah! What's it to you?" (positive)
Q. "And didn't you say it's the highest in the world?"
A. "Yeah!"
Q. "Well we got a buildin' in Sydney that's fifteen hundred and fifty feet."
A. "What's that?"
Q. "I said we got a buildin' in Sydney, Australia that's fifteen hundred and fifty feet tall. So how come you say this here is the highest buildin' in the world?"

A. (Doubt, uncertainty, discomfort) "Say, feller, now you must be wrong. Our building is the highest building in the world. I know that. But you wait here. I'll go and check."

Before the man came back, an elevator was ready to go up. Jimmy said "Cheese it!" to Ivan, and they went up to the tower. I never did find out what happened when they came down again.

On the holidays I went and dined with the Chisholms and we generally played bridge. Mrs. Chisholm was a wonderfully efficient woman who good-naturedly put up with a great deal of ribbing from Sheila. Harry Chisholm, Mr. Yearling Sales, was a charming old boy with white hair and ruddy cheeks.

I wanted to visit the wheat belt that stretches between Sydney and Melbourne, as there were many mills and grain elevators in that region. Telford Simpson was driving to Melbourne, and asked me to go with him. South of Bathurst were only dirt roads winding from one small community or one isolated station—the Australian word for ranch—to another even more remote. Terrific windstorms swept across this almost uninhabited country. They were so strong the car was nearly lifted from the road. Torrential rains followed directly after them, and since everything was dry, there was the danger of flash floods. Each low place in the road became a torrent where the water flowed over the hood of the car. At the first danger point we stopped before venturing across, packed a water-resistant protection around the carburetor, distributor and spark plugs, took a long breath, and charged through the flood waters. Around Bathurst, the market center for the whole grain-growing interior, were big estates producing wheat world-famous for its quality; but now we came to rougher lands where a village of five hundred people was esteemed big. We visited at Quandilla in Wesdalion and Tubbel Road, where the mail was delivered once a week, and so came to Cootamaundra itself, lying beside the powerful Murrumbidgee River that flowed from the Snowy Mountains a thousand miles away.

Cootamaundra was another inland metropolis, with perhaps two thousand population at that time. There Telford wanted to take a side trip that led us still further afield, to Coulburn, forty miles from Canberra, which in my days there was still in the blueprint stage. Here we approached singular country that had the remarkable quality of producing both gold and wheat. Telford's old uncle, Austin de Lauret, lived at Coulburn. He was a descendant of emigres from the French Revolution, one of the last of the Bourbon princes. He was known as Uncle Wuff.

We toiled over dirt roads to his station, a dilapidated old ranch house. No one was around but an aged colored servant. He told us that the boss was not at home, but might be found in the local inn at Coulburn itself. We drove on to the city, which turned out to be a sprawling community of a couple of thousand inhabitants. The hotel was a one-room structure with a bar and a poolroom. In the poolroom was a strange old gentleman like a character out of one of Dickens' novels. He wore a three-day beard, a bowler hat, and a dark gray frock coat. He spoke with an accent bordering on Cockney, and was absorbed in playing pool against the paid attendant of the poolroom. Thus lived the last descendant of the Bourbons in Australia.

We invited him to dine with us, and with great difficulty got him to give up the pool table. Telford and I tried to start conversations on any subject—world affairs, Australian politics, royalty in exile—but in vain. The old gentleman was only interested in the price of wool, and now that it was down he was only interested in playing pool. The meeting made a profound impression on me, if only for the living symbol of primordial insularity that sat before us. I was frankly appalled by his lack of concern and downright disinterest. He had no curiosity about anything beyond his own tiny sphere of influence upon our mortal coil. I posed myself a question: If I settled here, I asked myself, would any progeny grow up like this old-timer with his frock coat on his sheep ranch? In my own fateful Russian way, I still felt that signs are sent down to us, that they warn us if we choose to see. I saw a large sign in the equation of the Bourbons of France to the Obolenskys of Russia with the common denominator of this isolated spot.

From Coulburn we went on still another side trip, over the mountains to Canberra, the new Australian capital that was then being built. Canberra was being built as Washington was built, an entirely new city, and the greatest town planners of the world had entered a competition for its plan. The winner had been the person who left its magical site as little changed as possible—a beautiful site on the fringe of the Blue Mountains, with the Molonglo River winding through its parks and past its government buildings. We approached it over a mountain pass, through country that reminded me of an entirely unpopulated Bavaria.

We got to Melbourne, where the political situation was a little less chaotic than in New South Wales and I had hopes of governmental orders. Now, however, the Americans were really moving in with strong competition. Since they could not pay the heavy import duty and produce as fine machinery as we did, they revolutionized the business, dispensing with all the refinements, dropping the nickel and polished steel, and turning out rough serviceable machinery that was merely designed to do the work. They could now undersell us despite the forty-four percent duty they paid.

I spent my time visiting flour mills. Aside from working hours, I met Dame Melba, who had returned to Australia after her last triumph in London; I had known her well from the old days through her friend Mrs. Hwfa Williams. Rumors had been published, and then denied, that she was retiring. She had a beautiful house, Coombe Court, about twenty miles from Melbourne, where she lived as the uncrowned queen of Australia. I spent a couple of weekends there with an old friend, Bertrand Yorke, and with Brookes and Patterson, the two great tennis champions. Tennis champions, horse breeders and musicians, if they were the best and therefore in Melba's class, were Australia's equivalent of royalty in those days. The old tennis star, Brooks, and the new, young champion, Patterson, were old friends and great rivals. They wanted to play doubles, so a local doctor and I made up the four. I have never in my life seen tennis balls traveling so fast. The senior champion and I were defeated.

Melba gave a great concert at that time. As it opened she announced her retirement. The ovation was beyond anything of the sort I had heard or imagined. Then she sang with that thrilling sonorous clarity of hers, which made a listener feel as if, with her marvelous diction and her golden voice, she was sentencing someone to death. Perhaps the ovation was too much for Melba, for she went to London the very next year if only to announce her retirement again, and in fact did not retire for many years. She was a remarkable businesswoman.

Back in Sydney I found an invitation from Roy Chisholm to visit him at his station in New South Wales. Sheila rang me up and said she was going, too, as Molly would be there. We went to the ranch by train. Roy and I then left the girls to twiddle their thumbs. It was good for them, he said. So we took packs and a group of the men and Roy and I rode off into the country. For three weeks we lived on horseback. We rounded up cattle, branded them, and lived with the jackeroos, as the Australian cowboys were called. When we had first arrived at their camp they tried the old Australian cattle trick on me. An Australian stock whip was about twenty-five feet long. A jackeroo whirled it about his head expertly, and when it cracked the report was like a gunshot. The jackeroos delighted in letting foreign visitors get entangled in these whips. An Australian stock whip was not much different from the long whips the coachmen used when they drove sleighs in tandem down the Volga in winter. We had often cracked them in Krasnaya Gorka in my childhood. But I said nothing, and when they gave me the whip to try it, it worked perfectly. My stock went up with the jackeroos.

They also took me on a kangaroo hunt. Hunting kangaroos consisted in riding through the brush-gum trees, in a row, with wolfhounds running between the horses. All of a sudden the jackeroos gave a terrific yell. We could see the kangies flying through the air in great leaps ahead of us, at a speed it seemed we could never hope to match.

The brush was really jungle country. The huge gum trees had thick gum under them. Fallen trees, stones and rabbit warrens created every conceivable kind of hazard. A horse could break its leg very easily anywhere at all. I lay down on the saddle, gave my pony her head, and trusted to luck. I never saw anything in my life so agile as that pony. How she knew where to jump in that long grass and over those fallen logs was a mystery to me. There was a blur of twisting and darting movement, with the gray shapes of the kangies occasionally visible ahead.

Had it gone on for long we would have come to disaster, and gone down in country where falling was dangerous. But the chase was brief. Beyond a brief open grassy stretch an amazing sight opened up. Kangaroos get winded easily. Suddenly they stopped, braced themselves with their backs against trees. When we came up, they were fighting off the hounds with their hind legs. I jumped off the pony and started to run forward, but Roy galloped up and called me back in genuine alarm. The kangaroos could easily rip a dog to shreds with their powerful legs, and we were warned never to dismount, for these odd and timorous animals could easily rip a man to pieces in their panic in the same way. They were protected by the government, and could not be killed. Then we called the hounds off, without dismounting, and with yells and whips induced them to leave; the chase was over.

On the way home we rode up to a barbed-wire fence. There I earned a new technique for jumping a wire. We took off our coats, spread them over the wire, backed away, and jumped the fence. Those Australian ponies were like cats.

In the evening I did my best to make myself useful, helping with the fires, cooking, and washing the dishes. While I was finishing up, Roy came up to me chuckling. He had overheard the jackeroos in a discussion of someone they thought was royalty. "That son of a bitch ain't no prince," one of them said. "He's a Goddamned cook, that's what he is." I must say I was flattered. And after that I felt myself to be as good as any other Goddamned jackeroo in the camp.

We spent these remaining days going out on the range, rounding up the calves and branding them. The reason why we carried long Australian whips was that the wild cows became angry when their calves were taken, and often charged. The trick was to crack the whip in front of their noses as they charged, and then get out of the way on those dexterous ponies. We rounded up the calves, drove them to corrals, where they were herded one by one through a narrow lane called a crush. Then we branded them. When they were freed, they scampered back to their mothers, who mooed and licked them solicitously.

Our meals tasted wonderfully. They were cooked on wood fires in the open; tea was prepared in a billy that every man carried on his saddle. I found the country extraordinary. It was full of parrots of all colors and sizes, and laughing jackasses, which are really wild birds. They laughed exactly like human beings in the middle of the night. It was an eerie sound. Rabbits had honeycombed the ground with their warrens. They had multiplied by the millions after they had been imported, and they had become an intolerable pest. The big factories using their pelts for making smart felt hats made no visible dent in their tremendously increasing population. The country was full of large poisonous snakes. Roy showed me another local trick. When a jackeroo saw a snake, he jumped off his pony, grabbed the snake by its tail, whirled it around his head, and cracked it like an Australian cattle whip, which snapped the snake's head off. We were riding along together when we saw one gliding over the path. Roy jumped from his horse, whipped it around and cracked its head off. The next one he encountered he graciously left for me to kill. I jumped off the pony bravely enough, and approached the serpent, but then my nerve failed me as I stooped to grab it; I hesitated; and by then it was too late. The snake was prepared for its attack, and ignominiously I jumped back on my horse. I know my stock went down that time, but no one said anything.

When we got back home, the girls were pretty glad to see us. "You see?" said Roy, winking at me. "I guess we can still teach you Russians a thing or two."

Sheila was delighted to have me back, but I could see that something was troubling her. I asked what the matter was. "Loughie's coming to Sydney," she said. "I've to decide!"

In the station itself, the ranch house, there was a wood stove in the bathroom. Roy kept a can of kerosene there, and used it to start the fire—he poured it over the chips, threw a match in, and the bathroom warmed up. Toward the end of our stay it happened that Roy had been cleaning something with gasoline, and left the container, exactly like that which contained kerosene, in the bathroom. When I started a fire I took the wrong bottle. There was a terrific explosion. My face, head and eyes were burned. My eyelashes were completely gone. The doctor was hastily summoned. He arrived twelve hours later—that's how far from civilization we were. He picked from my eyeballs the scorched fragments of the eyelashes. He told me I had been very lucky and departed on a twelve-hour drive back to his office.

When I was able to travel Sheila and I went back to Sydney. All plans were up in the air at that time; the depression in Australia was worsening; the political situation had grown more confused than ever; and people were returning to England or going elsewhere. Sheila's husband then arrived from India. He was greatly better, and while I knew what it would probably mean, I consoled myself by thinking of his and Sheila's happiness and that of their beautiful children. Their plans for the future were now completely changed. Although Sheila had not said as much, I knew that they would soon leave for London. She intimated that she was going to give things another try, and she was right; but thereby my closest friendship in Australia would be broken off. Deep in my heart I knew I would be losing someone who would mean something to me for the rest of my life. It was then that I realized that I had been living in Australia for the sake of a dream. I had no idea until then, just how great a part of that dream Sheila had represented.

I took a small apartment not far from the club and returned to my regular working habits. I plunged into my work harder than ever, but it seemed to bear me less and less fruit every day. Each morning I walked to the office. On the way I stopped to pick up young Watts, who lived next door. Gradually it became a custom to meet him for breakfast. The Wattses had a delightful five-year-old daughter, Shirley, who used to climb on my lap while we drank our coffee and discussed the news in the papers. Through the strange mutations of this social world of ours, a decade and a half later, when I had become active in trying to help the Ballet Russe de Monte Carlo in New York, trying to keep its organization from falling apart, a brilliant young ballerina from Australia suddenly appeared to join the company: it was Shirley Watts at the beginning of her career. Then and there I took her out for an evening at El Morocco. She had great dreamy eyes and long eyelashes, and I was the envy of the company that evening at least. I never saw her again; she vanished as suddenly as she arrived.

Meanwhile, I spent each day combing through lists and files, exploring for possible customers or calling on officials of the agricultural department of New South Wales. But by now even the youthful ardor of my hopes that had borne me to Australia and sustained me there had vanished. If life was too easy I felt the incentive leaving me; I felt I was not working properly; and I began to blame myself.

But the truth of that time lay embedded in Australia itself. If life was too easygoing in the city—and I had come to realize that despite the outward show of early-rising hustle and bustle—it really was just that it was too hard out in the bush. There was no happy medium. Nothing did any good and my business was stagnating around me. Besides, everything seemed too far away, and I began to comprehend something—that one should never be too far removed from the font or hub of things that are moving and dynamic.

My answer lay somewhere in the fact that the turmoil of Europe had become unreal to me. I was lonely and loneliness is always worse when one feels that one really isn't proving anything. I needed stimulation and a sense of working for something that I believed in. I could no longer find this here. Europe was my answer.

As suddenly as I had decided to leave for Australia, I returned in spirit to the Old World. I told Sheila the day I booked my passage. She and Loughborough decided to stay another year, and give things another try. In two weeks I went back on the Orient line, and this time it was a long journey back. But this time at least I knew the kind of life that I wanted to lead.

CHAPTER XXII

I reached Rome in January 1922. My half sister Olga, who was living there with Mother and my half brother Max de Reutern, was marrying Captain Stroukoff, the officer of the Chevalier Guards whose bay gelding I had ridden in the Emperor's review. I remained in Rome for their wedding.

Mother had gotten out of Russia with a good part of her jewelry, the emeralds from her tiara, pear-shaped emeralds, sapphires, and the ruby pendants that fascinated me in my earliest childhood in Czarskoe Selo. It was strange to see these gems again, to recall the world of the court halls, and the glamorous image I retained of Mother and Father dressing for the court ceremonies.

Mother lived comfortably enough on the sale of her jewels, but there has been much nonsense written about the fortunes in jewels that people managed to get out of Russia. Intrinsically valuable many of them were, but when people had to sell them because they were in need, they could not get high prices. Mother learned she had to sell to the first bidder or at the price the first dealer offered. A ring formed as soon as word got around that she was selling one of her jewels. The dealers worked together. They never offered a higher price than the first dealer offered. I'm afraid Mother made some horrendous bargains.

In selling her jewelry she was helped by her son, Max de Reutern.

His career in those years consisted in traveling about and making the best bargains wherever he could. Subsequently, he went into the famous dressmaking establishment in Paris, Paquin, becoming its manager. He had, in the meantime, married an Italian girl, Luciana Aloisi, of a family prominent in political life. Her uncle was the very shrewd minister of foreign affairs in the government that Mussolini was later to establish.

Olga and her husband were going to stay on the Stroukoff estate in Poland, located on the very border near the Soviet Union. It was not a very healthy outlook for a young couple and I told them so. By that time the Bolsheviks were organized and were constantly sending agents across the frontier to liquidate anyone they suspected of operating effectively against them. That is exactly what happened to Stroukoff—two secret agents crossed the border, set up an ambush, and shot him. But that, too, is leaping ahead of the story.

For the moment we were cheerful and the return to Russian ways, customs and language, after nearly a year in the bush, was pleasant. Max's old tutor Pavel Ivanovitch was there as part of the household, the same humane, understanding individual I had met years before when Mother returned to Russia.

After I'd been in Rome a week, I received an answer to a letter I had written Catherine at Nice. She had been spending more and more time there with her mother. I was shocked and greatly saddened: Catherine told me that Princess Yourievsky had died just before I'd left for Australia. I was astonished that she had never told me this earlier. I had had great admiration for the old lady. She had lived to the exact moment when her money ran out. There had been nothing left, and so, God bless her, she found the time for her to die. My long bedside talks with her were truly historic. I immediately wrote Catherine a letter of sympathy, recalling her mother with deep affection. She had been wonderful to me.

By . the time I arrived in London again, I had already parted company with the grain-handling machinery business and so could not hope to keep up the Hill Street house where Catherine and I had lived. So I again joined Felix Youssoupoff in his Knightsbridge flat, and Vassily, our old chef, moved in to cook for us. Then I scouted around for a job. I found one with Byng, Foley. It was the brokerage firm of Lord Byng's, the hero of Vimy Ridge, who was also the London police commissioner.

My position there was that of a half-commission man. Each morning, wearing the London broker's stock in trade, a dark suit, gloves, umbrella and a bowler, I traveled by tube to the stock exchange, as impervious as any Englishman. It was more interesting than making hundreds of unproductive calls on public officials about nebulous projects for grain elevators. Here I was engaged in imminent, up-to-the-second business, and I was making a living. And Vassily helped. I firmly believe he was one of the greatest chefs that ever lived. Occasionally I asked some of my customers to dine. And so it came about that we had small dinner parties once or twice a week; Vassily cooked, while friends, some of whom were great musicians like Uncle Kotia, provided the music.

In those days the story of Rasputin's death was not generally known. Felix was still a man of mystery whose fame rested on his reputation that he had murdered Rasputin in a desperate effort to save the dynasty. At one of these dinners Felix was persuaded to tell the story. That night he really told it better than I have ever heard a story told. The room was lit by candlelight, with Tesphé the Abyssinian standing impassively behind him in the shadows. The effect was overpowering. When Felix finished, there was a long silence. Then the Duchess of Portland, one of our guests, said softly, "I felt I was there." What had emerged from Felix's account was the tremendous, building, overpowering strain on the Imperial court in the last days before the Emperor abdicated. "And I understand now," the Duchess went on, "what I never understood before—the atmosphere when Rasputin was given the poisoned wine to drink—the smell, the incense, the candle wax, the musty heavy rugs. It was like the atmosphere in this room—right now!"

As I was now leading a bachelor existence, I dined out a good deal. The talk was of hunting or horses or engagements and marriages and other everyday matters that made all kinds of Russian melodrama recede into the shadows. Weekends were spent in the country playing golf or tennis with my friends, or riding with Tommy Bouch with the Belvoir hounds. The Earl of Fitzwilliam, to keep up public interest in polo, had set up a stable where one could rent polo ponies—a pound a chukker, if I remember rightly—making it possible for enthusiasts to play without the expense of keeping up their own ponies. I played there often. But polo ponies are either good or bad and I never knew what I was going to get.

It was back at Rome during the holidays when I went to visit Mother that I met Millicent Rogers, an exquisite American girl with the wide, slant eyes of a deer, which I noticed she accentuated with eyebrow pencil. She was visiting Europe with her parents and her friend Leia Emery. I was introduced to her at a picnic given by Countess Tookie di Zoppola. I began taking her out when she visited London a little later and we got unofficially engaged. But I could never be sure of her; she had too many beaux; she was, apparently a past master at keeping one dangling. Millicent was terribly attractive, one of the most beautiful girls I have ever known. She was an exotic creature, with a curious languid manner. Even her voice, soft and pensive, was that of an Oriental, and she generally dressed the part. It was Millicent whose influence led me to ask Catherine to begin divorce proceedings. I was really fascinated by her. Catherine's Monseigneur was in favor of it, and it was largely through him that Catherine took the first steps toward our divorce. Catherine now had a going career and a complete life of her own, her own house, and Miss Lily Pickens to look after her.

At the end of the London season, Millicent's parents took a place in Scotland called Cortachy Castle, and I was invited to visit them there. It was the grouse-shooting season, and there would be a big shoot. Ali McIntosh was designated to be the escort for Leia Emery, and I was with Millicent. The moment that Ali arrived, the smell of the heather must have been too much for his Scottish soul, for he changed immediately into his kilts. They remained on him for the rest of the evident part of his stay. This was, perhaps, a mistake, for Ali was used by now to the relatively warmer climes of London clubs and houses; and Cortachy was cold. So cold, in fact, was Cortachy that we all bundled up, even indoors, something that Ali considered quite beneath him—even on the moors. It happened to be one of the coolest seasons in history for that part of the country—as we, and Ali in particular, were to find out all too well once we got out on the moors.

That day was really miserable. We were bombarded from dawn to twilight by a light all-enveloping drizzle that completely destroyed morale and seemed to freeze the very marrow of one's bones. Ali, who had scorned all our bundlings-up, wore his kilts with bravado for the first few hours. But by and by as a fierce little breeze sprang up the draft must have been terrific. He stuck it out and when we finally retired, he was the bluest Scotsman I had ever seen. Going back in the car I told him that I hoped he hadn't sustained any permanent damage, and he became speechless with rage; so I added, "Ali, I bet that was one time when you would have preferred to wear your Romeo tights!"

Cortachy Castle itself is a very ancient and revered edifice in Scotland, especially the keep; it is the seat of the Airlies. Millicent told us a story that night, which Ali quickly said he already knew. He was still thoroughly displeased with all of us, and Millicent naturally continued. Centuries ago, there was a drummer of Cortachy who had been a traitor to the Airlie during a war between the clans, and Airlie had had him hung from the keep during a siege as a warning to his enemies. Before he died, the drummer put a curse on the Airlies and swore that he would drum his drum around Cortachy every time an Airlie was to die.

Then Ali, never to be outdone, piped up with a sequel to the story: apparently, the summer before, Cortachy had been taken for the shooting season by Mr. Axel Wichfeld. Meanwhile there was a very gay house party going on at Glamis, where the present Queen Mother, then Elizabeth Bowes-Lyon, and Bruce Ogilvy, the brother of Lord Airlie, were visiting. Bruce thought it might be fun to play a joke on Wichfeld, so he got hold of a big drum, dressed up in full Scottish regalia, and then they all motored over to Cortachy. At exactly midnight, he got out of the car and drummed loudly around the keep. Wichfeld was woken up, and, furious, he threw open the casement, stuck his head out, shook his fist, and shouted down a stream of fruity expletive that would have gladdened the heart of my old sergeant major, Ivan Blajevitch.

The awful thing about it was that that very same night Wichfeld's mother, far far away in Denmark, died. I understand that when Airlie heard about it, he expressed considerable displeasure at the actions of his younger brother. As he said, "After all, one of these days you may be killing *me!*"

After the stay in Cortachy, things looked pretty bright again for Millicent and me. We saw each other constantly; although I must say she really was something. She was still talking to me in complete tangents—perhapses, maybes, we'll sees. Then she suddenly took off for Switzerland. Presently, via the grapevine there I heard rumors that she was seen often with a gallant young Argentine, blast him! Anyway that's what I thought at the time. She later married him, but must have led him a merry chase, poor fellow, because before she did, she married a man called Count Salm.

However, I had never cried over the spilling of milk, and I had no intention of beginning. I led a relaxed and pleasant life. Several of us went up to Oxford for the reopening of the Loders Club, closed throughout the war. We had an exceedingly good time, going back to Peckwater Quad one night and, in accordance with our age-old custom, blowing the hunting horns in the course of our celebration. There was a new generation of undergraduates at Oxford, very serious, hard-boiled, highbrow scholars, and I'm afraid we weren't at all popular with them. Many of the students were soldiers and officers whose education had been interrupted by war. They were now back at school, quite well along in years and experience. They were incensed by the noise we made that night.

Walter Dalkeith was there, and Eric Ednam who told me about the last charge of his regiment, the Tenth Hussars. It had occurred about the time of our retreat to the Dvina on the eastern front. Eric told me about riding flat out into the German lines, a very different thing from breaking suddenly out of the woods and charging as we had done. We had the element of surprise on our side. As Eric's horse cleared the first line of German infantry, he saw a German officer spring up and fire his carbine at him point-blank. The bullet missed, and just as it missed, Eric galloped past and slashed the German with his saber. Despite the confusion, he retained a vivid picture of the German officer's face, and at the moment that I talked to him, Eric believed that he had killed the man.

After the war, in connection with postwar problems, Eric was working on the steel cartel, and he had to go to Germany to meet Thyssen, the German steel magnate. As he went into Thyssen's office, he saw Thyssen's secretary. He thought, "I have seen that man somewhere before." It bothered him so much that he asked the man, "You know I believe we know each other. But *where*? I'm *sure* I've seen you before."

"Yes," said the secretary with a wry smile. "And I'm better now, thank you. I'm the German officer whom you cut down with your saber. I've got a very good memory, too." The man's name was Eddie Oppersdorff. He and Eric immediately became close friends. When Oppersdorff went to London, he met and married an attractive Boston girl, and settled down in New York. Much later, after Eric had become Lord Dudley, his son got married. Eddie was at the wedding reception, and the wedding cake was cut with the sword that Eric had carried on that cavalry charge.

I had taken a flat on Little Grosvenor Street. My neighbor upstairs was Evelyn Fitzgerald, whose wife, Ellen, was a sister-in-law of Lord Beaverbrook. Ali McIntosh lived across the way and except for him, it was a quiet, comfortable, relatively modest existence. I became a member of Bucks Club, and I lived the sort of easygoing bachelor existence that it sometimes seems London was specifically designed to provide.

At this point in my life, Paul of Serbia introduced me to a very bright young American called Henry Channon, then as always known as Chips. He was a good deal younger than I was and had graduated from Oxford with honors the year that I returned from Australia. Chips was the absolute double of the famous golfer Bobby Jones. His father was a Chicago manufacturer, making rope transmissions, hoisting equipment, garden tools, hardware, rigging for stage sets, and flags. Chips's mother was a prominent Chicago clubwoman related to the powerful McCormick family and Chips was their only son. He had just written a novel called *Joan Kennedy*, which was critically successful in England, but the American press was cool. Chips had always loved England, and thereafter he became a British subject. When he went into politics, becoming the candidate for the Conservative party for Southend-on-Sea, he was instantly elected.

Chips had a truly infectious charm. From my own point of view he was wonderful company and he hasn't changed at all today. I attribute his political successes of earlier days to his puckish sense of humor and plain hard work, of which he was eminently capable. He never lost a single election, even during the years when the Conservatives were losing one seat after another. But then again he always had a way of putting things that made everybody laugh. I know for a fact that during the London blitz in the Second World War, Chips was always down on the docks with his constituents, cheering them up, seeing to the destitute and homeless, and they loved him. He would drive down every morning in his great green Rolls-Royce.

He saw no point in apologizing for his wealth, preferring to use it wisely and to help. He was buzz-bombed himself later on in the war.

When I knew him first, Chips was sharing a bachelor apartment in London with Viscount Gage, who later married Imogen Grenfell, the youngest daughter of Lady Desborough. It was in that apartment at tea one afternoon that he told me about Alice Astor, who had lived much of her life in London and had come out that year. He was fascinated by the fact that she had been one of the first four people into Tutankhamen's tomb when it was opened. He said, "There was a curse on it, you know!" and went on to praise Alice to the skies. Meanwhile, I subsequently discovered, he was praising me to Alice.

I finally met her on a golf course. There was a foursome arranged by Baba Curzon one afternoon, one of the recognized great classical beauties of England, the third daughter of Lord Curzon. I was Baba's partner, and we played against Boy Browning, then a young lieutenant in the Guards, and Alice. Alice was better than all of us. She was twenty, brilliantly educated, and had the darkest hair I'd ever seen—she looked like an Egyptian high priestess as it swirled about her shoulders in great blue-black folds. Her tastes, I soon found out, were many and varied, although it was at first exceedingly hard to get very much out of her, she seemed so quiet and shy. And when I did get to talk to her after the match she spoke with a quizzical and deft amusement, with a curious upward inflection in her voice that came at the end of her sentences. I could see then that she had a fantastic knowledge of art and literature, music—anything you could think of—and she combined this with a fierce and wild determination to win at golf.

Alice's parents had divorced when she was sixteen years old, and Ava Astor had recently remarried. Her older brother, Vincent, stayed with his father, and

Alice had gone to live in England with her mother. Ava Astor was now Ava Ribblesdale, having married Charles Lister, the Fourth Baron Ribblesdale, in 1919, a gentleman whom King Edward had nicknamed The Ancestor because he looked so much like an old master.

Ribblesdale had been a great ladies' man, one of the gayest bachelors in England. Ava Ribblesdale had had visions of tremendous parties and much entertaining in London, but what she hadn't known was that all Lord Ribblesdale wanted was to settle down with the most beautiful woman he could find, take her out to his country place, where he could lead the quiet gentlemanly life, and read her the classics in the evening with the great sonorous bass voice that he possessed. Ava never forgave him. It was in this sort of atmosphere that Alice had been brought up, absolute Edwardian brilliance, profound knowledge of all things, but complete cold; and speaking about spoiling children, Ava Ribblesdale never believed in spoiling anybody.

I may say that while she and I were at loggerheads for years, we eventually became close friends. Although she was difficult, magnificently sharp, tremendously grand even to the last—as exemplified by her once turning to Nancy Astor on leaving Cliveden and saying, "*Isn't life frightful?*" with a devilish glitter—Ava Ribblesdale, God bless her, was one of the most courageously uncompromising females that ever lived. At the age of ninety early this year, she went out with her battle pennants flying—I dread to think what must be happening up there!

Nevertheless, her approach was hardly a help to her children—Alice, who suffered under the whiplash of her constant criticism to the very end, or Vincent, who was a fine and handsome young man, but embittered by it. Vincent, too, had received the double burden of having his father, Colonel John Jacob Astor, go down on the Titanic. Immediately, all his plans of studying to become a physicist were necessarily cast to the winds. Even his inherent desire to go into public service had had to be passed by. The demands of taking care of one of the greatest fortunes in the world were literally overpowering. Certainly they could be handled by a man of his extreme intelligence, and they were, but at that time they required no outside interference from academic studies. To me it is remarkable that either one of these two turned out at all, and as it is, they turned out magnificently through their own steam and will power. They were two of the greatest friends I ever had. I say "were," because Alice, poor darling, is now dead. Vincent, touch wood, is still hale and hearty.

After the golf match, Alice and Boy Browning, Baba Curzon and I went somewhere and danced. Since the days of my arduous training with Ceccetti, I had loved to waltz; and Alice, I found to my delight, was a marvelous dancer. Those were the days of the great waltzes. That night we ran the gamut from the works of the Viennese masters to such current favorites as 'Three O'Clock in the Morning."

Alice began to talk to me about her fascination with furniture, and she knew everything about it. When she came into her own, she said she was going to start a collection. The week before, I had gone to a party at Lord Curzon's, whose house on Carleton House Terrace was filled with fine examples of the Empire, Louis Quinze and Louis Seize periods. Lord Curzon was a great connoisseur. I recalled to Alice my interest in a splendid overmantel in one of his sitting rooms.

"Oh!" Alice said, I thought rather sharply; but I thought nothing of it, and I went on talking about the Curzons' rooms.

"Well, I see you don't remember," she said.

"Remember what?" I said. "There was also a fantastic clock . . ."

"We have met before, you know?"

"Oh?" I said. "It's quite possible. Were you at the Northumberlands' last week? Yes. You were. Now I remember . . ."

"I was not, and you don't remember at *all*" said Alice, chuckling. She had me on the run.

Then all of a sudden I did remember. It was that very last week at the Curzons'. I felt like a damn fool. I had been waltzing with Edith Mills, formerly Edith Cadogan. We were going strong, until I suddenly reversed and we smacked into a young lady and her partner. It was quite a smash, and the young lady hadn't been pleased at all. To my horror, that young lady had been Alice.

What else could I do? I immediately apologized. Alice accepted my apology in the grand manner and we both roared with laughter. After that Alice and I began to go dancing together a lot, and we became the best of friends. She told me she was going to the Curzons' fancy-dress affair next month. I asked her to go with me. We treated it as a kind of anniversary of ours. I remember Alice wore a Chinese costume and I wore a red *Cherkeska*, the Cossack uniform. I went head over heels for Alice that evening. Chinese costume or not, she reminded me of a Persian princess that I had seen on a mosaic in a mosque in the Middle East. She had entwined lapis and emerald bracelets on her wrists and she wore a very strange ornament at her throat, like a sun of many glowing semiprecious stones, and encircling it in a great half moon was a fantastic necklace. It was of hundreds of little gold rams' heads strung side by side on a single continuing filament. "My God," I asked her, "what is that?" I knew it was something extraordinary. I felt it. It was as if I was drawn to it; it seemed to have a power. I didn't like it, magnificent as it was, and I said so. She told me about it. It had come out of Tutankhamen's tomb. While it was not intrinsically valuable, it was a priceless museum piece. Each of the rams' heads were made of bitumen upon which soft gold had been laid, thousands of years before Christ. I begged her not to wear it again. I swear that evening I had felt the shiver of the unknown about us, and I began to give more than a second thought to Chips's laughing comment about the curse of Tutankhamen.

I am not a mystical person, preferring to stay away from such things. I believe that such things are better left alone, but the feeling is there within me. It has been a savior to me on numerous occasions. All during the war I had the conviction that Father, of all people, was around me whenever I was in danger. I have been steered in the right direction so many times that I would be a fool to say there was nothing to it. The danger is that if one gets too deep, one comes close to death within one's life. White magic, black magic, where is the dividing point? The black arts are a dangerous mystery, and they can encroach further and further upon one's personality to the time when they can well take over. In a sense, it is like unlocking Pandora's box, and as Andrew Lytle, the famous American writer, recently said to me: "What greater position is there for the devil to be in today than to have no one believe that he even exists?"

From that point on I became truly concerned for Alice; from that moment on I knew that, like my own mother, things spiritual could be Alice's Nemesis. I had the overpowering feeling that I was there to help. At the same time, there was nothing in this world that could have drawn us together more. We talked a great deal that evening and she told me all she knew or felt she knew. She had been very much affected by Kipling, especially his approach to reincarnation. She had met and talked with him and she had studied Hindu and Egyptian philosophy.

Then she told me a strange story. I will never forget the way she told it. It was as if she was transformed. Her eyes seemed distant, and her whole personality seemed to glow. She was convinced that she was the reincarnation of an Egyptian princess, the daughter of the High Priest of Heliopolis. He was the High Priest of Amon of the darkness and violently opposed to the short-lived reformation under Ikhnaton, whose approach was too close to Christianity. She herself had run away and become a convert to Ikhnaton's worship of Aten, the god of life-giving sun. When Ikhnaton died, she was recaptured and taken back to the dark imprisonment of her father. It was the strangest story I'd ever heard at a gay party in London, but I knew then and there I was needed because I felt that what she was saying was, incredibly enough, the truth. But events much later on must be the judge. In the meantime, I was convinced that a good time was the first order of business. So I whisked Alice off into the glitter of the dance and we forgot all about everything.

The social sensation of the evening was the resplendent arrival of a scarlet-robed Cardinal Richelieu and his retinue. The Cardinal seemed exceedingly frisky, and he pinched a couple of the girls. Then suddenly I was propelled by a sharp object from behind. I turned angrily around to see the Cardinal roaring with laughter and brandishing a hat pin. I looked closer, and it was Willy Kelly, my old friend from Australia.

After the party Alice and I made our way slowly back to the Ribblesdale house on Grosvenor Square. I took as long as possible for it wasn't far away.

Imagine, a Chinese princess and a Cossack horseman without his horse wandering hand in hand through the quiet and peaceful streets of sleeping London Town. It was a wonderful evening. That night Alice and I became engaged.

Ava Ribblesdale was strongly opposed, which is saying a good deal. She had never been known to be a weak adversary. She took immediate steps. Alice had a lot of beaux, and her mother began arranging things for her to do, so the following gentlemen, many of whom were friends of mine, began showing up at every possible opportunity: Arthur Wilson, Ivo Churchill, Pepe Merito, Lord Cochrane, and even an Annapolis midshipman who lived near the Astor country place at Rhinebeck, New York! His name was Bob Huntington, and he was Ava Ribblesdale's heavy artillery. Alice had known him for years, and he was extremely good-looking. Bob and I eventually became good friends, as he was Helen Astor's brother.

Actually, I quite understood Lady Ribblesdale's point; she felt that Alice ought to have more of a fling, but I was hanged if she was going to get away with it. Besides, I knew perfectly well that she had her heart set on Alice marrying a British peer, or at least a well-to-do Englishman, certainly not an impoverished Russian prince.

Pepe Merito was a foreigner, like me; so he was in disfavor. But at least he was wealthy, so Alice was hustled off to his place in Spain, with Ava Ribblesdale sacrificing herself as chaperon due to the extreme urgency of the situation. Alice and I corresponded regularly.

Actually Pepe was a very nice fellow. He raised baby bulls for the bullfights. Visitors to his place were entertained and entertained alike by getting out into a miniature bull ring with the calves, which were fierce little creatures, and executing veronicas and other mutations of passes at these baby bulls. Alice went there twice, which didn't please me at all, because I knew by then that she rarely did anything that she didn't want to do, Ava Ribblesdale or no Ava Ribblesdale! Pepe did a big business making a very fine sherry.

Ivo Churchill was the son of Consuelo, the Duchess of Marlborough, now Mme. Balsan. He was artistic, a good collector of modern art, a very quiet, highly cultivated Englishman. Knowing Alice, I considered him a worthy adversary, and then again, Lady Ribblesdale was smiling upon him.

Lord Cochrane I knew only slightly, not having run into him since the grouse shoot at Cortachy with Millicent. He was an outdoorsman, and a fine shot, but from the way he had bundled up and spared himself during that frigid outing and took care of himself afterwards and watched himself in drafts and things like that, I gathered that he was a little overcautious. I liked him, and I'm very sorry to say that he very incautiously called on Alice the very day that we were announcing our engagement. The situation threw Alice into a complete tail spin. She had been planning to tell him, when he had arrived at Grosvenor Square, before she could say a word, he was proposing.

Alice, quite typically, and wholly contrary to her mother's wishes, suddenly cut loose from them all. The more we saw of each other, the more I felt the parental opposition grow, and then Ava Ribblesdale whisked Alice off to the United States with her and no more nonsense.

That was the gloomy winter of 1922-1923. Alice was twenty then, but even at that tender age she was just as determined as her mother in her quiet inimitable way. She told me not to worry, that we would weather the storm, and besides, she said, her mother's custody would terminate when she became twenty-one on the seventh of July. She would come into her own on that day, and she would have control of her own funds. I was very touched by her remarks; at the same time I remember that my eyes widened. I had had my first taste of Astor will power in action. It's something not to be taken lightly.

Those days had their amusing moments, too, such as the times when Lady Ribblesdale and I with Alice on my arm would confront each other at the various parties. In true Edwardian fashion, nothing was to be demonstrated in public. We would bow politely to each other, smile faintly and then move gently on.

Helen Astor on the other hand was terribly fond of Alice. Realizing that Alice was hell-bent on marrying me, she tried to help us in every possible way. She had the most remarkable poise, something that I had not often seen even in royalty. She was calm, she had great common sense and gave good counsel, she kept her head at all times and ever since has been just about my closest friend. Helen was a beautiful creature. She had exquisite ash-blond hair and was devoted to music and musicians. Tall, statuesque, and outwardly a little forbidding even, Helen was underneath unbelievably kind, not only to us, but to everybody, and Helen hasn't changed a bit today. I know that if anything ever happened to me, I could rely on her completely.

At that time, Helen had taken a little house in the Bois at Paris. Alice would go off to visit her there and I would go to Paris over the weekends. I have a suspicion that Ava Ribblesdale caught on to all of this, hence her sudden removal to America. Needless to say, Alice and I wrote to each other every single day.

That summer Alice became twenty-one, Ava Ribblesdale abdicated gracefully in the grand Edwardian manner, brought Alice back to London, and was charming to me thereafter to the rest of her days, which were many and wonderful. Alice immediately bought herself a Rolls-Royce, and her chauffeur, Gilbert, became a great friend of mine. His driving was superb and fast. It had to be, since Alice was almost always late.

Still, we had problems. We had to wait for my British divorce, although my divorce papers in the Russian Church had been signed by none other than

Metropolitan Platon himself on January 1. It was a difficult time and we had to be very patient.

We had some very good friends like Lord and Lady Carlisle who invited Alice and me to visit them over the Christmas holidays at their castle on the border of Scotland, so that we could be together. We didn't want to offend Lady Ribblesdale, if possible. Our friends began to get used to the situation. Alice and I met quietly and we did our best to overcome the opposition of her family. The British press, however, is incredibly nosy. For us, secrecy was difficult to maintain because the English branch of the Astor family was so much in the news, partly because of Lady Astor's strenuous political career, and partly because the English branch of the family had just then reentered British journalism by buying control of the London Times.

Nancy Astor was something. When I first met her she had just come back from Bolshevik Russia. With a gleam in her eye she baited me: "And what a wonderful job they've done over there in such a short time!" she said. Of course she didn't mean it, but she was testing me. I went to the stock exchange each morning. Alice and I found ways of seeing each other during the day or in the evening. We played golf after working hours and met at parties at night. The costume balls that then flourished simplified things. Many of the parties were so big that one went entirely unnoticed in the crowd. Then again Helen Astor still had her house in Paris and Alice and I were sometimes able to get away for weekends and visit her there. We went sightseeing around Paris, hunting out little-known restaurants where we would not be likely to meet anyone we knew.

On one memorable occasion Alice and I went to a fancy-dress ball at the Duchess of Sutherland's. Prince and Princess Nicholas of Greece were there. Vere Bessborough and I were disguised as drunken waiters, with false noses and wigs. We brought along a lot of cheap crockery. During the supper we started waiting on the royal table, and very badly, too. I had my thumb in Geordie Sutherland's scrambled eggs, as I put the dish before him. He never moved a muscle, so I signaled Vere and he dropped the crockery. This time Geordie was transfixed with horror. He was using the royal service that evening in honor of Prince and Princess Nicholas. I knew what he was thinking—everybody did. And then I took his scrambled eggs away from him in the middle of a mouthful. He was livid, but since royalty was present, he didn't dare say anything. It was an interesting period in many respects, the Olympic Games in Paris that year, the great tennis matches in Wimbledon, the theater experiencing one of its high points, with Fred and Adele Astaire in *Stop Flirting!* George Robey in *Leap Year*, Constance Collier in *Our Betters*, Sybil Thorndike in *Saint Joan*, and Tallulah Bankhead in *The Creaking Chair*.

On June 23, 1924, I at last received an official certificate from the Royal Court of Justice of the County of Middlesex, certifying that Princess Catherine Alexandrovna Obolensky, widow of Prince Alexander Bariatinsky, was granted a divorce from Prince Serge Platonovich Obolensky Neledinsky-Meletzky, by the Judge, the Honorable Sir Thomas Gardner Horridge, Knight.

Alice's and my engagement was officially announced on the Fourth of July.

The American newspapers had announced that we were to be married on July 18. When that day arrived, the reporters called at the Russian Church on Buckingham Palace Road, and found nothing scheduled for the day except a memorial service for Emperor Nicholas II, which caused a lot of confusion. Vincent Astor wanted to give Alice a unique wedding present, and finally decided to give her the two great diamond earrings that had belonged to Marie Antoinette. She had sewn them into her corsage when she fled from Paris and was caught and brought to the Bastille and the guillotine. They had later belonged to Felix Youssoupoff. I begged Vincent not to buy them. I am superstitious in some respects, and those jewels were associated in my mind with bloodshed and tragedy—the duel and death of Nicholas Youssoupoff and the Rasputin unpleasantness. The earrings seemed to bring tragedy to whoever owned them. Marjorie Post owns them today, but she seems happy as a lark, so who can tell?

Alice and I were finally married for the first time at nine in the morning of July 24, 1924, at the registry office on Buckingham Palace Road, the civil ceremony. Paul of Serbia was my best man. Our car was caught in traffic and we were five minutes late, an unheard-of thing for the groom! We found Lady Ribblesdale and Alice ahead of us with one of the officials from the American Embassy. Alice then rushed home to change for the Episcopal ceremony in the Savoy Chapel. This time Paul and I were on time. Because quite a crowd was gathering and the church had to be entered through a long courtyard, Alice came in by a side door with her cousin Waldorf Astor, who gave her away. Only the family were present. Alice wore a bridal gown of ivory georgette, with a lace veil, fastened with a band of orange blossoms, forming the train. From there we hurried to the Russian Church of St. Philip, for the Eastern Orthodox service. Here, among others were: Prince Nicholas of Greece and Grand Duchess Helen, who were seated with my mother, my cousin Prince Dimitri, the Earl and Countess of Westmoreland, Viscount and Viscountess Astor, Major John Jacob Astor, Chips Channon, Lord and Lady Loughborough, Lady Emerald Cunard, and Colonel Paul Rodzianko.

The day was now long advanced, for the Russian service is a lengthy one. We then went to Lady Ribblesdale's house for a small wedding breakfast, and went off on the boat train to the Channel steamer. Our honeymoon was in Deauville. The trip across the Channel was a bit windy, but not rough, and we sat on deck, with Bishop Manning of the Episcopal Diocese of New York on one side, and on the other Louis Wiley, the editor of the New York Times, both of whom I had met before at Nancy Astor's. We plunged into an animated discussion, on one hand, of the problems of the Episcopal Church and the Russian Church, and on the other side of the internal situation in Yugoslavia.

After the crossing we spent a week at Deauville in the astonishing bliss of having no one we knew, or no one, apparently, who knew us, anywhere around. Then my old friend Saveli Sorine appeared. He said he wanted to see how I looked when I was happy.

Each morning Alice and I took horseback rides along the beach. Each afternoon we went for a motor trip over the summer roads. After a week we returned to London, and then set out for Canada. We planned to buy a ranch. I thought I knew enough agriculture from my days at Krasnaya Gorka, and my experience with the grain-handling, to make a go of it. After we decided to marry, Alice and I had agreed to live part of the time where we would not see too many people, somewhere in the country where we could be happy.

It was I who persuaded her to make the trip into Calgary.

Mr. Beatty, the president of the Canadian Pacific Railroad, happened to be on the Empress liner that carried us to Canada. Evelyn Fitzgerald, from the flat above mine, had introduced us. Mr. Beatty was charming. He arranged our whole trip. We crossed Canada in a private car to Calgary, with side trips all along the way. We went to Banff, then by car to Lake Windermere, where we camped at the remote end of the lake, very isolated and wild, and paddled over the lovely blue water of that mountain paradise each morning.

Back at Banff, we rejoined the more civilized world, and then went by train to Kamaloops, and into pretty wild country, deep in British Columbia, looking at ranch sites. We went far north along the old Caribou Trail into sub-Arctic weather. The winter had begun in August. The trip became too trying for Alice. The prevailing moisture-laden winds from the Pacific swept in gales around the peaks of the Canadian Rockies, and the search for a place to live became more and more discouraging.

I had hoped to locate in secluded country, for I knew only too well how difficult it was to make a success of marriage in a large city, but the country we saw was too remote. A steady wind blew across the plains. The western prairies were arid, with dry bunch grass and occasional pines. Even the most beautifully situated ranch stood in windblown loneliness, or loomed up out of rainstorms after hard drives over dirt roads. Alice didn't like it. My old Balliol friend Cuthbert Holmes, now married and with a family, had real estate interests in Vancouver and Victoria in British Columbia. We visited him, and then returned to Banff, from which we looked at Calgary property on occasional trips.

We visited the Dukhobors, those strange groups of Russian peasants who settled at Calgary in their own colonies, having as few dealings as possible with the modern world. They were uneducated, refusing to learn to read on principle. Yet their leader was a highly intelligent man, and the colonies were amazingly prosperous. We went from one to the other, villages thirty miles or so apart, real Russian peasant villages, and a feast was laid out for us in each. I saw Alice was getting more and more uncomfortable, and I didn't feel well myself. But they had lavished so much on this entertainment that we could not refuse them.

When we had recovered, and were back at Calgary, we went into the Ritz hotel dining room for dinner, and to my astonishment the orchestra began playing the Imperial Russian anthem. It startled me to hear it. The orchestra leader was a Russian emigre. And there was also present a Russian officer who had successfully arranged to locate on Calgary farms, a large group of White Russians from China.

Alice did not complain of the hardships of our search for ranch sites. But I realized the poor girl was not happy, and telegraphed Helen and Vincent Astor in New York to say that we were giving up the project and returning home.

My first view of the United States was of the old Astor mansion on Fifth Avenue. We reached New York at night, and were taken to the huge chateau at Sixtieth Street and the Avenue, really two houses rebuilt into one, the most imposing mansion in New York, if not in the New World. Entering the great hall, we passed through huge bronze gates, and came into a reception room whose walls were paneled with canvases patterned after Brussels cartoons. Facing the entrance was a big sculptured fireplace. Beyond it lay the ballroom, which was also the art gallery. This was the ballroom where Mrs. Astor, Alice's grandmother, held the great balls that had made her the leader of New York society in the days when she and Ward McAllister between them drew up the famous list of the four hundred people who were to comprise New York society. Now Helen and Vincent used it each January on the anniversary of Mrs. Astor's balls, for a charity benefit.

A hundred paintings were ranged on the high walls around the ballroom, principally Seventeenth-Century French art, with Corot providing the masterpieces of the collection, but the vast array of odalisques, dancing girls, cows in meadows, cottages, sleeping children, dogs herding sheep, sunrises and sunsets, Roman ruins, parting lovers, homecoming travelers, made it a monument of mid-Victorian taste. One of the huge canvases that caught my eye was Detaille's realistic painting, "The Russian Countryside" so exact that it might almost have been taken from scenes near Krasnaya Gorka.

Statues were everywhere, masterpieces like Houdon's "Voltaire, Greek and Roman works, sculptured groups; and the famous prizes of the Astor art collection, the six priceless Brussels tapestries, glowed with subdued color. The marble stairs and the enormous, heavily gilded drawing room created an impression of almost overpowering solidity and permanence. It was a magnificent relic. Vincent had just at that time decided to give it up, and announced plans to raze the old Astor house for an apartment to be built on the site. So I again felt that I was seeing the end of an era, as I had felt I witnessed the end of the Edwardian period in my Christ Church days at Oxford.

Alice quickly recovered her high spirits on leaving the high mountain wildernesses of Calgary. My impressions of the United States in the days that followed were hectic—I made tourist visits to the wonders of New York, the Metropolitan Museum of Art, the Museum of Natural History, the skyscraper canyons of lower Manhattan, and Texas Guinan's night club. Prohibition was the abiding interest of Americans in those days; in going out in the evening, the host presented each male guest with a flask to carry with him. From a few days of this amiable existence we moved suddenly to the solitude of the Astor estate at Rhinebeck, a couple of hours north of New York, overlooking the Hudson. The tennis house, built by Stanford White in his happiest period, was almost as magnificent as the main structure. It contained a huge entrance hall, with light, airy lines despite its immensity, a sunken swimming pool, and a covered tennis court, the first in the country, and a big dining room that looked out over terraced grounds to the Hudson. The mansion itself had already become obsolete with changing times, and Vincent planned to raze it and convert the tennis house into a residence.

All this sort of thing was very new to me, on a different scale than anything I had ever seen before. The New York friends I had made had more money to spend than anyone I had ever known, and kept up large yachts, houses in Newport and Long Island and in the South, as well as their mansions in New York, many of them properties more elaborate than those of the Czars of Russia. Their social life depended a lot on the night clubs of New York, to which their guests were invariably taken, along with the speak-easies, whose mixture of informal entertainment and law evasion I found extremely interesting. Vincent had been the benefactor of so many institutions that whenever Alice and I visited them, we were generally shown around by their officials. On our visit to the Museum of Natural History, Dr. Clarence Hay conducted us through the exhibits. Dr. Hay had gone on Vincent's first Galapagos trip on the *Nourmahal* and had discovered in the Galapagos Islands—or rather in only one of the Galapagos, the most remote and the least known—a rare spineless cactus which provided good food for cattle, and which, if it could be made to grow elsewhere, promised to be of a revolutionary importance to cattle raising in arid lands. I was not along on that particular voyage.

Alice and I returned to London, where we rented John and Momo Marriot's house on Hill Street. Alice wanted to buy a London house, and we took over the Marriots' place as a temporary residence until we could find a permanent home. We had not been in London twenty-four hours when a small square box, sealed with Cartier seals, arrived as a gift from Laura Corrigan. It contained a baby rattle. We never discovered how Laura learned that Alice was expecting a baby, as we had kept it a profound secret from everyone.

I returned to my desk at Byng, Foley, and Alice began house-hunting. She found the likeliest prospect to be Hanover Lodge in Regent's Park, the home of Admiral and Lady Beatty. It was on the market, but there was a mix-up about it. The Admiral had never wanted to sell, but his wife, insistent that they should, had put it up for sale. The purchase of the house was arranged without the buyer's name being disclosed. Alice signed the deed not knowing any of the above.

"Poor old Hanover Lodge," Admiral Beatty wrote to Lady Beatty from the Admiralty that night. "I shall be sorry to leave it, but you will be pleased, and that's all that matters. The Obolenskys have bought it and got it very cheap. Well, it's gone now, and there's no more to be said."[1]

But when Lady Beatty got the letter and heard that Alice had bought it, she wanted it back. In fact, she offered to buy it back at a very large premium. As we had barely taken possession, Alice suggested that we return the house, take the premium, and that I keep it as a nest egg. But I knew that she liked Hanover Lodge and wanted it. So we kept it and began accumulating furniture and possessions.

Our household of the day consisted of my chef, Vassily, who had married an English girl; Alice's maid, Boyak; Gilbert, the chauffeur, and his wife; Dean, our butler, who doubled as my valet; and a cairn terrier named Gin. We were a happy household, and the period that followed our settling in London included the happiest years of my life. We spent a lot of time shopping for furniture and to my amazement I discovered that the early training I had received from the instructors in the Art Institute in St. Petersburg, on periods of design and the work of the great craftsmen, was still with me. This became most helpful. We became familiar with the London dealers: Moss, Harris; Partridge, Lenihan, and their guild. Gradually we acquired a beautiful collection of old pieces.

One day a dealer called, saying that he wanted to see me confidentially. When we got together, he told me that he had been approached by an emissary from the Bolsheviks, a London dealer who did business with them. The Reds were selling old Russian art treasures, jewels, and all sorts of valuables. The Bolsheviks had decided that now that I was married to Alice it would be easy for me to acquire, for an astronomical sum, Philip Maliavin's huge portrait of myself that had hung in the library of our St. Petersburg house. They evidently believed that I had millions to spend. The very last thing I wanted was Maliavin's portrait; but there was an interesting bit of information that emerged from the discussion with the Bolsheviks' London dealer. He told me that the house on the Mitninskaya had been converted into an orphanage. Before it was taken over by the government, Ignatie, my old butler, had taken the silver and valuables and plastered them up behind the wall of a bedroom.

---

[1] *The Life and Letters of David Beatty, Admiral of the Fleet*, London: Hodder and Stoughton.

When Soviet officials had come to rifle the house, they found nothing, but there arose in Russia a legend of the fabulous Obolensky treasure. Since the house had always been watched, the Bolsheviks logically believed that whatever treasure was there had been concealed somewhere on the premises. They had searched and searched but had found nothing. Then the house was turned into the orphanage. Years later, a little orphan girl began poking at the plaster beside her bed. She and prodded a little at a time, until a hole began to form in the wall. Finally one night the plaster crumbled through into a deep recess. She poked her arm in, felt something inside, pulled, and out onto the floor tumbled a golden spoon. That was the end of the Obolensky treasure.

In the meantime, Maliavin's picture remained on the library wall. After I refused to buy it, the Bolsheviks moved it to one of their galleries to be included among their national art treasures. I think they made a big mistake, considering my opinion of the painting, but there I am, forever enshrined in my sailor suit and staring with an enraptured expression on my face at a model of an obsolete Czarist battleship for generations of Soviet art students to study.

Alice and I moved into our new house in the spring of 1925 shortly before Ivan was born. We were still shopping for a few things that Hanover Lodge needed. One morning we visited Christie's auction rooms. After lunch, first labor pains began. The doctors were called, and nurses began arriving in droves. I was relegated to my study downstairs. There I sat with the fierce bust of Ivan the Terrible glowering down upon me. Chips arrived for dinner, and exactly at midnight Ivan was born. Chips and I were allowed to see Alice and the baby, who, Chips said, looked exactly like Vincent Astor.

After the death of her sister Queen Alexandra, the Dowager Empress Marie Feodorovna announced that she was returning to Copenhagen to end her days. We got an audience, Paul Rodzianko and I, as representatives of the Chevalier Guards, of which she was the honorary colonel in chief. We presented her with the traditional bouquet—red and white, the colors of the regiment. She accepted them graciously, with a smile, and acted as if the whole regiment were drawn up before her, instead of two of its surviving officers.

Paul had opened a successful riding school near Windsor, where he taught horsemanship to a lot of famous people. It never ceased to astonish me that we had had in the same regiment Paul and his brother Alexander, who formed two-thirds of the team that had won the King Edward Cup three times running.

In those days Alexander had a famous horse called Eros, one of the great jumpers of the prewar years. Alexander rode him at Windsor, at Olympia, at the Vienna Horse Show, everywhere. Eros became a very famous horse. During the Revolution Eros had disappeared. Meanwhile, Alexander, now a general, commanded a division under Yudenich, making his way to Sweden after the collapse of the White armies. After he crossed the frontier, he met a Swedish officer riding along on a horse he recognized. It was Eros. Alexander stopped and chatted and asked about the horse, which the Swedish officer said had been sold him by the Bolsheviks. He knew the horse, had even seen him jump at Vienna before the war. "Rodzianko owned him, you know," the Swede said confidentially. "By the way, sir, what is your name?"

"Rodzianko," said Alexander, chuckling. Immediately, the Swedish officer dismounted, shook the general's hand, and gave him back his horse. Thus, Eros lived out his days in comfort in Paul's riding stable at Windsor, the only horse in our regiment, so far as I know, that got out of Russia after the Revolution.

Peter Zouboff also was in Yudenich's outfit and commanded a cavalry regiment. After its dissolution, Peter went out through Estonia. There he began helping the Russian Orthodox clergy to organize, and got the Church on a sound footing. As usual, he was thinking of becoming a bishop, but I told him to wait. Even then I had the feeling that he would be more valuable outside the church as a working layman.

By this time, my half sister Olga, who had married Captain Stroukoff, was living on the Stroukoff estate in Vilna, Poland; and by this time they had one daughter. They had been bothered by Bolshevik goons who were constantly slipping across the border from Soviet Russia. They had to go about armed—just in case. Persons of the old regime living on the Russian border were known to have been killed by such people. In fact, it was a common occurrence. News of this sort was coming our way frequently. The Bolsheviks were reaching out more and more to attack us in the countries of our exile. Thus the people we had known began to scatter widely. Many were already in Shanghai. A great number settled in Yugoslavia. The biggest colony gravitated to Paris, while a good many sought sanctuary in London, and every day more and more were moving to the United States.

Sonia Gagarin, to whom I had been engaged, reached the United States with her mother. Two of her brothers were also in the United States. The other brothers, both engineers, remained in Soviet Russia.

Natalie Narishkin, whom I had gotten to know in Yalta, made her way to England. She published her memoirs of the revolutionary period and included many of our group's experiences in the Crimea. Baby Bariatinsky, who married an Englishman, also wrote a volume in which Catherine and I appear at the time of our arrival in Kiev in disguise.

Colonel Levshin, who had gotten me into the Chevalier Guards and was the husband of my cousin Natasha Koutouzoff, escaped the Bolsheviks and lived in Paris. Their children settled in Morocco. And Serge Koutouzoff, who had headed the St. Petersburg recruiting stations, settled in the United States, his daughters marrying Americans. Sonia, the youngest child of my Aunt Vera Koutouzoff, married young, and her husband was killed by the Bolsheviks. After the Revolution she married a former officer of the Chevalier Guards, Serge Boutourline, settled with him in Boston, and raised her family. The eldest

Koutouzoff child was Countess Grabbe, the wife of a colonel of the Chevalier Guards. They, too, found their way to Paris. One of their daughters, Sonia Engalicheff, became a very fine artist, creating matchless miniatures; and she came to the United States and lives in Long Island.

The daughters of Uncle Alexis—the uncle who had been *Oberprocurator* of the Czar, the Eye of the Emperor in the Church—made their way out of Russia. Dolly married and became the Duchess of Leuchtenberg. They now live at a ski resort at St. Sauveur in the Laurentians in Canada. Most of the children of Uncle Alexander also escaped. Dimitri lived in Paris. The musical career of Aliosha I have already mentioned.

Aliosha had several daughters. His wife's, Luba's, dress shop on Park Avenue did well immediately, my wife Alice providing part of the capital. On the whole, then, it seemed that the people who escaped from Russia were establishing themselves. But there were many shaded areas in the picture. Over many of us lay the constant threat of violence like that which threatened my sister Olga and her husband.

Catherine's boys, Andre and Buddy, both went through unstable periods in their lives, dropping out of sight for long periods at a time. Buddy once visited me in England. He stayed a few days, and vanished. Andre was even less reliable. The only person who managed to keep track of them was their old nurse, Miss Lily Pickens, and she did so when everyone else gave up. From her I learned that Buddy had gone to the United States; she wanted me to find him a job. I did so, but he soon wandered off. Later, again, from Miss Pickens, I heard that he was in Hollywood. Presently it developed that he had married someone there. The name Bariatinsky is a magical one for many Russians. Buddy, I gathered, married someone in the movie colony who knew what it meant in Russia. But soon Buddy disappeared. He turned up in Shanghai, where he lived for a long time. The Japanese invasion of China set all the Far East in turmoil, and as nothing further was heard of him, I suspected that Buddy was dead.

While I was serving as a paratrooper in the Second World War in the American Army, my orderly appeared one day and said that a Corporal Bariatinsky wished to see me. It was Buddy. We had a nice talk, although I noticed that he didn't really tell me very much. The last I heard of him was that he was a sergeant at Fort Riley.

The third son of Uncle Alexander Obolensky was Peter, who was just my age, a strange fellow, quiet and withdrawn, who always kept to himself. He married Olga Obolensky, not my sister, but the daughter of the governor general of Finland. They had two sons, Ivan and Alexander. Peter Obolensky was arrested by the Bolsheviks and sent to a labor camp. Miraculously, he escaped to Paris. Still back in Soviet Russia, Olga, thinking he was dead, became engaged. Her fiancé was taken into custody and was sent to a whole series of labor camps. Whenever he was transferred, she followed after him, moving to the nearby towns, visiting him whenever she could, and getting him supplies.

The boys were then five or six years old. Cousin Olga had kept a few pieces of jewelry. She sold them, got in touch with two Finlanders, and gave them the money she had raised. They agreed to smuggle the two boys out of Russia. She did not have my address, but something about me had appeared in Bolshevik papers, so she addressed them simply to "Serge Obolensky, London, England."

The Finlanders moved openly with the boys to a place near the border. There, telling the boys they were all going to play Indians, they placed them in a canoe, covered them with furs, and paddled across the Gulf to Finland. Waiting in Finland until they found a trustworthy-looking sea captain, they made a bargain with him to transport the boys to England, giving him part of the money for their passage. He was an old sea dog of an Englishman, commanding a weather-beaten tramp steamer. He put tags on the boys that read, "Obolensky Boys, Ivan and Alexander. Deliver to Serge Obolensky, London, England."

While we were living in Hanover Lodge, a telegram arrived from Hull. It came from the captain of the tramp. It said that two boys had been placed on the train addressed to me. So I met the train and took them in. But there was really no problem. Their grandmother and an aunt were in London, and they were delighted at the prospect. Thereafter, the boys made their home with them. Alice and I undertook to provide for their education. They went to school in France, eventually finishing up at the Sorbonne.

In the interim, Olga, their mother, disappeared into the Arctic mists. Her fiancé had been moved to still another labor camp to work on the Onega Canal. This was the terrible one on which the lives of so many thousands of prisoners were expended. Here Soviet security was prohibitive. Olga trained herself to become a nurse on the chance that thereby she could find ways and means to keep near her fiancé. Finally, she got a note that he had died, and she was told to leave the area. She was allowed to establish some sort of permanent headquarters in the town of Tver. After that, nothing more was heard of Cousin Olga. Her sons grew up. Twenty years later, during the Second World War, Olga and her son Ivan met in Germany, both prisoners of the Germans, not even knowing that they were mother and son—the most amazing meeting of the sort I have ever heard of. But that belongs later in this account.

As a result of Alexander and Ivan, Alice endowed a school in France where the children of Russian refugees could be prepared for their education in the new world they were entering. Then she did other things for them, finding them jobs, helping them in business. She was amazing.

I had spoken so much of my old polo-playing days at Oxford that Alice also offered to buy me a string of polo ponies—or, more exactly, she started to give me the ponies, but I could not accept them. As I intimated before, there was so much distress, so much hunger and heartbreak about us that the very thought of the cost and upkeep of those unnecessary horses was too much. At my request, Alice used the money she had intended to devote to our stable to establish a foundation to provide for Russian emigres in need.

CHAPTER XXIII

The years after the war were as glamorous as any in English history. There were dinners and dances every evening during the London season, and the current of the times ran so strongly toward entertainment that one felt a little dull for even being interested in politics and economics when there was so much going on. London was bulging with royalty, they were still entertained in those days with the full prerogatives of their royal positions, even though many of their countries had been run by dictators for decades, like King Manuel's Portugal. Some indeed had even completely disappeared from the maps of the world. Quite a few of these royal personages, like Prince Nicholas and Grand Duchess Helen of Greece, were old friends.

Others, like the young Queen of Rumania and her sister, were new social favorites enjoying a tremendous London success. Their goings and comings furnished excuses for innumerable social gatherings; their affairs provided the raw material for endless gossip. It is a common error to believe that only the people of democratic countries are interested in royalty because they have no royal families in their own nation.

The reverse is also true. Royalty was London's business. The city was dedicated to royalty with a professional interest and flair, just as Hollywood is interested in motion pictures, or Detroit in automobiles. A good many of these royal visitors came to play tennis on the courts at Hanover Lodge. We had two courts, one grass and one composition.

Most afternoons there were many friends who came to play tennis and to tea—Duff Cooper; Michael Herbert; Jimmy and Toto, the Duke and Duchess of Alba; and Americans like Jimmy Van Alen, of Newport, whose wife was a cousin of Alice's, and Barbara Murray, one of Alice's closest friends, who had married an Englishman, Lord Francis Doon.

One royal family of a small principality threw a revealing light on the royal feelings of a time that is usually considered synonymous with freedom or royal prerogative in all respects. On the contrary, concern for one's people and propriety was put above all else. The queen of this Graustarkian realm was hopelessly in love with one of the British dukes, who was likewise secretly in love with her. Neither of the two was at all happily married. They saw each other rarely, but their devotion persisted over years and despite long separations. Consciousness of their royal positions led them to behave with more perfect dignity than ever. Whenever this queen was in London, they both came every day to play tennis on our grass court. I have the greatest respect for people like that. I felt terribly sorry for them.

We lived like this: in midsummer we visited the United States, first at Newport, then to Rhinebeck for the fall, returning to London for Christmas, and leaving in January for St. Moritz to ski, then stopping off awhile in Paris before going to the south of France for the spring and returning to London as the new season began. Sometimes we remained in England in the autumn, weekending with friends like the Duchess of Rutland at Belvoir, or Lord and Lady Curzon at Hackwood or Mrs. Greville at Polsden Lacy. We went to the great J-Boat races for the Astor Cup at Newport, a beautiful sight as these huge craft, never more to be seen, hissed through the water like gigantic geese in flight—then on to Scotland to stay with Lord and Lady Beatty and shoot grouse. I rode to hounds at Belvoir, and then, on returning to the States, went off to Bernardsville, New Jersey, at the invitation of Oliver and Mary Filley. There the Pines mounted me. They had good hunters. The hunt there was called the Peapack, and it sported a distinctly local breed of hound, able to pick up the scent of a fox even in dry weather. We had some fine hunts there. We were in full cry when I remember jumping a narrow gate between ugly wire fences on both sides, going over stirrup to stirrup with Jimmy Clark, a very fierce and gallant horseman. Our tandem jump was a topic of conversation. The hunt ball afterwards was a highly colorful event, with all the men in their pink coats, the evening variation of hunting dress similar to tails. I remember being very stiff that evening and it was hard for me to sit down. I had neglected to soap my behind for a smoother ride.

It was a life of sport and leisure and I would be exaggerating my interest in world affairs if I did not admit that I enjoyed it enormously. My recollections of the decade are a haze of golden memories: the Hudson in the fall, the banks blazing with all the green, red, brown and gold tints of the turning leaves; Newport with the glaze of summer sun over the sailboats in the harbor; the old Fall River Line; St. Moritz, where we skied every other day, toiling up to the heights with our food in packs on our backs; not to mention old ocean greats like the *Majestic*, *Olympic*, *Berengaria*, *Mauretania*, *Aquitania* and *Leviathan*.

Nothing world-shaking happened—which was pleasant for a change. Existence was simultaneously colorful and untroubled. I remember things like a ghastly rough crossing on the Majestic, or the explosion of an oil heater in Helen Astor's house in Paris, as being among the foremost of our trials of the time. But glamor is the most perishable of all commodities. All those parties and hunts and voyages have dissolved into generalized recollections of a very good time. I still had a job of sorts at Byng, Foley, and went occasionally to the office. A nagging inward weight at my own inactivity bothered me like an old wound. I got highly concerned at the news of Hitler's Putsch at Munich, if only because General Ludendorff was supporting Hitler. Any officer like myself who had fought against Ludendorff was bound to take anything that he was engaged in seriously. I recognized what a bold and ruthless military genius he was, and therefore I was certain that Hitler was a serious menace. My fears, however, were much in the minority, no matter how much I expounded my thesis that Ludendorff would not have been tied up with Hitler were he the complete fool he was then for the most part considered.

But in the midst of the general well-being that had settled over society there was not much room for matters of this sort. Politics were generally dull. History was not being made. Diplomats of the Locarno sort were no balls of fire. The possibility of another war was slight—except that Vincent Astor was gloomy about things. I must say he always seemed to know.

Alice and I had no difficulties in those early days aside from the problem of being late for dinner. She was famous for not being on time. Now, in England, when royalty was present, all the other guests were required to be present five minutes before the royal guests arrived. But Alice was always just as late as ever. With my "old world" upbringing, the strain on me was great. The protocol of court promptitude in my childhood and the vast care my parents and all my family had given to court functions, made the prospect of arriving after the royal guests a hair-raising one. One evening my nerve broke as the minutes ticked away. Alice was changing dresses, dissatisfied with this or that. I fled, and caught a taxi, arriving on time. Alice sneaked in after the first course. The next time the same thing happened, and I went on ahead. But after having to sneak in alone twice, Alice reformed and was thereafter on time.

She managed this by putting all clocks in Hanover Lodge forty minutes ahead; she had a make-up kit put in her Rolls, and then she ordered Gilbert to drive like the wind. It was an effective procedure and she frequently got dressed en route.

The years passed so lightly that when trying to segregate one sequence of parties from another I find them all dissolving into one, and I have to rack my brains trying to recollect what year each took place in, or who was present. I recollect that 1925, the year Ivan was born, was deemed a sort of vintage year of great parties, but Alice was kept in bed for a considerable period after Ivan's birth, and remained not strong, so we only went out a little.

Ivan was christened in a marble font at Hanover Lodge in the dining room. He disapproved strongly of the total immersion. The Russian priest from the Russian Church in which we had been married, officiated, along with various other clergy. His godparents were Paul of Serbia; Grand Duchess Helen, the mother of Princess Marina, later the Duchess of Kent; Chips Channon and Waldorf Astor.

Like most babies, Ivan proved to be a good sailor, but his superlative nurse, Miss Spiller, was a very bad one, and so was Alice's maid, Boyak; but Dean, the butler, made out all right, as I did, and we came into New York harbor in good condition. There Vincent and Helen met us with the *Nourmahal*—the old one, not the great *Nourmahal* he later built—and we started at once for Newport up the East River and out on the Sound. It turned into a trip even rougher than the one we had been on. As we plowed on, the weather darkened; it was obvious we were going to be seasick. Helen, my sister-in-law, never drank champagne. But she looked at the little yacht and the big waves, got a bottle of champagne and went to bed. "It's the only way," she said solemnly. My main recollection of the trip is of Helen sitting up in bed and giggling when the *Nourmahal* began standing on its bow and then its stern. I fled to my cabin, where Alice already was. Thereafter, I, in company with everyone else except Vincent and the crew, groaned in misery throughout the storm. Never have I been happier than when we were reported off Brenton Reef, the Newport narrows just ahead.

Each morning at Newport we met at Bailey's Beach. We swam. The families assembled, Goelets, Vanderbilts, Astors. It was a fantastic American panorama for me. There, Ivan and Miss Spiller joined the other children and their nurses. Daisy Van Alen's two sons were about Alice's age, and Jimmy Van Alen had been one of Alice's old beaux. Daisy was fond of Alice and exceptionally kind to me. One of the great ladies of Newport, she knew it like a book. Besides, she was a native, one of a hardier breed who lived there the year round. She had an old-fashioned electric phaeton which she drove around those shaded streets, up stately Bellevue Avenue, and into the drives of the great villas. They reminded me eerily of the villas of Czarskoe Selo.

In fact, Newport reminded me of Czarskoe Selo the more I saw of it, the great trees, the gardens, the avenues of villas, the same kind of architecture, even the smells. On the beach, or by the water's edge, the illusion vanished. The blue sky and water, the huge yachts (in which Vincent and his friends regularly commuted to New York) and the maze of slanting sails of an afternoon off the Torpedo Station gave Newport its own distinctive air. But again inland, the houses dating from the island's colonial era, stark and white and functional, the sandy roads and scattered fir trees, the quiet unobtrusive sense of leisure, all summoned up the vanished, colorful world of the old Russian capital. Newport in 1925 was more like Czarskoe Selo in 1895 than I can possibly hope to communicate.

We basked lazily at Bailey's Beach all morning, lunched with friends at Beechwood, the Astor house, or elsewhere, and in the afternoon the *Nourmahal* weighed anchor to go outside the narrows and watch the yacht races. Vincent was Commodore of the New York Yacht Club in those days. At night we danced in gaily decorated pavilions, tents that were put up for the various occasions that were held almost daily in the lanternlit gardens of the fabled Goelet, Brown, Vanderbilt or other mansions. In Russia things were neither as lavish nor as well organized. I have never seen such constant or easy sumptuousness, which led me to believe that great Russian fortunes had been much smaller. Frankly, it made Russian efforts look picayune by comparison.

I was also astonished by the way young couples danced in the United States—with their heads together and their behinds stuck way out. It really was terribly amusing to me. I even asked one of these young couples why they danced that way and without hesitation they answered, "It's easier, and our knees don't get in each other's way."

In late August we boarded the Nourmahal again, leaving at night, and sailed into Hell Gate off New York, just as sunrise fell on the sky-scrapers. To get to the Hudson River the ship had to go right around the island. By this time I still had seen almost nothing of the United States. A brief stop in New York on our honeymoon, the Astor mansion in Newport, the Newport Casino tennis courts, the beaches and gardens of Newport embraced my knowledge of the country, and now this idyllic glimpse of Manhattan. My astonishment at the first sight of another side of America, the towering heights of the Palisades, and the brilliance of the fall foliage, inconceivable in our wintry climate in Russia, where snow fell in Czarskoe Selo in September, was pronounced. We passed Bear Mountain and West Point, sailing between high cliffs on one side and rolling hills on the other. Most of the country was densely wooded, with little villages, each with its strange, sharp-pointed church steeple, ranged at regular intervals along the tracks of the New York Central.

That evening the *Nourmahal* anchored in the river off the boathouse on the Astor estate. We were bundled into the starboard launch and went up the long and curving hill to Femcliff. There was a solemn rural stillness in the country around Rhinebeck and the adjoining town of Hyde Park. The enormous mansions, really palaces, of the Vanderbilts, and the Ogden Mills and the homes of railroad kings and others that have now been converted into museums, stood on a crest on the east bank of the Hudson, surrounded by immense grounds, like English parks. Scattered here and there were smaller houses of the more truly patrician landowners, like the Livingstons, Delanos, Aldriches, Dowses, Dinsmores, Stuyvesants, and Roosevelts. Many of their lands came down from the great Livingston land grant from the King.

This is one of the earliest of the colonized areas of the North American continent. The people are tight of lip and are individualists to their dying day. They are a fair people, cheerful and kindly. They have been brought up to fend quietly for themselves with a minimum of fuss, and they are steeped in traditions similar to those of the old Russian and his land. They are a churchly, highly critical folk. All have read good books. In fact, the simplest of them is deceptive, for he or she will know a great deal. I almost think it is inherent. They may not talk much, but they think—think hard about everything.

The people around Rhinebeck are the kind of people who form the backbone of America, and then the land itself, its swelling countryside, and its productive farms provide a stalwart reason. Yankee, Republican, Dutch-English-German-Swedish stock, have the inviolable mores and tenets of the property owner—whether their holdings be a single acre or a thousand.

Nor are they soft. They have fought in all the wars, and are willing to fight again if need be. They are patriots, and they don't take kindly to having themselves, their families, their country or anything pertaining to their way of seeing things as things should be, stepped on by anything or anybody. In the meantime, they repair on occasion to a fine colonial structure for their evening's refreshment, the oldest hotel in the United States—the Beekman Arms.

Rhinebeck and environs is a land of artists: Thomas Wolfe wrote his Of Time and the River at the Dowses' Foxhollow Farm. Washington Irving inscribed many of his masterpieces to this region where the revolutionary armies marched in the shadow of Rip Van Winkle and his little dwarfs of the Catskills. John Jacob Astor wrote his novel there. Painters like Church abounded, still abound, and deep beneath it all there rests the feeling of a tremulous electric soil, bursting with the feelings of the past, that constantly recharges the batteries of those who dwell upon it. It is a land of Indian sacrificial grounds on the high bluffs above the river, of Indian wars frugally fought with only two of the best braves from each tribe, of the strange but just and savage ritual of the tribes of the Six Nations—the Great League of the warlike Iroquois. And sometimes, if you stop and listen in the Hudson River stillness, their sacrificial drums beat still.

Helen Astor, when she was later married to Lytle Hull, had a road on her property that passed directly over the body of an Indian. He was buried with his horse under a rough headstone. At that point on the road exactly there were constant accidents—ridiculous and unnecessary ones. Strange things happened, like a car suddenly swerving needlessly straight off the road. Helen and Lytle decided to shift the roadbed in order to bypass the Indian's grave. Since then, there has never been an accident anywhere on their place. Nowadays, common practice calls the Indian Victor. Nobody ever passes by the Indian headstone without raising a hand and saying, "Hello Victor." That is the way things are and have always been in Rhinebeck.

An interesting fact is that older residents of this Hudson River community have never gotten over their resentment at the influx of the railway titans in the latter part of the nineteenth century. And in truth the mansions which they erected were absolute eyesores and built on too large a scale to be comfortable, or even livable. When I arrived they were still being kept up, though in most cases the owners visited them briefly. When the depression came they were closed as habitable houses forever, and the descendants of their builders generally occupied the guest houses or other dwellings on the property. Many were taken over by the State of New York, for example the Vanderbilt and Mills estates are state-owned and crowds of sightseers are taken through them.

Alice and I once spent a weekend at the Millses', an enormous grayish-brown stone building, three stories in height and nearly a block long. A small army of servants was required to keep it up. I remember that the service was terrible according to standards of the day. Nothing was done for the guests, the bags were not unpacked, and the atmosphere within those thick and gloomy walls was one of grudging delay. I honestly don't think that many of the servants ever knew why they were there.

Elderly ladies of the region, dressed in Victorian costumes, dominated the social landscape. They were always under full sail: great hats, frills, gloves, parasols, and veils—anything to avoid the rays of the sun. I felt that there was something symbolic about it. They rode in curious-shaped automobiles, with very high bodies, driven by aged chauffeurs, obviously their former coachmen. The old ladies and their coachmen seemed still to regard the horseless carriage with considerable malaise.

The later mansions appeared to have been built in imitation of English country places, but there was no real social life to the region to compare to the hunts and parties that filled the English country houses with life. Country life abounded in compact and crowded England. Of course I realized that the tremendous spaces of the United States made the big difference. Rhinebeck in a way was very much like Krasnaya Gorka. From the moment I first saw it, I responded to its physical beauty. From the eastern bluff of the Hudson, where Ferncliff was, the river widened to an almost lakelike expanse. Mornings, its far shore was frequently invisible because of the mists that clung to the surface of the river. A small offshore lighthouse blinked its warning; a miniature beacon in a miniature sea. Upriver the Hudson narrowed between high rocky banks on both sides. On the western side the Catskill Mountains rose steeply, seeming sometimes close at hand, and at others far away. Often in the bright fall days when their pastel-colored faces gleamed most brightly, a great cloud would come and obscure the mountains temporarily from sight. Once it had passed, a frosty whiteness would have blanketed their peaks down to the foothills—the season's first snow. It would not fall in the lowlands, but it would tinge the Rhinebeck air immediately with the freshness of its wintry breath.

Almost all the way up along the Hudson, the New York Central Railroad hugged the river bank. Rail traffic was heavy and thunderous, and the nighttime was constantly startled by the mournful shriek of steam.

As a result, Alice wanted to build our house a long way back from the river itself. Vincent arranged to deed over to her ninety-nine acres of the Astor property, including the headland, as a site for a permanent house; and she and I set about planning it at once. When the deed was filed, there was a considerable newspaper stir because it was rumored that Alice was going to build another monstrosity in the grand tradition. Actually, all the Astor houses were cottages compared to some; Alice had exquisite taste. She knew exactly what sort of a house she wanted, and it was to be a manageable little beauty. Accordingly, she planned a gray stone Queen Anne manor house, set high up on the crest of a slope leading to the river. Simple to the point of austerity in its exterior lines, it was of surpassing warmth within. It was a place to be comfortable in, with cosy rooms where you could cock your feet up of a cold winter's evening and read by the fire. I'm not exaggerating—in some Hudson Valley places you couldn't think of doing that, or if you could think of it the light was often so bad you couldn't see.

While getting the plans worked out, we stayed at the old Astor mansion at 840 Fifth Avenue. One evening Vincent took a party of us off to Texas Guinan's. She came and sat down with me and Vincent introduced us. No sooner had she heard my name than she jumped to her feet, summoned her retinue and said, "Girls! This here is Prince Serge Obolensky. So let's show the Prince how we reee-ally entertain our guests in our great City of New York!" At once there was an act that had better be described as being in the very best "Let's go!" tradition of the day.

Helen and Vincent gave a swan-song party for the old Astor mansion in New York, the last to be held in the house before it was torn down. They also wanted to introduce Alice and me at the same time. Aliosha Obolensky, who had just returned from his world tour with Melba, sang at that party. I had never properly appreciated the grandeur of the old Astor mansion until I saw it crowded. As the people moved about beneath its gigantic chandeliers, I realized that this was what the house had been built for. Other times it seemed waiting, hushed and expectant. I remember talking with Jimmy Walker, the witty and debonair mayor of New York. We stood directly beneath a huge tapestry depicting the visit of Cyrus to the defeated Croesus. At that moment across the room a startlingly beautiful girl stood framed against one of the old-fashioned gilded panels. Jimmy immediately took me over and introduced me to Clare Boothe Brokaw, who had just come in with her great friend, the drama critic George Jean Nathan.

The atmosphere of the gathering was a pleasant mixture of the social and the practical. I can best express this by recounting my talk with James Gerard, the former Ambassador to Germany at the time of the First World War. Ambassador Gerard had been present at the wedding reception in Philadelphia in 1891 when John Jacob Astor married Ava Willing in what was described at the time as the greatest social event in the history of Philadelphia. He was a seasoned elder statesman who drew me aside to urge me earnestly, then and there, to join the Democratic party. He felt very strongly about it, and gave me an account of Democratic party principles, which on the whole I found to be what I believed in. As a result of this talk and many others before I became eligible to take the oath of allegiance, I was to register as a Democrat as soon as I became an American citizen.

As to the old Astor house, on its site today is one of the most prominent synagogues of New York City.

It was about this time that the much-talked-about, ever-impending trip to America of Sheila Loughborough, who was now unattached, and Poppy Baring actually took place. There was a whole host of gallant New York gentlemen anxiously awaiting their arrival: like Carroll Carstairs, an old beau of Sheila's;

Suydam Cutting (pronounced sir damn), who was a great friend of Vincent's and upon whom Vincent always played the most elaborate practical jokes; Dick Peters, who I believe had been in Jeb Stuart's cavalry and was pushing a spry ninety; Will Stewart; and Lytle Hull.

Carroll Carstairs decided to give a welcoming party for them—dinner and the theater the very evening that they were due off the boat. Alice and I were invited. Suydam was delegated to meet the girls at the dock, help them through customs, and escort them straight to dinner. It was all arranged and Suydam was delighted.

Suydam arrived alone at Carroll's party with a long face and muttering "Too damn many beaux. But they're coming. You'll see!" It was now extremely late for dinner. Bit by bit we got the story out of him. Apparently, Sheila and Poppy had also been met by a great retinue of gallants from an entirely different group who had refused to be outdone by Carroll. What's more, the girls had insisted on bringing two of these gentlemen along to our party. At that second they walked in, two extra gentlemen and all. Carroll was livid, and it was a "situation." Finally, Carroll agreed reluctantly that the two dark horses could meet up with us all later. We quickly rushed off to the theater. All this time I noticed that Sheila was saying, "Yes, Sir Damn!" and "No, Sir Damn!" and "What do you *really* think, Sir Damn?" Meanwhile Suydam was absolutely delighted. I don't think he caught on at all. After all, Sheila hadn't ever met him before that evening, and she was first-naming poor Suydam to death. Meanwhile, he was in seventh heaven. He was by now patting her hand.

I'm afraid I just couldn't resist it. During the intermission I said, "Sheila, how do you know Suydam so well?"

"What?" she asked.

"Well, you are being *extremely* familiar."

Poor Suydam looked at me angrily. I could see he was also puzzled.

"Oh, Serge, *really!*" she said frigidly. "I've never even met you before, have I, Sir Damn?" she asked.

"No," he said, visibly brightening. "No, Sheila, you never have." He was absolutely delighted with himself and he again took her hand and patted it. This time it was Sheila's turn to be shocked. Her eyebrows went straight up.

"Well, all I can say is you're both being familiar as hell," I said, laughing. And then a look of angry suspicion crossed her face.

"Sir Damn is a baronet, isn't he?" she said to me. "I mean, you are a baronet, Sir Damn, aren't you?"

I roared with laughter and told her. She was absolutely furious and I'm afraid that for the rest of that evening it was "Yes, Mr. Cutting" and "No, Mr. Cutting"—mostly the latter.

But Suydam and the girls soon became good friends. He really was a terribly nice and amusing man. He had one quirk that reminded me in a way of John de Salis; he was extremely careless about his dress. Also, although he was immensely wealthy, he was known for being close. He would get whatever he could of his wearing apparel at the five-and-ten. His suits he picked up at bargain spots off Wall Street; his ties were of the mail-order variety; and his shirts were of the cheapest. Sheila and Poppy ganged up on him one day. They had a perfect out: Poppy had just opened a millinery shop in London and was taking orders right and left and they decided to put the heat on poor Suydam. He was improperly dressed, they said. He should put his faith in Poppy and sign some of the little order blanks. That way they outfitted Suydam from head to toe in the most splendid and expensive clothes. I must say they did him a great favor, and in all fairness to him, Suydam put up with everything, even the horrifying bills—except for one item, which he talked about for months afterward. This was a bill for a pair of two-hundred-dollar pajamas. He never could get over that.

Our crossing to England on the *Majestic* in January was rough. We were playing bridge in our stateroom in the middle of a howling storm when there was a sound like a cannon shot over our heads and a huge crack opened in the wall, revealing the gray and stormy sky. We had hit a wave so enormous that the top deck cracked wide open. The steward rushed in, telling us breathlessly that all was well, and hastily transferred us to another suite.

As a result of the crack I expect, we reached England a couple of days late, found the weather there terrible and went on to St. Moritz. A lot of our American and British friends were there—Freddy Allen, Dolly and Jay O'Brien, Margaret Coates, Barbara Murray, now married to Lord Doon, and Grace Moore, the singer, who was so much in love with Chato Elisaga then that they used to disappear for days at a time. The Spaniards were there in force, Jimmy and Toto D'Alba and their friends, and several Italians, the Agnelli family, owners of the Fiat works. I knew the son from my London bachelor days, and also his beautiful wife Veronica, the daughter of Princess Jane di San Faustino.

The standard skiing practice in those days was to go up to Silvaplana toward the Bernina Pass, climb for a couple of hours to the col, and come back with a long, steady descent to the floor of the valley that ended with a stiff half-hour run to the inn. It was sometimes hard slogging to the col, but the run back was always wonderful. Sometimes we took the train and pushed up to Diavolezza, a couple of hours of easy ascent, and then after a few miles or so of hard going, we would be ready for the descent. The tremendous heights there are unforgettable. Every sound carries for miles and miles. The snow up there was always perfect because the ice fields nearby gave it a fine, gritty texture. Or we took the funicular to the glacier, quite a long climb above the cable car to the ice fields of the glacier itself, with a return over the ice field and then along the rim of the valley, finishing with a long smooth run over the snow-covered meadows.

Part VII

New World

CHAPTER XXIV

John de Salis reappeared at unexpected moments. At St. Moritz I was to learn of his more recent activities. The last time I'd seen him his mustaches were enormous. He had served in Russia with Denikin, returned, and won a gigantic bet in London. He was always hard up for cash because his father only gave him a pitifully small allowance. So he thought up a way to make some money. John was one of the finest shots in England, so he bet everybody that he could shoot a clay pipe out of his brother's mouth at a hundred yards. Everybody bet; they thought they really had him, and his brother. But John won. He did it by placing his brother behind the corner of a building with the pipe sticking out. He knocked it cold. Thus, he was able to live comfortably for a while, while he studied for his Foreign Office exams, which he passed with flying colors.

John was then sent to Washington, where he was a wow with all the Senator's daughters. His manic sense of humor required him to hire a bus one evening and make a date at the same time with all the girls who were interested in him. They were to meet him at a certain street corner, so he arrived with his bus, on which he had been kind enough to provide refreshments, loaded them on board, and waved good-by as they were driven off for a two-hour tour of the sights of Washington.

The thing that really did him in in Washington was his impersonation of Einstein. He thought it would be amusing to invite twenty important people to dinner to meet Dr. Einstein, and he got himself up in a disguise. After the coffee was served, John, as Einstein, got up and delivered a brilliant parody of the theory of relativity. To his horror they were all taken in, and parts of his "Einstein speech" were argued about in the Capital. Once again, his practical joke backfired through his own brilliance. The word got out, and he was fired.

Old Count de Salis, really furious by this time, then got John a job as A.D.C. to Lord Lytton, the governor of one of the provinces in India. At a tiger shoot for a highly influential guest, John was put on the flank. Beaters drove the tiger toward the center so that the guest could get a shot. John saw the tiger in the distance, raised his gun without even sighting it and fired just to shoo the thing along. The tiger dropped dead. John was sent back home.

That was the story that John told me after I came down from the ski run. I found him at the hotel, badly dressed as ever, plump, with the same owlish humor and the same absent-minded air. His mustache was shaggy and tremendous. As usual John never worried. He was in love with Margaret Flint, he said, but he worshiped her from afar and could never get up courage to propose. He wandered about, apparently idly, but he was very observant and actually tremendously well-informed.

He was really in trouble with his father this time, he said, and the old Count de Salis, now British minister to the Vatican, had exiled him to the de Salis castle at Maloja Pass, just up the road from where we were staying. The means of his exile were simple—John was kept on even shorter funds so that he couldn't wander around and do something that would displease the old diplomat. Rudyard Kipling, his father's great friend, was also living at the castle, and I remember John saying to Alice, "I love old Kipling, but when you never see anyone else, it gets a bit tiring."

I had skied too much, and suffered a painful attack of snow blindness after this meeting with John, necessitating an immediate trip to Paris. The doctors kept my room at the Ritz in complete darkness, for an inflammation of the iris developed. Miss Spiller, Ivan's nurse, took care of me and turned out to be a marvel; and Mother came up from Italy at that time. She lived in Viareggio, and had become a citizen of Italy. She was delighted with Ivan, loved to take care of him, and the upshot was that she returned to London with Ivan and Miss Spiller while Alice and I went to the south of France to stay with the Balsans.

Consuelo Vanderbilt after her divorce from the Duke of Marlborough had married Jacques Balsan, and they had built at Eze a Mediterranean retreat from an ancient monastery brought over from Normandy stone by stone. The monastery had become an exquisite French house, filled with the masterpieces of furniture and art they had collected. They had converted the cloisters of the monastery into a courtyard. Glass was placed between the columns, closing in a corridor that ran around a lovely formal garden.

Lord Balfour, the elder statesman, benign and well along in years, was the greatest speaker I ever heard except Winston Churchill. He could hold a crowd spellbound about philosophy, history, foreign affairs, literature, art, economics, with a relaxed and measured air that was like the art of a great actor. We certainly got an earful during our visit. He, too, was one of the guests, and an enthusiastic tennis player. During our stay at Eze, I was always his partner. He was sparing and deliberate, and only played the balls that came near him—I did the running. We played every morning. Harry Stoner, an old equerry of King George V, was on the opposite team and he made up the four with our host, Jacques. Harry was famous as one of the three best shots in England. (The other two were George V and Lord de Gray.) Harry was tall, thin, straight as a ramrod, and a stately tennis player. Alice was usually his partner. I ran all over the courts. The three others, the older generation, murmured "Well played," and waited placidly until something was hit near them. Harry Stoner had an odd eye defect. He saw everything double. And yet he played a good, if stationary, game, which mystified me: How did he know which of the two balls he thought he saw he should return? It was the same thing with shooting. How did he know which bird to shoot at? Especially in a covey, since each bird, for him, was accompanied by a double. He said he just knew by instinct. For me this was never a satisfactory answer.

Eileen Sutherland was also a guest of the Balsans. I had known her from my earliest days at Oxford. Her marriage to Geordie, the Duke of Sutherland, had been the great social event of 1912. Her mother-in-law, Millicent, the Dowager Duchess of Sutherland, was as beautiful as she was. Whenever the two duchesses appeared together, people said it was incredible that two such beautiful women should have married into the same family. Millicent was an amazing woman, an author of considerable ability, active in all kinds of charitable works, and a London hostess who reigned for many years without seeming to lose in the slightest the charm and beauty that were her birthright. Her portrait, with her two equally beautiful sisters, is considered one of Sargent's masterpieces and was placed in the National Gallery. When Geordie married Eileen Butler, the Dowager Duchess, who was then a widow, retired, saying there shouldn't be two Duchesses of Sutherland; she promptly went to Paris, possibly as an excuse, married a gentleman called Mr. Howes, and then settled down in a country place in France.

Eileen had now taken up painting and we saw some of her handiwork at Eze. Her sketches were good and she had an eye for color. She and Jack Woodhouse, another guest, spent their time painting the beds of varicolored flowers in the wonderful gardens that Consuelo had put in around the house. Jack was the international polo player. I was astounded that under Eileen's spell, Jack had discarded his mallets for a paintbrush.

We all went off occasionally to Cannes to play golf, or to Monte Carlo, where Alice liked to gamble at the Cafe de Paris. As I have said, I did not like to gamble. One day while Alice was playing, I ran into Barney Charlesworth, the captain of my Oxford polo team. I had not seen him since the victory celebration after our Cambridge match in the summer of 1914. Barney's wife was at one of the roulette tables, but he was not. So we reminisced, and then sat down at a vacant table, where we changed a thousand-franc note into hundred-franc chips. I decided I would stop when I had lost the thousand francs. Barney was luckier than I, and after I lost all my chips I stood by and watched him play. I noticed he had a big pile of chips on the black, next to us, and at each throw it doubled. Black came up about eighteen times, but he still left it on the black. I couldn't get over his courage. I remember hitting him on the back when black came up again, but he merely laughed a little nervously. But after the twenty-first time I said, "Barney, you're fantastic. You've got a courage I never had." He looked up in bewilderment. The croupier, who was watching us, said to me, smiling, "Monsieur, I really think you should take those chips off—this can't last."

"What do you mean?" I said.

"But it's your money!" he said.

I raked it in immediately. I realized it was fool's luck, but I marched triumphantly over to Alice, who was losing. She was furious, because admittedly I knew nothing about roulette. I've never played since.

We got back to London just as the British General Strike of 1926 began, and, strange as it may sound, this historic event seemed to me to be about as unreal as my brief involuntary gambling luck. The memory of the Russian Revolution and the savagery that followed the breakdown of authority had influenced me more deeply than I knew. I could not expect that crowds of strikers lined up against the government would conduct themselves as peacefully and as courteously as in ordinary times. It seemed to me amazing that there was no violence. The same respect for law and order was shown on both sides. And the preparations of the public for meeting the emergency impressed me like something out of *Alice in Wonderland*. Alice and her friend Alice Winn were enrolled as civilian assistants and worked every day for the two weeks of the strike in a canteen in a bus terminal.

At the Bucks Club we all enlisted as special constables and were attached to Scotland Yard as a flying squad. I was the driver of George Carlisle's open car. We all wore raincoats and bowler hats. I put two tennis balls in the crown of my hat, but luckily my invention was never to be put to a test. We really didn't have much to do. Food was unloaded at the docks by volunteers, and moved out into London proper in convoys, which we were there to protect. But no one interfered. The other members of my squad were Billy Bishop, later the famous air marshal, Michael Herbert, Eddy Grant, and Barney Charlesworth, all my old Oxford pals. I do not know how Lionel Tennison, who was the *bon vivant* of Bucks, talked himself into being a deputy police commissioner of the Yard, but he managed it. We lived like that for about ten days with Lionel in glorious command, till the strike was settled. I remember Sidney Herbert, who was then Parliamentary secretary to Prime Minister Baldwin, telling us at Bucks that the evening before at the government meeting they had had to choose a committee to negotiate with the general strike committee and the question came up of appointing Lord Birkenhead, who was then Lord Chief Justice, and whose brain worked so fast that he was always several jumps ahead of his opponent and everybody else besides. It was decided in the spirit of fair play not to appoint him, as this would have been eminently unfair to the strike committee. This is the kind of approach that makes England truly great.

In October, after the strike was settled, Alice and I went off to Paris with our whole troupe, Ivan and Nanny Spiller, Gilbert, and Boyak. It is important to know that throughout the period since the war and the Revolution, I had been fairly active in anti-Bolshevik groups. As a result, I have often been asked why we weren't objects of interest to the Bolsheviks. I think the reason is that we weren't considered important enough. The different White generals, who had their own organizations, kept the Bolshevik agents occupied. While we were in Paris, General Kouhtepoff, one of the ablest of the anti-Communist officers, got in touch with me. We met secretly, and he asked me to work with him. He made a powerful impression on me. General Kouhtepoff was a big man in every sense of the word, physically powerful, and clear-headed as to what he was doing and what he might accomplish. He had the complete loyalty of his followers, who trusted him implicitly.

Gilbert, our chauffeur, came to me only a short time after my meeting with General Kouhtepoff. He said he didn't want to alarm me but that whenever he drove Alice anywhere he thought the car was being followed. We decided to test this idea at once. I drove while Gilbert kept his eyes open for the people he thought he had seen. When he spotted them, I turned a corner to be out of their sight for a moment. He jumped out. I drove on, and presently I saw the car again, with Gilbert following it in a taxi. We tried to close in on them, but as soon as they became aware that we knew we were being followed, they drove away. Yet the sense of being under surveillance did not go away, and I suppose there was more than one car. I made a point of driving out after her when Alice went out shopping. And there they were again. Gilbert and I were now certain we were being followed almost all the time. However, we had nothing to report to the police, merely impressions, glimpses of a car with tough characters keeping us in sight. Then Nanny Spiller reported uneasily that there appeared to be an unpleasant group of people loitering around in the Champs-Élysées whenever she went there with Ivan. The same faces kept turning up in odd places. Again there was nothing concrete, but again my old sixth sense told me that there was something tough and worrisome about the atmosphere. The time seemed to have come to do something. The next time Gilbert and I were out in the car alone, we spotted the car that seemed to be following us and crowded it to the curb on a deserted street. Two hard-eyed individuals got out, saying very little, and anxious to get away from there. I had never seen them before, though I was sure they knew who I was. Later on, the police with whom we checked had no record on them of any kind. But for the moment the surveillance stopped, at least so far as we could tell.

Only a short time had passed since my meeting with General Kouhtepoff—a matter of days. When I made inquiries about him, as I was supposed to contact him again, I learned that he had disappeared, vanished into thin air. He had gone to a meeting at his office a short distance from his home, but never reached there. His disappearance became the greatest sensation among the anti-Communist groups working in Paris, for he was surrounded by every possible means of protection against the Bolsheviks' secret police. Subsequently his story came out as a result of a fight within the ranks of his captors. General Kouhtepoff had been abducted in the heart of Paris to be taken off to Russia. Three Bolshevik agents got to him by dressing as French policemen. He was so strong they could not keep him overpowered, so they chloroformed him. Placed in an ambulance, he was driven to the coast, where a Soviet freighter was waiting offshore. The evening he disappeared a girl and a young man were making love on a certain beach. Suddenly an ambulance came screaming onto the sand and stopped in front of them. A boat came out of the darkness; a stretcher from the ambulance was put aboard; the boat went out to sea, and the ambulance drove off.

Fortunately for General Kouhtepoff, he was given too much chloroform, and died from its effects. He was lucky, because he was spared the torture he would have received to force him to reveal his supporters inside Russia. He alone knew who they were. And the only records were those in his head. The officials of the Cheka were so savage at word of his death that they ordered his blundering kidnappers liquidated. Two were shot. The third got away, and finally carried the whole story to the Paris police, which is how the tragedy of General Kouhtepoff came to be known. Then the young couple also came forward and told their story.

I decided then and there to stop my anti-Bolshevik activities for the sake of Ivan and Alice. We left immediately for London and booked passage to the United States. When we were two days out at sea, I got a heartbreaking telegram from my sister Olga. Bolshevik goons had slipped across the frontier, had lain in wait for Stroukoff on their Polish estate, ambushed and murdered him.

Alice and I spent our time between New York and Rhinebeck. I was then suddenly deeply involved in a legal complication affecting the Russian Church. In Russia, the Bolsheviks had slacked off their frontal attack on the Church, but had decided to turn their eyes elsewhere. They had been unable to depose the head of the Church in Russia, the Patriarch Tikhon, who after having been imprisoned was released and returned to his monastery in Moscow. There he maintained his full prerogatives as head of the Church.

Many years before, parishes had been established in America under the old Imperial regime, and were basically a mission under the jurisdiction of the senior Metropolitan, who had his seat in New York. By this time there were 360 valuable parishes of the Russian Church in America. To get control of them would be a plum for the Soviet regime. The Soviets, despite Tikhon's disapproval, had organized a small synod of dissident priests and bishops and called it "The Living Church." Then they sent a bishop of this "Living Church" to New York with credentials that supposedly authorized the removal from his post of Metropolitan Platon and appointed the "Living Church" bishop as his successor. When I arrived, there had been litigation. The American judge, who had been unaware of the subterfuge, had ordered the Cathedral in 97th Street to be handed over to the new bishop and Platon to be removed. Metropolitan Platon summoned me when he learned that I was in New York and told me of these dangerous events. He said he was fearful because the deeds of all parishes were held under the jurisdiction of the legally recognized head of the Russian Orthodox Church in America. This head was now the bishop of the "Living

Church," and one by one this man could throw out the clergy, put in propagandists as priests and take over the properties of the churches.

Serge Gagarin and myself founded a committee, including Rachmaninoff and Sikorsky, to raise funds and appeal the court order. With the great help of Bishop Manning and the Episcopal Church, we achieved our financial goal and secured the assistance of George Zabriskie, the prominent attorney, Charles Sabin of the Guaranty Trust Company of New York, and Haley Fisk of the Metropolitan Life Insurance Company. Through their help, we won the appeal.

As a result, the Bolsheviks' "Living Church" withered away, and Metropolitan Platon, now back in power, turned over to their respective parishes all the deeds to Russian Orthodox church properties throughout the country. Thus such a situation could never arise again, and henceforth the parishes could elect their own priests and bishops come what may. I patted myself on the back, because it was one of the few times that the Soviets were really defeated.

During the lengthy fracas, the intricacies of Russian Church law became too much for me, and I got Peter Zouboff to come to the United States from Estonia to help us. I got him a visitor's visa through the intercession of Bishop Manning, who recognized his importance to the Church. I went to meet Peter at the boat along with his former troop commander, Serge Boutourline. I had already arranged with Dean, my butler in London, to have Peter taken to my tailor so that he would be properly appointed on his arrival in the States. As a result, he was indeed perfectly dressed, bowler hat, cane, gloves, spats, and all, but to my amazement he was sporting a gigantic black beard, well squared and clipped, but a beard all the same. When Boutourline and I saw this apparition coming down the gangway, we looked at each other and said "That has to come off!" We saw him through customs, performed all the niceties that are expected from old friends; and when he was cleared, we took him to an apartment that I'd arranged for him with some mutual friends, dropped off his luggage, and whisked him away again in a taxi.

"Where are we going?" he asked cheerfully.

"Oh, it doesn't matter," we answered. But there must have been something in the tone of our voices that wasn't reassuring.

"Where are you taking me?" he asked, nervously this time.

"You'll see," we said grimly.

At that moment, the taxi stopped outside my barber's. His red and white cylinder was spinning gaily. Before Peter could protest we gave him the bum's rush, and he was plumped into the barber's chair. "No! No!" he cried as the barber's sheet enveloped him. He struggled to his feet, but Boutourline and I pushed him back down. I winked at my barber friend who immediately grasped the situation. With a dexterity that I have rarely seen, his shears were out, and half of Peter's beard was gone. From then on things went smoothly and "Our Bishop" of the good old days was resigned to his fate. Two minutes later he looked thirty years younger and was actually delighted with himself. "Well," he said wryly, "I'm certainly ready for the New World now!" He certainly was, and in our proceedings against the "Living Church," Peter provided us with the greatly needed ecclesiastical background and information so necessary to the winning of our case. Peter remained in the United States. He became a professor at Columbia, and then at the Naval Academy at Annapolis.

Kerensky arrived about this time. Nine years had passed since his Provisional Government gave way to the Bolsheviks, but this was his first trip to attempt to present the case of the moderates in Russia to the American people. He was so successful that thereafter he, too, stayed on, and is still here today. I understand that he lives in California.

Vincent Astor's new yacht, the *Nourmahal*, was being built at Kielgoorden, in the Field and Krupp yards in the Kiel Canal in Germany. For generations there had been a *Nourmahal* in the Astor family—the name is Arabic for "Light of my soul." This was the first American yacht of such proportions ever built in the Kiel yards and it was built there for a purpose. Vincent foresaw even then the coming of the Second World War. Thus, he built a ship that was really designed to be a raider, with the two six-inch gun emplacements forward. If war did come, he expected to command her. Actually, when the Japanese attacked Pearl Harbor, he held the permanent rank of Captain in the Naval Reserve, far too high for such a small command. He became a Convoy Commodore.

When plans for Vincent's yacht became known, there was a thorough study of the ship published, stating "the era of super pleasure has begun." I imagine that even in the booming mid-twenties most people were satisfied with the ordinary pleasures open to mankind since time immemorial, without striving for super-pleasure. I know that Vincent for the reasons above stated was primarily concerned with the design, speed, and seaworthiness of his new vessel. It had to be a magnificent ship, the finest, most seaworthy ocean-going yacht ever built. The New York Times exaggeratedly announced that it was so large that an airplane landing field had been built on deck.[1] Vincent was aided by the depression in Germany and the fact that he had taken a flier and bought a third interest in a remarkable movie called *Ben Hur*.

The *Nourmahal* was more than 262 feet long, with a forty-one-foot beam, and she drew seventeen feet of water. She was really a miniature ocean liner, with a sharp bow, a cruiser stern, and lines like a coast-guard cutter. Her two balanced engines turned up 3200 horsepower, and she had a cruising radius of nineteen thousand miles without refueling, the longest cruising radius afloat. There were three decks, eight guest cabins, a master's lounge with a fireplace and sofas, a library paneled in Norwegian pine, a dining room on the upper

---

[1] *New York Times*, June 8, 1928.

deck paneled in American walnut and seating eighteen, a main lounge with a fireplace, teakwood desk, and a huge kind of sofa on the awning-covered quarterdeck aft. The crew had splendid quarters, and each officer had a separate cabin. The *Nourmahal* was equipped with fathometers, a gyroscopic compass, an automatic pilot, controlled ventilation, and all sorts of new nautical devices that Vincent wanted to try out. Her wireless plant was one of the largest afloat. Twin heavy-duty diesels were designed to take her across the Atlantic at sixteen knots, nearly passenger-liner speed. A nine-day boat, she reportedly cost more than a million dollars in those hard-currency days.

While the *Nourmahal* was building, Vincent was constantly going back and forth to superintend its progress. He had taken a flat in Paris with old Dick Peters, his great friend and cousin, who was better known as Cousin Dick. Cousin Dick was pushing ninety, as I said before, but he still considered himself the ladies' man that he had been ever since the greater days of the Confederacy, for which he had fought. He had held the Confederate rank of cavalry captain. Vincent was always playing terrible jokes on Cousin Dick. He had devised a fictitious character called Countess Ramona, her full name being Countess Ramona Gomez y Sepulveda. And she was married to a man named Butts. She was constantly writing Dick indiscreet letters. Three or so a week arrived, all heavily perfumed, which Vincent had dictated for his secretary to transcribe into her own handwriting. If Vincent ever had to leave, he made sure that his secretary had a sufficient backlog to cover the period that he would be away. These letters went on for twenty years; and presents from Countess Ramona, very often rather off-color ones, would arrive for Cousin Dick at the most inappropriate and compromising moments. She seemed to know his every move. He really didn't know what to make of it.

Alice and I in the meantime made our annual pilgrimage to St. Moritz, then visited the Balsans, and traveled to Viareggio by car along the Mediterranean, to visit my mother. We stopped at Florence and Paris before returning to London. By then Vincent was holding trial runs of the *Nourmahal* off Southampton. Toward the end of June, Vincent decided to take the Nourmahal across the ocean. He asked me to come along, and although Alice was not quite happy about it, she let me go. The party consisted of Vincent, Charley Winn, Duncan Harris, Jack Yates and myself. As we sailed we hit one of the greatest storms in the Atlantic. We had to heave to and ride it out. I remember going up to the sitting room and finding Charley in a dejected mood. I told him that I had the best cure for any seasickness and rang for a bottle of vodka. I remember giving a large jigger of it to Charley, although he was a bit dubious about it, and drinking one myself. Charley later told me he saw my face going pea-green and I disappeared down to my stateroom not to appear until the next day. Everybody was down except Vincent and Jack Yates. Duncan never appeared for all nine days until we sailed into New York harbor, on July 4, 1928. The night before, Vincent had made an inventory of wine and beer on board and to our great regret, to obey the ridiculous prohibition laws, ordered all the liquor dumped overboard except a minimum amount which was declared medicinal. I'll never forget the chagrin on the face of Duncan Harris as two cases of Bollinger 1917 went flying out into the drink. Speaking about drink, that day we all had terrible hangovers, because we had valiantly tried to eliminate the need of spoiling Father Neptune.

George Baker on the *Viking* sailed out to meet us. It was a beautiful sunny morning. Helen Astor, Edith Baker, the Filleys, Will Stewart, Vincent's great friend, and Harriet Post were on board.

We left the same day we landed for Rhinebeck, which was very interesting for me, as our house, which is now Ivan's, was then in the process of being built.

I stayed in the United States a week, and then I sailed back to England on the *Majestic* with a very gay group; Will Stewart; Tookie di Zoppola; the Bill Crockers; George Grossmith, the British actor; and Bubbles Ryan, the daughter of a British chief justice; and Charley Winn. It was quite a crossing. We played charades in the evening, and one evening Charley Winn had to act out the part of a drunken sailor. He found some lipstick and applied it liberally to his nose and cheeks. The next morning he was horrified because it was still on his face. What he hadn't realized was that he had picked up Bubbles' indelible lipstick, then a very frisky thing indeed. Rather than show himself in such condition, he sent a message of desperation to the ship's doctor: "The compliments of Captain Winn, but would the doctor be kind enough to come to his cabin to remove some lipstick from his face?" The doctor was livid. He sent a very haughty message back: "Compliments to the Captain Winn indeed! I have much more important things to do on board!" When finally Winn had to show himself in all his flaming glory, the doctor realized what had happened and took pity on him. But no amount of medication would do the trick and despite the fact that we arrived in Southampton a day late, Charley Winn looked every inch the part of the drunken sailor that he had impersonated so well, when he came sheepishly down the gangway.

In the summer of 1926 our friends, the Ward girls, Cyril Ward's daughters, had an old aunt who lived in a beautiful old house in the outskirts of The Hague. Chips Channon, the Wards and Alice and I rented it for the month of August. It was right on The Hague Golf Course. Alice then asked me if it was all right to bring Naps Allington along. I'm afraid that that was the beginning of all the trouble between Alice and myself. While I liked Naps personally, I got rather upset and then angry, although I acceded to Alice's wishes. I should have known better, but it hurt me very deeply, and his presence only served to get me on edge. Come hell or high water, we all embarked together. But I must say we did have a wonderful time sightseeing in Holland.

Chips was writing his new book on Ludwig, the Mad King of Bavaria, the fabulous monarch whose mistress was Lola Montez. He wanted to do more research on the subject, so we all got in our big Packard touring car with the double windscreen, and Gilbert drove us up the Rhine to Cologne. From there we went to Munich. Here Chips became interested in another story, and changed his book to a collection of biographical essays—one long one about Mad King Ludwig, and another about a man called Arco-Valle, whose cousin, Luigi Arco-Valle, we both knew. When the German revolution had begun in 1918, Munich became socialist. But the extreme Reds under Kurt Eisner, better known as the Spartacus movement, started a Lenin-like uprising. Arco-Valle killed Eisner. He was himself shot and left for dead. Somehow he recovered, and though sentenced to death, he was saved once again by the tumult of revolution. Thereafter, he lived in seclusion, a man of legend, hated by some and venerated by others. Chips wrote up his story as a parallel to Felix's killing of Rasputin.

We spent several days looking over various palaces built by Ludwig, including Kimmsea, the replica of Versailles, except that it was on a small island, completely mad but beautiful. From there we went on to Salzburg where Dr. Rudolf Kommer, the famous lawyer and adviser of society, took charge of organizing our excursions around the various beautiful baroque castles. He was a great personal friend of Max Reinhardt, who eventually left him his library at Leopoldskron. The main thing I had against Salzburg was that, while we were there, it rained so much.

From there we motored to Yugoslavia, where we stayed a week with Paul and Olga, near Bled, their charming place in the mountains with wonderful trout fishing. King Alexander, who lived nearby, entertained us several times and was most hospitable.

When we got back to Salzburg we ran into Count and Countess Mercatti with their daughter, Atlanta, who was bored stiff, so, by God, Chips and I persuaded Alice to invite her to join us in Venice, which she did. It was fun driving on those rough Dolomite mountain roads, with their terrific hairpin turns, to Venice and the views were breathtaking.

In Venice we stayed at the Grand Hotel. Atlanta Mercatti joined us a few days after we arrived. We went to fetch her at the station, and on returning, when our gondola came alongside the float at the hotel, Michael Arlen was there waiting for a gondola. We asked him to have a drink; he accepted; and from that moment on he never left Atlanta's side. Finally Alice, who by now had fully sensed my annoyance at all things, got quite worried, as she was her chaperon. She told me that old Michael had a reputation for being a very naughty boy. She was afraid of her responsibilities toward the Mercattis.

There in a nutshell is one of the ironies of my life; Alice became considerate again. She had a talk with Atlanta, who told her Michael had proposed. They were intending to go to Florence, and Michael was going to ask her family's permission to marry her. All ended well, and they were married shortly. From then on I am afraid something happened to Michael Arlen. He used to have a very distinctive, cynical style of writing, as is found, for instance, in *The Green Hat*, but, after his marriage, that quality evaporated. Perhaps happiness is a bad thing for a writer. Whatever, Michael never wrote anything striking again. He must have become really happy.

Venice had the usual round of parties given by various people, including Elsa Maxwell with her famous treasure hunts. Finally Alice and I motored back over the St. Gotthard pass, a lovely interesting drive. We stayed in Paris only a short time and returned to our routine life in London. But the trip, I'm afraid, created friction. I was still associated with the firm of Byng, Foley on the stock exchange and used to go to the City in the morning and lunch at Bucks Club. At that time Mrs. Buckmaster opened a flower shop in the building next door and started selling members of the Bucks dark-red carnations. That was the beginning of the fashion to wear them. She got two very beautiful models as salesladies. Their names were Lollypop and Smut. Ladies were soon getting furious all over London whenever their men turned up with those dark-red carnations. Our boutonnieres were prima facie evidence that we'd been chez Lollypop and Smut. Unfortunately, they soon got married: one became Mrs. Player, the name of the famous brand of cigarettes in England. I honestly don't know what happened to Smut.

In the United States Alice and I again stopped in New York with Vincent and Helen Astor. Helen had a charming admirer, Clary Mackay, of the cable company, a great collector of primitive armor. He had a museum on Long Island. He once gave a great ball there for the Prince of Wales, and a guest took away a stirrup of the famous Cumberland Armor, which was never found. He had a wonderful estate at Gardiner's Island where he bred every year about five thousand pheasants for shoots to which a few privileged friends were invited. I was very lucky to be one of them. These shoots typified that period of American life that will never come back. Clarence Mackay was a most lovable, simple and accessible man, very fond of good jokes; an incredible host. He always had the most perfect food service, and his whole life was one of the best-organized things I ever saw. The same applied to his shooting parties. We were sent instructions a week ahead of the hour of departure of the special train at Pennsylvania Station, on which tea and drinks were going to be served during the trip. Mackay's yacht was waiting for us at the far end of Long Island; we embarked and the yacht brought us precisely on time to Gardiner's Island. We received instructions as to what to take in the way of clothes, amount of cartridges, and the exact plan of the three days of our stay. On the trip back, lunches at 12:30 were served in a tent between beats. Food was kept piping hot in thermos containers, and wine, beer, brandy and cigars were offered.

I had been to some royal shoots in Europe, but never saw such well-arranged hospitality and service as Clary gave us. My first visit to Gardiner's Island was with a party consisting of Mr. John W. Davis, Mr. Norman Davis, head of the Red Cross, Percy Pyne, Morgan O'Brien and a couple of others.

The excellent shots were Clary (the best), Percy (the next best). We killed a lot of birds and then were put into blinds on duck and geese. We were taken there at 3:30 in the morning, whilst it was still very dark. I was detailed with Mr. John Davis. We found the blind stocked with cartridges, hot-water bags at our feet, bearskin rugs and an enormous hamper of food from soup to coffee and cigars, and we fired away at the birds that came in great numbers until we got our quotas. (A strange thing happened this last summer of 1958, and it was very sad. Lady Ribblesdale had died, and at her interment, I noticed that she was buried right next to my old friend, John Davis.)

Another great shoot of those days was at Marshall Field's estate on Long Island. Marshall was then married to his first wife Evie, the sister of Buddy Marshall. They had just finished building their house, which was a magnificent Georgian structure overlooking the Sound.

The guests were nearly always Percy Pyne, George Baker, Will Stewart, Benny Moore, who was married to Alexandra Emery, sister-in-law of Grand Duke Dimitri. The best shot there was Waddy Lewis. Marshall generally also had about five thousand pheasants. These shoots were mostly stag parties except for our hostess.

My life with Alice, in the United States, had the same routine. Finally our house at Rhinebeck was ready and we moved in just before Christmas. Mott Schmidt, the architect, had done a magnificent job, and it was fun furnishing it. I brought over from England a number of Russian portraits of Borovikovsky and Levitsky that I'd bought, and they were hung up. Alice still did not like them but made a concession to my ancestry. The way we finally moved in was quite funny. The house had furniture and draperies but there were neither household utensils nor pillows nor bedcovers. There were not even pots and pans for the kitchen. Someone recommended us a firm that would undertake to supply them for a fee. Alice got them two days before a weekend. Typically enough, she'd already invited six guests and was desperate!

Mercifully, the firm delivered everything on time. The guests arrived on Friday, the next day. I was amazed at this instance of American organization. It was our first cozy Christmas in our own American house. I remember decorating the Christmas tree. Alice gave me a lovely pair of crystal and diamond turtles as links. I still have them. They were replicas of those I had inherited from Father which disappeared during the looting of Mordvinov Palace at Yalta in the Revolution.

We left at the end of January for Europe again.

Ivan had grown into a serious but happy child, strong and healthy. He loved the big gardens around Hanover Lodge in London. When Alice and I were going out, he was fascinated by our preparations and used to run from one room to the other, watching Alice and me getting ready to leave—Alice usually late. He reminded me of me. At Rhinebeck he had a gray Egyptian racing donkey called Cleopatra, and he loved to ride on Vincent's miniature steam railway that ran on a half-mile loop on the grounds of Ferncliff. Ivan was bright for his age. Both Vince and Helen were fond of him, and he adored the chance to go aboard the *Nourmahal*. He was no trouble whatsoever, and his nurse, Nanny Spiller, was wonderful with him, the best nurse I have ever known, even better than Miss Lizzie who cared for me in those remote days at Czarskoe Selo. I used to say prayers with Ivan in the evenings in front of an icon that Metropolitan Platon had inscribed to him. I would take him to the Russian Church on Sunday. That was quite wonderful. Once he saw an old lady who knelt every so often, crossed herself and then, while kneeling, bowed and touched the floor with her head. For a long time afterward Ivan followed her example while saying his prayers.

Mother had not been feeling well for some time, and she finally died in Paris, after an attack. She waited until we arrived, and shortly afterward she just gave up. Luckily she did not suffer, although we had known for some time that she had contracted a form of cancer. We buried her just outside of Paris near a farm that her nephew, Alec Narishkin managed.

I am afraid I was getting pretty restless in my life of great leisure. When we returned to London I felt I needed something constructive to do. Although I was still connected with the brokerage firm of Byng, Foley in London, my position was not very demanding. Soon we went back to St. Moritz, where I again got a case of iritis and snow blindness. This time it was terribly painful—I couldn't bear the slightest light. This was a disaster, and Alice took me to Paris to recover. But then we found that I also had to have a cyst removed from my nose. It was an operation that had to be done. Nanny Spiller nursed and took care of me. She was wonderful. After a while, Alice didn't stay around me much; I became hurt all over again, and I began to brood. I spent my convalescence at Eze with the Balsans before we went back to Paris where the season that year was particularly gay. There were parties every evening, but I couldn't go out too much. I'd been very ill. Alice went to almost all of them. I went to one or two. I liked to dance, especially after being cooped up so long, and Alice got very irritated when Paula Cosa Maury, one of my favorite waltzing partners, and I waltzed together a great deal. Alice and I went out to play bridge occasionally, but she was usually bored with that. Lady Ribblesdale had always made her play.

It was in Paris that time that Alice walked out on me during a bridge game. Alice had a famous older cousin called Marie Louise de Saint See. She was an extraordinary character, and a great bridge player. She spent her time reading and was a collector of weird objects and books; she only collected first editions. She also had a great collection of rare books that were not only to read but had historical value of one form or another. For instance, to my horror that same bridge evening, at Marie Louise's, she showed us a book that came from the library of the Marquis de Sade. It was bound in human skin. The skin, she said, came from the backside of one of his favorite mistresses. Anyway, it didn't help my bridge at all. I know it made Alice jumpy. The very atmosphere about the place made tempers flare.

Alice's table finished first, but our game dragged on and on. Alice asked me to give it up, but out of politeness I thought I ought to finish the rubber. I have never known a rubber to drag out so long. When it finally ended, I found that Alice had left long before.

There was one other source of contention, and aside from my periodically uncontrollable stupidity at hitting back, Alice was extremely jealous of Nanny Spiller with Ivan. I frequently defended Nanny, and Alice was furious. I still had to take it easy, and Alice would often go out to dine with friends. To my annoyance a rather unpleasant, I thought at the time, Frenchman kept turning up. I couldn't wait to leave Paris.

There were two large fancy-dress parties in London that season, one at Lady Curzon's, while Lord Curzon was away. Malcolm Bullock (husband of Victoria Stanley) was filling in for the host. Vere Bessborough, Harry Rosebery and I put on a show in which twenty of us dressed up as Klu Klux Klan men and marched in with flaming torches and abducted the Spanish Ambassadress, Mme. Merry del Val. She was a wonderful sport and really enjoyed it. We also staged a three-cornered fight in which we had layers of clothes on, and gradually discarded them, remaining finally in tights while a colored sun set on the backdrop behind us. Harry Rosebery got so excited that he didn't realize that the tights were his last garment and started pulling them off. Luckily, somebody stopped him. The other ball was at the Sutherlands. I remember being the bull in a bullfight in which Duff Cooper was the picador.

The summer went by very quickly. Nancy and Waldorf Astor gave a tremendous party at Cliveden, and there were many affairs at Ascot. After a spectacular row with Alice over Nanny, Naps, my operation, my waltzing partners, everything, I decided that we needed a breather. Alice and I made plans to go by car to the Riviera. Originally, Alice was going with Chips Channon and me, and Brinda Kapurthala whom she had insisted on taking along. But at the last minute Alice backed out. She told me to go anyway, because I needed to. I reluctantly agreed, and Brinda, Chips, Gilbert, our chauffeur, and I left one day for Limoges, Carcassonne, Arles and Cannes. It was very funny. When we stayed somewhere for the night, the hotel people could not quite figure out our relationships. There was much winking and Gallic conjecture going on in the domains of the various concierges.

The days were very hot and our maharanee complained bitterly about the heat. We finally persuaded her to get up very early and get to Toulouse about lunch time. It was a scorching morning, and she told us that she wanted a room in a hotel to sleep until six in the evening before going on further to Carcassonne. Chips consulted his Baedeker and found a hostelry marked with three stars, in Toulouse. I asked a policeman the way to that hostelry. I thought he gave me a queer look, but I didn't pay much attention and proceeded to drive on, following his instructions. We disembarked and spoke to a very fat lady, who seemed to be the manageress or owner. We wanted only one room for Madame, we explained, and that one only for a few hours. We had to be leaving by five P.M.

We also asked if in the meantime we could have lunch. We were served a very good meal in a very ornate room at the back of the house. Finally Chips and I departed on a sightseeing tour and told Brinda to be expecting us back about five. Having surveyed Toulouse, we finally got back and asked for Brinda's room. To get to it, we had to walk up a couple of flights on a very narrow staircase. We found it with difficulty and knocked at her door. After repeated knocking, we heard a faint and rather frightened voice asking who it was. When she recognized our voices, we heard furniture being removed from the door and a very, very angry Brinda Kapurthala appeared. She told us that a number of irate gentlemen kept pounding on her door. Chips said "Good gracious!" and took out his Baedeker again. Chips inadvertently had guided us to a kind of place that had other functions than mere innkeeping. It was a place that Frenchmen call a *maison pour les sports*. I am afraid instead of being sympathetic with poor Brinda, we roared with laughter and kidded her unmercifully from then on.

I was already by this time feeling pangs for home. I kept thinking about Alice, and it made me feel wonderful, for it meant that the trip was serving the purpose that I had meant it to serve. By this time I had gotten everything out of my system and I had written and telephoned to Alice constantly. I was very much in love with her.

Having inspected the beautiful ramparts of Carcassonne, we went on to Arles and Santa Maria, the shrine where all the gipsies come once a year to worship their patron saint. From there we arrived at Cannes, where Alice had already arrived by train. Catherine Condon, Chips, Brinda, and Alice and I shared a villa, and there we remained until the latter part of August. We had a marvelous time. There were parties constantly. One festivity started literally before the preceding one was over. Then, as if that wasn't enough, someone had the brilliant idea of going in a body to Venice, where Elsa Maxwell's costume balls and treasure hunts were making things amusing. It really was getting to be too much for me. Nevertheless, we all set out in a blaze of good spirits—sixteen automobiles in a caravan. We swept down on the little hotels and made the trip one long continuous party. We reached Venice, and moved into the round of Elsa's parties, the first one, I remember, a costume ball, at which I appeared as a gondolier and Alice as a gipsy.

I was looking forward so much to being with Alice in London and Rhinebeck again. Only on our return to London was I to receive the real shock of my life; for there I was to learn how deeply she had resented that summer in the Riviera.

CHAPTER XXV

One morning at Hanover Lodge, Alice told me she wanted a divorce. She felt she could remake her life. She was still young and she could do it. I could see she was terribly determined. She then said that she wanted to make over to me a very large amount of money, which I naturally refused. If she really wanted to go through with it, I said I would still like some time to be able to get back on my feet and be independent. I hoped that in time, during this intervening period, she might change her mind. That day, full of self-recrimination, I arranged to go back to the States and find a job.

Vincent did not want Alice to divorce me. Back in the United States I started looking for work, but he intervened. He got me a position in the Chase Security Corporation, which had merged with Chase Harris Forbes. I finished with the foreign department, under Mr. Rovensky, remaining there three years. I began to work there shortly before the stock-market crash of 1929, and the beginning of the depression.

That fall, Alice came to the United States and was even more definite about wanting a divorce. Vincent was against it, and tried to bring about a reconciliation, while I continued to work in the Chase. Rumors of our separation were now appearing in the papers, and quite a bit of notice was paid Alice's return. It was a hair-raising arrival. God bless her, she had brought a lot of baggage, thirty trunks; and the frantic customs people held her up for hours at the pier. Helen drove down to get Ivan; and Henry Greenberger from Vincent's office rushed over and tried to speed things up and pay the duties.

Early in 1930 Vincent made the first famous cruise in the Nourmahal with a group of scientists headed by Dr. Eugene Pool, the director, and Dr. Clarence Hay, of the American Museum of Natural History—Kermit Roosevelt, Suydam Cutting, the ornithologist James Chapin, the botanist Henry Svenson, Dr. Charles Townsend, the director of the New York Aquarium, and others. They were going to the least known of the Galapagos Islands, to search for the rare *testuda portieri*, a gigantic tortoise found only there, to bring back coral-reef fish, and to continue research on the unique Galapagos Island spineless cactus, which was being tested as a food source for cattle in arid regions.

I stayed on and worked in New York, where Cousin Dick Peters got me elected to the Knickerbocker Club. I think that he and Frank Crowninshield and old Mr. Stotesbury wanted to be sure of a fourth for bridge. This was the only period of my life in which I went in for bridge in a big way. Those two years I lived at Sorine's apartment at 26 West 59th Street and, rather than stay home all the time, found a certain relaxation at the Knickerbocker—nor was it too expensive. I really loved playing with those old gentlemen, except that the cardinal rule was to try not to be the partner of Cousin Dick. He thought he was playing hearts most of the time. He had an unfailing inclination to shoot the moon.

One afternoon Dick Peters called me up at the Chase with a sense of great urgency in his voice. "Serge," he said, "tonight is the Beaux Arts Ball."

"Very interesting," I said.

"I've got two tickets, and I'm in love."

"Well, have a good time," I said.

"But you don't understand," he said. "Mrs. Sam Goldwyn will be there."

"Oh?" I said.

"And I'm in love with *her*."

"Well, good luck!" I said laughing.

"Serge, dammit, you don't understand at all. I don't know her, and you do. The two tickets are for you and me and you can come along and introduce me. It's a fancy dress, you know."

I told him I was tired. I told him that I had a terrible day coming up. I told him I had plans. I told him anything I could think of.

"We're even invited to a dinner!" he said.

I really couldn't refuse him any longer, so I said all right, I would put on my Cossack uniform.

That evening we dined at Whitney Warren's—he was the man who had built the New York Central and off we went to the Waldorf, with Dick all decked up as Louis Seize, beauty marks and all—"A much maligned king, Serge," he said, "a much maligned king." The trouble was that he was wearing a fine gray wig, which by and by he got bored with, taking it off from time to time and shoving it back on. Frequently, he got it back to front, and once, like poor old Countess Kleinmichel, he got it upside down.

We went through the entire place over and over again looking for Mrs. Sam Goldwyn. She wasn't even there. But Dick with his old Confederate stubbornness would not give up. No, we had to make a tour of *all* the parties that were being held upstairs in various suites. And in a jam-up in one of the elevators I lost Cousin Dick. He vanished. I looked everywhere for him, because I was a little worried, and he wasn't feeling any pain. He just disappeared, so I went home to bed.

The next morning was Sunday, and I went over to the Knickerbocker Club for lunch, and there stretched out on one of the couches and covered with a great plaid rug was Dick Peters. He was still Louis Seize. He opened one eye and said furiously, "Serge! These doggone boys kept me up. Good fellers though, but they kept me going to six in the morning. I'm getting too old for that sort of thing. Hell, I'm ninety-four!"

Alice went back to stay more or less permanently in London. In 1931 Edward James, the brother-in-law of Marshall Field, married the dancer Tilly Losch, who was an old friend of Alice's and mine. Tilly was then the star of

George Balanchine's ballet in Paris. Tilly became sort of an ambassadress between Alice and me, trying to straighten things out; and during those days I saw her a great deal. It seemed strange to me, because Tilly was not happy herself, and in a year's time she got a divorce. Still, she was a good counsellor and a beautiful one. Today, she is a first-rank painter and is living in New York.

By this time, Vincent and Helen had fixed up their new house at 130 East 80th Street, and they had asked Cousin Dick to move in with them, as he was hard up. Vincent, of course, adored him and the activities of Vincent's brainchild, the mysterious Countess Maria Ramona Gomez y Sepulveda with amorous intentions toward ninety-four year-old Captain Dick Peters of the Confederate States Army, were growing daily more insistent. Unmentionable portions of her clothing would arrive for Dick periodically at the most appalling moments, at a dinner for instance, and little cards from her would say such things as "Souvenir, my darling. I saw you today outside of a saloon. Your own, your adoring, Ramona S."

Vincent, however, had had a shock when Cousin Dick moved in to stay, for he brought with him all his ancient and battered furniture. Some of it was good, and all of it had come from down South. Dick was very attached to it, and to Vincent's horror it was stored in rooms all over the top floors of 130 East 80th. It really created a mess, and Vincent immediately began a campaign to get Dick to auction it. At first he got nowhere. Dick was just plain attached to his furniture, he said. Finally, Vincent said he would pay the cartage and the commissions to the auctioneers if only Dick would get all the stuff the hell out of there. Dick was also a good businessman, and he instantly agreed.

So everything was set at an auction house of good repute, catalogues were printed, the furniture went out of 130 to Vincent's great relief even if he was paying for the transport, and the day for the auction approached. But Dick began to brood. He was attached to that furniture, and he felt that it was now really beyond a matter of mere price. He felt he was a damn fool to have let Vincent persuade him to do such a thing. By the day of the auction, Dick Peters had worked up a full head of steam. He went over to the auction rooms and bought the whole lot back, outbidding everybody else. The next day, all the furniture arrived back at 130 East 80th Street, and Vincent had to put up the fees for the cartage both ways, and the commissions to the auctioneers, because Dick really didn't have a cent. Vincent was very unhappy about that.

Alice then went to a remote town in Nevada where she finally applied for a divorce in the summer of 1932. Vincent kindly offered me the services of his lawyer, Cass Ledyard, of Ledyard and Milburn, and the agreement was worked out that I had custody of Ivan and Alice had the custody of our daughter Sylvia, who was born after the divorce proceedings had begun.

I took a small flat in 79th Street. I will never forget how lonely I felt, but I could only blame myself. In cases like this it is generally the man's fault. I ought to have been able to handle our lives better. I tried to persuade Alice to give it one more chance, but failed. The divorce was a long-drawn-out affair for only one reason: she wanted Ivan to be educated in England, while I wanted him to be educated in the United States. After all, she was an American citizen and the United States was my new adopted country and I didn't believe a child brought up internationally could have a happy life, as he would be torn by conflicting ways of life.

Vincent at this point made me a very good offer to work for him in his real estate company, with Gerry Chadwick and Jack Gates. I accepted. In the meantime I worked hard and soon became well acquainted with Vincent's holdings. I found my Russian training invaluable and not too different. I think I made two contributions to him in my work. One was the suggestion to rebuild or offer the City of New York his downtown tenement buildings, which were in awful shape, which he did. The municipality tore them down and built a housing project on the site.

The second was the remodeling of two blocks of brownstone houses on East End Avenue. They were in terrible shape, but had a beautiful view over Carl Schurz Park and Hell Gate. When Vincent Astor gave me the green light I had them renovated one by one. By degrees we put in new plumbing, electric wiring and steam heating, dolled them up both inside and out. Each house had a different-colored door and window boxes on each window sill; at the back of the houses I had the laundry poles painted various colors. We rented these small apartments for from forty dollars a month to one hundred dollars. We were very careful as to whom we took in as tenants and soon we got an amazing lot of attractive people living there. It was still the depression period, quite a few newlyweds rented these apartments, and soon there was not enough room for perambulators. We had to build a special place in the back gardens to house the prams. We called one block Poverty Row, and the other Busted Row.

I was so engrossed in the uptown section with these activities that finally I practically transferred my activities to the uptown office at 120 East End Avenue. I also rented one of the apartments in Poverty Row, and I lived there for a year. Nanny Tiffany and Eleanor Barry, a fine painter and now the wife of Larry Lohman of CBS, rented apartments in the house next door. We all had a very gay time. This lasted until the moment I got the divorce. As I say, I was given the custody of Ivan, and my daughter Sylvia, born during the divorce, was left in Alice's custody, but I stipulated that Ivan should be educated in the United States and that I should have him only half the time, especially the period when he was at school during the winter. As it worked out, I always let Ivan stay with Alice any time she wanted him, if she was in New York and he could go to school. I felt that a child should see his mother as often as possible, especially whilst he is small. I had learned that the hard way when I was little, and did not want the same thing to happen to Ivan.

It was during this unhappy period that the United States gave me a present. On September 24, 1931 at the District Court of the United States at New York I was granted one of the world's greatest gifts, American citizenship.

All Russians have a strong affinity for America. In many ways our great sprawling countries and their peoples are very much alike. Except for the Soviet regime today, there would be no problems between us. I was honored and overjoyed at being accepted by America, a generous and understanding, friendly land—my new home on earth.

CHAPTER XXVI

Our divorce came through on the 7th of December 1932, and Alice married Raimund von Hofmannsthal early in 1933. He was the son of the fine Austrian poet Hugo von Hofmannsthal, who was the librettist for Richard Strauss, the composer of *Der Rosenkavalier*. Raimund von Hofmannsthal was a bon-vivant writer who had been connected with Max Reinhardt in Vienna, and was later with United Artists and Paramount in Hollywood. Vincent was violently opposed to Alice marrying von Hofmannsthal, but they were secretly married in Newark, with Dr. Rudolf Kommer the witness. They planned to leave at once for Europe before the news was out, as there had been quite a bit of unpleasant newspaper discussion of our divorce. But Ivan became seriously ill on the day set for their departure and Alice stayed on to be with him, their trip to Europe taking place after his recovery.

I am happy to know that in time Alice came to realize that I always would be her very good friend. In the summer, Ivan asked if he could go and stay with his mother in Austria. I had rented a small house in Sands Point, Long Island for him, but I sublet it and he went off. I left my New York apartment and moved in with a friend of mine, Bert Taylor, who had a beautiful triple penthouse on East 57th Street. He had collected two other bachelors, Gary Cooper, who was making a film, and Lucius Ordway.

The four of us were under the wonderful care and hospitality of Bert, who was one of the greatest gourmets and connoisseurs of wines and cigars in the United States. He was also one of the most able brokers in Wall Street and was then actually president of the stock exchange.

I remember a series of parties that he gave in his penthouse. They were always very gay and the most beautiful and attractive ladies attended them. Some of these parties were given exclusively for the theatrical world, and the choruses of Ziegfeld and Earl Carroll. It was the period when the markets had recovered somewhat after the crash, and some people again had a lot of money to spend.

I had a funny episode that happened to me and involved a pretty nifty girl that was dancing in the Earl Carroll chorus. She is now a very well-known international beauty. Bert Taylor took a shine to her, but was unfortunately heavily involved with another girl. Both the girls, each in complete innocence as to the other's existence, were asked to a beach party at the old Atlantic Beach Club on a Sunday afternoon; and then we were all going to Nelson Doubleday's dance that he was giving for the Ziegfeld and Earl Carroll choruses at his house near Oyster Bay. He had just gotten a divorce from his wife and was trying to forget her, and I must say he chose a pretty relaxed way of doing it.

Bert came to me and asked me to take the Earl Carroll girl along in my car, as he had to take the other girl, and he was planning to dump the latter at the earliest possible opportunity. He knew I was then fancy-free. I naturally obliged, although I made a few remarks that hardly put him at his ease with regard to my own intentions. However, any port in a storm, and he said that he knew he could trust me. So the girl arrived. I was highly amused, because she also brought a small suitcase with her.

We lunched and swam at Atlantic Beach and about six o'clock left for the party in Oyster Bay. I locked the suitcase in the trunk of my car, and we all had dinner at Doubleday's. There was a wide dance floor and a beautiful marquee in the garden in which Emil Coleman's orchestra played continuously. Everyone was having such a good time that I saw that the party would probably break up in the early hours of the morning: so I went and warned Bert that I was going to leave and he'd damn well have to look after the girl he had had me bring. After all, I had to be in my office at nine the next morning. He said, "Serge, you're a brick!" and I left thinking that I'd done my good deed for the day.

I drove home and left my car at Helen Astor's garage. I went to work next morning and came home about six. There the butler told me that Mr. Taylor would like a word with me. I went into his room and he asked me what the hell had I done with the suitcase of his girl? As she was in such desperate need, he had had to take her out on a shopping expedition, which had ended up with a mink coat from Maximilian. Bert pretended to be furious with me for months afterward.

To add insult to injury, the girl went to her theater at show time that very evening in her mink, and, naturally, she made Walter Winchell's column the next day. It contained a few pointed remarks as to her possible beau, which got Bert in Dutch with his other girl. From then on the young lady rose to fame, forgot him and married one of the multimillionaires. I prefer to blame it all on a suitcase in the trunk of my old Ford.

Bert gave me a party on October 3rd. It was my birthday, and George Gershwin came and played his famous *Rhapsody in Blue* and parts of the score of *Porgy and Bess*, which he was just in the process of writing. He had hired Emil Coleman and rolled up the rugs for a dance. Carroll Carstairs was there, the Di Frassos, the Chaqueneaus, Jules Glaenzer and his beautiful wife, Kendall Lee, who presented me with a gold pencil that I still have. Kendall and Kay Chaqueneau were my extra special waltzing partners of those days.

There was another time when we had a riot with all the Earl Carroll and Ziegfeld girls. Some of my gayer bachelor friends that evening came to realize that the Ziegfeld girls were generally far more priggish than those to whom they had been heretofore accustomed. The boys at that winging were Earl Carroll, Flo Ziegfeld, Larry Doyle, Carroll Carstairs, Lytle Hull, Jack Baragwanath, Will Stewart, who was then in love with a wow of a show girl called Eileen Wenzell, and of course the four of us. Bert Taylor had taken a shine to a chorus girl called Betty Sundmark.

During the course of that one, somebody, I think it was Will Stewart, suggested that we all play "murder." In the course of the game, I drew the short match that designated me as the murderer. The lights were put out, and I was just about to put my hands around my victim's neck when I heard a terrific giggle, and then immortal stage whispers, "Relax, darling! Relax! It's only Will!" Naturally, I murdered my victim immediately and slammed on the lights. After that, Will decided that we should all play "statues," which is a game, and he got even with me.

In 1933 Vincent invited me to join his party on the *Nourmahal* for the ship's second expedition to Galapagos. The plan was for the ship to travel around to the West Coast where Vincent and the whole group would go aboard her in Hollywood. I had seen Doug Fairbanks at a party in New York and had told him about the plans, and he asked Doc Holden and myself to come out to Hollywood and stay with him for a couple of weeks beforehand. Doc was also going on the trip and this seemed a fine enough arrangement, so he and I accepted.

We went out together on the train two weeks before Vincent; and when we got to Hollywood, Doug's chauffeur met us at the station and drove us to Doug's studio. There Doug's male secretary conducted us straight to the steam bath. When the steam cleared, we saw Sam Goldwyn being pummeled on a marble slab. Then we saw Doug, and he introduced us to Charlie Chaplin, Doug Junior, Johnny Fell, Raymond Guest, David Selznick and Jock Whitney, most of whom we knew. Charlie, whom Alice and I had known in London, had just made a film in which he portrayed a toreador. Without a stitch on but with a towel in his hands, he regaled us with his act against a mythical bull.

After that, it was considered that we were in sufficient health to begin the unbelievable round of parties. Doug was tremendously hospitable. He had even bequeathed Doc and myself each a black limousine with a chauffeur, just to move comfortably around in. He had gotten us invited to every conceivable party, saying "By golly, we're going to get you New York glamor boys going around here. Besides, the stars around here need some new cannon fodder!" He had high hopes us all right. "And if you have to get photographed, Sergie," he say "just moisten your lips and say 'bitch'—it'll give you a wonderful smile."

The first party, which took place that very night, was given by Bill Haines, the well-known decorator. At Bill's blowout, the people present may be familiar: Carole Lombard; Ronald Colman; Cary Grant; Loretta Young, who was my real friend there; my old stablemate at Bert's, Gary Cooper; Mary Pickford; Clark Gable; Marlene Dietrich; Marian Davies; Paulette Goddard; Connie and Joan Bennett; Johnny Weismuller; Charlie Chaplin; Lupe Velez— almost all the stars you could think of. Doug got us shuttled around and then left us on our own. He came looking for Doc and me around three in the morning. He was always very concerned about us and wanted to be sure that we were having a good time. When he saw us, he was disgusted. We were with two of Bill Haines's exceedingly cute but lowly secretaries. "You so-and-so glamor characters from New York should be able to do better than *that*!" he said, and he took us home in disgrace.

Doc and I decided that in those next thirteen evenings we would extend ourselves to the limits of our endurance and shine in Doug's eyes. Actually, the stars that Doug had gone to such efforts all evening to introduce us to were really not interested in Doc or myself at all. All they were concerned with was their producer, or future producer, or possible producer. I swear that during the next thirteen days and nights there was a party every single moment of the day: breakfast, lunch, tea or dinner. The two Dougs, Doc and I were physical wrecks by the time Vincent was due to arrive. In fact, the pace had been so terrific that we'd actually all lost our voices—but completely. All four of us had gotten to the point where we were actually passing notes back and forth to one another. We couldn't even croak.

One morning we learned that the fine sight of the *Nourmahal* had moved into the harbor of the naval base and was now tied up at a dock. Doc and I looked balefully at each other. I knew what he was thinking—that Vincent was due in any moment on the train. Our condition could displease him, so we went out and got a whole lot of nose drops, throat sprays, gargles, anything we could think of to relieve our speechlessness but none of which did us a particle of good. We were just dead-beat, and that was that.

Vincent came straight to Doug's and bellowed for us. I'll never forget the scorn with which he looked us up and down. He was simply scandalized at our condition. He asked us what the hell was the matter with us, and my God we couldn't answer him. Doc and I sheepishly passed him a note. This got Vincent really displeased. He gave us holy hell, gave us our embarkation orders, and left. I'll never forget Doc passing me a note saying, "Sergie, we're in for the brig!" Once we were on board, Vincent didn't talk to us for three whole days, and meanwhile he regarded us with out-and-out disgust. We spent a good twenty-four hours in bed and the next twelve with our gargles and throat sprays. I'm sorry to say that Doc's voice returned sooner than mine, for it meant that for the rest of the trip Vincent's pointed remarks with regard to Hollywood producing were directed more or less straight at me.

The goal of the expedition was Indomitable Island, the least known and accessible of the Galapagos, where the previous expedition had gathered some rare specimens. Strangely enough, on this trip the spineless cactus of the Galapagos could not be found again, and the plant was known only through the specimens which had already been brought ashore and planted in Panama. But we found rare golden groupers and all kinds of exotic fish that were placed in the special tanks with which the Nourmahal was fitted. These tanks provided proper water temperatures whatever the ship's latitude and air temperature might be. The fish were to be brought back on the return journey to the government aquarium at Bermuda, then in charge of a first-rate scientist, a wonderfully jolly and rotund fellow called Louis Mowbray. Louis was one of Vincent's guests on the voyage, and he taught me how to tie bowlines and other more complicated knots. He also tipped me off about trawling for the big fish. "You must always trawl across a riptide," he said, "not with it or against it. You should direct your boatman to head for all the rips and cut straight across." I must say he was dead right. He also showed me how to harpoon.

The other guests were Patsy Ward, Doc Holden, Nancy Potter Bourne, Minnie Cushing, George St. George, and a fine surgeon whom we all nicknamed Selassie, because he looked like Haile Selassie. I don't remember his name. The *Nourmahal* had a whole operating room on board, and Selassie, who was also George's doctor, was there to saw or sew anybody up if need be. Actually, he was a hell of a good barber and, luckily, this was the only cutting he ever had to do.

Our first stop was off San Juan at the lower tip of the Californian peninsula where Doc and I caught our first marlin. Mine was 186 pounds. Then we went halfway up the Gulf of California and stopped at Acapulco. The fishing there was very poor, so we went ashore and took a motor trip to Mexico City via Cuernavaca where we had lunch. In Mexico City we did a lot of sightseeing and went through the palace of Emperor Maximilian. I was really disappointed in Mexico City, because I wanted to see some of the great Aztec and Mayan ruins. There was nothing there that remotely reminded one of Mexico's real past, although everywhere one could find traces of the much more recent conquistadores. We flew back to Acapulco, a very dangerous flight indeed, boarded the ship, and then sailed straight to our first ocean stop off the Cocos Islands.

There is a huge pirate hoard from some Spanish treasure ships from the Philippines supposedly buried on Cocos. I have a hunch that Vincent, in his precise way, was more interested in this than he professed to be. He knew all about the treasure clues and mythology of the place. The islands were a logical hiding place. He was sure there was something to it. Ashore on the islands at that time there was an expedition of treasure hunters, so Vincent wasn't entirely alone in his beliefs. The treasure hunters were a bunch of really cutthroat Englishmen, most peculiar people, shifty, ragtaggle, psychopathic, and seemingly dangerous. There were six of them in all, and one by one each of them behind the others' backs told us what he would do if he found the treasure. Each said that he was certainly not going to tell the others. It was a very explosive situation indeed, and the atmosphere was horrible. Perhaps as a result, the Costa Rican government had sent a squad of troops to the place under the command of a really charming officer. He wasn't happy there at all, but if the treasure did turn up, his government, so far as he was concerned, was going to get its rightful share, even if he had to shoot.

All the talk about a treasure gave us a strong romantic impetus, and on Vincent's direction, we climbed the peak of the island, and even located a cave not known to have existed there. We located some of the clues. "It must be in this general area," said Vincent. His knowledge of geology made him sure that a landslide had taken place at the crucial spot.

We did some fishing off Cocos. It was wonderful for wahoo.

Then we were off to Galapagos. Here it was a seventh heaven. Nature in its every curious state abounded. Galapagos had animals and reptiles there that ranged from ancient remnants of the dinosaur age all the way to monkeys. There were all sorts of creatures—exotic birds, strange flora and fauna, and fantastic fishes. We had fishing of every description.

Doc and I went harpooning in a school of giant manta rays that were sleeping on the surface. There were so many that we went from one to the other to find the biggest. We found him all right. I drove the shaft home and off we went. The port launch, the one that we were in, was a very heavy boat, and after I got three harpoons into the ray it towed us for four and a half hours with the engine in reverse. The beast had to be hauled up the side of the Nourmahal by a winch. It measured twenty-one feet from tip to tip and weighed over two thousand pounds.

On his previous trip Vincent had found a German couple living on Galapagos, a former dentist and his wife. They had fled from civilization, and were now savages in every sense of the word. The nearest people were seventy-five miles away by water. They had cleared a little ground, and built a rough hut. Vincent had given the man a rifle, which he had accepted morosely. There was a mystery involving them. There had supposedly been another man who had gone away to live with them. Despite expeditions there to find him, he was never found. And now, by the second trip of the *Nourmahal* all three had disappeared.

If you want to learn something about the true horrors of the sea, here it is. To me there is nothing more frightening. At night we would occasionally put a marine lamp just above water level by the starboard gangway. Big flying fish about a foot and a half in width would come scooting out of the darkness toward the light and strike the side of the ship with a resounding thump and stun themselves. Immediately, the sharks came up and went after them—I mean really huge sharks and barracuda and smaller sharks besides. Then we would go down onto the gangway platform just above the seething water and spear a big shark from back to front, so that as it sped away it would slip off the spear. There the terror would begin. I've never seen anything like it. In a flash the water beneath the lamp would become a frothing thrashing blood-red color as all the sharks in the area, excited by the blood, went after the wounded fish. In thirty seconds there would be nothing left of him. The sharks are tough creatures. I once caught one of the big fellows on a trawl. I had to empty twenty shots into his head before he finally died.

We always had a competition between our various boats. I thought I'd got something of a record when I caught a gigantic tuna one afternoon. It took me four hours to get him in. We towed him over to the ship and hooked him onto the winch. Somebody yelled, and I saw a huge fin shooting toward my catch. A monstrous white belly turned upward. There was a tremendous crunch and the water all around us went scarlet. When the winch hauled in, all that was left was one immense head. A single bite of that shark had done away with a tuna weighing upwards of two hundred pounds.

We brought a lot of penguins and turtles and turtle eggs aboard, and these eventually colonized Bermuda; because of the fish in the tanks, off we went as fast as we could go to Bermuda, via the Panama Canal. We stayed in Bermuda for ten days before returning to New York.

Vincent had always been interested in politics, and Helen was also, as a Republican. But Vincent was a Democrat, and he enthusiastically supported Franklin Delano Roosevelt. He was a member of the fabled Brain Trust. After Franklin's election, Vincent practically placed the *Nourmahal* at his disposal. A special ramp was built up the side of the ship so that the President could be taken aboard in his wheel chair without embarrassment. The President often went on cruises over the weekend in those first turbulent days of the New Deal. He fished, relaxed, and returned to the White House rested. When he went to Florida to speak soon after his inauguration, he sailed with Vincent and his party on the *Nourmahal*. A strange thing—Vincent had a premonition. Roosevelt's success had been so striking that Vincent began thinking that an attempt might be made to assassinate the President. Then he was sure that something like that was going to happen. He notified the Secret Service men to be doubly watchful. As the President and Mayor Cermak of Chicago drove through the streets of Miami, a shot rang out, and the mayor, beside Roosevelt, dropped dead. Afterwards, Vincent personally took the President back to the yacht.

I remember going to Franklin's Val Kil Farm near Hyde Park. It was about the time that Litvinoff was here and the diplomatic recognition of Soviet Russia was being discussed. The event was a picnic given by Mrs. Roosevelt for twenty members of the press at the Roosevelt estate, and we all sat around the pool and went swimming, including the President. He was very affable that day—in fact whenever I saw him he was extremely cordial. I asked him point-blank if we were going to recognize the Bolsheviks. He smiled, regarded me searchingly a moment and then said, "No, but perhaps some trade agreement will be worked out." Then he changed the subject. The very next week the United States recognized Soviet Russia. That was the way Franklin was.

In 1935 the St. Regis Hotel, which Vincent had sold to the Duke interests, was returned to him for default on the mortgage which he held. We never understood why the Dukes did this, as they were wealthy and it was a fine property. Besides, the Dukes had added a whole wing. For Vincent, of course, the St. Regis was free and clear. While there was no financial superstructure to cope with, occupancy was low. We had to think of ways to beef it up. The Peacock Room, designed by Joseph Urban, did a very poor business. The Oak Room, while it had a traditional standing, was dark and gloomy. The old-fashioned lobbies were also dark and uninviting. There were no wine cellars, and the food was conventional. Yet the building was an architectural masterpiece of its sort. When Colonel John Jacob Astor had built it, he had wanted to make it the great luxury hotel of the New World. Colonel Astor was an inventor and many other things as well. He was extremely able. His many marine engineering devices were awarded patents, all of which he gave over for the public use. In the St. Regis he had installed an air-conditioning system of his own design. On each floor there was a room in which sheets of dampened cheese-cloth were hung, and powerful fans drove the air through these sheets and into ducts that went to every room. And of course that kind of cooling system works quite well, as anyone who has ever placed a damp cloth before an electric fan well knows. Vincent put coils and compressors in these cooling rooms and, presto, thanks to his father's foresight he had the first fully air-conditioned hotel in the world.

The property was in receivership and the manager appointed by the receivers was Mr. Roney. Vincent suggested that I look things over and make my suggestions, as I had lived much of my life in the best hotels of Europe. He made me a sort of general consultant, promotion man, and trouble-shooter for the St. Regis, aside from my other real estate duties. That is how I started in the hotel business. I found it captivating and a challenge.

My sister-in-law, Helen, suggested Mrs. Cameron (Nanny) Tiffany as a decorator. Nanny and I got into a huddle and gradually planned the whole scheme of redecoration of the St. Regis, including the bar, restaurant, roof and finally the basement, which had been known before as the Seaglades. Vincent built the bar around the famous Maxfield Parrish painting of Old King Cole which Vincent's father had once commissioned for the bar of the old Knickerbocker Hotel. It was then on loan to the Racquet and Tennis Club. The restaurant was made into the Oak Room with the original oak paneling extended and pickled, to jazz it up, and a new ceiling was put in. The roof garden was done in baroque design to represent a Viennese fête champêtre. It was conceived by Vava Adlerberg and myself to resemble one of the temporary structures that Catherine the Great of Russia or Ludwig of Bavaria had built for their parties. It was beautiful and gay with a little pavilion and garden on one side, and I am happy to say that it is still one of the handsomest rooms in New York. Finally, an intimate *boîte* called the Maisonette Russe was created out of the Seaglades, and the Iridium Room emerged with a full-fledged ice show. This was Vincent's idea—a rink that rolled out onto the dance floor. The whole effect of the change in the hotel was a sensation.

We put in a good wine cellar. I hired for the Maisonette Russe a man who had been the Czar's chef at Livadia, a friend of Vassily's (he had stayed on with Alice), and, like Vassily, one of the best chefs in the world. Emil Coleman provided music in the Iridium Room, with a variety of suppers. In the Maisonette we got Yasha Nazarenko and an ensemble of Russian singers, and a gipsy orchestra of Cadolban. On the roof we took on, during the summer, my friend Jacques Fray. He had just parted company with Braggiotti, with whom he had toured in the United States for several years.

The hotel became the talk of the town and our reputation spread through the nation and abroad. We made a great success of it. Needless to say, the St. Regis became the center of a great deal of wonderful social life. A hotel quickly acquires a distinct personality. The St. Regis became a meeting place not only for society figures but for visitors from abroad, ambassadors, diplomats, foreign representatives of all kinds. And all my lady friends would come in to say "hello" to my little Welsh Corgi called Woggie. Woggie was a fabulous dog, who recognized everybody I knew, and received them even when I wasn't at my desk. They would often take him out for walks. He also played the piano, getting up on a piano stool and pounding away with his paws. The strange thing about it was that he knew a piano even in a place that he had never been to before. Upright or grand, it made no difference, he would go straight to it on command. Woggie soon became an institution, and that wonderful little dog's public relations value was more than anyone will ever realize. He helped pull people in.

The hotel occupied me much of the time until 1939. I went on several trips of the *Nourmahal* up the coast and over to Bermuda during this period. I went abroad a couple of times on public relations for the hotel, visiting Chips in London, and kept in touch with my many old friends.

Quite against my better judgment, in the mid-thirties I became a ballet impresario on a small scale. In the early days in London, Juliet Duff had kept the Ballet Russe, Diaghileff's old company, from breaking up, raising about three thousand pounds a year for them. Now the company, run by De Basil, was in trouble. Sorine called me, and said that the organization was falling apart and couldn't I help. I said I could try, and I found myself heading a finance committee. We decided to build up a full-fledged American ballet, a difficult venture in view of the high cost of any ballet in the United States at the time. We made an arrangement with Sol Hurok to arrange for a tour.

There was another company, known as the Ballet Russe de Monte Carlo, headed by Serge Denham and Junkie Fleischman. Since we were in competition in a limited field, I felt that the sensible procedure for both companies was to merge. Sorine and I laid the groundwork for our merger. Everything seemed all set, and thereafter I could never discover exactly what the source of the trouble was. De Basil's argument was always that the others wouldn't agree, and were blocking further negotiations. At last a verbal agreement was reached between De Basil, who was now with his company in London, and the others. To complete the deal I too had to go to London. The lawyers for the Monte Carlo Company were also in London. In fact, ridiculously enough, both companies had engagements in London at the same time. It proved my point. The Monte Carlo people were pleased with my arrangements, and nothing remained except that I needed De Basil's consent. He was now oddly reluctant to grant this. Still I went to the meeting full of fight, determined to save De Basil's company. And then, my God, I discovered that the Monte Carlo people were the agreeable ones and De Basil was the only person who was holding everything up. I think he wanted to be the absolute boss of both companies. The net result was that Sorine and I ended up in reverse positions to those which we had occupied before, after having spent a long and fruitless period as spokesmen for a man who had no intention of doing anything different anyway.

However, through my activities I came to know most of the ballet greats of that time—Danilova, Baranova, Massine, the Fokines, my old friends from Russia, Vera Zorina and many others. At least this side of it was exhilarating, except that few prima ballerinas are really good ballroom dancers, *very* few!

By 1937 and 1938 the depression was lifting. Society became gayer as the world became prosperous. America was back on its feet again. I went often on the weekend cruises of the *Nourmahal*, which were pleasant and exhilarating, for Vincent was always an excellent host.

In the meantime, in Europe war clouds were gathering. Hitler's star was rising. In Spain Franco was defeating the Reds, which was a god-send, as the United States had been taken in by fake democracy in being sympathetic to the Loyalists. We actually supported the Reds who were camouflaged as democratic people. They had Red army officers and commissars and Communist secret police operating with them. In May, 1939, Germany and Italy announced a military and political alliance. At the same time, in the Far East, the Japanese were slowly consolidating their grip over Mongolia and were fighting Mongol troops backed by the Soviets. Hitler was getting more and more belligerent. Neville Chamberlain was doing his best to appease him.

There was never any real sympathy for Hitler among the Russian refugees I knew. But at the same time, those who had suffered at the hands of the Bolsheviks were disposed to wait and see, if only on the grounds that Hitler had fought the Communists in Germany and was opposed to Communist Russia. I understood how they felt. They naturally felt about the Communists just as the refugees whose families were later tortured by the storm troopers were to feel about the Nazis. To them, at any time, any means of destroying the Communists seemed right. But I could never accept that view. I said that the Soviets would be our allies and that while that lasted, we had better learn to put up with them.

It was obvious a long time before the war that war was coming, a situation altogether unlike the period before 1914. I remember the good-will trip of the King and Queen of England to the United States, and the famous hot-dog picnic at Hyde Park. I was invited by President and Mrs. Roosevelt, and King George and Queen Elizabeth were extremely kind to me on that occasion. I had seen him often at parties in London since the period right after the war, when he had been known simply as Prince Albert. Alice and I had dined with the Yorks in our London days and seen them often at parties. But now it was ten years since I'd had the pleasure of seeing them. Showing his amazing memory for people, he came right up and buttonholed me at that picnic. We talked fondly about the old times. I was delighted by his and the Queen's happiness—they both literally radiated. He was truly a happy monarch, with a wonderful family life, despite the many shattering demands that he was daily forced to face—a remarkable fellow, quiet but unswerving, and filled with courage. I remember thinking "God bless him," as he moved away. I never saw him again. The Queen had the great quality of talking to one as if she were interested in no one else. She really made me feel wonderful. She was always unbelievable that way. She asked me what I was doing, how I liked my new country, and whether I missed my many old friends in England. We talked about old times, and then she too had to move on.

The outlook for France and England was very gloomy. I took a quick trip to England that summer and stayed with Chips Channon in his lovely house in Belgrave Square. Chips said that their armament situation, like ours, was frightful. They were going to rely on their navy, but the German air force really worried everyone. Chips was as usual in Parliament. He took me to lunch there, and I met a few of my old friends who were Members of Parliament, like Alen Lenox-Boyd, Philip Sassoon and others. I remember telling Chips, in case of war, immediately to send me his son Paul, that I would be very happy to look after him. He actually did so later.

I talked with several people there. They were in the same position with regard to Hitler that the United States has recently come to occupy with respect to Russia. Hitler could twist their tails. They didn't have the arms; they were just then putting the Bren gun into production. They had nothing! They were not scared, but they were hoping to prolong the uneasy status quo as much as they could, and the only thing they could do was appease and try to keep things on an even keel.

At this point I will merely call to attention the close similarity between the England and America of that day to the England and America of this very present moment. The Soviets are a dangerous adversary. Today I feel the same apprehension that I felt in England before the Second World War. Then there was Stanley Baldwin, who has since been pitied for the mistakes that he made.

Today I am extremely alarmed by certain of the recent decisions taken by our own Supreme Court who have forced us to rehire in key places, such as our communications system and even in the government itself, Communist sympathizers who had once been fired as "risks." I am also fearful of our terrible lack of preparedness for war, or for peace if only to keep the Soviets at bay. Before the Second World War there was a time of ease and prosperity. Everyone lived off the fat of the land, just as we are living today, with an army undermanned and untrained, as the English army was, and the Russian army in peak condition, as the German army was.

During that last trip to England before the onslaught, I had some gloomy talks with Michael Berry, the son of Lord Camrose, who was married to Pamela Smith, Lord Birkenhead's daughter. The fabled wit of her father had been passed on to Pamela. With her sharp tongue and sometimes biting humor, she also possessed her father's political clarity of mind. And Michael, of course, coming from the family that controlled the *Daily Telegraph*, was tremendously well-informed. As a close friend of Butler, who was then the Foreign Secretary, Chips also knew what was happening, and he was gloomier still. After visiting him, I went to Holland. Mrs. Adelaide Leonard had a villa near The Hague. I stayed with her a week, at the height of tulip time. She had many friends among the Dutch, who came to dine. In the evening, after dinner, they all talked quite freely. Preparations for war in Holland meant flooding part of the country. They were on constant alert, and then it was a complicated matter to decide what areas were to be flooded, and when. Their militia was all called up and on twenty-four-hour duty.

I took a trip to Hayling Island and saw Catherine, who I must say looked very well. I also went for a few days to Deauville and Paris, where I saw Dolly Radziwill, and we talked lightly about St. Petersburg days, when I used to give parties at my house during the war. But everywhere there was a feeling of impending disaster and subdued fear.

Still, we had a wonderful reunion of a few Russians at Dolly's. She got a Tzigany orchestra and we sang and played all the old tunes of the past.

I returned on the *Queen Mary*, with Jimmy Roosevelt, Lady Ward and Susan Ward. It was a gay crossing. We were met by a group who came out on a coast-guard cutter, including Betsy Cushing Roosevelt, Jimmy's wife, and her sister Barbara Cushing, whom I had been seeing a lot of. I was very fond of Barbara herself, but I was wary because all three Cushing girls were ruled by their mother.

Vincent and Helen were divorced, and Helen returned to her own estate at Staatsburg. It was the old Dinsmore place, which had been in her family for generations, going back to a date long before the Revolution and older than many of the old estates of England. There she built a marvelous house on the curve of a road overlooking the Hudson, with a concave front. It was pale blue with white trim, and Helen called it "Hudson baroque." She later married

Vincent's and my old friend Lytle Hull. Because she had done so much for music for so many years, the members of the New York Philharmonic Orchestra, on their own initiative, once chartered buses and rode to her house and gave a concert on the lawn. Helen kept the grounds wooded, but she planted wild flowers everywhere under the trees, and these, with the crab apples and dogwood, made the place enchanting.

That fall, Vincent married Minnie Cushing, who had been to the Galapagos with us. She, Betsy and Barbara were daughters of the celebrated Boston brain surgeon Harvey Cushing. I was by this time very much in love with Barbara, the youngest of the three Cushing sisters.

On weekends I would go up with Barbara to Darien, where her mother had a house. I've a slight suspicion that Mamma didn't relish the thought of having me as a son-in-law. Anyway, Barbara was always being pushed away from me; and I must say I laughed and thought that all that sort of thing had been done to me much better before by Lady Ribblesdale. Then Barbara married Stanley Mortimer and later Bill Paley of CBS.

When Hitler and Stalin made their famous pact in the summer of 1939 and partitioned Poland and the phony war began, I was nearly fifty years old. It was at this point that Cousin Dick Peters had his fabulous swan song. It seemed that the older Dick Peters got, the spryer he became. For years on end he had engaged in a running battle with the governors of the Knickerbocker Club to have a ladies' day. Never in the history of the club had a lady set foot within its portals. However, the governors finally relented, and that year they even gave Cousin Dick a Christmas present. They notified him that his suggestion with regard to a ladies' day had been acted upon, and they were now pleased to inform him that on January 27, 1940 a ball would be held in the clubhouse, and ladies would be invited. When the night of his great victory over the governors finally arrived, Dick Peters got carried away. He took Margaret Lawrance as his dancing partner for a Virginia reel that was played especially for him. He did such a dosedo at one point that he slipped and fell. When he was rushed to the hospital, it was found that he had broken his hip. Pneumonia developed, and he died within forty-eight hours of the gayest and most gallant moment of his long life.

By this time I had found that I had no chance of getting into the army. When France collapsed, and the Battle of Britain was under way, I thought I might get into the state guard, and I tried to enlist in the 17th Regiment, New York State Guard, because it was now a matter of time. But they told me that I needed references. I went to Colonel Robins, who was a partner in the law firm of Secretary of War Stimson. And he very kindly wrote a lot of letters of recommendation for me. Then I did the rounds of all the people who had received his letters. I said I wanted to join. They asked me why. I said the war was coming, which I'm sure they realized better than I, and I wanted to learn the drill, the infantry drill. I explained that as an old cavalryman I didn't know anything about infantry, let alone American infantry. So they told me to write down my life history. After that I don't know how many times I had to write my life history for the army. Then I was sworn into the regiment as a buck private.

I hurried from the St. Regis to the 34th Street Armory to drill. We drilled one night a week. I was dropped into H Company. There were several recruits lined up. I happened to be chewing gum. I often chew gum after dinner. The outraged sergeant came by, stuck his finger in my mouth and took the gum out. I was rather startled. But I thought he was a good soldier. He was a great guy, that sergeant, and we became good friends. He later became a captain. My captain then was Freddie Cromwell. My platoon commander was Lieutenant George E. Brewer. I was in the first squad of the first platoon. I went through all the rigmarole of drill, squad drill, platoon drill, company drill, manual of arms, bayonet training, rifle training, field stripping of rifles, machine guns, that kind of thing.

It was much different from the Chevalier Guards. During parades I was a guidon bearer. After Pearl Harbor and the beginning of the war, we were put to work guarding the water pumps in Brooklyn. I thought, my God, I'll never get overseas. I've got to get out of here. I studied everything I could get my hands on, and when officers' examinations were held, I took them and passed, and was made a second lieutenant in the Third Battalion under Major Wiess.

The officer in command of the Regiment was General Goodyear, Conger Goodyear, a great old boy, a fire-eater. He also wanted to serve in the regular army, but they wouldn't let him; he was too old. I was made a captain and took over K Company. This was my chance. As a company commander I could get training in some other branch. I had been pretty efficient in the White guerrillas, and I thought of the commandos, but I didn't know how to get into them.

Then I met David Bruce at a party. I asked him point-blank, "How can I get into a commando unit?"

Dave said, "Why, that's easy. Why don't you talk to Bill Donovan? He's living in your hotel."

When I got back to the St. Regis, I called Bill. I said, "Listen, I want to join the commandos. How can I go about it?"

"Well," he said, "I am recruiting commandos now. I'll be delighted to arrange for you to see one of my colonels. I'll just take you over to OSS."

I sent him another life history. I signed a lot of papers. Then I went to a commando school for officers of the state guard, near Boston. It was run by British officers. They were officers of the home guard in England, and they were first-rate. We were older men. We got up at five, went into physical drill, and got into pretty good shape. We organized raids, and we were schooled in modern techniques of demolition, and we attacked under fire—very close to real commando training, but not so strenuous. I was very tired when we came in at night.

While I was at the commando school, I was commissioned a major in the United States Army and ordered to report to Washington. I went to Q Building and General Donovan, to OSS, the Office of Strategic Services. General Donovan assigned me to Colonel Goodfellow, who from then on was my commanding officer. Colonel Goodfellow intended to train uniformed guerrilla units which would jump in behind enemy lines. I didn't know it at the time, but that's what I volunteered into.

I was sent immediately to a commando school in Virginia. None of us had names. We were all given nicknames, which were printed on badges. Nobody knew who we were. My name was Sky. This was a physical toughener as well. We got up early and went to bed late, training in special tactics, shooting at sounds at night, guerrilla tactics, memory tests of smell and configurations of places in total darkness, and especially demolition work.

I came back to Washington, and then we started work on tables of organization of the guerrilla units. I had to write up a lot of reports on the latest information about Africa. I did not know what that meant as we had not landed there as yet. I also was given a copy of the official *Soviet Russian Guerrilla Manual*. It had been smuggled out of Russia. I got it translated by General Barmine, who was then a private in the OSS. Barmine was the famous Soviet general who came over to us during the great Soviet purge of 1933. His English in those days wasn't altogether clear, so I eventually edited his manuscript, while the book became the basis for our own manual and our training for what we called operational groups, or OGs.

General Donovan was not allowed to have an army of his own. After the Spanish-American War there had been much resentment in the regular army at Teddy Roosevelt's having recruited and led the Rough Riders, where he was a law unto himself. Since then, strict laws had been enacted, preventing anybody from assuming a command in that fashion again. As a result, General Donovan was permitted only operational groups. That is the way the army thinks. Above all, General Donovan was not going to be allowed to lead another bunch of Rough Riders. We had a hell of a time getting the concept through, just to get permission. We were not even allowed to call our units platoons, companies, or battalions, so we called them groups. This was just another example of sheer red tape.

A company was our "group." A battalion was a "headquarters detachment," etc. And the table of organization was approved, each group a little smaller than a company, about forty men, two or three platoons. We increased them gradually; they stretched. We got everything we wanted, the newest and most secret weapons. We had the bazooka long before anyone else, high explosives, pliable plastics, quite safe without detonators.

Colonel Goodfellow got an idea I should train officers, and become familiar with the training given in the other services, like the courses being given to raider battalions in the marines. There were being given at that time at Fort Benning special combat courses. There were also paratroop courses being given at Fort Benning. For the moment I was not to do any jumping. The idea was for me to observe everything and participate in the training, so that I might get some good ideas for instructing our future units.

I was given an itinerary, first to the paratroop school at Fort Benning, and then to Fort Bragg, where they had glider training. That's the damnedest thing I have ever seen, those gliders coming in. They were as flimsy as racing shells in boat races. Each glider held a full squad of men. I put my foot right through one accidentally. I felt that I would much prefer coming down in a chute to riding in the gliders.

From there I went to Fort Knox, to study tank tactics and to familiarize myself with the way tanks operate. There they had hardening courses, combat courses, and tactical lectures, which to me were highly interesting, especially since their tactics were close to those of the cavalry which they had superseded. I stayed there three weeks. I then was sent to Indio, California. Tanks were on actual maneuvers there. I had three weeks out there in the desert. Iron Mountain Camp was a godforsaken place, but I learned General Patton's tank manual from back to front. They called it "Patton's Bible." I traveled in tanks and jeeps, right through the maneuvers, to ascertain how we could destroy German tank lagers (tank formations for bedding down at night) by parachute descent. It was very interesting, and every night I felt as if I'd been on horseback. I was stiff, and I ached all over. Thus I found that tank men, like cavalry, got very tired from a day of pounding around inside a tank. Every bump is delightfully translated to one's nether regions. As a result, tank men sleep like logs. I felt that our paratroops might someday be able to utilize this one simple fact and do a lot of damage.

Lest such a fate befall our boys, I taught them a cavalry trick that we had used in the Chevalier Guards. Whenever we had been away on leave we had softened up. The first few days back in the saddle were always sheer hell for all the aches and pains. We would soap our behinds heavily in the morning, and by evening we would have worked up a fine smooth lather. A ride with a good soaping was always much improved. Our tankers found this out, and were delighted.

Every night the tank men slept in the shadow of their tanks, directly alongside or under the tanks, because if there was an alert and the men weren't awakened the tanks in motion might run over them, or at least over their feet.

Then I was given a jeep and a driver. We lived at Iron Mountain Camp. In the morning we were each given a water bag and rations, and off we went for one or two days alone on maneuvers. This was a problem of navigation more than anything, and it was extremely difficult to find one's way around in those barren spaces.

My orders were to proceed on a certain day to San Diego and report to the Marine Corps for training purposes with the raider battalions at Camp Pendleton. By this time we were miles out in the desert with a small tank force. I said good-by to the commanding officer of the tank corps, and my jeep driver and I took our course by the compass through the desert. There were no roads anywhere, and it was a very frightening experience. The country was absolutely dry. We just had our water bags and a day's rations. If something had happened to the jeep we'd have been miles away from help. We had two shovels, and some boards to put under the wheels if we got stuck, which was frequent. At one point we had to dig our way out of the bed of a dried-up watercourse for hours, and the heat was as intense as I'd felt anywhere else in the world. After about seven or eight hours, we came to the top of an escarpment which abruptly dropped off a couple of hundred feet. We had to find a way around it and get across. We went along the crest, and finally, in the dim distance, we saw what might be a road. Like the movies, it actually was; and on that road we were able to drive straight back to Iron Mountain Camp.

I telegraphed Elsie and Charles Mendl in Hollywood, and asked to stop off with them for the night, and then I took the train to Hollywood. Elsie was away, and Charles had arranged for me to join his party at a night club, as my train was to arrive late at night. I'll never forget the joy of getting into a bath, drawn by a British valet, who laid out my uniform and polished my boots. I then joined Charles, who was with Harry Cushing; a couple of starlets; Johnny McMullen, Elsie's factotum; Greer Garson, and my old friend from Bert Taylor's party days, Virginia Bruce. Coming in after those weeks in the desert, and after sleeping in flea bags on the ground, that night's good bed was an amazing treat.

After recouping at Charles and Elsie's, I reported to the headquarters of the marines in San Diego, to General Howland (Howling Mad) Smith, who received me pleasantly. But there was a glint in his eye, and I realized that it just might be tough sledding here, seeing as I was an army man. An officer was assigned to me to show me around.

The marines had their own rifle; they disapproved of the Garand. They liked certain tanks only, and they preferred their own equipment. Their chutes seemed better than ours, with pilot chutes to help them open; and they had great esprit de corps. Their discipline was superlative, and I hope to God that no ill-advised mother or fellow traveler ever manages to put sufficient pressure on the marines to force them to change their ways. They are some of our best regular troops, and that is recommendation enough. Besides, such training saves lives in combat.

At San Diego, dust from the red clay permeated everything. It filled one's clothes, nostrils, hair—I've never seen such dust. General Shepherd, later commandant of the marines, and then marine chief of staff, assigned me to the training staff of the raider battalion then in training. I was told to report to a marine major at Camp Pendleton, who offered me a cot in his tent. Here there was even more of that red dust. Like General Howling Mad Smith, the major, too, had a gleam in his eye when he told me that we'd be up bright and early at 5:30 A.M., if I didn't mind.

We certainly were. We had calisthenics for half an hour ending up with the duck crawl for a hundred yards, with our rifles held high above our heads. It nearly killed me. I had been riding around in tanks and jeeps for a long time, uncomfortable enough, but riding all the same. So I was out of shape. I knew it would give the marines a lot of pleasure to see an army man cave in, and a lot of satisfaction at my trouble if I got through it. I was determined to give them the lesser satisfaction of seeing me keep going.

I must say I was very much interested in the training that the marines gave in their combat courses, especially the training with toggle ropes, descents from cliffs, and mountain climbing. Their makeup and camouflage was good, better than we had in the army.

From there I went to Fort Hood, at Temple, Texas, again stopping overnight with the Mendls in Hollywood. At Hood was the tank destroyer school. I familiarized myself with the thinking of the planning board, which was working on changes in tank design as a result of experience in combat. The last time I'd been in Washington I'd run into Cabot Lodge who had been in Africa and told me that the German tanks were outgunning us and that the silhouette of our General Grants was far too high. I noticed that the planning board was going on its same merry way. And our silhouettes would be just as high as ever.

At Hood they had a commando training camp, funnily enough very similar to ours, and also a combat course, in which we had to crawl through barbed wire directly under live machine-gun fire. The machine guns were set the same way as Fort Benning's. They were zeroed in on targets, and they had a wooden parapet built up beneath their muzzles so that they couldn't be depressed and the bullets couldn't go lower than a certain elevation and hit us. It was a strong incentive to learn a really flat crawl. We were quite safe, if we didn't lift our heads up. Again, it was all red clay, only this time it wasn't dusty and dry. Here the climate was such that it poured every single day, and we slithered around on our bellies covered from head to foot in an all enveloping and slimy ooze. Elizabeth Arden could not have done an iota better.

At Hood they also had a pistol course similar to ours. We would enter a dark labyrinth, and all of a sudden, forms would spring out at us from various angles and distances, including from behind. We would fire at them. To save time we learned to fire from the hip—just like they always have done in the westerns. The best technique of hip-firing is a burst of two shots—pop-pop, pop-pop. As a result, later on when we were behind the German lines, we could always tell when some of our boys were in action by the sound of these strange double bursts. At our training center, we eventually got so proficient we generally hit the targets right in the middle.

From Hood I went to further commando training in amphibious operations at Camp Edwards on Cape Cod. There we made a couple of amphibious landings on Martha's Vineyard, before I returned to Colonel Goodfellow in Washington. From there I was sent to the OSS camp close to the marine base at Quantico, Virginia. Colonel Livermore was our training officer and with him I worked on the further organization of the OGs. It was here that I made my five parachute jumps and earned my wings as a paratrooper.

Having assimilated quite a lot of information and know-how, I was then assigned to the new OSS headquarters near Washington, where I was to prepare a camp for training our OSS commando combat teams in guerrilla warfare. My chief instructor there was to be a very able British major called Fairbairn. Fairbairn was an expert in the art of silent killing, dirty fighting, and general stomp and gouge. He had been the former chief of police in Shanghai. He was old, but with super-judo he could throw anybody anywhere and kill him at the same time. The place assigned us for these gentle activities of ours was the Congressional Country Club and grounds outside Washington, not far from the Potomac.

It was while I was in Washington on this trip that I had to go to the British Embassy on official business; and there I saw a tall, slender, gray-haired girl who seemed familiar. It was Irene Boyle, my waltzing partner from the days of the peace conference in Paris in 1919, whom I'd met with John de Salis. She had been a secretary to the British delegation then and had remained in the foreign service ever since. She had been mostly assigned to the United States and was now private secretary to the British Ambassador, Lord Halifax. She was a great admirer of things American, which by that time many of the English were not. After they had gone through the blitz, they were complaining that they needed more aid than we supplied. Irene and I talked of Cuthbert Holmes, John de Salis, and the tea dances that used to be held for the delegations at the conference.

The Congressional Country Club was really an excellent site for a commando training school. Barracks were built around the clubhouse. Our combat course ranged over gentle fairways, bristling with machine guns and booby traps. Only a short distance from the immaculate greens lay a couple of hundred acres of extended woodland. I have never seen a jungle as thick as that in Africa, Russia or the Galapagos Islands. Underbrush, briars, swamps, muck, fallen logs, rocks, deep holes, impenetrable thickets, tangled weeds, steamy phosphorescent swamps—there was everything in the jungle wilderness there, twenty minutes from Washington. The thickets were so dense that the men could hardly cut their way through with machetes. That made it a wonderful place for training.

We established five different attack areas in that wilderness. Major Fairbairn trained us in all the most advanced Oriental methods. For instance, do you know how to keep unbound prisoners safely without putting a guard on them? You seat them straddling the bases of small trees, in such a fashion that they cannot get up unless lifted off by two people. They'll sit there until they die if need be. Major Fairbairn had learned all these things and many others besides from the Chinese underworld. All the men thought he was terrific. He was extremely interesting.

At that point our objective was to build up cadres of experienced young officers who would in turn train other detachments. We were also recruiting the services of Italian, Norwegian, Yugoslav and French detachments that were beginning to arrive. I asked to be sent to Fort Benning to the infantry school again to secure volunteer infantry and engineering officers for special hazardous duty behind enemy lines. To do this I secured the permission of General Donovan and General Weems, commandant of the infantry school at Benning. I was permitted to address the graduating class of young lieutenants and describe for them the kind of warfare that we were developing, and what they would be in for if they volunteered. I understand that my talk was very persuasive. I recruited twenty of them. Then in addition I picked out two key men: Captain Joe Alderdyce and Captain Cox. They'd been through everything, and I naturally asked them specifically to volunteer.

We did not form units immediately. Some of the young officers had not been through paratroop school, and all had first to complete our training course. Others, who were ready, began recruiting men. In the meantime, Barmine had completed his translation of the *Russian Guerrilla Manual*. So Alderdyce, Cox and I utilized this and adapted it to our specifications. Out of our work emerged the *United States Army Guerrilla*, which we wrote. In this task Alderdyce was invaluable, as he also knew the infantry's special course.

It was at this point that the Norwegian troops arrived at Area F, the Congressional Country Club, for indoctrination. Fairbairn, Alderdyce, Cox and I took them smartly in hand. We took the men out at seven in the morning, and we came in at eleven or twelve at night. Then a small marine raider unit was assigned to simulate the Germans. Our boys and the marines used blank cartridges, and the whole operation was very close to actual warfare. The marine sergeant was an extremely able man, and they were good. Many of them were veterans from the Pacific. At night our squads had to locate them, creep up on them without being seen, and jump them, while Cox, Alderdyce and I observed and made notes. The officers, who came from Benning, were also observers and judges. Afterwards, the marines moved on to another place.

The second unit we trained was an Italian group. In our outfit national groups were organized first, which proved to be a mistake because they were all too homogeneous. It was then like old home week. The Italians in this respect were a little difficult to handle *en masse*. The Yugoslavs appeared, and next we had a group of fifteen French reserve officers, so we boiled them all together, and the unit became something very close to American.

It was pretty rough training. Two more groups of Norwegians came in, recruited from ski battalions in California. Many were from Norwegian ships that had been interned, and by this time our training was pretty well shaken down. All kinds of nationalities now fought side by side, and the men were enjoying this and getting good. In fact, they thought they were pretty hot stuff.

I assigned one or two of the French officers to each group. They were generally older men—one had been on the *Normandie*. They were easygoing fellows, so I told them that if things got too strenuous and their hearts began to pound, they should fall out. But I have never seen more fiercely determined men—at least never since I saw Peter Dolgorouky preparing to jump the Greek corporal in the Crimea. They would not give in, those French officers, no matter how tired they became. They took their preliminary parachute training there, ground training, everything that could possibly be given to them, so that nothing remained for them to do but jump from a plane.

The esprit de corps of the boys in the ranks by this time had become far too high. They thought they were the salt of the earth, and they were tough. Every time we let them out they got into fights with the military police. As I say, we were observing them every step of the way in their training. Whenever they moved through the underbrush over a training course, they were not to be seen or heard. They received demerits every time they were spotted. One day I was watching a merged group of Norwegians and Italians in action. I had walked to cleared ground at the edge of the wooded area, which was near the target area of a group engaged in moving through the woods. There was a little side road there that connected with the main highway. I heard some conversation going on, and I went over to investigate. On the side road there stood some tanks with military police lounging around. They were being trained for tank operations. They had nothing to do with us. But I realized that if my boys, who had no love by 'his time for the MPs, saw those military police fellows they might put their training to good use. There was certain to be some trouble, so I rayed hidden in the bushes. I must say I didn't even see our unit approach, and I was watching for them. The boys were getting really good, or maybe it was the incentive provided by those MPs. They just materialized out of the woods and gave them the business. I was able to stop the slaughter before too much harm was done. This was the group that I now took off to Camp Edwards.

The big LSTs had then been built, and we used assault boats. We had one real piece of excitement. Our boys were to go over to Martha's Vineyard at night, to raid the Gay Head radar station, supposedly behind enemy lines. They were to put marks on ammunition dumps and shops and so on without being detected, and withdraw—the equivalent of blowing them up. Then they were to embark in the boats and return to camp. Naturally, they were all in blackface and camouflage. It all went well, and they were landed without an alert. But then they found a fence they didn't know about, and were having trouble getting through it, as it was patrolled. A truck happened to come along, and they jumped the driver, tied him up, and the whole bunch of them rode merrily into the area they were supposed to be destroying. They had a wonderful time. The next day every conceivable building had marks all over it. Then they got in the truck, rode back, slipped into the boats and came home. They were all very innocent the next day.

But the truck driver was sore as hell. When he finally got untied late that night, he went racing over to the police and said a huge army of goons had taken over Martha's Vineyard. He said that black men all covered with grease had climbed out of the ocean and attacked him. The authorities there had one immediate reaction: they pulled all panic switches, sirens blew, searchlights were turned on, and telephone calls went into Washington, to the army, air force, navy and marines. We got into a lot of trouble about that.

When I was promoted to lieutenant colonel, we had quite a celebration in Washington at the Mayflower. We generally allowed the men out every two weeks, and at that with our fingers crossed. But this time I relented. They all wanted to give me a party, which I accepted. Several of them had their wives living in Washington. Many others put up at the Mayflower. When the party was going strong, one of them said to me, "Colonel, what's the matter? We never see you with a girl."

"Well," I said, "I've given that up for the duration."

He thought awhile, and said, "Maybe it's all right at your age, but we can't do it."

CHAPTER XXVII

Our OG commando school was a very hush-hush affair, but the word soon got around. Presently I noticed that whenever I went to Washington, a man followed me in the streets. He certainly was not an inconspicuous shadow, because he was an infantryman, about six and a half feet tall. He never spoke to me, but he was always hovering around. Finally I went up to him and asked him what his trouble was.

He saluted eagerly and blurted out, "Colonel, how can I get into the paratroops?"

It turned out that he had been turned down once before because he was too big. He was a Harvard man, he said, and somebody had told him that I was training paratroopers. He had hung around all this time waiting for a chance to talk to me, but he had hesitated several times. He was afraid that I would turn him down. Well, we got him into the OSS, and he did very well.

It was about this time that I attended a reception given by Sumner Welles for the diplomatic corps. Ben Welles, his son, was also in the OSS. At one point I was standing talking to Grace Vanderbilt, who had come down to Washington for the occasion. It was at exactly this fortuitous moment that Sumner came up with Maxim Litvinoff and his wife, Ivy. He introduced the Litvinoffs to Grace, and he was about to introduce them to me when Grace buttonholed Litvinoff and said loudly, "Oh! So you're the Russian Ambassador, Mr. Litvinoff."

"Yes, Madame," said Litvinoff.

"How very interesting! You know, your dear Emperor was so kind to Neily and me when we paid them a visit on our yacht."

"But, Madame!" said Litvinoff.

"Yes, and they took us to Czarskoe Selo with them. Such a lovely place. And that dear, dear Empress! She was so wonderful to us.

"But Madame!" said Litvinoff again. He was perspiring.

"And those *beautiful* children," Grace went on. "Oh, Mr. Litvinoff, I'm so delighted to see you."

"Ah! Madame!" said Litvinoff hopelessly, and in desperation he turned to me, a safe, quiet American officer. Then he saw the Russian ribbons on my chest. He turned on his heel and fled, while Grace was puckishly delighted.

About the end of August, 1943, high-priority orders came to me to get ready to go to Algiers. I was told to take Captain Bradish J. Smith and radio operator Second Lieutenant James W. Russell with me. That was a bombshell to the camp and everyone was very envious. I got a short leave to arrange my affairs. I went to New York, saw Ivan, who was waiting for orders as a cadet in the navy air corps, and I was stopped by a speed cop in New Jersey on my return.

"What's the big hurry?" he growled. "Where are you going?"

"To North Africa," I said. "I'm on my way there now."

"Well, go ahead and good luck," he said, and he didn't give me a ticket.

It took three days to be processed. I felt like a pincushion after some terrible injections, and there were innumerable papers to be checked and rechecked. We left with a number two priority, pretty good, since number one was the highest, and even went in a comfortable plane, a luxury plane. With us were two technicians from OSS, specialists in geography, who knew every detail of the country, most important if we jumped behind enemy lines.

We landed in the north of England, where I telephoned Chips Channon to say hello. We next took off in a transport with bucket seats, flying on a big dogleg to avoid interception, and coming into Marrakech from the west about dawn. There we were taken to a Moorish-style hotel where American officers were quartered. We washed up, had breakfast, and were loaded into a conventional air liner for Algiers. On board, unknown to me, was Bogomoloff, the minister of the Soviet Union to the temporary French government in Algiers. I always wore my ribbons from the First World War. This was standard procedure, as the United States and Russia were allies, and I was ordered to wear them. The Soviet minister noticed these decorations, and while I knew nothing of his sharp eyes then, something very interesting developed later on as a result.

We arrived at Algiers in the evening and went directly to a villa that served as OSS headquarters. Who did I run into but Warrick, one of my old friends from the 17th Regiment of the New York State Guard. The executive officer of the OSS detachment was Major Pfleiger, and he took me immediately to see Colonel Eddy, a marine colonel, who was the commanding officer at the time. He said that General Donovan wanted to see me in the morning at nine o'clock. When I walked into the General's office the next day, Colonel Eddy, Major Pfleiger and the adjutant were with him. They all looked very solemn. They explained that at that moment General Mark Clark was going into Salerno and that Sardinia and Corsica, on the flank of the Salerno operation, held about 270,000 Italian and 19,000 German troops. These had to be neutralized. To avoid a costly invasion, it had been decided to send a mission, with letters from General Badoglio and General Castellano, deputies of the King of Italy, and another letter from General Eisenhower to General Basso who commanded the Italian troops in Sardinia. The letters proposed that the Italians should come over to our side and help push the Germans out toward Corsica.

The officers with General Donovan looked at me expectantly.

So I asked the General, "Do you want me to volunteer?"

He said, "Well—certainly."

"I'd be delighted," I said, and I must say they looked relieved. I asked when the mission was to leave.

"Tomorrow," the General said. My eyebrows went up at that. I asked if I could choose some of my officers to go with me and pointed out that it was pretty short notice.

General Donovan said, "Yes. You should take two radio operators and an interpreter. You've got one radio man who came over with you, and we'll give you another radio operator from here." And then an excellent British radio operator, Sergeant William Sherwood, was assigned to me.

I had heard that an Italian contingent, one of the first operational groups I had trained at our Congressional Country Club combat training course, had just arrived in Algiers. I said, "Could I pick out an officer from them as an interpreter? I know them; I trained them; and I have one in particular that I'd like to have along."

"Has he jumped?"

"I don't think so. But I gave him all the preliminary training, and it's only a question of jumping."

"Just tell me who you take," the General said.

General Donovan said his staff would give me all the information when I decided where I wanted to jump, the disposition of the enemy troops, the order of battle, and the location of the Italian headquarters.

I went out and drove to the OSS camp, where I asked for First Lieutenant Mike Formicelli and Second Lieutenant Jim Russell. When they appeared, I asked them. "Have you ever jumped?" Neither had. I told them about the mission. "It's a very hurried thing," I said, "but I'd like very much to have you with me. If you go, your first jump will be a combat jump. But you've had a great deal of training, and you can get all necessary instruction today at the jump school."

Both were delighted with the idea, and I dispatched them to the school, which was about seven miles away, a joint American-British training school on the Mediterranean. Then I returned to headquarters, where Colonel Eddy took charge of me. Upstairs was the research department, where I was briefed before a big relief map of Sardinia. He next conducted me to Colonel Jenkins at General Eisenhower's headquarters, who was the plan officer. He in turn took me to General Rooks, the head of G-3, who went into minute detail on the whole operation.

Meanwhile, General Castellano had just arrived at General Eisenhower's headquarters as the personal representative of the King of Italy. Colonel Jenkins explained what help headquarters could give me, including a letter from him in General Eisenhower's name and one from General Castellano. He thought that I should meet the Italian general before leaving, which I did.

The next steps were to meet the pilot who was to fly the mission in, to select the area where I would jump, and to visit the headquarters of the escape department to see about getting out of Sardinia in case we failed. The escape department had a complete network of what they called "safe houses" behind the enemy lines. They had prepared a whole plan for our escape. We were to be taken off by submarine in that event, and the plan involved flashing light signals and the arrangement for meeting the submarine. Strangely enough, that was the thing that bothered me most. I have claustrophobia, and the idea of being cooped up in a submarine was unnerving.

We then began planning the technical details of the operation. The best place to jump was a big waste land near Cagliari, the largest city on the island. To the west between Cagliari and the highest peak on Sardinia lay a stretch of sand dunes, like a desert. I picked out a place there, about ten miles from Cagliari. The highest point of the island would provide a wonderful target for the pilot. Cagliari had been bombed several times. The troops had left, but the five local airfields were entirely in the hands of the Germans. I knew I had to avoid the airfields and the German patrols if I was ever to get through to the Italians. That was why I selected that particular spot.

In the meantime, Formicelli and Russell had received instructions at the parachute school. Oddly enough, the Canadian sergeant who instructed them had once served as a jump master for us. We had had a training exercise, in which I had led an OSS group into Canada in a simulated attack on a railway. The sergeant was a good man, but that particular exercise had been a failure. It was our own fault. We had made too much noise and were detected.

We had a Halifax at the ready to fly us to Sardinia. But on the next day it developed engine trouble and the flight had to be postponed. The day following was the 13th of September. None of us liked that at all. We were superstitious. During that extra day I got some additional information and was given Italian money and other essentials. One of the officers at the paratroop school had wanted to come with us. He had trained in our combat course near Washington under me. When I said we could not take him, he said, "Well then, can I be your jump master?" I asked and got permission for him to be assigned to our plane as jump master. The way the bombers were fixed up for jumping was simple: their belly turrets had been removed and replaced by sliding covers. Before jumping, we would slide the covers back, the first man would sit down at the edge of the hole, with the next man standing directly behind him, and so on. Then one by one we would drop out into space.

Our team was again ready, but the next day the weather was bad over the target. Meanwhile, where we were, a hard slanting rain began, and hour by hour the weather grew worse. Finally we took off in the teeth of a storm after being told there was now good weather over the target. As it turned out, had we jumped any earlier, we would have dropped straight into a German troop concentration—but those are the lucky things in life.

As we were going to the plane, Colonel Eddy came rushing up to me with a white towel. We had forgotten to take along a flag of truce. After I thanked

Colonel Eddy, and we were off, I remember Mike saying to me, "Colonel, I hope you won't have to carry that damn thing!"

"Mike," I said, "that is exactly what you're going to do!" And I bequeathed it to him.

After an hour or so, we flew into quiet air, and by the time we reached Sardinia the night was calm; there was a beautiful moon and the stars were out. A few minutes after eleven o'clock the red light flashed on in the plane. The jump master hooked us up and slid the cover off the hole.

Down below, as I sat on the brink dangling my legs into space, I saw the lights of a great convoy of vehicles moving along a road. I thought, "My God! Those people don't seem to be worried about bombing or strafing or anything like that." It seemed like a bad omen. Then we flew into a quieter area, and there was absolute darkness on the ground beneath. The green light flashed on.

The jump master counted, "One, two, three, go!"

I went out by slipping off the edge and coming to attention, looking up. I counted, "One thousand, two thousand ..." I heard a terrific rustle. Apparently my chute was twisted a bit, and then it opened with a bang, and I descended in a great and eerie quietness. The air was a flat and wonderful calm, and I was bathed in intense moonlight. Alongside me, I saw the line of the chutes of my men opening. How pretty the chutes looked. They were gleaming like pearls. I thought ominously, "They're gleaming too goddam bright!" Then I felt my heart catch, as I saw the plane disappear into the night. The blue lights of its engine exhausts flickered away. And then all around us there was nothing except silence and the shadows on the Sardinian landscape beneath.

We were in an enormous valley. On one side was the dark shadow of the mountain. On the other side was a cone and on the top of the cone was an old castle. It was the most fantastic sight I've ever seen, a veritable fairyland. I looked around to orientate myself and see where, after landing, I would have to find my men. I began looking down, trying to see where I was going to land. For some ridiculous reason I thought of cactus. Paratroopers always hate the thought of cactus. Then to my horror I saw something on the ground. It was moving toward me very fast. I grabbed my submachine gun, and I really sweated that one out—until I realized what it was: the shadow of my chute.

I could see sand dunes between some bushes, and I guided the chute toward them. I made a perfect tumble on a little dune, landed, unhooked my chute, rolled it up and hid it in the bushes. All around things were awfully quiet. I found the men. They had all landed without any kind of trouble whatever, including the two who had jumped for the first time.

Four packages had been dropped with us, including the radio and other equipment. We looked for them and found them very close by. He had been a fine jump master to us, that man. Our plan was for Formicelli and myself to try to contact the Italians on the road to Cagliari and by hook or by crook get them to take us to General Baso. If we did not return within twenty-four hours, the others were to try to accomplish the mission. They had also been given copies of the letters that I carried.

We started walking, Mike Formicelli and I. We traveled by compass. We went quite a distance. When dawn was breaking, we saw a farmer going out to his fields. He took one look at us and ran. We didn't like that, and so we avoided a couple of other farms nearby, where the inhabitants were evidently still asleep.

We came to a road and met another farmer and a boy, riding in a big donkey cart. He was very friendly. We gave him a package of cigarettes, for which he was grateful, and some money. I asked him where the Germans were.

"Oh," he said, with a sweeping gesture, "they're in all the airfields." He told us that there was a village directly ahead. Above all, he said, we must avoid the village. A German patrol was stationed there. But there was a rumor that they were going to leave.

The sun was about to rise when we said good-by to him. We skirted the village and hurried through fields in which the people were beginning to work. They would look up at us, stare at our American uniforms and hastily go back to their labors, pretending they had not seen us. That only meant to me that they were afraid of being civil to us. The whole place smelt of the enemy. I told Mike that I didn't like it. Then we met another man who was friendly. We asked him two questions: the way to General Basso's headquarters and whether or not there were any Germans around. He said yes, there was a patrol. But he told us of another town, further on, called Decimomannu where the Germans had pulled out the day before. We decided to go there. On the way we came upon another donkey cart. In it were two Alpini. Our approach to the problem of lack of manpower was always to appear as if we had a whole regiment behind us. We went directly up to them, gave them some cigarettes. I said we had a letter to General Basso from the King of Italy. It was absolutely essential that we deliver it in person. They were immediately anxious to help. They, too, said that the Germans had left Decimomannu the day before. Only Italian troops were there.

Mike and I reached the outskirts of Decimomannu about eight o'clock in the morning. We came to the railroad station, where a train was standing at the platform between ourselves and the station. The town proper was beyond it. The railway coaches were the old-fashioned kind with a door to each compartment. We opened a compartment door, walked through to the corridor and, pointing our sub-machine guns, suddenly stepped out the other side of the train onto the station platform. I felt I was on a stage, and the curtain had just risen.

One minute people were milling about everywhere. Next minute everyone had frozen at the sight of the guns and our American uniforms. A carabinier had been talking to someone right in front of me as I stepped out. I have never seen such astonishment on any man's face. Before he could recover, and again playing the part of having a regiment on the other side of the train, I went straight up to him. "Where is your commanding officer?" I said loudly for all to hear.

He saluted hastily. "Right here, sir. Right in the station."

"Then call him!" I said. "I want to see him!"

Never have I seen a man move so fast. He left on the double and almost immediately a carbinieri officer scurried out to us. Everybody was watching the performance, rooted to the spot. As loudly as I could without appearing forced, I said, "I have a very important message from the King of Italy and General Badoglio to General Basso. Where is your commanding officer?"

"In the barracks."

"Take me to him. I must see him immediately."

"Please come inside," he said quickly, glancing apprehensively at the civilians. We followed him, and he began a wonderful nervous Italian conversation, during which he asked me questions which I answered or did not answer: I would only give him my name, and my rank of colonel, which I think led him to believe we had at least a battalion. Then, even more disturbed, he made another call. As he waited impatiently for the connection, he asked, "How many are you?"

"Two," I said confidently. I heard afterwards he had understood two battalions.

Outside, I could hear an uproar going on. The crowd had grown as the word spread that the Americans had come. They were cheering.

This was most reassuring. The civilians at least were delighted to see us, and this would not fail to be noticed by the authorities.

A very disheveled colonel then appeared. Poor fellow, I'm afraid we had really disturbed his schedule. He smelt faintly of perfume. I gave him the letter from General Eisenhower, which said in effect that we carried an important message to General Basso that had to be delivered by hand to the General as quickly as possible.

I really felt sorry for those carabinieri officers. They were in a ticklish situation, right in the middle of the Germans and ourselves, not knowing where their allegiance lay. The Germans hadn't even pulled out completely. The colonel said he would of course have to report to headquarters. In the meantime, he diplomatically covered his bets by asking us to breakfast.

The carabinieri were first-rate soldiers, well-disciplined and responsible. We were taken to their officers' mess in their barracks and they were most cordial. They said quite frankly that they would like to be fighting with us. We had an excellent breakfast. When it was over, word came that we were to be taken to the nearby airfield, which, they assured us, had just been vacated by the Germans. We were driven there by car, with an escort, and there we met a number of officers, of higher rank. All of them were friendly, with one exception, an intelligence colonel who grew truculent. I felt that we had better be on our guard, as he was a real Fascisti. Happily for us, he was almost immediately superseded by Air Force Colonel de Martire, who had seniority. The intelligence colonel took us to de Martite's office and began explaining his doubts about us. Colonel de Martire cut him short. "I have orders to take you under my protection," he said directly to me, "and conduct you to General Basso's headquarters." Then he looked meaningfully at the other intelligence officer. "There are German patrols everywhere around here. I don't want *anything* to happen. It's too important. So shall we go?" he said. "I'm putting a heavy guard around you."

He got us quickly away from the hostile intelligence officer, who, he told us, was working closely with the Germans. "But now," de Martire said, "everything has changed." He added that he knew that the Italians were coming in with the Allies very soon. In the meantime, he said, every hour that we waited before going to General Basso would be safer. The Germans were moving north. Meanwhile, he wanted me to visit Cagliari as I ought to talk to the commandant there. He had also arranged for a tour of the airfields, as things were happening so fast. Then he would escort me to Bordigali and General Basso.

De Martire was a fascinating man, highly educated and well-informed. We talked freely to one another. With the new agreement, he said, big Allied shipments would have to come into Cagliari. "It's too bad," he said, "but you have bombed the port to pieces." Also, he added, Cagliari was mined. But the commandant was an admiral and a good friend of his. I would show him my letters, and the admiral would order boats to go out to meet the ships bringing in American supplies to guide them through the mine fields.

At Cagliari, the A.D.C. to the Commander Count Greppi, greeted me most cordially.

I said, "You know, I knew a Count Greppi in St. Petersburg in the old days."

"What?" asked the Commander.

"Yes. He was the Italian Ambassador and . . ."

"My uncle!" said the Count, beaming. "No!—you knew him—" "He was quite old when he was in St. Petersburg," I said. "And I met him again in Rome after the war. He seemed very old indeed."

"He was! He was!" said Commander Greppi, obviously delighted by this unexpected turn of events.

"But I saw him at the races even so."

"Why, he just died the other day," he replied. "He was more than a hundred years old. And he died at the races!"

The Italians were now extremely friendly, and the mission was turning into a social occasion. We could feel the atmosphere growing lighter by the hour. Count Greppi took me to the admiral in command of the local naval units, who was already fully aware of the situation. Then and there arrangements were concluded for guiding our supply ships into the harbor.

I sent Mike back with an Italian escort to pick up Sherwood and Russell and their radio equipment in the hills. The mission was proceeding smoothly, almost too smoothly. Theoretically, since I was moving around under General Basso's auspices anyway, I could have radioed that it was accomplished by three that afternoon. But Bordigali and the General's headquarters were well in the center of Sardinia, eighty miles away. A lot could happen in eighty miles. They put me in a car, carabinieri with submachine guns on both sides of me, literally blocking me from sight. They didn't want my American uniform to be seen by anybody that might notify the Germans. And, as if that were not enough, ahead of me was a truck, packed with soldiers with machine guns, while another one of similar strength followed close behind.

We drove very fast along the roads. When we got to General Basso's headquarters, I learned that the German liaison officer had departed only half an hour before, driving north at a great rate toward Corsica.

It was now mid-afternoon, less than twelve hours after we had jumped. At Bordigali Colonel Bruno, the Italian chief of staff, received me at headquarters. He was a tall, good-looking man. "Rest assured that we will comply with the command of our King," he said.

On behalf of General Eisenhower I expressed thanks.

"Everything will be attended to," he said, and he explained that General Basso would not arrive until that evening, and that I was to dine with him. "In the meantime," he said, grinning, "I shall ask you to remain very quiet and, please, out of sight. You've shown yourself enough. The place is in sufficient uproar and the Germans are leaving. I've arranged a quiet headquarters for you at the next village, but even there it will be better if you do not show yourself."

When I went out to my convoy to go into hiding, I began to understand General Bruno's concern. All around headquarters were a great many tough-looking Italian paratroopers of the Nembo Division, wearing blue berets. A large number of them had been in the crack Fulgere Division, which had served with distinction in Africa. They had fought in the battle of El Alamein and all the rest of it. My briefing earlier at Algiers had told me they would probably be very unfriendly; their temper was bad, and the almost general good will of the Italian troops toward us was nonexistent in their bailiwick. I was hurried off to the next town and quartered with an Italian family, a mother, father and daughter, all of whom spoke perfect English. The carabinieri from my escort trucks immediately surrounded the house, their machine guns at the ready.

When I was safely in my temporary headquarters, a commotion started. The commanding officer of my carabinieri escort came rushing in. A battalion of the Nembo at General Basso's headquarters had mutinied, and was going north to join the Germans. General Basso had sent one of their senior officers, Colonel Becci, who had tried to talk them out of it. Before he had finished, a captain of the paratroopers had shot him in cold blood. The rest of the Nembo was now in a state of utter turmoil. They were highly unreliable and a danger to the entire area. I was to be on my guard. They were under orders to move to an area twenty miles away. Whether they would obey was anybody's guess. I must say I could not blame them. Head and shoulders above most Italian units, they had been fighting alongside the Germans every step of the way. Now they were suddenly expected to turn against them. Little wonder that the morale of the entire Italian army was affected as the news spread like wildfire. The situation was touch and go.

Thanks to the efforts of General Basso and Colonel Bruno, a compromise method of operation was worked out: the Italians did not actually fire on the Germans, but after German troops relinquished a village, the Italians moved in.

Meanwhile, the balance of the Nembo did obey orders, and sullenly moved away, while the Germans hurried toward Corsica. A makeshift ferry arrangement of small boats had been assembled to take them over the straits between the two islands. Then they hoped to get to the mainland to join the German army in the north of Italy.

That evening a car and a heavy escort arrived to fetch me to General Basso's headquarters. The General showed the strain of these days, but received me cordially. I delivered my letters to him. He too said, "We will abide by the orders of the King."

I could then radio back that the mission was accomplished. Except for the Germans retreating in the far north, Sardinia was ours. But Mike Formicelli had run into trouble. When he got back to the hills Sherwood and Russell thought that Mike and his carabinieri group were an enemy patrol. He had an unpleasant time getting close enough to let them know who he was and still remain in one piece. However, no harm was done and they all reached Bordigali the next night. It was a fine reunion.

The next day we were given new headquarters nearer General Basso's. All of us were moved in with another family. The carabinieri this time literally surrounded the place shoulder to shoulder. We rigged up a makeshift antenna in the back yard. Then it developed that our batteries were not functioning properly. Basso's radio men got some automobiles that the Germans had abandoned and adapted their batteries to our transmitter. They were most helpful. Thirty-six hours after we left Algiers, I was able to report that our mission was accomplished.

CHAPTER XXVIII

My first task thereafter was to establish good relations with the Italian staff. I met for breakfast, lunch and dinner with General Basso and his officers, and this part of the work was not difficult. My second job was to make a survey of Sardinia's economic needs, to see what supplies should be sent in to provide immediate help and start the economy refunctioning. An office was given us directly across the street from the Italian headquarters.

First of all, however, high-octane fuel had to be flown in for our planes. Formicelli went back to the Decimomannu airfield to arrange for our planes to come in; then I went there myself. We sent back detailed instructions for landing approach, the condition of the field, and so on, and a system of intricate recognition signals to use. Our planes were to waggle their wings in a certain way, and circle the field once.

It was amazing. Almost immediately two fighters appeared. They signaled, and circled the field. And then an immense convoy of C47S came in, all loaded with gas. One after another they landed, all day long. I've never seen anything like it. When we move, we really move.

Maintenance crews were landed, and within half an hour after the first plane came in there was a full-fledged American airfield functioning there.

Once only were we attacked. A single Fokker-Wolf came in, dropped bombs, and hit a few Italian planes on the ground. There were none of ours there at the time. The Germans flew low, and the Italian gunners downed the plane. The pilot had been stationed there before the Germans pulled out. They all knew him, and gave him a funeral. I think he believed that they would not fire at him.

My own relations with the Italians developed into friendships. They were interested, for instance, in the fact that my mother had become an Italian citizen; and then, too, we had many points of contact from my trips there to see her before the war.

Among the Italian troops on Sardinia there was one other hostile division. They were Fascisti, and they were far from considering the war over. They were all still fanatically supporting Mussolini. If there was to be any real trouble, it would plainly come from them and from the Nembo paratroop division. I made a point of trying to get to know their officers. They were commanded by a Milanese, who was tough and sore. We had bombed Milan and destroyed two houses he had owned, which made him very resentful. He kept harping on it. I began to pull his leg. I told him that the Italians who had taken part in the bombing of London did the most damage there, and destroyed a whole block of houses belonging to a friend of mine. We were even. He became less irritable, and even friendly.

One thing the Italians were famished for was coffee. They had not had any for months. The coffee and cigarettes we distributed were so appreciated that I radioed for large supplies of them to be sent in, which was done immediately. In those days I myself did not smoke cigarettes. I had an old corncob pipe. The Italians had never seen one before, and certainly not the way I managed it. I would pack the bowl with tobacco rolled up in a ball of toilet paper. Then I made a hole in the top of the paper with a match and lit it. The pipe wouldn't go out even in the highest wind. This operation never failed to interest my hosts and former enemies.

Word came through that General Theodore Roosevelt was arriving at Cagliari. I radioed that his PT boat would be met outside the mine field, and be guided through by a tugboat. Ted Roosevelt was a close friend of Vincent. Both had gone to Harvard, and were lifelong companions. I had met Ted often before the war, and I knew him well. I was waiting at the pier in Cagliari when the PT boat came in with Ted, his aide-de-camp, and two OSS officers from our operational group. Their arrival was a pleasant boost to my morale.

When Ted stepped onto the pier, "Sergie," he said, "you are going to be my executive officer!" He was delighted with everything that had been done. My economic report was finished—an analysis of what I felt the Sardinian economy needed, what the people lacked. He read it and approved it, and we went on to General Basso's headquarters. Thereafter we took our meals daily with the Italian staff. Ted got on exceedingly well with them. Like myself, he talked a little Italian—very broken Italian—which amused and pleased them. Our public relations were excellent.

At night he made me tell him in detail everything that had happened from the time we jumped. When I came to the part about the Nembo, Ted looked thoughtful. "I'll tell you what we'll do, Sergie," he said. "Let's review that Nembo Division."

"When?"

"Tell them tomorrow morning. At eight-thirty."

I went to Colonel Bruno. "With the compliments of the general, sir." I said. "He wants to review the Nembo."

"*What!*" said Bruno. He nearly fell out of his chair.

"I said, sir, that General Roosevelt wants to review the Nembo."

"My God!" said Bruno, "they'll kill him!—When?"

"Tomorrow morning."

"Oh, my God!" said Colonel Bruno. "You *must* change his mind."

"You don't know the General," I said. "He's a very determined man. Those troops must be in formation by eight-thirty."

"A Roosevelt killed!" cried Bruno. "A Roosevelt murdered!—reviewing *our* troops!—and you, too!" He was absolutely horrified.

"Yes," I said, "but that won't happen." It was a discomforting thought.

He gave the orders, and very early next morning Ted and I drove to their encampment. There, beautifully drawn up on a field, stood the grimmest array of scowling soldiers I'd ever seen. "Take your gun off, Serge," Ted said, easily. "We'll use our swagger sticks." We were still in the car, and Ted was smoking a cigarette. He threw it away, and we got out and walked slowly up to the formation of troops. We approached it from the extreme left. On the right flank was a sergeant major, one of the biggest men I've ever seen, a huge, bearded veteran, bristling with ribbons. Ted wasn't very tall. He went right to the man, and looking up at him, said loudly in Italian, "What a magnificent soldier! Where have you served?"

"In Africa, sir."

Ted tapped the decorations with his swagger stick. "And what are those ribbons?"

"I'm afraid, sir, those were won fighting against you."

"What battles?"

He named them—an astounding list.

Ted chuckled. "Splendid!" he said. "If we'd had troops like you on our side, we'd have really done a job. You gave us one hell of a time! I congratulate you on your accomplishments."

The sergeant grinned and some of the men chuckled.

"What *else* do you do?" Ted asked.

"I'm a boxer."

"A boxer!" Ted stepped back, cupped his hands and called, "How many men here are boxers? Put up your hands! All boxers, break ranks and step forward!" He talked about boxing with each, joking with them in his bad Italian and making them laugh. Then he went and looked over the troops, chatting informally with a very large number about the battles they had been in, congratulating them, and asking them about their home towns, gathering good will by the minute. It was an astonishing thing, what that man did, and they gave him a cheer when we left.

On the way back I asked him how in hell he did it. He said, "Sergie, it's really very simple. When I was a boy, Father (President Theodore Roosevelt) always took my brothers and me on his campaign trips. I learned a few helpful things on those trips. Father always had to have a rope put up ten feet away around his observation-car platform, to keep the crowd back. They always pressed up against it, and when Father came to the proper moment in his speech, he would shout, 'Take away that rope!' The people always cheered, and when the rope was removed they all rushed up to shake his hand. Serge," Ted said, "I tell you. You can't do without that rope!"

The officers of the Nembo had meanwhile asked us to breakfast. We of course did so, and one after another of them volunteered for service with the American army.

There was a very interesting sequel to the story. Ten years a Captain Minietto of the Italian army, now the purser of an Italian Line ship, came to see me at the Sherry-Netherland. He had one of the Nembo paratroopers. He told me that he and five others been designated to kill us when we came to review the division. The plans were all set. When Ted and I arrived, they were so impressed by his manner and the fact that we were alone and unai that they were delighted to become our allies.

Still later, I was invited to a party at the Byron Foys'. There was an exceedingly attractive woman I didn't recognize, across the room, and I asked to be introduced. The name didn't mean anything to me. I sat beside her, and she said, "You are a man I have always wanted to meet, and you don't know who I am."

"I'm afraid not," I said.

"I was the wife of Colonel Becci."

"Oh, no!" I said. "He was a brave man."

"Yes," she said, "he was loyal to his king. But such things cannot be helped. I have since heard a great deal about you from my husband's friends who were there, and they ask to be remembered." She had since married Enrico Piaggio, a leading industrialist of Italy.

I then began making trips all over Sardinia with General Roosevelt. We started by going to the little island of Maddalena, the headquarters of the Italian navy in the north. The admiral there was married to an English girl. It was the place where Mussolini had been held until the Germans came in by parachute and took him to Como, just before I landed. It was also the site of the tomb of Garibaldi, upon which Ted Roosevelt laid a wreath, after first putting it on Mme. Garibaldi's by mistake.

The admiral was friendly. We dined with him, and he gave us a fast Italian version of the PT boat to take us around the coast. The Germans were now moving out of Corsica, skirting a road on the east coast, and the French were coming up on the west coast. We joined the French who had a cruiser there. One of our OSS operational groups, the Italian contingent, was in the area, working with native French troops from Morocco.

General Roosevelt and I met the French commander, General Martin, had dinner with him, and put up at a hotel. The Germans had only recently left, and they knew everything about the town. They also knew the French. They knew where the French would logically be on the first night they took a town. So they bombed the *maisons pour les sports*. That caused a terrible commotion. The Germans had literally caught the French with their pants down, and the French were outraged; they thought it violated all the unwritten rules of war.

The countryside thereabouts was lovely. Our OSS contingent was in the hills, and Russell, my chief radio operator, was now with them. So we went there. The *Goumiers* the native Moroccan troops, were everywhere. They dressed like monks, in big, flowing robes, hoods over their heads. Every axiom of warfare went by the board with them. They brought their sheep and their women with them when they went to war. Instead of keeping out of sight, they built big fires at night, cooked their meals and relaxed. About eleven o'clock at night they just disappeared into thin air. They scorned the use of weapons other than the great sharp knives they carried. They were magnificent night fighters.

One of them had asked Russell, "How many ears do you have?" "Only two," he said, laughingly.

"I have nine," the Moroccan said, and he reached under his robe and drew out a string of nine ears. Whenever they killed a German they cut off his ears, as proof of what they had done. Since our American helmets looked a lot like German helmets at night, we had to be very careful around the *Goumiers*.

Our main mission in Corsica was to arrange the evacuation of the Italian soldiers back to Sardinia. When this was done, we started back. The only transport we could get was an old Savoy-Marchetti plane that had once been strafed. The French pilots refused to fly it. Nobody would fly it except the Italian pilots. It was as close to a wreck as a plane could be and still get into the air. It was held together by baling wire. But we had to get back to Sardinia, so Ted told the Italian pilots to get ready. The French then made a fuss because they didn't like the idea of Italian pilots taking off in an Italian plane. But General Martin gave orders for the Italians to fly us, and General Roosevelt, Lieutenant James Lawrence and I started out.

We had a snappy escort of French Spitfires. The Savoy-Marchetti flew slower than their stalling speed. It was, in fact, so slow that they had to fly miles ahead and miles back, circling round and round. They finally left us when we got over Sardinia itself.

The mountains of Sardinia are quite high, and we then realized that our Savoy-Marchetti had an ominously low ceiling. We sailed along as if we were going to run smack into them. But then a pass opened up. It was wide enough, but with an unpleasantly high saddle-back in the middle. We flew right toward the saddle-back with the peaks extending high above us on either side.

Lawrence and I were in back, sitting by the antediluvian machine gun. Ted was forward with the pilot and copilot. The pass contained quite a bit of foliage for mountain country. I noticed that the grass was long, and there were many daisies growing there. I could see the daisies much too plainly.

"Oh my God!" said the copilot.

"Don't worry!" said the pilot.

"You'll never make it!" yelled the copilot, suddenly clutching his hands together in an attitude of prayer.

"I've got to try!" said the pilot, and we wallowed along so close to the ground that I could see the petals of the flowers. Then we came to the ridge, and the copilot covered his eyes with his hands and jumped in the air to try to lighten the plane, and we went over with the wheels just missing the grass. Then the ground dropped away and there was grass all around us, like a pasture.

There was an Italian airport beyond the pass. The Italian pilots said they were going to land there and recover from their experience. We landed gratefully, bumpily, and spent the day.

We were at dinner when we were raided, and the whole mess around us ran like hell for shelter as the Germans made a few passes, not many, and shot up the Italian planes on the ground, missing ours, unfortunately. Ted got up from the table and motioned to me. We walked out into the field. He looked at the German planes buzzing around, and said, "Sergie, what caliber guns do you think they're popping at us?" He was the coolest guy in that town.

We flew back to Decimomannu where a military government was presently established under a British brigadier. The Catholic Church had arranged a cardinals' mass, to celebrate the deliverance from the Germans. It was very impressive, with General Roosevelt, General Basso, the Brigadier and their staffs, and the great detachment of Italian frogmen—of the San Marco Battalion—the boys who had swum under water and put bombs under the British battleships in North Africa. When the mass was over, I saw Ted on the steps out in front of the church, with a great crowd of Italians down below him. He bounded right down the steps into the crowd, shaking hands, and they hugged him and, cheering, threw him into the air for five minutes.

When he got away he turned to me with a delighted smile on his face. "I'm an old hand at this business, Sergie! That rope, remember? Take away the rope!"

After that we flew back to Algiers in a B25. It was a routine staff life. I received a citation for my Sardinia operation:

> "Lieutenant Colonel Obolensky volunteered to lead a small parachute unit which undertook a hazardous mission on the Island of Sardinia while the German Army still controlled the island. With exceptional initiative and despite the presence of enemy patrols in the neighborhood, he made his way to the Italian Commander-in-Chief, and was the first element of the Allied forces to contact him. He inspired such confidence that he at once became the General's adviser and during the vital days that followed he acted as representative of the Allied Commander-in-Chief, and cabled valued intelligence to his base regarding the German evacuation and ports and airfields available for Allied use. As Executive Officer for Brigadier General Theodore Roosevelt, upon that officer's arrival on 18 September, Lieutenant Colonel Obolensky participated in an extensive survey which resulted in the compilation of a valuable report on existing conditions in Sardinia, thereby contributing materially to the success of the Allied Forces in the Mediterranean Theatre. . .

CHAPTER XXIX

When we landed in Algiers the reporters had heard about our Sardinia coup. They swarmed around General Roosevelt, who was always good copy, and well known to them. "You'd better talk to Colonel Obolensky," he said, and gave me a terrific build-up. That was how the story came out in the American newspapers—otherwise, our work in the OSS rarely received any publicity.

Ted was pleased about the whole thing. He slapped me on the back and said, "Sergie, when another dangerous mission comes along, let's do it."

I saw a good deal of him in the days that followed. One day he said to me, "Sergie, you and I like to live dangerously. I really think we're a good team. We ought to go into Yugoslavia. Let's try it. We'll work the same way. You go in first, and I'll follow. We'll get to Mikhailovitch."

His idea was that I could make the original contact because I had known King Alexander of Yugoslavia in the old days, through Paul, and had trained Yugoslavian guerrillas in our OSS training course. I could get in and arrange a landing field, and he would follow with planes. The situation in Yugoslavia was pretty bad, with Mikhailovitch under fire from Tito's partisans, and a civil war beginning between the two guerrilla forces. Ted's idea was that we should reach Mikhailovitch first, and from him get to Tito, and work out a means of cooperation between them.

The more he worked on it, the better the plan seemed. Finally he decided to go to Harold Macmillan, later the British prime minister, who was then attached to General Eisenhower's staff in North Africa. I had known Macmillan at Oxford, and Ted and I went in to see him together.

When Ted outlined the project, Macmillan looked startled.

"I'm afraid decisions have already been reached, at the very highest level," he said, "and this wouldn't fit in at all with them."

In retrospect, it is easy to see that Churchill and Roosevelt had already decided to support the left under Tito and cast Mikhailovitch to the wolves. The responsibility for the deed is primarily Churchill's, and he relied mainly on Brigadier MacLean, who was then in Yugoslavia. I believe it was one of the greater mistakes of the war. Mikhailovitch was accused of playing along with the Germans. The Germans were breathing down his neck; he had to give them support if only to survive. Besides, he wasn't a Communist. His leftist enemies used this to undermine Mikhailovitch with the Allies, but the truth was that his sympathies were always with us, and the decision to back Tito delivered into the hands of the Reds some two million Yugoslavians—good, stable, religious, conservative people, who could have formed a solid support for a pro-Allied government in Yugoslavia.

Ted Roosevelt was more than disappointed. He began asking questions, raising hell everywhere, about it. Of course, this got him nowhere. There was always an effort going on somewhere to put me into staff work, but I wanted to stay in operations with my men. So I kept my nose to the grindstone, and stayed out of sight as much as possible. My work was principally the dropping of our men into Italy. We called them bodies. I can't write about it, even now. One reason I didn't want staff work was that I wanted to jump into France, and there was a rule that we could not be dropped into a country if we had anything to do with our men already dropped there. In case we were captured, it would not do to have highly important names disclosed under torture. Consequently, I refused to know anything about France, an English officer was handling that, and I only knew about our Italian operations.

It was by now November. Word of our mission, and its success, had got around in military circles, and my name became known in Algiers. Through a third person I learned that Bogomoloff, the Russian minister to the French government in Algiers, had been on my plane when I flew in; that he had noticed my Russian ribbons from the First World War; and that recently, he had heard of my Sardinian mission. He wanted to meet me.

I asked Colonel Eddy what I should do. "By all means, go," he said. "Find out what they want."

My invitation was to dine at the Russian ministry, the sort of place that I had once avoided at all costs. It promised to be a big evening. I knew the Russians never made an invitation of this sort unless they had directives. And I also knew enough of Russian hospitality to know that I was likely to get plastered. I got into my best uniform, the one with the brightest ribbons from the First World War, drank a large jigger of olive oil to decrease the effect of the vodka, and made my way to the villa where the Russians had their ministry.

There I was introduced to Minister Bogomoloff, a large and professional Soviet diplomat, with huge spectacles; General Vassilieff of the Red Army, quite a well-known officer in Russia; and Admiral Frolov, a cultivated and distinguished individual and two or three others. At 'inner I was seated on Bogomoloff's right.

But the vodka was served in tumblers instead of little vodka glasses, and I knew I was in for it. The chances always are that the rest of them are only drinking water. The minister proposed the first toast: "To the American army!"

We downed our tumblers and the servants refilled them.

I then lifted my glass. "To the gallant defense of Stalingrad by the Russian army of which America and all the Allies are proud!"

That went down. And so it went. But I knew something was going to happen, and I began to get a bit intoxicated in spite of my olive oil. We chatted in a friendly enough fashion, the minister and I. He commented on my ribbons from the First World War. And I described briefly some of the engagements. Then he raised his glass and said, "To the old Imperial Guard!" I thought I couldn't be hearing right. "Yes," he said, "to the old Imperial Guard, who taught us how to do it!"

We drank, and I couldn't help making a remark. I said, "Where's the NKVD?"

There was an immediate lull, and I noticed all eyes steadily regarding the Minister. Bogomoloff cleared his throat and said, "It is perfectly all right. We recognize the military quality of the old Imperial Guard. One of your ancestors was Field Marshal Suvorov. We recognize his military genius. He is a national hero, the precursor of all our tactics. We think so highly of him that the military academy of Soviet Russia is named for him."

I must say I was very pleased by this speech, but I knew there was something behind it. I thought, let's see what's to come.

At this point Bogomoloff explained that erroneous ideas prevailed about conditions in Soviet Russia. Then he asked pleasantly, "Wouldn't you like to become a Russian again?"

Unfortunately, I said "No!" too quickly. I should have asked more questions, pretended to think about it, but I was now tipsy.

"Why not?" he asked, laughingly.

"Well," I said, "you didn't want us once. You may remember. I had to leave."

"Don't say we didn't want you. You didn't want us."

"I won't haggle about it," I said. "I know what happened to me—and the others."

"But you are completely wrong," he said. "You can have private property, people are allowed to own their own houses in Russia, their own bank accounts, everything of the sort."

"I am very happy in America," I told them. "Russians like America, you know. I have my family there. I am able to work and earn a good living, and the Americans have been very kind to me from the time I arrived. I consider myself an American, and besides, I know that to go back to Russia would be a very great mistake."

He said politely, "I am very sorry that you feel that way."

General Vassilieff had little to say. He was very grave, very subdued. I don't think he liked any part of it. But Admiral Frolov, on the other side of me, was most amiable. We talked and became quite friendly. He was not well, he said. Trouble with his kidneys made it unwise for him to drink like this any more. He liked to drink, and it was a shame. He was naturally high-spirited and enthusiastic. I learned that he was a graduate of the naval academy. He didn't seem much interested in politics. He was the sort of Russian with whom one could easily have been on good terms, had it not been for the cleavage of ideology. We both got pretty tight. He proposed a *Bruderschaft*, the old Russian custom of drinking as brothers, in which we linked arms, gave each other our names, downed our glasses, and kissed three times which made us blood brothers. So we did that.

By that time I was awfully tight. I managed to get away without disgracing myself, but my car wasn't there. The driver hadn't come for me. They got one of their cars, and they drove me back to the villa. Fortunately, there was no one around to see me stagger in.

Aside from a bad hangover, which I weathered, there were no ill effects. As a polite gesture, I had asked the Minister to dine with me. I called him, and he said he would be delighted. So I invited several of our colonels. Colonel Jenkins was there, our plans officer. The war room was under his command. Then there was Colonel Mann, who was the liaison officer with the OSS on the staff of General Eisenhower; and Colonel Pfleiger, the assistant to Colonel Eddy. We had a pleasant dinner. I had to translate, for, while the Minister spoke perfect English, he insisted on talking Russian. Colonel Jenkins had been in Siberia in 1919 as a young lieutenant protecting American equipment that had been shipped to Russia as war supplies. They were talking about Kolchak's retreat, and Colonel Jenkins asked, "Did we Americans cause you much trouble in Siberia in 1919?"

The Minister peered at Colonel Jenkins through his spectacles, and replied in English; he forgot to reply in Russian. "You?" he said, "No. They—" he pointed at me, "a great deal!"

I said, "Thank you, Excellency. That's the first official recognition I've had of my good work in those days."

A few days later I sent a message to Admiral Frolov asking him to dine with me. To my surprise, he accepted. He had become famous in Russia as the head of the naval commandos. He had inaugurated the course, and trained the first commandos. He told me he was a Bolshevik by faith; he was raised under that system, went through the academy under it, and believed in it. We began to talk politics. He again repeated the Minister's request for me to come back.

I said, "I have been accustomed to a wholly different way of life. I believe in democracy. That's why I fought the Bolsheviks. I fought for a democratic, parliamentary form of government."

He gave me an interesting revelation of the state of mind of an intelligent Bolshevik. "We don't feel that the Russian people are ready for democracy," he said. "You knew it better in those days than we do now. They need the lash. They're lazy and peace-loving. They need a driving power to make them do things."

"That's exactly what I don't believe," I said. I realized that he was expressing what he thought the old conservatives believed in, myself included, and he was a victim of his own propaganda. "We never believed in the lash," I said, "and without it we could have achieved a great deal more than you."

Frolov and I had a long argument on precisely this point—what Russia could have done with the steps toward democracy that had been taken under the old order. He felt I should know better. "The Russian," he said again and again, "must be coerced. He is too much of an individualist. Every Russian thinks he's a genius. The only way to make him work is to coerce him."

That was an interesting discussion. He never gave any quarter, and neither did I. But it was easy to talk with Frolov. We talked objectively and openly, one military man to another. But there was another type of Russian in Algiers. The representative of the control commission of the USSR was a general named Solodovnik and I suspected that he was the NKVD officer. He was the pure Karamazov type. If you said anything to him, he immediately turned it in such a way that you could never recognize your thought—an amazing example, requiring a high level of ability, of the type of Russian mentality that I had known to exist since college days. I have always considered that type of person to be the physical manifestation of sheer evil at work.

I saw Admiral Frolov again, at a party given by the English in Algiers. He was with his adjutant, a young naval lieutenant, perfectly disciplined, and with pleasant manners. Shortly after this he disappeared, and I never saw him again. He was said to have been called to Russia very suddenly, and it was speculated that he was in disfavor. I hope his meeting with me had nothing to do with it, for he was a good representative of the Soviet doctrine, about which I constantly annoyed him, taking the position that it was in utter disregard of what was good for the Russian people, or any people for that matter. I heartily disapproved of his ideology, but I liked him.

I believe the Bolsheviks' interest in me came solely from my work. I was operations officer for the OSS in Algiers, occupied with preparing drops behind the German lines.

In the middle of January I was sent to Caserta, Italy. There we of the OGs carried on the same work more intensively.

One day I was in the courtyard of the Caserta Palace, and a car arrived. General Alexander, the British commanding general of the Allied armies, got out. He was considered by far the best general the British had. I had met him when I'd been at Oxford, and he had been a young subaltern in the guards. He had since learned Russian, which he spoke fluently, having served with the British forces in Russia during the Revolution. He had become a colonel when still extremely young.

He saw me, stopped in astonishment, and said, "Serge, it's wonderful to see you. But, good heavens, what are you doing here?" I could see him looking curiously at my paratrooper's wings. "Surely you don't do that sort of thing?" He pointed at the wings.

"Well, I am with the OSS, sir," I said, chuckling.

"At your ripe old age?" He laughed and said that he wanted to hear all about it, and asked me to dine with him that night.

He was using a villa near Caserta for his H.Q. and his quarters were a special railway car on the tracks. I was to dine with him at his villa.

That evening his whole staff was there, including General Cannon, who was commander of our tactical air force. This airforce outfit was then under Alexander. Before dinner, General Alexander introduced me as Colonel Prince Obolensky. I said, "I'm sorry, sir, but we don't have titles either in America or in the American army." He chuckled, but let that pass. However, at dinner he still placed me on his right, with General Cannon on my right. That sort of thing happened occasionally in Europe, but it was often very embarrassing.

During dinner an adjutant came in with a dispatch. General Alexander read it through right there and said, "I guess we'll have to do it," and passed it to me to give to General Cannon. They had a short discussion. The longstanding trouble at Monte Cassino had come to the breaking point, and there was only one way for it to be resolved. Alexander gave the order then, to send in both the tactical and strategic air force. And then we went back to our dinner. The bombing took place next day.

When I came to know later on of the rubble to which the ancient abbey was reduced, and the controversy that surrounded the bombing, I realized that I had actually seen one of the historical decisions of the time.

CHAPTER XXX

I went back to Algiers under orders to take several operational groups to England and to prepare to jump into France before the invasion. As I have said, John de Salis turned up whenever I would least expect him and at this moment he somehow passed through Algiers. He rang me up, but missed me. He left a message; and I called him back, but missed him. We finally spoke on the phone just before he left, and I heard his voice for the last time, for he died soon after the war. He was on some hush-hush mission. I had no idea what he was doing, where he was going, or where he had come from, and it had always been that way. He seemed to me to be always moving around the world, friendly, funny, good natured, absent-minded, having done something no one quite knew what, and on his way to something else equally obscure.

Getting the operational groups to England was a top-secret affair. The boys went by ship; I flew to Casablanca, and then to an airfield in England. There I ran into Angie Duke. We had a great reunion for a couple of hours. Then I had to take a plane to London, but alas, I was there only a short time, to pick up further orders. Camp was being established at a place called Brock Hall near Northampton, and I was appointed commanding officer there of the operational groups of the European theater.

We had two Norwegian groups under Major Larson, coming down from Scotland, and two French groups. The Norwegians had been preparing to jump into Norway, but plans for the invasion of France were now maturing, so everything was transferred to that. At the same time, the SAS regiment (the British equivalent to OSS), which had covered itself with glory in Africa under the Sterling brothers, was now in England preparing for the invasion.

I had to see if quarters were adequate to receive our operational groups. The house was an old manor house, cold and empty, but with good plumbing. We got plenty of coal and warmed it up, and put in as many cots as it would hold. Later, when we were overrun, we sent the men to the camp area nearby, while the house doubled as official quarters and headquarters.

Up to D-day we were kept pretty busy. Leaves were suddenly restricted to nine miles from camp. We were put on the alert. A couple of German paratroop divisions had concentrated at a coastal area in France. It was possible that they would make an attempt to jump into England to paralyze our airfields. We were to protect our airfields at all cost. In the meantime we were getting ready to go into France ourselves behind the German lines. We had been assigned to invasion headquarters as Special Force troops under SHAEF.

The Norwegians came in by truck. They had had no parachute training, so I got permission for them to attend the jump school at Ringway. Then I learned that we were going to jump from Liberators, whose stalling speed was much higher than that of our C47S. I was afraid that our American parachutes, which opened very quickly in the slip stream, would blow their panels. I wanted to take no chances, so I asked and got permission for all my men to be trained at Ringway using British chutes which had long drops and thus would open well below the slip stream. We used these when we jumped into France.

In arranging this, I went to the headquarters of the British airborne forces to see Brigadier General MacLeod. Headquarters were on a golf course near London. He asked me to lunch. Going through officers' mess, we passed someone vaguely familiar. It was Boy Browning. "My God, Boy," I said, "I haven't seen you for ages." I remembered the day we had played golf and I had met Alice.

"What are you up to here?" I asked.

"I'm C.O. of the British airborne troops," he said.

"Good Lord," I said, "You're a general."

"And an old one at that," he said.

"Well" I said, "I'm just a bright young lieutenant colonel looking for help."

I explained my problem. Boy said, "I'll give the orders." They arrived the next day. He certainly did us a good turn.

Boy Browning became well known to Americans for his military prowess. After the war he married the famous novelist Daphne du Maurier and became the treasurer of the royal household of Queen Elizabeth.

Thanks to his magic word, I took the men to Ringway for a period of intensive parachute training. Jumping from a plane isn't so bad, but jumping from a balloon is terrible. In a plane there is always a lot of noise; the wind catches you, and you slide on your fanny into space before you have time to think about it. But jumping from a balloon is in complete silence, from the motionless basket, and you have to step out into the air and drop straight down, with no roar of the propellers and the wind. Under the British training system each man made two balloon jumps and five jumps from planes. We all qualified as British parachutists and were given permission to wear their paratroop wings on our right shoulders.

By this time I had a lot of prima donnas under me. Some of the boys had had fifty or sixty jumps and were as hard to handle as movie stars. They were also popular with the girls. Their pay was much higher than in the British army. They could take the girls out and spend money on them, with the result that they had a lot of fights—black eyes were frequent sights on Monday mornings. And yet there was a certain mutual respect as well, between them and the British. For instance, some of the boys came to like one of the British jump masters at Ringway. They asked me if he could be their jump master for every training jump. The British are fantastic in trying to improve troop morale. I took a tip from them, and requested that jump master. The night we took off for France, there he was waiting to hook the boys up. I think they really appreciated having him around.

I went to London quite a lot for orders and briefings. Alice was living at Hanover Lodge. She remained in London throughout the war. She was amazing. She had made her home in England and she saw no reason why, just because a war came along, she should leave England in the lurch and rush off to America. She drove an ambulance all through the London blitz. Then she organized a mobile canteen for the anti-aircraft batteries and drove it personally all around the coast. She was making highly intricate electronic equipment in a factory, when I went to dine with her.

Just as we sat down at the table, there was an air raid. We didn't want to go to the shelter, so we got under her steel table and waited it out. I dined with Alice often, and realized that we were truly friends to one another. I was just as fond of her as ever. Von Hofmannsthal had departed, was divorced, and Alice had a new husband, Philip Harding. She told me that she wasn't happy.

I went to London to get my orders at SHAEF, stopping sometimes to see Chips or other old friends, once in a while going to a night club or a theater, and once taking some of my young American officers with me to Parliament, where we listened to debates in the House of Commons. Laura Corrigan had sold her jewels to help France and its wounded when the Germans swept to Paris. Then she had escaped to England. She loathed the Germans. She was an extraordinary woman. Once Chips and I stopped in to see Laura who, like Alice, stuck by England when things were tough. She was famous for her malapropisms. A buzz bomb had landed in Regent's Park and sheared off the front wall of her house just before we called. It was one of the first of the buzz bombs, still called doodlebugs in those days. Laura was pacing fiercely up and down in her drawing room, now wide open to the weather, saying, "Those damned doodlebuggers!"

In the country, near the camp, we went to parties, one at Melton Mowbray where, in the old days, Tommy Bouch had kept the Belvoir hounds. The British went out of their way to be pleasant to us. We gave a party in return near our camp. There was something weird about London social life and night life in those days, with all the theaters and the night clubs open and going full blast in the midst of all the wreckage. The British had a lot of guts.

Before the invasion itself our situation was also strange, as we simply waited for orders to come while everything was in motion around us. The roads were chock-a-block full, with whole convoys of infantry on the move. A few days before D-day we held a practice night drop. We of course had to cooperate with the home guard, or they'd shoot us up. Everyone was alerted for German paratroops. We decided to simulate an operation. We would be the Germans, destroying airfields and railways, which they, the home guard, were to defend.

We had devised a new technique of leaving the plane fast, at "fast stick" intervals, one man practically standing on the head of the man who went out before him. That way the whole platoon was strung out only about 200 yards when we landed.

I looked up the colonel of the local home guard. He turned out to be my old friend from the Loders Club at Oxford, Geoffrey Lees, now a gentleman farmer in the area, a typical retired British officer with a beautiful estate and with a first-class unit of the home guard defending his territory.

From about nine-thirty on a beautiful late June night until five the next morning, our paratroopers and his home guards played hide-and-seek over the countryside, simulating combat, security and everything else that we would likely encounter behind enemy lines in France. The operation was very successful in building up morale in the men, who were restless waiting for orders.

We took off for France in three separate operations. I went with the third. The night before, two platoons left, one to the east of Liège, the other near Bordeaux.

My group flew in three planes, twenty men to a plane. When we got over the target area, the weather was bad. No signal from the ground was visible, nothing below us but an enormous hole of darkness. The pilot would not drop us. We waited, at the ready, for nearly an hour, while the plane circled round and round. Then the pilot told me that it was clouding up at home, gas was getting low. He turned and took us back to England.

We finally came down near Oxford. All the other fields were clouded in. We had some time there, and I went to Christ Church College to look at my old room in Peckwater Quad. The Quad itself had been modernized. The old front of the Quad, with its crumbling half-columns, had been faced. It looked much less ruined, but to my mine much of its charm was gone.

Our other two drops, at Liège and Bordeaux, were successful. At that time it was expected that Patton would break through the Germans hourly, and one of our objectives was to secure an airfield, to have gas and equipment for him when he arrived. The specific job of my group was to hold a bridge to enable tanks to get to the tip of Brittany. The men whose drop had been successful held the bridge and stayed there. I had to rig another operation for those of us who had been brought back. So I went to London. There I found time to call Alice, who said she was having a dinner party that night. She had some extra food, she said, and I must come and share the wealth. And so I did. Chips was there, and several others.

It was a very funny evening, and I had fond memories of the early days with Alice. That night we saw a perfect example of the lengths to which she would go to make her guests comfortable. Vassily was with her, of course, and she was determined to provide us with a meal in the old grand manner.

It was a difficult proposition to get the smallest luxury items during those lean war years in England, let alone the basic food. Before dinner, Alice had proudly told us all that she had actually gotten some oil for a salad dressing. This was to be a great treat, and when we downed our martinis, I saw Chips licking his chops at the prospect.

I must say Alice outdid herself. We had Vassily's famous sorrel soup. We had plenty of chicken, and the salad was delicious, and Chips asked for more. Then Alice presented us with the real triumph of the evening. She had had Vassily cook a souffle, something that many of us hadn't seen for a very long time. I certainly hadn't, and Chips was tucking it away as if there was no tomorrow. Then suddenly he stopped. His eyes looked vacant and surprised. He plonked down his spoon and fork and rushed from the table. We all went on eating, chuckling about Chips, when one of the other guests did exactly the same thing. Do you know that by the end of the dessert every single one of us except Alice underwent that same experience? Not one of us except Alice finished that souffle. By questioning Alice, whom we accused of poisoning us, we finally found out what had happened. Alice had innocently bought some mineral oil to use for salad dressing. She never ate salad herself.

"I thought it was the same as olive oil," she said.

This was a very unusual period, during which we were four times over enemy territory. Only on the fourth time were we allowed to jump. After each abortive attempt I had to return to London to rerig a new operation. Those operations took an endless amount of planning, and sometimes we planned jumps that were suddenly countermanded with no explanation given. The crux of the matter lay in the fact that we had always to jump ahead of General Patton, take an airfield and hold it, so that our planes could land and bring in gas for his tanks.

During that period, I spent a lot of wonderful evenings in London. I saw such old friends of mine as Margaret Sweeney, Popsy Ward who was then Eddie Ward's wife, and a few others. I would stay at Chips's in the lap of luxury in Belgrave Square. How curious it all was, one day dancing in London, the next day over France, standing over that shrieking hole in the belly of a plane. During this period I became very good friends with a tough American sergeant from Brooklyn who had taken a shine to me. He apparently got himself appointed as my jump master, so as to take care of me. It was very touching, and it was always comforting to see his smiling, friendly face.

I was always worried about Alice now that the buzz bombs were coming in. Chips's house and Hanover Lodge were right on their trajectory. I kept telling her for God's sake to take shelter in the evenings now. The whole St. John's Wood-Regent's Park area was getting pulverized. Whenever I was staying at Chips's, I would listen to the bombs putting toward me. If one cut out before it was directly overhead, I took cover fast. But if it passed overhead, and cut out anywhere near the zenith, safe though I was, I had a horrible fear for Alice, who adamantly refused to go down into her cellar. The bombs that cut out over Chips's were the ones that were hitting Regent's Park.

One of the evenings that I went to dine with Alice we were literally blown away from the dining table. We never heard that bomb coming. It was a near miss of tremendous proportions. We all went out to see where it had hit. There was a shambles down at the bottom of the garden, near the tennis courts. There had been a little rose garden with a sundial there. Alice shouted, "Gilbert always walks down there around this time!" There had also been a huge copper beech with a swing under it, where Ivan had played as a child. It had completely disappeared. The bomb must have struck the top of it. To our horror when we got there, we heard groans. I saw somebody, or what looked like somebody, and then I realized that it was Miss St. George, Alice's secretary. She told us that they had all gone for a walk, she and Gilbert and his wife, and they had stopped there for a swing. "Are they all right?" she asked, and then she died. We never found a trace of the others.

I was terribly upset, realizing that Gilbert, my old friend, was suddenly, needlessly dead. We had driven everywhere together in the good old days. He was a great companion to me and loyal to Alice throughout everything. He also was a hero, having done an incredible job during the blitz as head of A.R.P. detachments in the area. He had performed countless feats under enemy attack beyond the call of duty. Again a rose garden, I thought, and I remembered the rose garden in the Crimea, the place of gentle childhood memory, become a charnel house.

My orders this time were to prepare for a jump into the forest of Rambouillet, only about thirty miles from Paris. But this was one of the plans that was changed at the very last moment.

In the Indre region, about a hundred and fifty miles south of Paris, there was a big electric transformer station, with a main cable to Paris. There was a balloon barrage there. My new job was to take one company, or rather one operational group, and hold that station and prevent the Germans from blowing it up as they retreated.

We went in again, but again we ran into trouble—this time it was heavy flak, and the pilot wouldn't drop us. Back in London I went dancing—again a strange sensation: over France one night, and dancing in London the next.

We tried a second time, but the same thing happened.

My tough American jump master was kidding me now about my unfruitful operations, and we were talking freely about the girls of Brooklyn versus the girls of Manhattan. Before the third try—he was sure we would make it that time because, as he said, "Third time lucky!"—he came up to me as we were about to get our chutes and paraphernalia strapped on.

"Coynel," he said. "I like you. I'm going to do something for you that I've never done before. But you got to follow me to my quarters."

"All right," I said.

There he opened his locker and proudly showed me a very detailed display of quite a few young ladies, pinned to the back of the door.

"There are twelve of them there," he said, proudly. "All American, every one of them a beauty. Now you pick out the one you like, Coynel, and I'll pin her right up in front of you, and as you go out into France it'll make you feel good because the last thing you'll see will be a beautiful American goil."

I really picked out a beauty, and I knew that all the boys would go out with a grin.

The sergeant was right. The third time we went in we did jump. Because of the delay, we had lost our moon; everything was black as pitch. It was altogether unlike Sardinia. We were rigged up in a quick stick. Our harnesses were fixed with a slide that ran along the plane leading to the hole, automatically opening the chute as we jumped. The packages of equipment went out first, our radios and supplies. I went last, because I wanted to see the stick go out. We went out in seconds, each of us looking at the sergeant's pin-up girl. I counted; I heard the boom as the chute opened; then I floated down into darkness as black as the Black Hole of Calcutta must have been.

We had no names. I was "Colonel Butch." The Maquis were waiting for us. We piled in cars and trucks, and were taken to a farm about twelve miles away. There the Maquis fed us magnificently. I must say the men never ate so well as there in France with all the food they had smuggled out of occupied towns. We slept in a barn.

There was one company of Germans under a captain at the power station in Eguyzon, and there was a French force of the Petain government to defend the balloon barrage and the electric transformers. I arranged a meeting with the French officer, and told him I had orders to take and hold the power station. I had, of course, placed my men in echelons in the countryside to give the impression that I had a big force with me. The French captain was stunned when I told him I had direct orders from General Koenig of the French army to take and hold Eguyzon for France. Then I said that under no circumstances must the Germans be permitted to destroy the station.

In return for assurance that the electric station would not be blown up, I would permit safe passage to Argenton for the Eguyzon Germans to withdraw. I told him they should be out before dawn. "Otherwise, I said, "I'll attack at six in the morning and I won't guarantee anything until they have passed beyond Argenton." I said this for fear that the plant would be blown up after they pulled out. If they double-crossed us and destroyed the station in that fashion, we would take care of them as they retreated. I arranged that part of it with the Maquis. I sent a platoon to help them cut the road, and fell trees, with a colonel of the Maquis working with us, to hold them up if necessary.

We went into battle formation about three miles away. We left open the fork of a road through which they would have to pass. Sure enough, they came by and disappeared up the road to Châteauroux. After a time the French captain appeared. "They're gone," he said.

He said they had not planted explosives, and he was right, but at that time I still did not know if they had or not. We then established quarters in a farmhouse and started getting acquainted with the Maquis colonel of the region and his operations.

The Germans were still in possession of Paris. I think one factor that saved the station was that it supplied so much of Paris and they did not want it destroyed until they pulled out from there. The big German column that we knew about was coming in from the west, but was now passing north of us. After the German contingent pulled out from the power station, the mayor of Châteauroux, a nice little man, delighted at our appearance, wanted to hold a victory celebration, and I agreed. Châteauroux was the biggest city of the area. There, after the Germans left, the Maquis had taken over the local newspaper. They were all Reds, and when I came in as the representative of the Americans, they gave me the clenched fist, the Bolshevik salute.

The next day was the victory celebration at which the mayor, the Maquis colonel and I reviewed the parade of the local Maquis. I made a speech from a balcony, and placed a bouquet of roses on the grave of a Maquis hero. Then we went back to our headquarters.

A group of Maquis lived with us in our hideout on the farm. The men got along well. The Maquis varied greatly: the conservatives were well-informed, very responsible, and good soldiers; others, most of these in leftist groups, were trigger-happy, cocky, and foolish. So there were really two lines in the French underground, one serious and disciplined, but inclined to lack initiative; the other reckless, dangerous, and veering over to the complete dominance of the Reds. There were about a thousand Maquis in the area where we were, which was almost the geographical center of France. We got our food and supplies through them, paying them for each man's daily needs, fifty francs per day per man. The astonishing thing was that the countryside was so prosperous. Food was plentiful, and economic conditions were far better than anything I had heard had led me to believe.

In the meantime a large German column was retreating from Bordeaux. As it rumbled past along the road through Châteauroux, only a few miles north, I thought we ought to see what we could do to cause them trouble. This was the main line of the great German retreat, although we did not know it at the time. Simultaneously, another German column was coming up on the other side of us from the south.

Hundreds of thousands of German soldiers were on the road. I went back to Le Blanc, a few miles west of us, to reconnoiter. Beyond Le Blanc the road forked. One road led to Châteauroux, and I realized that the Germans would have to take it; the other led to Le Blanc itself.

When I got to Le Blanc some prisoners were brought to me, including two Italian naval officers who had been in Bordeaux. They had been retreating north with the Germans. They were an unhappy lot. Italy had capitulated; for them the show was over; and their morale was non-existent. We picked up quite a bit of information from them.

The Maquis put up ambushes along the road to Le Blanc, on the near side of the fork in the roads, and in Le Blanc itself. We did not dare attempt any action along the main road with its enormous concentration of troops.

A good-looking girl was planted beyond the fork in the road. She went out there whenever there was a German unit of manageable size approaching. She busied herself with something in the yard of a house there. When the Germans came by, usually an officer in a jeep first, or a truck with prisoners, they asked the road to Châteauroux. She pointed to the road to Le Blanc. They passed on out of sight, to where the Maquis were waiting to pick them up. I stayed and watched the German traffic on the main road as long as I could. What I saw convinced me that the Germans were going hell-for-leather out of there, all the way home.

The next night I went back with the men. A priest there, at an estate along the big road, gave us more invaluable information about the German movements. His cousin was in the Maquis, a young, extremely able soldier, very helpful. As a result, we deployed along a ridge running parallel with the main road, my men on one side of the road. On the opposite side we placed a group with mortars. The mortars were zeroed on the road itself. We figured that when the firing began, the Germans would sweep around a hillock to outflank my men on the ridge. "They never make a long sweep," I was told, "but always a very short one." So I put two men with a machine gun on the flank, behind the hillock.

In the middle of the night there was a lull, and then traffic on the road ceased. The last German trucks vanished. We could not hear anything approaching. And then suddenly a lot of Germans on bicycles appeared.

Our men and the Maquis on the ridge opened fire. The Germans returned it. Then our mortars opened up with sulphur shells. We could only strike like that and then retire. We were only fifty men and a handful of Maquis, while there were thousands of Germans.

So we went to a rendezvous where lorries were waiting, about a mile back. We never used main roads, ploughing through fields from one farm to another. Later, I went back alone to see if we could make another sortie.

I watched the Germans along the same big road. But the end of the column was approaching. It had been trickling down gradually, and this was really the end of it. The great lines of trucks, jeeps and men ended. An occasional isolated truck, or a few together, raced along. And all the time, along the road, the most virulent of the Maquis groups were chasing the column, ambushing and killing off the men at the end of it. They took cars, bodies and everything into the woods. There they stripped bodies of clothes, and then raced on to catch up with the column again—a gruesome business.

That night we were bedded down at one of their control points in the deep woods. All around us, womens' clothing was hanging on branches of trees: mink coats, dresses, slips, ladies' shoes, everything you could think of. "What happened to those girls?" I asked the Maquis colonel. "Don't ask!" he growled. "They were Nazis and French collaborators we caught fleeing with the column." It was at this same control point that I learned that when the head of the retreating German column had broken into Châteauroux, the little mayor had been taken out and shot.

We left our headquarters and went in the opposite direction from Le Blanc to hit the column in the forest of Varennes, where it was moving through a beautiful, parklike woods. Then we went back to Le Blanc. Soon after we arrived, a lot of our trucks swarmed into town. And there were our own men, the group that had been dropped near Liège just before we jumped. Their mission was completed, and they were now with a British contingent. They were entirely separate from us, not even under my command, and were on their way to another exploit. I learned later that they captured a German headquarters, for which Captain Grunset received the Croix de Guerre.

There were embarrassing moments to this kind of warfare. When we came into a town, women ran out and kissed us. And everywhere people gave us wine—they handed bottles of their best local wine to us when we passed, or threw them into the trucks when we drove by. A wonderful gesture, but wine is not good for men in combat, and I had to put a stop to it. Once a dazzlingly beautiful blonde ran up to me and gave me such a whacker that I was dizzy. Then she ran off. Whew! The next day I was at the command post I had just established, about thirty miles away when my orderly said that a Maquis captain had arrived with a contingent and wished to report. He was a young Frenchman, very agreeable, and after he concluded his business he said, "I believe you know my wife."

"Oh?" I said, "I don't think so."

"She tells me," he said, "that she met you yesterday at the square in Le Blanc . . ."

"Was that your wife?" I exclaimed perhaps a little loudly. Then I recovered myself, and said, "Was that lovely creature your wife? My dear friend, congratulations. You are indeed fortunate."

The country grew quiet after the German column passed, and we made arrangements with the *garde mobile* of the French, already coming into the region, to set up joint patrols. We gave the men leave to enjoy themselves in Le Blanc. To the south and west of us there was an isolated contingent of Russian and German troops—Russian prisoners who had gone over to the Germans to escape the Reds—hurrying to reach the main column of retreating Germans. We stopped them at a road block, and I sent the German officer a letter under the flag of truce recommending that he surrender. Unlike the Maquis, I promised to respect him and his men as prisoners of war. He replied, "I'm going to shoot my way through!" which he did. We didn't have enough power or the right under our orders to stop him.

They were now about fifty miles from the rear of the column. Further on, after undergoing continual harassment from the Maquis, who made attack after attack on them, they finally surrendered to another officer of the OSS, Colonel Grell, our plans officer, who had been my assistant manager at the Hotel St. Regis in New York.

There were no more German troops to be found, and our mission was over. We received orders to that effect. Practically all operational groups in the area converged on Le Blanc, our assembly point, including the contingent that had jumped at Liège. For a day or two we put up at a pleasant country estate for a rollicking reunion before we were flown back to England. Our group was the last to go. We flew back in a C47, piloted by a former fighter pilot. He was so exultant that he buzzed all church steeples of Argenton. Flying back, we saw an extraordinary sight, wave after wave of planes and gliders going into Holland, in the great airborne operation that was to be the largest ever created by the Allies.

CHAPTER XXXI

We returned to England in high spirits, and we immediately received the present of a leave. The boys took off like wild men. I dreaded to think what London would be like for the next week, but they had certainly deserved it. I made out my reports, and went to stay with Chips.

That evening I was walking in Piccadilly when I got a tremendous wallop on the back. I turned and saw the beaming face of my friend, the sergeant with the pin-up pictures.

"Coynel!" he said. "Why! You're alive! You're back! I never thought I'd see *you* again!"

The mission was, I believe, generally accounted a successful one. The French government very kindly awarded me the Croix de Guerre for my part in saving the power station. I was told that my men were all going to be reassigned to the Far Eastern theater. I called them together to say good-by; I told them that I had put them through a very severe course of training and that I would appreciate their honest answers about that course: Did they think that training was all right? I must say that I happily heard a unanimous opinion that the course was okay, that the training colonel was okay. I told them I was more than pleased to hear their verdict.

My own orders were to report back to Washington for reassignment that meant the Far Eastern theater also. On the way back I thought about my possible function in this theater of war. I became a little discouraged. My fifty-fifth birthday was approaching. Age in itself did not bother me, but I had noted in myself an increasing tendency to be hit by communicable diseases. The thought of those Oriental and tropical ailments (which had been fatal to many of our younger men in the Orient) was a little too much for me. I had long since passed the age at which I was eligible for retirement; I had contributed to two successful operations of some importance; and I concluded that I had done enough. So when I was asked if I would like to go to China, I replied that I thought I was too old to risk it.

I have told about the two sons of my cousin Olga Obolensky, the daughter of the governor general of Finland, and how she smuggled them out of Russia addressed to me. Before the war, the boys had finished their education at the Sorbonne. One of them, Ivan, had gone to Hungary, where he became a salesman for a porcelain factory. The other was inducted into the French army at the beginning of the war. With the closing of the frontiers during the war, I had lost sight of them, just as we had lost contact with their mother twenty years before.

The Americans had just entered Munich and word was brought to me of an Obolensky living there, a lady who had been a prisoner of the Germans. Gradually I learned an extraordinary story. That lady was Olga, my cousin. After her fiancé had died at the Onega Canal and she had been sent to Tver, she was guarded and not allowed to leave the town. For twenty years she devoted herself to her work as a nurse, and became head of the local hospital, with no real knowledge of what was happening in the world. Suddenly the Germans arrived. Olga continued working at the hospital. The Germans kept her at her post. After a time she noted that the invaders were uneasy. She suspected that they were preparing to pull out. That meant that the Soviets must be advancing—if they returned to Tver she would be shot for having worked with the enemy.

At this moment a German prisoner-of-war convoy passed through the town, heading west. Olga joined it. Slowly they made their way across Russia and Poland and into Germany. By this time she had become known to the Germans as a White Russian and an Obolensky. She was not molested by them; in fact, she was treated quite well.

Eventually she reached Berlin, and from Berlin she made her way to Munich. Then the Americans took the city. When she reported to the American authorities, she learned of still another Obolensky living there. It was her son Ivan, who had fled the Russian advance. The two met not knowing they were mother and son. Then within a week, my brother Vlady appeared, having been released from a German camp. Vlady somehow knew that Alexander, the other brother, was safe in Paris.

Olga's sister, who married one of the Zvegintsoff family, was in London when the boys were shipped to me after they were smuggled out of Russia. In fact, she was present at the wedding of Alice and myself, and she had cared for Olga's children. Her son, Teddy Zvegintsoff, a very able young fellow, had been my son's tutor before the war.

I had tried to persuade Teddy to come to the United States and go into business with me. But he wanted to be a soldier. He joined the British Army, serving at the Khyber Pass, and in Burma against the Japanese. Still extremely young, by the end of the war he was already a British colonel. It was through his assistance that Olga and Ivan Obolensky were identified and released. But it proved to be difficult to get Vlady out. The authorities believed he had contracted tuberculosis as a result of his hardships in the concentration camp. He was living in a D.P. camp when I found him. I was able to send him supplies, but it was a long time before he was permitted to leave.

Meanwhile Olga and her son lived with a charming old German couple, near the extreme point of the Russian advance into Germany. And while they were there, the Russian kidnappings began on a large scale. One day the old German came to her, saying two American officers were asking to see her. Olga looked out of the window, and there was something funny about them.

She told Ivan to go out the back way and call the American patrol. She kept them talking until the MPs arrived. The men were Soviet agents.

My own leave-taking of England after the war consisted of a wonderful flight in an army transport from Scotland, our whole group in the OSS flying together to Goose Bay and then to Washington. As we neared Washington, a fog closed down over the eastern United States. We circled a long time. Every field, it seemed, was closed in. We had the single alternative of going back to Goose Bay and waiting. The pilot came to talk to us. He said he was a native of Baltimore, and if we wanted, he could bring the plane down there despite the soup. He'd done it hundreds of times. Of course, he was partial. He had a date that night. Otherwise, well, back to Goose Bay. We voted unanimously to try it. The plane went down through the fog and made a perfect landing on the runway. When we got out, we discovered that it had stopped five feet from the end of it.

In Washington, at OSS headquarters, Colonel Goodfellow told me he sympathized with my decision not to go with the operational group to China. He said I had done my share, and this was the time to get out. So I tendered my resignation and on March 11, 1945 was processed out and returned to my apartment in New York. My daughter Sylvia, and Alice's daughter Romana von Hofmannsthal, were staying there with their governess, the invincible Sheelagh MacDermott of the Irish Free State. They were already young ladies going to the Brearly School each morning. Sylvia had sent me the funny papers all through the war. These had done a real service and went right through the unit. By the time everyone had read them, they were in shreds. Two other people had been terribly good about sending me things and writing me during the war. Irina Lazareff Blaine, my childhood friend, and Thelma Foy. I shall always be grateful to them.

Almost as soon as I returned, my son came home. His training as an aviation cadet in the navy air corps was almost complete, but the navy was already cutting back its forces. He had been given a choice of going on and spending four more years in the service, or completing his education. I advised him to return to Yale, just as my own father had advised me to finish my education when the question of military service came up, and that is what he did.

My first problem was to decide what I was going to do. I saw my good friend, Arthur Krock, of the *New York Times*, in Washington, and talked to him about getting into public relations. He suggested I see Eddie Bernays, the famous public relations man, as the man best qualified—and, in any event, Eddie was an old friend of mine.

I had a long talk with him, and we went over all the different things I had done—real estate management with my father, broker, agricultural machinery salesman, hotel man. Eddie said, "You can do public relations anytime, Serge, but you've been closer to hotel-keeping than anything else! That is public relations. What's wrong with that?" The result was that I stopped in to see Byron Foy, who saw Boyd Hatch, a director of the Plaza Hotel, who in turn discussed the matter with Conrad Hilton, who had just bought it.

At this moment I was presented with three alternative careers. One in Washington—a group wanted me to live there, to work on what were called "deals," one big deal a year being enough to live well on. At the same time Will Hays, the head of the movie industry, offered me a post through Eddie Bernays, a representative of the industry in Europe, extremely interesting, but involving a lot of travel. "Do you want to fly around?" Eddie asked me.

"No," I said, "I'm sick of flying around."

And at the same time, Vincent came back from his convoy duty in the navy. He said that I could return to work with him.

Hilton offered me a position directing public relations and promotion for the Plaza Hotel. It was like my St. Regis job. So I went back to hotel-keeping, where I have been ever since. These intervening years have been filled with interest for me, more so than I could ever have expected when I began my postwar career.

Building up a hotel is a human enterprise. You have to be known and liked by its rank and file, the waiters, the captains, the clerks, the manager—it all adds up to esprit de corps. This is great for the customers. Despite a good building and a good location, everything still depends upon people—on good will, good service, and, in a sense, on personal friendships. When I got there, the grand old Plaza in New York, with its magnificent setting on Central Park and Fifth Avenue, and its hallowed associations dating from innumerable balls and coming-out parties and the stories of F. Scott Fitzgerald, had lost something of its prestige. The rooms were still beautiful, and of proportions that contemporary builders no longer find profitable. We had to get people to want to come there, to feel that they could rely on us to provide them with the extra little things, to get them into the habit.

One of the very first things that happened was that my son and I gave a ball in the Crystal Room of the Plaza. It was our coming-back-from-the-service party. It was one of the first of the big parties given in New York after the war, and everybody, starved so long for that sort of thing, had a tremendous time. Ivan had invited all the younger belles of the debutante vintage, and I had asked my friends. It was an incredible mixture but an effective one. I took Connie Woodworth to it. I had met her on my first weekend back in the States with the Warren Pershings at Narragansett. I was most indebted to them, for she was a very young-looking almond-eyed girl with white hair. I'd never seen such coloring. Also, she was terribly funny, especially whenever she was teased. She rose beautifully to every occasion.

After our party, I got Hildegarde to come and sing at the Persian Room. I had known her since she was eighteen, during my bachelor days with Bert

Taylor before the war. Will Stewart had really promoted her and he had brought her often to Bert's parties. He got Jerome Kern and Cole Porter interested in her. In those days she would always sing Will's theme song with her: *Ich liebe nur eine, der eine bist du.* Hildy was a big hit at the Persian Room, and business began to pick up immediately.

I drew up a plan designed to provide better service for our guests. We beefed up the decor, and put in a sensational new night club called The Rendezvous, with an excellent Russian chef, also a friend of Vassily's, and we began bringing in shashlik on flaming swords. Unfortunately, Alice, who had just come back to the States, was one of the first to try it. We weren't exactly shaken down, and the skewers would come in with seared tomatoes on their tips. Seared tomatoes are dangerous on a sword, because the tomato skin has lost all its firmness. One of them dropped off right on poor Alice's head. I gave orders that they should never sear the tomatoes again.

The first bachelor postwar ball was held at the Plaza; and it was a great event, although our ranks were sorely depleted by many of our cohorts being still away in uniform, or even married. It was, of course, a white-tie affair, and there were only four of us: Charley Cushing, Doc Holden, Lauder Greenway and myself. It was very amusing as there was a tremendous smell of mothballs everywhere, and all the starched fronts and collars were yellow with age. I took Connie Woodworth to this one too. I had fallen in love with her, hook, line and sinker.

Throughout the war Vava Adlerberg had been at the Plaza. He was tall, courtly and very correct. He had never gotten over an occasion when he was an assistant manager at the St. Regis; there was an urgent call from the Gotham for the manager on duty, which Vava happened at that time to be. Apparently, we had a girl on our eighteenth floor ledge overlooking Fifth Avenue. She was totally nude and dangling her legs over the ledge. Vava was of course elected to go up and remonstrate with her. He was so successful in his persuasion that she came back in immediately. He never lived it down.

One morning in the Plaza Vava came to me with a very worried face.

He said, "Serge, Mrs. X wants to see you."

"Oh," I said. "Why?"

"She just wants to see you," he said. He looked more worried than ever.

"All right," I said. "I'll go."

"Serge?" he said. I was already going out the door so I stopped. "Whenever I go to Mrs. X's room, I never go in. You understand, Serge? I stand in the doorway, smiling, and bowing politely. And I never close the door."

Vava never lived that one down either.

Renewing the spirit of the hotel comes down to one's own friendly feeling for people, and I have found that the successful managers are a special type of individual—people with a natural liking for others, a personal interest in them, and with a deeply ingrained concern for their well-being. Those I have known well, like Mr. Ross of the Plaza, who has now retired, or J. B. Herndon, who followed him, a friend of Hilton's, were among the pleasantest people I have ever known. Boyd Hatch and his wife were really the moving spirits of the rejuvenation of the Plaza. I gave them the idea of having important persons decorate specific suites in their own names. Boyd thought this was great; he was an idea man always ready to accept an innovation.

After a year or so, I was made vice-president of the Hilton chain in charge of all promotion and public relations. I began traveling around to the hotels Hilton had acquired or was acquiring, the Stevens and the Palmer House in Chicago, the Town House in Hollywood.

While in Hollywood I again stayed with Elsie and Charles Mendl. This time Elsie said, "Serge, it's time for you to get married and I have just the thing!" That evening Elsie produced a beautiful Greek divorcee called Adrian Helis. She was extremely wealthy, but I thought she had a very determined chin. I must say I was taken with her, and I took her out in Hollywood, but as to marriage, well, I was rather scared of her. Many years later I met her again at the Ambassador. She was now married to a very nice man called Malvin, and they came to dine. During dinner, we talked about our courtship in Hollywood, and when I admitted that I had thought she had been a bit too domineering for me and got scared of her, "Scared?" she said and laughed. "I was petrified. I thought you were one of those wild men from the steppes of Russia!" She knew by then that since I had known her, I had become very devoted to Connie Woodworth.

We tried to work out a unified theme in all our hotel promotion, from the letterheads to the billboards and magazine advertisements, to set a standard of good taste. And the tone of the hotels in turn depended not only on these good things, but upon the sort of parties and charity events and celebrations that were held in them.

It was an interesting and an important work. The old tradition in American hotel rooms was of grimly utilitarian quarters, with stereotyped decorations—or with none at all—and no further solace for the occupant than the Gideon Bible. The new trend of good taste in hotel decoration, as exemplified when we got Elsie Mendl to do over some rooms at the Plaza, gained momentum very fast. Elsie was, of course, the chief exponent of chintz. And, believe me, you can do things just as cheaply in good taste as in bad, and you can do an awful lot with a paintbrush. That was Elsie's idea—bright curtains, lyrical furniture with attractive upholstery that was comfortable as well. It was only up to us to provide good service from the bellboys on up. Then the new spruced-up condition of the public rooms, the restaurants, even behind scenes in the kitchen, the wine cellar, all added to a general feeling of movement. We stressed air conditioning, piping-hot water, the mechanical side of the operation, as well, for plumbing and kitchen equipment are all linked to aesthetic factors, to the intangibles that go to make up a happy place for people to stay. And a cardinal rule is, if the help are happy, then it's a good hotel. I think that by and large we had a happy esprit de corps at the Hilton chain.

In the actual operation of a hotel, the art of management consists in delegating responsibility, securing assistants who can do the work that is necessary, or training people for the work if none with the required training is available. Our accounting system operated on a twenty-four-hour basis, so that any significant change was immediately noted and steps instantly taken to correct it. I was fortunate in being able to pick good assistants. Once in a while I had a rude awakening—for the most part the men who worked with me flourished in their posts. I was delighted when many of them followed me when I moved to another hotel.

One of the last interesting occurrences that happened to me at the Plaza was the arrival of Gromyko. I was standing near the reception desk at the time; his aide, a Soviet general whom I'd met in Washington at various functions, came rushing up to me and took me over to meet Ambassador and Mme. Gromyko. Gromyko was very cordial, and I wished him a comfortable stay. I saw them several times, and at one dinner, at the Mills's, I was put next to Mme. Gromyko. She seemed very nice, and had been a cattle expert on a huge state farm near Minsk. We had a lot in common. The more I questioned her about it, the more certain I became that this particular farm was one that had belonged to Paul Bouteneff, a cousin of mine. It was called Schorssi and it was a place where Father had sent me once to learn about cattle farming. Even then, it was one of the largest in Russia. Bouteneff had been in the Ministry of Foreign Affairs under Uncle Valerian. I am not certain that I am right, but there's more than an even chance that she had operated Schorssi.

CHAPTER XXXII

It was shortly after we had all returned from the wars that an institution was formed in Southampton. It was a bachelor's summer haven, and it was conceived by my friend Angie Duke. It was called the Duke Box.

Angie donated the unused stable on his farm to the cause of unwed gentlemen. I do not want to give the impression that a lonely-hearts club was formed on the Duke estate. None of us was lonely in the least, although all of us, to a man, abhorred the thought of marriage—at least that was what we had to say, since I think it was written in the Duke Box charter. It was a kind of protection, that charter. One thing was certain from the ground rules of the place; once we got married, we couldn't stay there any more, and for any of its members, that should be incentive enough.

In the beginning there were seven: Angie Duke, Jay Rutherfurd, Serge Obolensky, Alfred Clark, Craig Mitchell, Vava Adlerberg, and Constantin Alajalov. These were the charter members. Under their auspices, the stable stalls became five little rooms each with a bed, dressing table and a basin with running water. Angie lived in his house next door, and Ala (Alajalov) had a little two-room bungalow next door, which he decorated inside with a brilliant trompe l'oeil series of frescoes. Then he hung up a sign outside that read:

Garden of Allah

He was quite content to leave the stalls to Vava, Alfred, Craig, Jay, and me. Meanwhile, we all shared costs, and a floor was put down in the main building over the packed stable earth. The Duke Box was in business. We began receiving immediately. To start things off, we gave a few parties and then a dance. We found that we had created a kind of Southampton social center almost overnight. At first I think all the tried-and-true Southamptoners came out to see the fun, just as they might go to watch a match at the tennis club. The group we invited to our parties was more of an artistic and international category than anything else. Our guest book began to record names that ran the gamut from Greek shipping magnates to Ginger Rogers and Hedy Lamarr.

In the beginning the Duke Box was tremendous sport, but also tiring. In the evenings the mosquitoes made it very hard to sleep. They breezed in unimpeded through the open top-half of our stall doors—I remember Vava complaining bitterly about this. So we got some mosquito netting for the five strategic places. At the same time, we fixed up the saddle room as our bar and kitchenette, and every morning we would have breakfast "in the patio," which a little earlier had been the stable yard. And thus the Duke Box was created.

Ever since it has been an absolute godsend. The older I get, the more I need the sun and salt water and the exhilaration of all things.

Not long ago I was on the dance floor with a young and very pretty girl called Mary Maude McKim. I saw a horrified expression come over her face when I was waltzing with her. She was looking at me intensely. One thing that I know I can dance reasonably well is the waltz, and that look of hers disturbed me. Before I could ask her what the trouble was she said, "Serge, what in hell is all that creaking?"

I couldn't help laughing. I, of course, knew it was the wax on the floor. "Darling," I said, "it's my poor old knees!" But I must say I went down to Southampton very early that next Friday to take the sun and air.

A good part of the Plaza staff followed me to the Sherry-Netherland. Hampshire House on Central Park South and the Sherry-Netherland opposite the Plaza had been on the market for some time. Boyd Hatch was offered the Sherry-Netherland at a price that he accepted, and he wanted me to team up with him to operate it. About a month was required to conclude the deal, so I left the Hilton chain, established myself in a small office as Serge Obolensky Associates, hotel consultants, and waited. Hilton, in his restless way, scouting around for another property, also saw possibilities in the Sherry-Netherland, and decided to buy it, only learning to his chagrin that we had bought it the day before.

In the hotel we found violations galore. We incurred heavy expenses; one of the unpleasantnesses was that new plumbing was required throughout the building, but then I put my formula to work.

It was once again a matter of getting people to come to a new hotel. You always have to make that place the thing to go to, especially if you are a reasonably small operator. There is no earthly point in trying to compete with big commercial chains, which Hilton and all the rest can operate infinitely better since they can absorb costs and defray charges in many ways and increase efficiency. With a single hotel like the Sherry-Netherland we had one approach to make and that was to try to establish the best luxury hotel in the city, and to become known for that. It's logical that even if we didn't become the best, we had only to compete against the Pierre and the St. Regis, and the percentage is far better that way than competing commercially with twenty or so well-run commercial establishments.

Accordingly, we increased our inventory, added extra staff, spiffed up the uniforms, put in key men whom I knew could do the best job for the luxury and continental trade. We got Cecil Beaton to decorate some suites; we pushed up the prices of our food, and our room rents; and we began making money, but we still needed one other factor. The Sherry-Netherland was a small hotel and a relatively little-known one, though in an excellent location. What we needed most of all was to create habit. So we decided to put in a night club. I asked Ivan to bring over as many of his friends as he could. I have always been a firm believer in enticing the young into my hotels. No business is good if its strength is dependent upon the older people. When we opened our night club, which we called the Carnaval, I made a rule that the younger people would not get a cover charge. It worked. My son Ivan passed the word around to his friends, and they all began coming in in droves.

In public relations I had Sasha Tarsaïdzé primed to arrange our parties and banquets. His job was to be sure that there were as many movie stars and celebrities around as possible. After all, they bring in trade if they are known to frequent a place, and Sasha was to send in news and press releases to the columnists about them. This is perhaps one of the most important factors in the hotel business—to be able to get things in the columns about your hotel. This was one thing which we were lucky enough to be able to do quite effectively, thanks to the interest of people like Gigi Cassini, Charles Ventura, Bob Considine, Dorothy Kilgallen, Hedda Hopper and many others.

And then in the cellar I created the first atomic shelter in New York. I equipped it with oxygen, geiger counters, shovels and picks, stretchers and surgical equipment. I hoped that other places would follow this example, although I prayed that the shelter would never have to be used.

While I was at the Sherry-Netherland, I got Jim Forrestal intrigued with a plan that I considered terribly important for the safety of our country, namely the organization of a special state guard force in the United States, similar to the British home guard during the last war.

SUBJECT: Mobilizing the state guards for the purpose of protecting vital war defense installations in the United States such as dams, water works, electric plants and war defense factories.

Plan
Each state will organize state guard units from a platoon in a small community to a regiment and brigade in a town, depending on the size of the community. These units to be organized primarily in the vicinity of installations vital for our defense. Close coordination and liaison with regular forces—army, navy, etc.

The operational function of these groups would be nearly identical with that of the British World War II home guard.

Purpose
1. To guard and protect the plants in time of emergency. The problem of defense will be in rural and in urban areas; villages and small towns with platoon groups and special arsenals located centrally for easy access and if alerted will make the defense of vital installations a very simple operation.

2. To have primarily an alert INTELLIGENCE NETWORK in the area for the purpose of intercepting inside and outside saboteurs (the men would be specially trained in intelligence work). At the present moment undoubtedly the Communists are infiltrating their agents into the various plants of national defense and ringing those plants with men that could carry out sabotage whenever the signal would be given. A well-organized group of local citizens that would either work in the plants or have key men in the various companies in the surrounding townships and villages. They could do a sterling job in gradually locating them and report them to the FBI.

Also in case of new persons appearing in the community they can be reported to headquarters and their activities screened. In other words, we would have a constantly alert organization in a network right across the United States that would be on the lookout for any possible subversive activities in the local communities that could hamper our war effort. On M-day it would be the key to our entire home defense.

3. In case of enemy airborne attack to delay the access of the enemy to war plants and installations in the vicinity by guerrilla tactics, road blocks, ambushes, destruction of bridges, and thus give the opportunity to regular army troops to come up and deploy in the area.
4. All activities against enemy forces to be in liaison and close coordination with the local or area regular army or navy commanders.

Recruiting
Members of the state guard ought to be carefully screened by the FBI for communist affiliations and would consist of the most dependable citizens of the community. Veterans of the two World Wars would be encouraged to join.

Training
1. Intelligence training and counter-intelligence—to be organized under FBI supervision and manuals.
2. Guerrilla training—In the archives of the OSS there exists a manual called *The Operational Group Manual* (#0499520) for the United States army guerrilla-trained units that was prepared by Major J. E. Alderdyce of the infantry school at Fort Benning and myself. This manual could easily be adapted to the training of the state guards. In addition to the OSS literature, British home guard manuals could be adapted to United States functions and nomenclature.
During the last World War, I was trained in the OSS schools and subsequently was training officer for the special operational group of

United States army parachute units that fought with the Maquis (the resistance) behind enemy lines. I was in command of these OSS units in ETO and jumped with them into France during the invasion. I was able to test this training which proved effective.

Equipment

The accent for state guard detachments ought to be on *mobility*. The equipment ought to be light and consist of Garand rifles, submachine guns, Browning automatics, light mortars and bazookas, and all requisite demolitions material. It would be recommended that each platoon should have a jeep, a weapons carrier and a motorcycle.

Such equipment to be held in arsenals roughly as follows:

Area Arsenal

Special arsenals for platoons in villages or small towns to be centrally located with reference to the vital installations to be guarded.

Colonel Serge Obolensky, USAF (Res.)

It was to be made up of older reliable men who were to protect their various villages and townships in time of national emergency. They were to be properly armed and trained to prevent looting and pillaging in their communities, to have a special intelligence section for work in their areas, and in the case of any attack upon the homeland, to be prepared to protect vital installations from saboteurs. I submit this plan in the back of the book as an appendix, as I now consider it more vital to our safety every passing day. Jim couldn't get anywhere with it at the time, due to politics, but I do know that he was concerned as much as I. To take one specific case in point: if a bomb dropped anywhere near New York, or was even threatened by a foreign power, what would happen? Wouldn't millions of people begin swarming out through the countryside? What would they do? Would they all be peaceful, law-abiding? Would the hope that they would be law-abiding be sufficient? I merely submit that the outlying areas around New York had better start thinking about this fact, and decide before it is too late that it might be wise to have a trained and active home guard force of local citizenry just standing by if need be.

It was in line with this kind of thinking that I applied for admission into the air force reserve. I was accepted, and every week, I went out and trained at Mitchell Field. I was attached to Intelligence. They can give us a lot of eye openers, those young air force fellows. Through Stu Symington's interest, I was given the chance of making some of my ideas known through military channels, and I hope that some of these have been helpful. I was made a colonel under Colonel Ernie White, a wonderfully bright young air force officer. One day I saw him with his arm in a sling. I said, "Ernie, what have you done to yourself?"

He looked at me wryly and said, "I had to bail out yesterday, and dammit, Serge, I didn't know how to land!"

I must say it made me feel pretty good. "Ernie," I said, "I'm at your service any time you want to learn."

One thing that upset me greatly at the time was Alice's sudden marriage to David Bouverie. When Alice divorced Philip Harding, I had really hoped to remarry her, although I knew her tremendous pride, and therefore had not come to mention it. With Alice, you always had to find exactly the right moment for things like that. I did know, however, that she was still quite fond of me, and I really had the feeling that we might have worked things out at last a second time.

It really is a tragedy about human beings sometimes; once they make a mistake they can never quite recoup the ground that earlier was lost. They can never quite get back. It was exactly that with Alice and myself—terribly fond of each other, terribly concerned, and yet something somewhere was unwilling. Or perhaps it was in the cards and willed that way. I knew she was unhappy, for she had gone racing hither and yon, and had only been wounded all the more. Yet all the time, single-handed she had done so many things for people. For example, she was the one who kept the Sadlers Wells Ballet going through its dark and arduous years. And there was a host of writers, artists, and needy friends whom she befriended.

When I was the President of the Sherry-Netherland, the directors decided to expand here and abroad. I went to Beverly Hills to negotiate the purchase of the Beverly Hills Hotel, which we unfortunately missed by a hair's-breadth. I stayed at the hotel at the invitation of Hernando Courtright, the President and General Manager. In the evenings I saw many of my old friends. Doug Fairbanks, Jr. and his lovely wife, Mary Lee, asked me to dine. They were giving a party for their house guests, Lord and Lady Airlie. Ronald Colman and his wife and David Niven and his wife were there. After dinner, we saw a preview of one of Ronald's movies.

Archie and Shirley Preissman also had me dine with them, and they considerately provided some of the great beauties of our country that evening: Kay Aldrich Cameron, Betsy Bloomingdale, and Elaine Hollingsworth. It was difficult to figure out which of them was the most attractive. Kay Aldrich's husband was away. I learned later that she was very nervous when I took her home. I was gratified to find that I was still considered dangerous! Back home again, I plunged into my work at the Sherry-Netherland, which had become New York's number one glamor spot. And then, suddenly we sold it to the

Kimelman interests in 1953 for one of the highest prices per room in hotel history.

Jules Stein had asked me to come to England and have lunch and view the Coronation parade of Elizabeth II from the M. C. A. building on Hyde Park Corner. Jules' invitation was an unexpected pleasure, and it was a wonderful chance. I had a good vacation coming to me and I was free to go. So I accepted, and went to stay with Chips in Belgrave Square.

Chips also had seats for me opposite the Abbey, but Jules' M. C. A. vantage point was far superior. So I called up Merle Oberon and Paul Louis Vellier, who were also invited to Jules', and we all went to M. C. A. together.

We had a magnificent view of the parade from the balcony on the second floor. I'll never forget what a wretched day it was. Merle put a waterproof coat over her head. Of course we got wringing wet, but we had been well fortified by Jules' excellent bill of fare, so we didn't feel it. Afterward, we all went off into Hyde Park to watch the troops going home. What impressed me tremendously was their great enthusiasm; their marching was a beautiful thing to behold, and they moved like clockwork: the territorials; the life guards, cavalry very much like our old Russian Chevalier Guards; the old home guard, who still stepped smartly and with great precision; the Dominion troops; and, of course, the guards and countless other regiments in their full dress. I had not seen such colorful pageantry since my days in St. Petersburg, and that gave me a pang about the heart. The people went wild as each unit passed by them—the wonderful British people who had been so good to us during the war.

I went to two parties that evening. Chips gave a gramophone party for all the royalty that hadn't been asked to dine at Buckingham Palace. Chips was always thoughtful, and this is just another example of his kindness. Many of the guests had come in off the streets in damp street clothes, and warmed themselves by the fire. The young Duke of Kent and Princess Alexandra were there and their aunt, the Countess Toerring. I hadn't seen Wooly for a long time. We had a wonderful time reminiscing. She looked so well that I never suspected that I would never see her again. She died very soon afterward.

At Chips's party, I also saw Margaret of Greece, the Princess Hohenlohe, who was the Duke of Edinburgh's sister. I hadn't seen her since those very happy days at Bled when Alice and I had visited Paul of Serbia. Chips had had the rug pulled up in his magnificent bric-a-brac-encrusted drawing room, and we all danced to the gramophone. Chips was remarkable that way, managing always to create an easy informality. He was a magnificent host, and it was a fine party.

The second party that I went to that evening was at Londonderry House. It was a white-tie affair. All the ladies wore tiaras, and Eleanor Whitney and Marjorie Davies, both Americans, had on diamonds and emeralds that outshone the days of the Imperial court at St. Petersburg. In fact, fantastic jewelry was everywhere. At Londonderry House that evening I waltzed with many of my old flames from both sides of the Atlantic Ocean.

Almost immediately after the Coronation, I flew back home, and that summer I recouped the wear and tear on my old bones in the sun at Southampton. The Duke Box was in full swing.

As all organizations go, things have frequently to change within their framework. If they don't give a little at the seams they dwindle away and soon exist no more. The Duke Box was no exception. Since we all were bachelors, the membership by this time had often undergone a few changes due to the inroads of womankind. Of course, we were always very sorry to see one of our number leave our ranks and marry, but we always wished him a speedy return. Frequently that is exactly what happened, Jay Rutherfurd and Alfred Clark being notable in this regard.

However Vava Adlerberg, the great sybarite, left us for quite a different reason, preferring the luxurious and well-run household of Rosie Gaynors to our more rustic ways (Rosie's stepfather was Willie K. Vanderbilt). Besides, I was the cook, and Rosie had a magnificent chef. I was not offended. In Vava's eyes I understand that there was no choice to be made in the matter, no choice at all.

Still, we were delighted when, after he left us and Jacques Fray moved in to join our little group, Vava ran into trouble at Rosie's. One weekend Rosie had given a huge party, and Vava happened to be her only weekend guest, of which he was quite proud and in the course of the party told us so. That evening Rosie looked as beautiful as ever and she wore all of Mrs. Willie K. Vanderbilt's jewelry. The next morning she couldn't find the jewels anywhere. She frantically telephoned the police. They arrived and demanded to question everyone. The servants were all old family retainers. The police were especially interested in Rosie's guest because they were certain it was an inside job. So Vava was waked up and before orange juice, even before coffee, he underwent a very stringent cross-examination. That afternoon he sought sanctuary at the Duke Box. He was horrified. "Police! Imagine!" he kept saying. He said they'd even told him that he wasn't allowed to leave Southampton.

Naturally, we didn't want to do anything to increase his worries, so we told him that if he had to spend the night in jail we were sure he'd be comfortable. We were certain that the beds there would be far more restful than the Duke Box's—or maybe even Rosie's soft luxurious ones this time. Poor Vava got redder and angrier at us by the minute. Finally he couldn't take it any longer, and he left.

That evening he called me up, much relieved. The jewels had been found, he said. When she'd taken them off the night before, Rosie had put them on a towel and forgot about them. Next morning, the maid had rolled up the towel and dumped it in a laundry hamper—Vava never made the files of the Southampton police.

Jacques Fray, who had taken Vava's place, became our great lover. This was evident from the day he arrived. Girls began calling up the place from London, Paris, Hollywood—everywhere. They also began appearing at the Duke Box in large quantities. We raised our eyebrows a little when he insisted on putting in a private phone. We put a piano in the Duke Box for him, which he has since used to great advantage whenever ladies came to call. Once, when we gave a dinner before the big ball of the season at the Beach Club, a number of us asked him to play for us. We sent a couple of beautiful girls over immediately to look as if they had gravitated toward him. Jacques became more and more enchanted with the girls—and with his playing. They asked him for this and that, and he was really outdoing himself when we all slipped out, leaving him playing to an empty Duke Box.

But gardening more than girls is Jacques' hobby, and he manicures our lawn, plants bulbs, and sprays our rambler roses. He is as careful about his flowers as he is about his ladies, and with his infallible Gallic charm, Jacques has probably become one of the most sought-after and choosey bachelors in Southampton. His voice after following the strains of *Der Rosenkavalier* all those long years on Radio Station WQXR is well known and he had perfected it by now to impart a soft and amorous texture. "Le brave Jacko," as we call him, is our Duke Box lover par excellence. He won't go anywhere any more where either the food or the girls aren't up to snuff.

Jay Rutherfurd, who is our noble secretary, is a Republican who started as a buck reporter. He is brilliant underneath his irrepressible and bouncy exterior, and he would give you the shirt off his back if you asked him for it, although I think he might try to stop you asking first. I've always said to him that he ought to be in politics, which he adores. He knows so much about it, but for the present he is a businessman spending his off-again on-again bachelor summers in Southampton at the Duke Box. He can sell anything to anybody, from three tons of toothpicks to a can of Snow Crop, while the girls sell him a bill of goods. He has been married once. That is enough. We always tell him that the Duke Box is the safest place for him.

Alfred Clark is the Singer Sewing Machine Company and he has a first-rate mind with a voluminous knowledge of art. His father got together one of the finest collections of modern painting in this country. Alfred is our great marrier, which is of course a disadvantage at the Duke Box, but I must say he always returns in his off periods to take up summer residence with us. Each occasion of his return has been immortalized by Ala with a tombstone painted on the living room wall. Today, however, Alfred is no longer at Duke Box. He really is married, very happily this time.

As you can see, our curious Duke Box summer place is one of wit and heart, gentle teasing and good cheer. There is almost constant activity there throughout the balmy weekends at Southampton.

One time I brought a very attractive girl called Norma Munroe up for the weekend. I'd only just met her. Since we have no ladies' quarters at the Duke Box, we always arranged for them to stay at one of the Southampton inns.

On Saturday we gave a party. I was, as usual, the cook, working outside on our open range. While I was turning over a steak, I noticed that Alfred was being extraordinarily attentive to my girl—I turned over another steak.

Driving her back to her inn much later on, I casually asked, "Did Alfred propose to you?"

"How did you know?" she said.

"Well, I certainly hope so!" I said, laughing.

Alfred is certainly a charming man. Two weeks later Norma married him. Six months later they were divorced. But now, as I said, Alfred is at last a happy man.

Very often in the mornings, Angie Duke appears to breakfast with us. Long ago he too left us, and got married to a wonderful Spanish girl, Lulu Arana, and there is no lady who has ever helped the Duke Box contingent more with our intricate and varied problems. She is our confidant and counselor, and quiet as a church-mouse, thank heaven! Mornings, as I say, Angie appears and often with his little two-year-old daughter, who has great blue eyes and golden hair. She is our mascot, and I predict great things for her.

We bought the Ambassador Hotel in 1954, forming a company of which I was to be the president, just as I had been in the Sherry-Netherland. Mrs. Joseph Davies, the wife of the ex-Ambassador to Moscow, was one of the first to make the hotel her permanent residence; then came Count and Countess Bismarck, who was formerly Mrs. Harrison Williams, the fabulous Mona of Daliesque fame; and Gloria Vanderbilt Stokowska. What the newspapers began to call my personal group made the hotel their meeting place, and this was news—and business. My friends from all over the world came and tried us out. Most important, they came to stay again. This is how the word-of-mouth begins—good, bad, or indifferent. Apparently we were "good," or so the reports came back from society, the sporting field, the military and diplomatic service, the international scene and the United Nations. Thus the Ambassador Hotel acquired its "tone," something intangible, a quality that cannot be acquired except through human associations and the good will accompanying them. We established the Embassy Club, a new night club, which Eddie Bismarck decorated; banquet rooms, the life-blood of hotels; ballrooms; a totally new decor for a run-down old hotel; and good publicity—in short, the "formula" began all over again.

As always, in the most carefully planned events the worst periodically happens. During one of the first large functions we gave down in the Embassy Club, a disaster occurred. Or maybe one of my waggish friends had played a joke on me. I had to give a little welcoming speech; and Chauncey Gray, our band leader, signaled a chord on the piano to clear the floor. I couldn't believe my eyes. There directly in front of me was a pair of ladies' unmentionables. Everybody began to giggle. I had no choice but to pick them up and say, "Any gentleman who has lost anything can find them again in the ladies' powder room!" And I went on with my speech. I felt very proud of my delicacy. But I understand that nobody wanted to be seen going to the powder room that evening, and, at any rate, nobody put in a claim.

In May of 1955, Bob Christenberry and I took a trip to Rome, Athens, Istanbul and Beirut. There were some hotels available for purchase or that needed to be built in these cities. At Athens I telephoned Grand Duchess Helen, my old friend, and she asked King Paul to tea, as she said he wanted to see me. His Majesty was personally interested in having a top rank hotel in Athens. We talked business and discussed the time we had met during the last war at Chips's. Grand Duchess Helen made a wonderful effort. I knew she wasn't well but she was as gracious and dynamic as ever.

The financial set-up of our Athens projects were headed by Mr. Bodossakis, a fabulous financier with a finger in every Grecian pie, and Mr. Stavros Niarchos, neither of whom felt it safe to go into a Greek venture without the other! They were a tremendous combination, until Bodossakis pulled out and the deal fell through.

That October, the Shah of Iran wanted to build a modern hotel in Teheran. His Majesty requested that I come to see him there, and I went with Drew Dudley, who had been attached to the Shah's and Queen Soraya's party during their stay in the United States. Drew knew His Majesty very well and was a wonderful escort. Teheran I consider one of the most fascinating cities of the Near East, and there, His Majesty the Shah proved to me what a truly unassuming and attentive monarch he was. I talked at length with His Excellency Mr. Ala, the Prime Minister, and also to the most able of all the cabinet ministers in charge of the Plans Organization of Iran, Mr. A. Ebtchaj, considered in New York circles one of the top-ranking financial minds of the world. It was an instructive trip. One evening, the A. D. C. of the Shah, Mr. Manucher Gharagozlou, with his beautiful young wife, gave Drew and me a tremendous party. I never ate so much fresh caviar.

The year 1956 was one of the most fateful years of my life. The first reason was the pride that I had in my son Ivan, on the completion of his long and ambitious novel, *Rogues' March*, about the Hudson Valley. On the day of its publication Alice and I got together and threw a party for him at the Ambassador. I must say that while I personally felt the book a bit too "strong," it had tremendous power. The critics bore me out, because he was praised to the skies by some and fiercely attacked by others for his candor. I'm very much afraid that my son turned out to be a crusader. I say afraid, because that sort of thing never leads to happiness but often, as with Jim Forrestal, to despair. However, I've done a good bit of that myself in my time and weathered the storm. So more power to him.

No sooner was he through his saga than he was divorced by his wife, the former Claire McGinnis of San Francisco, a very lovely girl. I must say they handled everything extremely well, and with regard to their three beautiful children, made a very good arrangement quite similar to mine with Alice.

But the tragedy of all time for me was yet to come. Little did I know that at that happy party for Ivan and his book, I was to see Alice for the last time. She always disguised her problems so beautifully. Ever since she had divorced David Bouverie she had been moving into dangerous company. I can't help thinking of the unfortunate Czarina and Rasputin in this context.

Talk about Tutankhamen! The strange thing is that she had gotten herself deeply into the hands of mystics. I firmly believe that they were preying upon her psychic needs for financial ends. I know for a fact that at the end she was almost utterly alone, at least she thought she was, which is more to the point. Imagine, a person who has done so much throughout her life for everybody—artists, writers, musicians, painters—everybody, thinking that she was alone!

All I know is that bit by bit the pressures of the lore of the past began to prey upon her, as she delved into it. She was an expert in Egyptian hieroglyphs. Who knows what secret doors might have been opened?—if indeed any such secret doors actually exist. Or do they even have to, when the mind itself may be the very largest door of all?

All I know is that Alice died suddenly, unnecessarily and before her time, put upon by the pressures of this life, and cursed by the pressures of the past. God bless her, for I know in my soul that she has found at last happiness and rest. We buried her in Rhinebeck, and there was a void in my heart. I began to work, hard; and bit by bit there was life once again.

My old friend, Vassily the chef, was broken-hearted. He pined away and died almost exactly a year after Alice. He asked to be buried next to her in Rhinebeck, and he was.

We received a lot of offers for the purchase of the hotel, but they were on-again-off-again deals and bad for the morale. But sold it was, in 1958, and at one of the last functions there, I performed a Russian dagger dance. I do this every Russian New Year's Eve. I first do a dance with five flaming daggers, well known in Russia. At the end of the dance I stand on a table, and below me on the floor people put dollar bills down on a bread board (to save the parquet). I have to hit the bills with my daggers, which I throw, one at a time, from my mouth. I guarantee to hit the bills with three out of the five daggers. If I succeed, then all the money that was placed on the board goes to the Tolstoy Foundation. If I lose, the money is returned.

There is one further part in the ritual. I drink the *horn of plenty* dry before I do my dance. The horn of plenty is a ram's horn, a big one, and its contents are supposed to fortify me for the New Year and my dance. It is usually filled with champagne. This time Vava Adlerberg and Sasha Tarsaïdzé filled it up with a half-and-half mixture of vodka and champagne. I was really fortified. I could have killed them. My eyes began to run. I got through the dance all right, but by the time I had to throw the daggers I could hardly see. I gritted my teeth, and I somehow made it. My discomfiture is immortalized in a photograph on one of the pages of the volume.[1]

In the interim, the Sheraton Hotel chain had acquired the Hotel Astor on Times Square, and put it in good condition. Since the Sheraton people wanted a hotel on the east side, and the Zeckendorfs had bought the Ambassador from us, an advantageous trade was worked out. Early this year, the Sheraton group took over the Ambassador; the Zeckendorfs, who wanted me to work with them, moved into the Astor, and I found myself guiding the Astor. The hotel had originally been owned by Waldorf Astor, of the English branch of the Astor family. It is a superb old building in the heart of the theatrical district.

To give you an example of its strong construction: I have an apartment on the third floor on the corner of 45th street and Broadway right opposite the shining waterfall, one of the big signs on the Great White Way, but I can't even hear a sound from the street. It's much quieter than the Ambassador or the Sherry-Netherland ever was. Bill Astor told me that he had been sorry to part with it, and Bill was terribly kind to me when he gave the first big dinner there under our auspices. He asked eighty people to dine, and it really was a case of "The Astors are coming back to the Astor!" At least, that's what the press said. I must say I am very grateful for that.

Today, at the Astor, there is a whole world of conventions opening up. President Eisenhower's suite in New York is in the Astor, and on his visits to the city the hotel takes on a different aspect. The secret service men are everywhere, police abound. In short, there is activity, constant, moving, dynamic, at the Old Astor once again. The hotel business is a fascinating thing if you like people, as I do. And who knows? Maybe the trend is back to Broadway, as it once was, in its heyday and its great and splendid past.

Yet, I remain one man in his time, simply an ex-Russian of a particular background and family, the foundations of whose existence were destroyed. I believe that for myself and for millions of Russians who once lived under Communism, the terror and the hardship of those days did not for an instant destroy our faith, our interest in the world, and our love of life.

And, certainly, we all had our memories, and traditions that were strong and sufficient to keep us going. From my own point of view, the little that I saw of Russian Imperial Court life was a vivid spectacle, as it was to many

---

[1] See Publisher's Note

Russians in all walks of life, something adding variety and glamor to existence. But I had further stimuli. The divorce of my parents meant that I spent much of my time in the country—where, in fact, most Russians lived—and which I learned to love. Like most Russian children, I had peasant boys for my playmates. In the First World War I was a buck private, carrying my own saddle, caring for my own horse, eating the food that the privates ate; and thereby I came to understand the difference between their point of view, and that of an officer class which was still largely hereditary.

I do not mean to imply that I was a typical Russian, but that the attitudes I expressed, and the qualities I possessed were those of many Russians, and they exist in Russia now. On looking back, my life seems to have been several things all at once: a political life in the emerging Russian democratic institutions that was ended by the war and revolution; a military life in the last great war of horses and men, the swan-song of cavalry warfare that dated from the days of Genghis Khan; a social life amongst people all over the world, to whom I was allied by heritage, but from whom I was removed by circumstance and by the end of the role that the princely families had played in Russia.

Those of us who escaped from Russia had, perhaps, quite a bit of reason to be discouraged about the future. But on the whole, I think, we still tried to give what we could in our varied fields of endeavor, whether they were literature, art, music, science, or simply the service of society. And I think we successfully overcame any tendency in ourselves to despair.

I, myself, feel it to be a work of consequence to do what one can to provide pleasure for people, to serve others; I take it for granted that a primary objective in the lives of men is to have a good time. If, in my own small way, I have added to people's enjoyment, then I have succeeded. Whatever the completely opposite successes of the Bolsheviks, we can be certain that for many Russians in Russia today, a desire for the enjoyment of life still exists, and their basic quality of human friendliness is still an inherent part of their existence.

One of the main things that I hope I have accomplished in this chronicle of my life is to make the American people aware of the great human quality of the Russian people that lies hidden today behind the gigantic fictions that the Communists have created. I believe we should bear in mind that the Russian people, forced to live under Soviet minority rule, still possess qualities that are not foreign to us. I believe that they hate oppression—most of them—and many do not even understand the role their present government plays. I believe that they still possess tremendous vitality, a strong, resurgent optimism and high spirits, which the most savage attacks of the Soviet regime have not destroyed.

So I feel that while we must arm against Russia, we should make every effort to understand her people, and try to get through to them. Every means of cultural interchange with Russia should be explored with all the fervor we possess: our plays, our books, our athletes, our musicians, our films. We must strive to make the Russian people see us as we really are, and not as we are caricatured to them by the Soviet regime.

I do not say that our own government in the United States is perfect. We have our own failings. Democracy doesn't always function as it should, but it is certainly the best form of government that has yet developed on this earth, more pleasant to live under than any other, and offering more freedom and promise for a better life for all men, under the law.

I wrote this book because I believed that there was a story to tell, and one which may in some small way explain an ex-Russian's point of view toward the world. I have wanted in this volume to clear up some misconceptions about the old Russia that I knew. I have tried to show it as it truly was, with its fun-loving, ebullient people. God knows why they are always considered so gloomy over here, although I suspect that it's greatly due to Chekhov, badly played. In my time, they were moving relentlessly along an evolutionary path to plenty; and they were getting there, without the lash, despite what Frolov said. I always believed in a parliamentary and a democratic system for Russia, as did my father and grandfather before me. Most educated Russians felt exactly the same way, and as far as I am concerned, this story is a reavowal of my faith in such a system.

My father always used to say to me, "Learn, do things, but when you do, remember you must always put your country first, your family second, and yourself third."

I would be remiss in my obligations, therefore, if I did not include a word of warning to my new country, the United States. For she is coming to another period in her history that will call for heroism. There are such moments of crisis in all countries, and they must face up to them, or perish, either physically as Rome did, or spiritually as Russia did in the Revolution of 1917.

Forces of good and forces of evil have always been in juxtaposition in the world since time immemorial. We are presently in a struggle to the death. Our position is made precarious by the fact that today the forces of evil have in their control, Russia, a physically young and virile nation—Russia, my old country, which, in my time there, was only permitted the beginning of its economic upswing. When the Bolsheviks took over they gave themselves a present. It was all there, and they capitalized on it.

In one sense Admiral Frolov was right when he spoke about the lash, but he made the mistake of complicating the Soviet regime with the Russian individual: the only thing that the Soviets will ever respect is the big kind of stick that Teddy Roosevelt always held behind his back. It takes a strong wrist, but we must learn again to carry it. More than that, we must learn that at times we will have to appear to be friendless and alone. And so, it is time for us to face the facts, unpleasant as they may seem to be.

We are confronted by an indefatigable enemy, the Soviet regime, which is prepared to use every means at hand to snuff our spirit out, if only to impose on us a form of government that is obnoxious to every sense of human decency. I can say so, because I know them.

I myself, as an American citizen, am prepared to give more of my time and income to our defense. It is not too late, but the time is now. Their stakes have been death for years, whilst ours are still rooted in our comforts and our family units. What good are these if we are neither able nor willing to protect them? What good indeed, unless we begin to put our country first?

Our problem in the next few vital years will be these: to wage a successful peace, we shall need manpower, a lot of it, properly trained to handle our very very complicated hardware. All the missiles in the world will be to no avail unless we have the facility to use them, lots of them. We must get rid of the concept of a "citizen army," where a man can just take down the flintlock from over the fireplace and go to war. At all cost we must have a standing army, navy and air force with a strong commensurate armament. All the electronic brains in the world will be useless unless they have sufficient missiles standing by, and just in case, atomic shelters must be built to house our people, all of them. Finally, each hamlet, town and city must have its own state guard unit of older reliable men equipped and ready to protect the citizenry from the ravages of city mobs that may be swayed by rabble-rousers in the Reds' employ. It happened in St. Petersburg and Moscow. It happened in Czechoslovakia. It just happened in Bagdad. Can we be complacent enough to say, it can't happen here? Thinking of my country, my new country, I wonder.

Once again the future of the world is obscure, yet it holds for us the promise of beauty. When we jumped into Sardinia, there was a moment when our parachutes seemed to hover motionless over an unknown world. I could see the vanishing shape of the plane we had left, and the floating silvery chutes of the men who were with me. On one side lay the shadow of the mountain; on the other was the strange volcanic cone with its fairy-tale castle topping it; and deep down below us lay a future which we could not penetrate. We did not know what we were going to find; but for an instant, as we descended, I realized that I had never seen anything more beautiful than the scene that lay before me as we poised over the unknown. As far as I am concerned, this is the story of democracy, a way of life that has grown stronger through wars and through revolutions and is unshaken, despite the seeming recent successes of the anti-democratic forces of my Russian homeland.

ABOUT THE AUTHOR

Prince Sergei Platonovich Obolensky Neledinsky-Meletzky was an American aristocrat, guerilla, socialite, tycoon, and paratrooper. The child of Prince Platon Sergeyevich Obolensky-Neledinsky-Meletzky and Maria Konstantinovna Naryshkina, Serge was born in Tsarskoye Selo on November 3, 1890. After completing his primary schooling in Russia, Obolensky studied at Oxford, where he was a acclaimed polo player.

He returned to Russia on the outbreak of World War One, volunteering for a calvary regiment and marrying Catherine Yourievsky in 1916. Recognized for his enormous bravery, Obolensky was quickly promoted and decorated on three separate occasions with the St. George's Cross, the highest award for military service in the Imperial Russian Army. After Russia collapsed into civil war, he fought for the White Army before evacuating with his family.

Finding safety in London, Obolensky's marriage could not survive the strain of these chaotic events and the couple divorced in 1924. That same year, after wandering through Europe and America at the height of the post-War economic boom, he married Ava Alice Muriel Astor, daughter of one of the wealthiest men in America. The couple had two children, Prince Ivan Sergeyevich Obolensky and Princess Sylvia Sergeyevna Obolensky, before divorcing in 1932.

His commanding presence translated well to the business world, where he found enormous success in the public relations and sales. Obolensky befriended some of the most prominent Americans of the period, and was a fixture at high class social events.

When war broke out again in Europe, he volunteered immediately for service in the American military. Initially a member of the reserves, he was soon selected for the special forces. Even at 52, he still was in excellent physical condition and was one of the oldest men to complete parachute jump school. He personally captured the island of Sardinia without loss of life, then later lead a daring raid to save one of Paris's only electric power stations.

After retiring from the military, Obolensky continued his life of distinction, becoming Vice Chairman of the Board of the Hilton Corporation while continuing his enormous success in public relations. He married Marilyn Fraser-Wall in 1971.

Obolensky died on September 29, 1978. He led a rich and full life.

Made in the USA
Monee, IL
22 May 2021